HUMAN SEXUAL
RELATIONS

HUMAN SEXUAL RELATIONS

Towards a redefinition of sexual politics

Edited by

MIKE BRAKE

PANTHEON BOOKS, NEW YORK

LIBRARY OF CONGRESS CATALOGING IN PUBLICATION DATA
Main entry under title:
Human sexual relations.
  Includes index.
  1. Sex—Addresses, essays, lectures. 2. Sex customs—Addresses, essays,
lectures. 3. Sex research—Addresses, essays, lectures. I. Brake, Mike.
HQ19.H85 1982   306.7   82-47865
ISBN 0-394-71109-2 (pbk.)   AACR2

Manufactured in the United States of America
FIRST AMERICAN EDITION

CONTENTS

ACKNOWLEDGEMENTS

1. *The Sociology of Georg Simmel* translated by Kurt H. Wolff. Excerpts from *The Isolated Individual Dyad.* Copyright 1950, renewed 1978 by The Free Press, a Division of Macmillan Publishing Co., Inc.
2. Max Weber: Excerpts from *Religious Rejections of the World and Their Directions.* First published in *From Max Weber—Essays in Sociology,* edited and translated by H.H. Gerth and C. Wright Mills. Copyright 1946 by Oxford University Press, Inc., and renewed 1973 by Hans H. Gerth.
3. Max Weber: Excerpts from *The Sociology of Religion.* Copyright 1963 by Beacon Press. Reprinted by permission of Beacon Press.
4. Sigmund Freud: Excerpts from *Introductory Lectures on Psycho-analysis.* Translated and edited by James Strachey by permission of W.W. Norton and Co., Inc., for the USA. Copyright: 1965, 1964, 1963 by James Strachey; copyright 1920, 1935 by Edward L. Bernays.
5. Wilhelm Reich: Excerpts from *The Sexual Revolution.*
   Wilhelm Reich: Excerpts from *The Function of the Orgasm.*
   Wilhelm Reich: Excerpts from *The Mass Psychology of Fascism.*
   Reprinted by permission of Farrar, Straus and Giroux, Inc. From *The Sexual Revolution* by Wilhelm Reich. Translated by Theodore P. Wolfe. Copyright 1945, 1962, 1969 by Mary Boyd Higgins as Trustee of the Wilhelm Reich Infant Trust Fund. From *The Function of the Orgasm* by Wilhelm Reich. Translated by Vincent R. Carfagno. Copyright 1973 by Mary Boyd Higgins as Trustee of the Wilhelm Reich Infant Trust Fund. From *The Mass Psychology of Fascism* by Wilhelm Reich. Translated by Vincent R. Carfagno. Copyright 1970 by Mary Boyd Higgins as Trustee of the Wilhelm Reich Infant Trust Fund.
6. Herbert Marcuse: Excerpts from *Eros and Civilization.* Reprinted by permission of Peter Marcuse. Copyright© 1966 by Beacon Press.
7. John David Ober: *On Sexuality and Politics in the Work of Herbert Marcuse.* First published in *Critical Interruptions,* edited by P. Brienes (Herder and Herder, 1970). Copyright J.D. Ober.
8. Jean-Paul Sartre: Excerpts from *Being and Nothingness.* Copyright line: 'First published in 1943 under the title *L'Etre et le Néant* by Gallimard. © 1943 by Jean-Paul Sartre. First published in English 1958 by Methuen & Co. Ltd. English translation © 1958 Philosophical Library.'
9. Simone de Beauvoir: Excerpts from *The Second Sex.* Translated and edited by H.M. Parshley. Copyright 1952 by Alfred A. Knopf, Inc. Reprinted by permission of publisher.
10. Thomas Nagel: "Sexual Perversion." Journal of Philosophy, volume LXVI, no. 1, 1969.

11. Alfred Kinsey, Wardell B. Pomeroy, Clyde E. Martin: Excerpts from *Sexual Behavior in the Human Male.* Saunders 1948. Alfred Kinsey et al: *Sexual Behavior in the Human Female.* Saunders 1953.

12. Alan P. Bell and Martin S. Weinberg. Excerpts from *Homosexualities: A Study of Diversity Among Men and Women.* Copyright line: '1978 by Alan P. Bell and Martin S. Weinberg. Ack: Reprinted by permission of Simon & Schuster, a Division of Gulf & Western Corporation.'

13. William H. Masters and V.E. Johnson: Excerpts from *Homosexuality in Perspective.* Little, Brown 1979. Reprinted with permission of the authors. Also excerpts from *Human Sexual Response.* Little, Brown 1966. Reprinted with permission of the authors.

14. J.H. Gagnon and W. Simon: Excerpts from *Sexual Conduct: The Social Sources of Human Sexuality.* Aldine 1973.

15. Ken Plummer: *Symbolic Interactionism and Sexual Conduct: An Emergent Perspective.* Ken Plummer: Copyright 1982.

16. Meaghan Morris: (review article) Michel Foucault, *La Volonté de Savoir.* First published in *Working Papers,* Feral Publications, Australia, 1976.

17. Ros Coward, Sue Lipshitz and Elizabeth Cowie: *Psychoanalysis and Patriarchal Structures.* First delivered at the Conference on Patriarchy held in 1976. Copyright: First published in the *Papers on Patriarchy* (1976) by the Women's Publishing Collective.

18. Jeff Weeks: *The Development of Sexual Theory and Sexual Politics.* Copyright Jeff Weeks 1982.

19. Michèle Barrett: *Female Sexuality.* Copyright Michèle Barrett 1982.

20. Monique Plaza: *'Phallomorphic Power' and the Psychology of 'Woman': A Patriarchal Chain.* First published in *Questions Féministes* 1 (1978). This translation by Miriam David and Jill Hodges was first published in *Ideology and Consciousness* 4 (Autumn 1978)

INTRODUCTION

Mike Brake

Sexuality as Praxis – a consideration of the contribution of sexual theory to the process of sexual being

There is no longer any place in present-day civilized life for a simple natural love between two human beings.

Sigmund Freud,
Civilization and Its Discontents
(London: Hogarth Press, 1930, p. 77n.)

The nature of sexuality has always been of central concern to human beings. Literally the essence of life, it has been a subject of contentious debate in religion, ethics, philosophy and the arts, as well as an arena of conflict for ordinary people swimming against the tide of mainstream morality. The epistemology of human sexual behaviour has been of interest to the social sciences and most of us take a prurient interest in it. Because of its intense emotional nature, the ecstatic moment it offers in a drab and arid existence, it is a subject which ranges into the difficult area of the personal and the political. It represents the struggle of civilization against animalism, of the spirit against the body. A common theme is the necessity to make sexuality subservient to labour discipline, to subdue hedonism in the interests of progress. Sexual passion is the wild card in the pack, the one area where the trappings of respectability and success have been thrown away for pleasure, and often the chord struck in us has been an uneasy envy. Yet sexual activity is shrouded in mystery; everyone has subjective experience of it, but little objective knowledge. It is surrounded by myths and taboos. The passions alien to our nature are incomprehensible to us, and those which attract us overwhelmingly exciting. An appreciation of the orientations and interests of others is consequently very difficult when there is no shared desire. We are also caught in the double bind of a capacity to be censorious about that which does not attract us, and even more censorious about that which does excite us. We are in addition sexual beings caught up in ideologies, roles and identities which owe much to a structured definition of sexual power. Feminism has revealed the power relations between the sexes, both within a conscious, taken-for-granted world and at an unconscious level. Homosexual people have revealed the far-reaching consequences of heterosexual domination in a sexuality which bases itself on biological reproduction. Sexuality has its political dimension in a very distinct way, and sexual relationships have always been a struggle. At first these were concerned with the spiritual versus the animal nature of human beings, then an obsession with decency and purity against pollution by the senses. Feminism has revealed these as part of the concept of women as sexual property, and despite accusations of a 'new puritanism' has shifted the argument to one of countering attempts to reduce women to sexual objectification. They have made out a viable case against pornography, sexual relations between adults and children, incest and other areas by raising the important issue of exploitation. Because contraception has separated their sexuality from reproduction, they have laid the foundations of a new self-determined sexuality.

Since the nineteenth century the biological, social and psychological evidence concerning our sexuality has altered its epistemology. The development of knowledge in the field of human sexual relations has been inevitably extended in an atmosphere of controversy. Consequently much of its application has been part of radical discourse. To counterpose new concepts of sexuality is to challenge at some level the dominant moral order. One central issue is the definition of the nature of sexuality itself. Is one speaking of a concern with forms of sexual desire, is one speaking of genital sexuality or a more generalized eroticism, or of gender identity with appropriate behaviour? Nothing as complex as sexuality can be reduced to biological functionalism. Our knowledge of sexuality is restricted by our accessibility to different partners. Simmel[1] reminds us of the special intimacy of the dyad, especially in marriage. The intense privacy of this is emphasized by the feature that for its continuance the dyad needs two, but for its end one must leave. It is a group which feels 'endangered and irreplaceable'. We invest heavily in our sexual relationships; it is an area where we are, however briefly, outside the alienation of work, where we feel accepted and loved. Weber[2] has pursued how the erotic sphere is institutionalized in particular ways in particular societies. For him sexuality and religion are linked in a tension where mystic union with a deity is a substitute for sexuality. We connect with our animality through eroticism, which offers us an escape from the iron cage of rationality. Indeed it is its very irrationality and animality which attract us. The importance of desire as an antirational, passionate force is present in the work of most writers on sexuality. Freud argues that human beings have to sublimate their sexual feelings to develop civilization,[3] even though not all libido is sublimate-able and not all people, indeed only a minority, are capable of sublimat-ing extensively; and he is doubtful of the satisfactions sublimation offers.[4] For Freud, psychoanalysis is in fact a method of shifting repressed sexuality and sublimating it into higher spheres of activity.[5] The child has a full range of erotic behaviour; polymorphous perversity abounds. The child must, however, as time progresses, develop through stages of erotogenic organization (pleasurable body areas not necessarily genital) to a genital organization of its sexuality. Genital-focused heterosexuality is seen as the mature stage of development. Another aspect of sublimated sexuality is its relation to work. Civilization overcomes nature because the pleasure principle (absence of values concerning instincts) is replaced by the reality principle. Culture controls instinct; ontogenesis is related to phylogenesis. The question of repression is of interest to many radicals who feel intuitively that this is a neglected area in radical political thought. Castel,[6] however, is highly critical of psychoanalysis as a subversive, political exercise, seeing this view of it as 'one of the greatest contemporary mystifications'. The professional neutrality of the analyst disguises the social and economic context of analysis; for example, the cash payment for services essential to the analysand (but not the analyst) is reduced by psychoanalysis to being merely of symbolic significance in the transaction.

The degree to which society represses sexuality is a matter of interest-ing speculation. Freud certainly agrees that it is excessively strict; the point of psychoanalysis is to reduce the effects of its strictness. Reich argues that culture represses sexuality unnecessarily, but he is speaking of 'normal' adult genital sexuality, and this occurs for him particularly in cultures based on patriarchical domination, rather than, as Freud implies, in all societies. Reich sees the remedy of this in sexual educa-tion. Repression would disappear if full genitality was established earlier in life, so that pre-genital modes of erotic organization would fade away. Work would be entered into as the results of an unrepressed life. Brown,[7] however, raises an important issue:

The crux of the problem is not the repression of normal adult genital sexuality, but what to do with infantile perverse sexuality.

He suggests that what is required is not the genital-focused superior orgasm of Reich, but a return to the polymorphous perverse – to anarchic sexuality. Not only are all parts of the body involved, but also an androgynous 'Dionysian ego', synthesizing male and female, Self and Other, life and death. The Freudian myth – the primal horde – is replaced by the myth of the primal androgyne. He implies that God is a hermaphrodite, and the unconscious is androgynous, our lives becoming a mission to recover our lost androgynous self. Despite this revolutionary psychology, there is no sense of history, of the need of material production to harness human energy, no sense of ideology or the political economy. It is Marcuse who pursues these ideas, raising some interesting questions about the nature and form of sublimation. Marcuse traces a relation between alienation in labour and the suppression of libidinal freedom. Freud had suggested that the pleasure principle (unrepressed libido) had to be sublimated to allow the reality principle (repressed civilized behaviour) to operate. Marcuse, however, argues for a prevailing historical form of the reality principle (the performance principle), a particular form of repression under capitalism which required surplus repression. There was a greater, more varied repression under capitalism than was required for the continuance of civilization. Under it, both body and mind became instruments of alienated labour. Sexuality is genital-focused because it leaves the rest of the body free for use as an instrument of labour. 'Genital tyranny' exists in the service of capitalist production, and hence the view that Reich held of intense genitality missed the point for Marcuse. The body had to be eroticized more generally, to return to a form of polymorphous perversity; otherwise it was left open to further economic exploitation. He also saw Reich's failure to distinguish between repressive and non-repressive sublimation, and repressive and non-repressive desublimation. This is a sophisticated attempt to relate the private sphere of sexuality to historical forms of the mode and relations of production. Marcuse sought a release of sexuality into Eros, into a situation of total bodily eroticism. He warned us that we are moving not towards an eroticized and sexually liberated society but towards a situation where permissiveness is confused with freedom.[8] We are becoming repressively de-sublimated (rather in his sense of repressive tolerance); sex is becoming more open in advertising and in general culture as a further means of tying us to the work process, not liberating us. The 'Playboy' culture does not sexually liberate women in any real sense but further enslaves them through their objectification. This is why Marcuse recognizes the importance of what heterosexual genital tyranny sees as 'perversions'. Homosexuals are involved in sexuality for hedonistic reasons; there is no reproduction of the work force involved in their sexuality. As such they are living symbols of threats to the dominant moral order. This, combined with heterosexual men's fear of their own homosexuality, may do much to explain homophobia. He sees homosexuals as having revolutionary potential in the sexual sphere[9]:

> In a repressive order, which enforces the equation between normal, socially useful and good, the manifestation of pleasure for its own sake must appear as 'fleurs du mal'. Against a society which employs sexuality as means for a useful end, the perversions uphold sexuality as an end in itself; they place themselves outside the dominion of the performance principle and challenge its very foundation.

Noticeably absent from much of the literature is the unspoken world of women's desire, subsumed under male definitions. Like that of gay people it has been mediated through patriarchy – the Law of the Father. Only recently has woman emerged as a desiring subject. Most writers have ignored her sexuality as 'mysterious'; little is known of her heterosexuality and even less of her lesbianism. Female libido and its directions have been only speculated about. Woman's sexual potential freed from fears of pregnancy is an unfinished theme. For similar reasons, gay people have only recently explored their own definition of the situation to account for their desire. Homosexuality is relatively unexplored. The degree to which people who apparently are predominantly heterosexual have homosexual feelings is uncharted. It is probably more useful to conceptualize a continuum between homosexuality and heterosexuality rather than qualitatively different categories. There is also confusion between masculinity and femininity and homosexuality.

It seems more useful to see that there are various types of human sexualities, and that there are homosexualities rather than one vague category of homosexuality. It may well be true, then, that those who see themselves as homosexual in our society are those who maintain this identity despite everything heterosexual society does to programme them otherwise. Kinsey[10] suggested that our sexuality can be conceptualized on a continuum from no homosexual experience to no heterosexual experience, with variations which suggest a predominantly heterosexual or predominantly homosexual behavioural pattern. Kinsey's data roughly suggested that 25 per cent of American males and 15 per cent of American females had at least one homosexual experience to orgasm. Hunt's 1974 survey[11] found similar figures; yet only about 2 per cent of females and 3 per cent of males considered themselves exclusively homosexual. Weinberg and Williams[12] found in their sample of the gay community in Holland, Denmark and the U.S.A. that only half of their respondents actually saw themselves as exclusively homosexual. Plummer[13] has indicated how homosexual people actually resist the homosexual label. Their behaviour may be homosexual, but they may not see themselves as homosexuals. Blumstein and Schwartz[14] found that many of their bisexual sample in fact had sexual relations with only one sex. However, they also found that their sample which was self-defined as homosexual had nearly all had heterosexual relations at some time during their life. Few people had relations with both sexes during a similar time span; most had intermittent periods of either homosexuality or heterosexuality. The important variable is self-definition of sexual identity. There are complex responses politically to bisexuality in the gay world.[15] Homosexuals feel that bisexuals are trying to claim an alliance with the gay world; yet when heterosexual sexist oppression occurs they retreat hastily into the straight world. Only too often men who claim to be bisexual are making a machismo claim that they are so sexually powerful that they make love to (rather than are made love to by) men as well as women. Politically what is important for bisexuals to recognize is that it is their homosexuality which is oppressed, and that they should publicly declare their membership of the gay world. What emerges is that, whilst only a minority see themselves as exclusively gay, this depends on their interpretation of exclusively homosexual.

From this it can be seen that homosexuality is not one simple form of sexual orientation but a vast array of orientations. Among women, some feel they have always been lesbian, some feel they want to relate to women more closely because of their feminist principles, and others feel they no longer wish to pursue the structural contradictions of heterosexuality. The situation is a confused one, but it does appear that more people are exploring their sexuality than previously, and that this has changed traditional definitions of sexual identity. Phantasy raises a problem for simple views of the homosexual–heterosexual dichotomy. If a man making love to a woman phantasizes that she is another man, or that he is a woman, is this basically a homosexual or a heterosexual act?

This takes us beyond the observables of data collected by survey or in the laboratory; it takes us into the meaning the sexual act has for the actor.

The nature of our sexuality has been recognized as more complex than the determinism of nineteenth-century theories of sex suggested. McIntosh[16] has raised the interesting question of the extent to which people, in particular women, shape their own sexuality. Lesbian women can be seen as those who struggled against their homosexuality ('old gays') and those who struggled towards it: is this merely different accounts of the same phenomenon or are they distinctly different experiences? The 'new gay' person is puzzling not only to the conventional wisdom of heterosexual views of sexuality but also to the 'old gay' community. We begin to see the real meaning that the politics of the personal has as part of the human project. We also begin to see fundamental differences between men's and women's sexuality. Few hitherto heterosexual men have given up heterosexuality to explore the homosexual mode of existence. Heterosexual men's interests are too structurally entrenched in masculinity: for them homosexuality is a distinct threat, with phantasies of anal rape and fears of demotion to the second-class role of woman. Effeminism is not a source of self-exploration and emotional support. Masculinity remains a privileged position in both the homosexual and the heterosexual male world.

A difficulty with the concept of human sexual identity is the role of the self. We are reflexive beings, and as such we are both the subject of our own desires and the object of others' sexuality. Nagel[17] suggests a paradigm of desire which involves an arousal of desire in the self by firstly being aroused by the sight of the other. This involves an awareness of this arousal, a sensing of the other, which leads to an interaction where the other senses one's desire for him/her. This schema suggests this leads to furthering of desire in both, an intersubjectivity of desire, which is the basis of sexual relations. The self, however, does not exist in any ahistorical, acultural sense, outside of a social context. It is essentially a social being. The directions it takes reflect the questions we ask of ourselves and our world. It is related to our consciousness in the political sense. As such this is developed through our ability to question ideological issues embedded in our culture concerning sexuality, and these may well be related to our relations to material production. Sexuality is praxis in a very basic sense. We develop through our perceptions, cognitions and understanding of our relationship to the world and to others within it. These are reflected back and mediated by our emotions.

The subject–object division in human relations is a distraction here. Our self as subject is part of the living relationship we have to others and they have to us.

The problem for any concept of self as an autonomous ego is that from the moment of our first perception we enter a world of prestructured subjectivity. Lacan has drawn our attention to the fact that at the same time as we enter the symbolic world of language society also enters us through the same media. As we begin to inhabit the world, so it also takes up habitation within us. This is not to argue that our subjectivity remains determined. Any reflexive being must initiate a dialectical relationship to the world once the precarious element of social reality becomes apparent. Our sexuality is obviously shaped by the limits of our knowledge concerning biology, psychology, ideology and so forth. It is De Beauvoir[18] who reminds us that

> It is only in a human perspective that we can compare the female and the male of the human species. But man is defined as a being who is not fixed, who makes himself what he is. As Merleau-Ponty very justly puts it, man is not a natural species: he is a historical idea. Woman is not a completed reality, but rather a becoming, and it is in her becoming that she should be compared with a man; that is to say, her *possibilities* should be defined.

Woman for De Beauvoir is the supreme Other, against which man defines himself as subject. The relation is not as Nagel (or indeed Sartre) seems to suggest as necessary for an 'unperverted' relation, that of inter-subjective reciprocity. She exists in De Beauvoir subjected to an act of psychic oppression.

> Woman is the archetype of the oppressed consciousness: the second sex. Her biological characteristics have been exploited so that she has become the receptacle for the alienation all men must feel; she *contains* man's otherness, and in doing so is denied her own humanity. However the important point is that sexuality is a *lived* experience.[19]

> The tremendous advance accomplished by psychoanalysis over psychophysiology lies in the view that no factor becomes involved in the psychic life without having taken on human significance; it is not the body-object described by biologists that actually exists, but the body as lived in by the subject. Woman is a female to the extent that she feels herself as such. There are biologically essential features that are not a part of her real, experienced situation: thus the structure of the egg is not reflected in it, but on the contrary an organ of no great biological importance, like the clitoris, plays in it a part of the first rank. It is not nature that defines woman; it is she who defines herself by dealing with nature on her own account in her emotional life.[20]

There is, then, a basic concrete biology; there is the received world of appropriate behaviour, and the strange set of introjected ideological notions – the emotions.

Lust, possessiveness and jealousy are the irrational forces which we have constructed partially through values mediated to us by significant others. Not all of our emotions are conscious; we learn them during a period of great vulnerability in a highly emotional context – in childhood. These are necessarily repressed in their raw form, but manifest themselves under stress. The self is an ongoing process, involved in a constant dialectic with a prestructured ideological world, located in a distinctly economic system. Sexual freedom, like sexual identity, is a battle with restraints, with a recognition not only of one's own oppression but also of one's relationship to the oppression of others. This is why the sexuality of men and women must be different. They live in different worlds, women caught up in sexual objectification expressed in fashion, the media and everyday encounters in the street, or captured in domestic relationships. Our behaviour may be scripted, but we must ask who writes the scripts, and where can we improvise? Where do we oppress, where do we take responsibility? It is de Sade who sees that love has no place in the realm of the true libertine. If we are to consider the question of sexual liberation, we must recognize that it may have different forms for men and women. It certainly raises questions of responsibility for our role in oppression if we are male or heterosexual.

From the 1890s, through the work of such thinkers as Ellis, Carpenter, Hirschfield, and of course Freud, we see a reaction against the dominant 'official' morality of the Victorian era. This period supported a stern moral attitude to sexuality which was at variance with the actual sexual behaviour then prevalent. The prostitution of women and children was common; pornography, in both fiction and photography, abounded; and rural working-class life was considerably sexually relaxed. Nevertheless it is fair to argue that the sexual orthodoxy of the bourgeois family, symbolized in the family of the Queen herself, was the respectable face which Britain in particular chose to offer to the worldly attitudes of France and Germany. The work of the earlier sexual writers self-consciously challenged this. Havelock Ellis's enthusiasm for a lyrical, romantic erotic love is an example; so, too, is his recognition of the prevalence of masturbation in women as well as his sympathy towards homosexuals. He criticizes the contractual elements of marriage as empty, and implicitly encourages the open marriage.[21] Drysdale's

Elements of Social Science, written in 1854, advocated birth control and attacked celibacy as a primary social evil. He was conservative about masturbation, taking the view suggested by Tissot's work on onanism in 1760 and Acton's work earlier in the nineteenth century: masturbation is a disease; 'spermatorrhoea', which is progressive, leads to stupor, lethargy, depression and even death, though for Drysdale, at least, this could be prevented by sexual intercourse. Masturbation, perhaps because of its suggestion of self-love, 'selfish' pleasure and its relation to phantasy, was viewed with suspicion and stern disapproval by many earlier thinkers. Its phantasies cross class and sex barriers. It is an area of sexual anarchy. As the old joke reminds us, with masturbation you meet a nicer class of person. It has been called the thinking person's television, and you certainly do not have to look your best! Krafft-Ebing (1840–1902), working in Germany, saw it as a loathsome disease; Freud argued up to 1925 that masturbation led to neurosis ('neurasthenia') and he saw even nocturnal emissions as bad. Elizabeth Blackwell, writing at the end of the last century, had spiritedly defended women's sexuality as being as lustful as men's, but she felt that masturbation could start as early as two years old and should be controlled. Even today masturbation is an area of embarrassment and guilt. The core of this taboo seems to have its roots in feelings that it is 'loveless', or 'animal-like'. (Schaefer[22] found this attitude in her study (1973) of women born in the 1940s and 1950s.) Amongst sexual educators and therapists, greatly owing to the work of Kinsey and Masters and Johnson, masturbation is recognized as a prime trigger in learning to have an orgasm. It is especially true for women, who have been traditionally taught to regard masturbation as sinfully hedonistic and unrelated to romantic love. That these attitudes have persisted for so long is hardly surprising considering the assaults on women's sexuality in previous times. Ehrenreich and English[23] remind us that in the nineteenth century the 'psychology of the ovaries' prevailed, where women's entire personality was considered to be dictated by the ovaries. Masturbation as a symptom of inappropriate sexual appetite in women (colloquially known as 'the vice', as opposed to 'le vice Anglais') was seen as leading to menstrual dysfunction, uterine disease, genital lesions and even dementia and tuberculosis. This is a long way from today's view that if women are to have orgasm it is essential for them to masturbate in order to teach themselves to recognize and respond to their own erotic feelings. A self-programmed orgasm responds to the pace of the woman's own erotic rhythms, and provides an anxiety-free atmosphere. The debunking of the vaginal versus clitoral orgasm in favour of the clitoral-triggered orgasm has helped women to define their own sexual feelings. Interestingly enough, even early sexual surveys revealed that, despite the moral deploration of self-abuse, it was common amongst women. Dr L. Dickinson, author of *A Thousand Marriages* and *The Single Woman*, written in 1932 and 1939, concluded that four women in five had practical experience of autoerotic manifestation, and as early as 1890 he had argued that it was natural and rarely physically harmful, and that no bad results had been noticed from 'moderate' masturbation. In *Factors in the Sex Life of 2,200 Women* Dr Katherine Davis, also writing in the thirties, found that, in a sample of over one thousand college women in America, 65 per cent gave definite histories of masturbation.

What we begin to see in the late forties onward is a distinct interest in what people actually do, due to the empirical breakthrough of Kinsey and his associates, and a focus on biological and behavioural aspects of sexuality. Robinson[24] sees this as the 'modernization of sex'. The German and English Romantics of the early nineteenth century opposed the traditional Christian ideal of chastity in favour of desire, but a desire set in the context of love. The Modernists, who Robinson sees as Ellis, Kinsey and Masters and Johnson, separate the sexual experience from its emotional associations, although Robinson makes important differences between the three viewpoints. Kinsey was eager to stress the physical naturalness of sexuality, and to remove this from the restrictions of either religion or love. As such he was a student of desire, an advocate of the view that just about everything is 'natural', so that to speak of pathology and normality is scientific nonsense. Kinsey collected a massive amount of data, still the major sexual survey resource material, revealing interesting correlations between age, class and sex in men, the widespread prevalence and relativity of homosexuality and the sexual potential of women. Indeed he distinctly debunked the phallocentrism of the penis. He laid the empirical foundations for much of the more enlightened work on women and gay people. It has a distinctly anti-moral flavour; normality was statistical, naturalness that which is found in the animal kingdom. For Kinsey a girl who was not taught to masturbate was at a distinct disadvantage orgastically in sexual intercourse later in life. Homosexuality was as natural as heterosexuality; people had much more homosexual experience than had ever been realized. Kinsey's radical empiricism ignored the meaning sexual acts had for the participants. Sexual identity was a summation of orgasms, rather than a reflection of one's relationship to the world.

Kinsey's influence was considerable. Weinberg's work on homosexuals with his colleagues Bell and Williams,[25] also working at the Kinsey Institute, is in essence a continuation of the Kinsey Reports. Gay people are shown to be no less well adjusted and no less happy than heterosexual people – perhaps a not very conclusive result for the effort involved, but it does attack the persistent myth of the homosexual as a tragic failed human being. The radical empirical tradition reached new proportions with the work of Masters and Johnson in the laboratory. By direct observation, and by the use of film and electrical recording, they gathered a mass of details concerning human sexuality. The sexual response of human beings passed through four stages – the excitement phase, the plateau, orgasm and resolution. They revealed that all women were not only potentially orgasmic, but potentially multi-orgasmic. The debate on clitoral versus vaginal orgasm was replaced by the notion that one could only speak of a sexual orgasm triggered by clitoral stimulation. Not only was penis size immaterial to female excitement and orgasm; the penis was immaterial. Masturbation is a primary feature in training sexual response, a coital partner even being seen as a 'psychic distraction' on some occasions.[26] Masters and Johnson are predominantly therapists, and they vigorously defend the sexual life of women and the old. In their work on homosexuals[27] they use the Kinsey categories to examine the sexual response of homosexuals, and their response to therapy aimed at improving their performance. We have, they note, primary sexual characteristics, which obviously affect our sexual performance, but we have similar orgasmic patterns, whether these are homosexually or heterosexually stimulated. Their failure rate was lower for homosexual dysfunction (12 per cent) than for heterosexual dysfunction (20 per cent). They were considerably less successful in their attempts to reorient from homosexuality to heterosexuality (35 per cent failure; most of the sample were married or in long-term heterosexual relations). Presumably this may be due to a combination of adult conditioning, and to failure to consider the influence of the fear of one's own homosexuality and homosexual self-hatred. Plummer[28] has written interestingly on the complex ways in which people avoid the sexual identity of homosexual by resisting the self label of homosexual. The meaning of an action in the context of sexual stigma seems to have been overlooked in Masters and Johnson. Their work on women has led Mary

Jane Sherfey[29] to develop her radical position that woman's multi-orgasmic potential, her prospective insatiability, meant that a patriarchial civilization must coercively suppress women's sexuality. The sexuality of woman must be kept a secret from her. The iron Law of the Father under patriarchy, stemming from a fear of independent women, means that a sexually demanding and insatiable woman can only be controlled by economic servitude and pregnancy – 'barefoot, pregnant and in the kitchen'.

The work of Gagnon and Simon[30] moves to an interpretation which includes an element left out of the empirical studies. They consider the meaning a sexual act has for the actor. Sexuality is a social construction, learned in interaction with others. Plummer[31] gives two examples: a naked woman lying on a couch being fingered by a man; and a boy watching football. The common-sense view is that the former is a sexual act. However, the man fingering the woman could be an interaction in a gynaecological examination, and the boy watching the football match may well be phantasizing the players in sexual acts. Despite the problems with this simple example, it makes the point that sexual meanings have to be negotiated. They are 'not universal absolutes but ambiguous and problematic categories'.[32] It is not sufficient that we have feelings and knowledge about those feelings; we respond to this information from and about our body. How are these meanings modified, constrained and altered by culture, by biology and by the interaction process itself? Who do we cast in the role of sexual object or sexual partner? Phantasy adds further confusion which takes us beyond the observables of data provided by surveys.

Central to this is the creation of sexual identity, and the processes involved in the social construction of this: how we become defined by others and ourselves as sexual beings – how we manage and negotiate these meanings. Gagnon and Simon see sex developed as a social construction with biological foundations. Our biology does not possess intrinsic meanings in its own right. These arise through interpretative, interactive procedures. There is a mix of public meanings given to sexual acts, situational, contextual meanings and the personal meanings involving the phenomenology of the actor. Gagnon and Simon (both have been senior researchers at the Kinsey Institute) have moved from empiricism to the notion that sexual behaviour is scripted, that there is a repertoire of publicly recognized acts and statutes with rules and sanctions attached. The routinized organization of mutually shared meanings involves both verbal and non-verbal behaviour – the 'courtship ritual' is an example. These are learned over time and reflect patterns of stages of development. The same sequence may, however, have different meanings for different actors. The state of physiological arousal is dependent on situation; it has to be recognized as sexual. This is reminiscent of Nagel's rather different interpretation of sexual encounters.

In contemporary France, because of different intellectual traditions, sexuality has been heavily influenced, firstly by the existentialism of Sartre and De Beauvoir, by the historical approach of Foucault and the structuralism of Lacan, the 'French Freud'. Lacan moves away from the American humanistic emphasis, a philosophy and psychology which portray people as volitional subjects, and sees people instead as transcended by processes. Central to this is the role of language, conceptualized as a mechanism for a prestructured subjectivity. As we inhabit the world, so it inhabits us. The penis, an organ of the body, takes on a set of meanings conferred upon it and becomes a symbol, the phallus. It becomes a signifier, separating two classes of objects – men and women. Penis envy becomes not a psychological imperative, but a socially shaped jealousy concerning sexual inequality. There is thus a potential for political analysis, a feature recognized by Althusser, who was pivotal in extending Lacan's political reputation amongst Marxist intellectuals.[33] Deleuze and Guattari[34] have extended Lacan into a political analysis of schizophrenia, drawing heavily upon Lacan's interpretation of the Oedipus complex, and Hocquenghem[35] has used a similar analysis for homosexual desire. In the unconscious, according to Lacanian theory, the child carries the structures of patriarchial society. The mother, the child realizes, is not the real authority in life, but is subservient to the authority of the father. As the child enters the social world, the Symbolic, the world of language, the roles learned are related to the central signifier, the phallus. Desire, for Lacan, is not a biological drive, but something symbolic which can never be satisfied; the desire firstly to complete the mother, to complete what she lacks (the phallus), and then to be the father, is always frustrated because it is a desire for a symbolic position which exists only to arbitrate authoritatively the direction of desire. Irigaray,[36] herself in the Lacanian tradition, has argued that Lacan's acceptance of the universalism of language – for example in his often-quoted notion that the unconscious is structured like a language – means that this can only lead to a traditional position concerning the feminine.

For her, the unconscious of women operates differently from that of men. This raises an important issue that even such empiricists as Kinsey recognized, that the sexuality of women is quite different from that of men. The failure in Freud to recognize this, or to give it any great credence, runs through many theories of sexuality. As Irigaray puts it,[37]

> When J. Lacan bemoans: 'I beg them on my knees to tell me what they want and they tell me nothing' why does he not hear what is at issue here. It is because he situates himself in the functioning of language and desire in which women cannot say anything, and in which he cannot hear them, even if they were to begin to speak to him.

Foucault[38] takes a very different view of sexuality. Here, as with Lacan, it is hard adequately to summarize a complex theoretical position. Foucault is interested in the apparatus of power, whether in the prison, on the scaffold, in the mental hospital and clinic, the school, the military academy or the court. He pursues the development of epistemologies and techniques prevalent in progressive treatments, and shows how they both liberate and contain patients, criminals, the mad etc. Sexuality, like mental illness, is linked to a wider morality. People become more innocent and more guilty. Sex for Foucault 'was a means of access to the life of the body and the life of the species.' The sexual family is the bourgeois family, but the bourgeois family has become obsessed with sex, which both distinguishes and affirms it. Sex has become more important; an explosive discourse has arisen around it. As our knowledge of sexuality changes, so does the specification of individuals. Whilst heterosexual monogamy remains the major point of reference, new figures, children, madmen, perverts, homosexuals, advance to reveal their presence. They are incorporated into new species. The sodomite becomes the homosexual, a species with a history, criminalized and pathologized but existent. There is a struggle for the body and its pleasures, a power struggle, with a power which comes from everywhere, and is sustained everywhere; yet there is always struggle. How this is manifested concretely is obscure in Foucault, although he sees the historical apparatus of sexuality as being predominantly that of bourgeois sexuality. Sexuality can only exist at one level because of the law. Its medicalization only increases control over the body. Power is not a superstructural effect, but a complexity of relations of force presented obscurely in Foucault. The domain of this power lies in the hysterization of woman's body, the pedagogization of the child's sexuality, socialization of procreative behaviour and the psychiatrization of perversity. This is what the achievement of sexual freedom has brought us, surveillance in newer forms. It has become rationalized not liberated. Our sexuality has become medicalized: a verbose discourse has occurred. It has become organized into a set of insights into socialization, family life and psychosexual development; it has evolved theories of 'normalization'.

The difficulty in writing about human sexuality is one's own involvement in it. The thrust of feminism has been to challenge the taken-for-granted and often unconscious sense of superiority which has hidden the sexuality of women, and by extension of homosexuals and sexual minorities. The more sexuality is brought into the open, into a 'liberated zone' freed from puritanism, the more women are open to exploitation by men, unless they too contribute to the sexual debate. Much of the basis of women's resistance to sexual objectification during the last century was related to their inability to earn a living for themselves, and also because they feared pregnancy. Any resulting children would become their responsibility, unless they protected themselves through the marriage market. In contemporary times, they are freed from this concern but by a contraceptive technology which as yet has unknown effects, and is centred on changing the body chemistry of women. The new openness about sexuality is to be applauded, but there is ever the presence of a 'repressive tolerance'. Most pornography, both hard-core and soft-core, is based on a form of rape; certainly on male power. The penis has too often become a weapon: virility and skill used to glorify masculinity rather than to contribute to equality. Kelly[39] argues

All heterosexual relationships are corrupted by the imbalance of power between men and women. In order to maintain superiority, males must feed on the emotional care and economic servitude of women. To survive in a male supremacist social order, women must cripple themselves in order to build the male ego. Due to the stifling effect of this culture and to the damaging roles it enforces, women cannot develop fully in a heterosexual context.

This superiority has to be destroyed to develop an equal and caring relationship already in danger of corruption by a form of material production which favours men. Sexuality for men is intimately connected to their concepts of masculinity; they see it as essential to their being. They form alliances with each other. Stoltenberg[40] comments

Male bonding is institutionalised learned behaviour, whereby men recognise and reinforce one another's bona fide membership of the male gender class, and whereby men remind one another they were not born women. Male bonding is political and persuasive ... male bonding is how men learn from each other that they are entitled under patriarchy to power in the culture.

Men have not yet learned to develop an analysis which recognizes sexism as an entity and which, instead of presenting an apologia for being men, develops a dialogue with women's criticisms. There needs to be a recognition of the differences between male and female sexuality. The contentious issue of sexual relations between adults and children in our society can be used as an example. It is possible to conceive that a relation between a young gay person and an adult could be a solution to the gay person's sense of isolation and difference. For a young female child, the situation of sexuality with an older heterosexual male is almost certain in our society to be exploitative. Male heterosexual phantasies concerning the sexuality of prepubescent children seem to be common, but have little to do with how those children perceive sexuality themselves. Children are highly sexual beings, but until we have some idea of how they conceptualize their sexuality, any relations they have with adults are doomed to be defined by the adult in a sexist context of exploitation. This is usually coloured by the sexual phantasies of adult males. Men have to surrender their obvious advantages if they are to develop new forms of sexual being. This means accepting responsibilities in sexuality, ending male competition, responding to women as people, attempting to deal with the feminine side of social life. It means exploring and relating to their homoerotic feelings, not cutting themselves off from them. This means giving up the half-human mode of living called masculinity. They need to remember that

Patriarchy then is grounded in a cultural norm of masculinity perpetuated by the sexual politics of heterosexual men ... All 'Men's liberation' which in form and content is masculinity-confirming is thus an escalation and permutation of masculine aggression. And its victims ultimately are women, whether or not they are taken to bed.[41]

This gives us some hint of the way in which patriarchal power, the Law of the Father, is embedded in personal life. Freud accurately saw his theory as subversive just because it told 'unacceptable truths'. He was indeed worried by its easy acceptance in America ('They do not understand that I am bringing them the plague'). Only when there is resistance in the person (or in society) is there any revelation of these 'unacceptable truths', that our sexuality is not civilized but a potentially destructive force. We have seen the development of the 'politics of the personal' as a breaking of new ground from the economism of the traditional Left. Sexual power, like any other form of political and social power, is corrupting. The extremities of these powers are seen in the sexual nature of torture, or the sexual atrocities of the concentration camps where ordinary people were given full rein for their sexual feelings of power and dominance. Socialism, in order to escape the perversion of it found in the Gulag, needs to question not only economic dominance but dehumanized bureaucracy, cultural oppression and sexual exploitation. The latter is more pervasive because it depends on legitimation by the victim. It counts on the willingness of the oppressed person to be exploited. A socialism which in a libertarian tradition challenges personal life, sexuality as it is lived, and reveals the oppression underneath our relationships is a humanistic socialism which can free us not only from others but ourselves. This is the real meaning of sexual politics.

Notes

1. Simmel, G., 'The Isolated Individual Dyad', reprinted in this volume.
2. Weber, M., 'The Erotic Sphere', reprinted in this volume.
3. Freud, S., *General Introduction to Psychoanalysis* (London: Allen & Unwin, 1953), p. 463.
4. Freud, S., op. cit., p. 355; *Collected Papers*, II (London: International Psycho Analytic Press, 1925), p. 83.
5. Freud, S., *Group Psychology and the Analysis of the Ego* (London: International Psycho Analytic Press, 1922).
6. Castel, M., *Le psychanalysme: L'ordre psychanalytique et le pouvoir*, Collection 10/18 (Union Générale d'Éditions, 1976). See also Gordon, C., 'The Unconscious of Psychoanalysis', a critical review of Castel in *Ideology and Consciousness*, Vol. 1, No. 2 (Autumn 1977), pp. 109–26.
7. Brown, Norman O., *Life against Death* (New York: Vintage, 1959).
8. Marcuse, H., *Eros and Civilization* (Boston: Beacon Press, 1955), reprinted in this volume.
9. Marcuse, H., op. cit. (1968 edn p. 46).
10. Kinsey, A., *et al.*, *Sexual Behavior in the Human Male* (Philadelphia: W. B. Saunders & Co., 1948).
11. Hunt, M., *Sexual Behavior in the 1970's* (Chicago: Playboy Press, 1974).
12. Weinberg, M., and Williams, C., *Male Homosexuals* (New York: Oxford University Press, 1974).
13. Plummer, K., *Sexual Stigma* (London: Routledge & Kegan Paul, 1975).
14. Blumstein, B. W., and Schwartz, P., 'Bisexuality', *Journal of Social Issues*, 35.2, 1973.
15. Brake, M., '"I may be queer but at least I am a man" – ascribed and

achieved gender', in Barker, D. L., and Allen, S. (ed.), *Sexual Divisions and Society* (London: Tavistock, 1974).

16. McIntosh, M., 'Sexuality' in *Papers on Patriarchy* (Brighton: Women's Publishing Collective, 1978).

17. Nagel, T., 'Sexual Perversion', reprinted in this volume.

18. De Beauvoir, *The Second Sex* (London: Penguin, 1972), p. 66.

19. Mitchell, J., *Psychoanalysis and Feminism* (London: Penguin, 1974), p. 306.

20. De Beauvoir, op. cit., p. 69.

21. Ellis, H., *Studies in the Psychology of Sex* (Philadelphia: F. A. Davis, 1928).

22. Schaefer, L. C., *Women and Sex* (New York: Pantheon, 1973).

23. Ehrenreich, B., and English, D., *For Her Own Good – 150 years of the expert's advice to women* (London: Pluto Press, 1979).

24. Robinson, P., *The Modernisation of Sex* (London: Elek, 1976).

25. Weinberg, M., and Williams, C., op. cit.; Bell, A., and Weinberg, M., *Homosexualities – a study of diversity between men and women* (New York: Simon and Schuster, 1978).

26. Masters, W., and Johnson, V., *Human Sexual Response* (Boston: Little Brown and Co., 1966), and *Human Sexual Inadequacy* (Boston: Little Brown and Co., 1970).

27. Masters, W., and Johnson, V., *Homosexuality in Perspective* (Boston: Little Brown and Co., 1979).

28. Plummer, K., op. cit.

29. Sherfey, Mary Jane, *The Nature and Evolution of Female Sexuality* (New York: Random House, 1972).

30. Gagnon, J. H., and Simon, W., *Sexual Conduct* (Chicago: Aldine, 1973).

31. Plummer, K., op. cit.

32. Plummer, K., 'Some Relevant Directions for Research in the Sociology of Sex: an interactionist approach', paper given to British Sociological Association, 1974; unpublished.

33. Althusser, L., 'Freud and Lacan' in *Lenin, Philosophy and other essays* (London: New Left Books, 1971).

34. Deleuze, G., and Guattari, F., *Anti-Oedipus: Capitalism and Schizophrenia* (New York: Viking, 1977).

35. Hocquenghem, G., *Homosexual Desire* (London: Allison & Busby, 1978).

36. Irigaray, L., 'Women's Exile – interview with Luce Irigaray', *Ideology and Consciousness*, Vol. 1, No. 1 (1977), pp. 62–76.

37. Irigaray, L., op. cit., p. 71.

38. Foucault, M., *History of Sexuality*, Volume 1, *An Introduction* (London: Allen Lane, 1979).

39. Kelly, J., 'Sister Love; an exploration of the need for homosexual experience', *Family Coordinator* (October 1972).

40. Stoltenberg, J., 'Towards Gender Justice', *Social Policy* (May–June 1975).

41. Stoltenberg, J., op. cit.

SEXUALITY AND SOCIOLOGICAL THEORY

Georg Simmel

Excerpts from 'The Isolated Individual Dyad'

First published in *The Sociology of Georg Simmel*, translated by Kurt H. Wolff (Free Press, a division of Macmillan Publishing Co. Inc., 1950).

The Dyad

We see that such phenomena as isolation and freedom actually exist as forms of sociological relations, although they often do so only by means of complex and indirect connections. In view of this fact, the simplest sociological formation, methodologically speaking, remains that which operates between two elements. It contains the scheme, germ, and material of innumerable more complex forms. Its sociological significance, however, by no means rests on its extensions and multiplications only. It is a sociation. Not only are many general forms of sociation realized in it in a very pure and characteristic fashion: what is more, the limitation to two members is a condition under which alone several forms of relationship exist. Their typically sociological nature is suggested by two facts. One is that the greatest variation of individualities and unifying motives does not alter the identity of these two forms. The other is that occasionally these forms exist as much between two groups – families, states, and organizations of various kinds – as between two individuals.

Everyday experiences show the specific character that a relationship attains by the fact that only two elements participate in it. A common fate or enterprise, an agreement or secret between two persons, ties each of them in a very different manner than if even only three have a part in it. This is perhaps most characteristic of the secret. General experience seems to indicate that this minimum of two, with which the secret ceases to be the property of the one individual, is at the same time the maximum at which its preservation is relatively secure. More generally speaking, the difference between the dyad[1] and larger groups consists in the fact that the dyad has a different relation to each of its two elements than have larger groups to *their* members. Although, for the outsider, the group consisting of two may function as an autonomous, super-individual unit, it usually does not do so for its participants. Rather, each of the two feels himself confronted only by the other, not by a collectivity above him. The social structure here rests immediately on the one and on the other of the two, and the secession of either would destroy the whole. The dyad, therefore, does not attain that super-personal life which the individual feels to be independent of himself. As soon, however, as there is a sociation of three, a group continues to exist even in case one of the members drops out.

This dependence of the dyad upon its two individual members causes the thought of its existence to be accompanied by the thought of its termination much more closely and impressively than in any other group, where every member knows that even after his retirement or death, the group can continue to exist. Both the lives of the individual and that of the sociation are somehow colored by the imagination of their respective deaths. And 'imagination' does not refer here to theoretical, conscious thought, but to a part or a modification of existence itself. Death stands before us, not like a fate that will strike at a certain moment, but, prior to that moment, exists only as an idea or prophecy, as fear or hope, and without interfering with the reality of this life. Rather, the fact that we shall die is a quality inherent in life from the beginning. In all our living reality, there is something which merely finds its last phase or revelation in our death; we are, from birth on, beings that will die. We are this, of course, in different ways. The manner in which we conceive this nature of ours and its final effect, and in which we react to this conception, varies greatly. So does the way in which this element of our existence is interwoven with its other elements. But the same observation can be made in regard to groups. Ideally, any large group can be immortal. This fact gives each of its members, no matter what may be his personal reaction to death, a very specific sociological feeling.[2] A dyad, however, depends on each of its two elements alone – in its death, though not in its life: for its life, it needs *both*, but for its death, only one. This fact is bound to influence the inner attitude of the individual toward the dyad, even though not always consciously in the same way. It makes the dyad into a group that feels itself both endangered and irreplaceable, and thus into the real locus not only of authentic sociological tragedy, but also of sentimentalism and elegiac problems. The fact that from the beginning it is defined as one that will die gives it a peculiar stamp – which the dyad, because of the numerical condition of its structure, has always.

Characteristics of the Dyad

Intimacy

In the dyad, the sociological process remains, in principle, within personal interdependence and does not result in a structure that grows beyond its elements. This also is the basis of 'intimacy.' The 'intimate' character of certain relations seems to me to derive from the individual's inclination to consider that which distinguishes him from others, that which is individual in a qualitative sense, as the core, value, and chief matter of his existence. The inclination is by no means always justifiable; in many people, the very opposite – that which is typical, which they share with many – is the essence and the substantial value of their personality. The same phenomenon can be noted in regard to groups. They, too, easily make their specific content that is shared only by the members, not by outsiders, their center and real fulfillment. Here we have the form of intimacy.

In probably each relation, there is a mixture of ingredients that its participants contribute to it alone and to no other, and of other ingredients that are not characteristic of it exclusively but in the same or similar fashion are shared by its members with other persons as well. The peculiar color of intimacy exists if the ingredients of the first type, or more briefly, if the 'internal' side of the relation, is felt to be essential; if its whole affective structure is based on what each of the two participants gives or shows only to the one other person and to nobody else. In other words, intimacy is not based on the *content* of the relationship. Two relationships may have an identical mixture of the two types of ingredients, of individual-exclusive and expansive contents. But only that is intimate in which the former function as a vehicle or the axis of the relation itself. Inversely, certain external situations or moods may move us to make very personal statements and confessions, usually reserved for our closest friends only, to relatively strange people. But in such cases we nevertheless feel that this 'intimate' *content* does not yet make the relation an intimate one. For in its basic significance the whole relation to these people is based only on its general, un-individual ingredients. That 'intimate' content, although we have perhaps never revealed it before and thus limit it entirely to this particular relationship, does nevertheless not become the basis of its form, and thus leaves it outside the sphere of intimacy.

It is this nature of intimacy which so often makes it a danger to close unions between two persons, most commonly perhaps to marriage. The spouses share the indifferent 'intimacies' of the day, the amiable and the unpleasant features of every hour, and the weakness that remains carefully hidden from all others. This easily causes them to place the accent and the substance of their relationship upon these wholly individual but objectively irrelevant matters. It leads them to consider what they share with others and what perhaps is the most important part of their personalities – objective, intellectual, generally interesting, generous features – as lying outside the marital relation; and thus they gradually eliminate it from their marriage.

It is obvious that the intimacy of the dyad is closely tied up with its sociological speciality, not to form a unit transcending the two members. For, in spite of the fact that the two individuals would be its only participants, this unit would nevertheless constitute a third element which might interpose itself between them. The larger the group is, the more easily does it form an objective unit up and above its members, and the less intimate does it become; the two characteristics are intrinsically connected.

The condition of intimacy consists in the fact that the participants in a given relationship see only one another, and do not see, at the same time, an objective, super-individual structure which they feel exists and operates on its own. Yet in all its purity, this condition is met only rarely even in groups of as few as three. Likewise, the third element in a relation between two individuals – the unit which has grown out of the interaction among the two – interferes with the most intimate nature of the dyad; and this is highly characteristic of its subtler structure. Indeed, it is so fundamental that even marriages occasionally succumb to it, namely, when the first child is born. The point deserves some further elaboration.

Monogamous Marriage

The fact that male and female strive after their mutual union is the foremost example or primordial image of a dualism which stamps our life contents generally. It always presses towards reconciliation, and both success and failure of the reconciliation reveal this basic dualism only the more clearly. The union of man and woman is possible, precisely because they are opposites. As something essentially unattainable, it stands in the way of the most passionate craving and fusion. The fact that, in any real and absolute sense, the 'I' can *not* seize the 'not-I,' is felt nowhere more deeply than here, where their mutual supplementation and fusion seem to be the very reason for the opposites to exist at all. Passion seeks to tear down the borders of the ego and to absorb 'I' and 'thou' in one another. But it is not they which become a unit: rather, a *new* unit emerges, the child. The parents' nearness, which they can never attain to the extreme extent they desire but which always must remain a distance; and, on the other hand, their distance which nevertheless to an infinite degree approaches their becoming one – this is the peculiar dualistic condition in the form of which what *has* become, the child, stands between his creators. Their varying moods now let one of these two elements play its role, now the other. Therefore, cold, intrinsically alienated spouses do not wish a child; it might unify them; and this unifying function would contrast the more effectively, but the less desirably, with the parents' overwhelming estrangement. Yet sometimes it is precisely the very passionate and intimate husband and wife who do not wish a child: it would separate them; the metaphysical oneness into which they want to fuse alone with one another would be taken out of their hands and would confront them as a distinct, third element, a physicial unit, that mediates between them. But to those who seek immediate unity, mediation must appear as separation. Although a bridge connects two banks, it also makes the distance between them measurable; and where mediation is superfluous, it is worse than superfluous.

Nevertheless, monogamous marriage does not seem to have the essential sociological character of the dyad, namely, absence of a superpersonal unit. For, the common experience of bad marriages between excellent persons and of good marriages between dubious ones, suggests that marriage, however much it depends on each of the spouses, may yet have a character not coinciding with either of them. Each of the two, for instance, may suffer from confusions, difficulties, and shortcomings, but manage to localize them in himself or herself, as it were, while contributing only the best and purest elements to the marital relation which thus is kept free from personal defects. If this is the case, the defect may still be considered the personal affair of the spouse. And yet we have the feeling that marriage is something super-personal, something which is valuable and sacred in itself, and which lies beyond whatever unsacredness each of its elements may possess. It is a relationship within which either of the two feels and behaves only with respect to the other.

His or her characteristics, without (of course) ceasing to be such, nevertheless receive a coloration, status and significance that are different from what they would be if they were still completely absorbed by the ego. For the consciousness of each of them, their relationship may thus become crystallized as an entity outside of them, an entity which is more and better (or worse, for that matter) than he or she is, toward which he has obligations and from which he receives good or fateful gifts, as if from some objective being.

Translator's Notes

1. Never Simmel's term, but shorter and more convenient than his, which here, for instance, is 'Zweierverbindung' ('Union of two').
2. cf. the more detailed discussion of this point in Simmel's chapter on the persistence of groups.

Max Weber

Excerpts from 'Religious Rejections of the World and their Directions' (Essay XIII)

First published in *From Max Weber – Essays in Sociology*, edited and translated by H. H. Gerth and C. Wright Mills (New York: Oxford University Press).

The Erotic Sphere

The brotherly ethic of salvation religion is in profound tension with the greatest irrational force of life: sexual love. The more sublimated sexuality is, and the more principled and relentlessly consistent the salvation ethic of brotherhood is, the sharper the tension between sex and religion.

Originally the relation of sex and religion was very intimate. Sexual intercourse was very frequently part of magic orgiasticism or was an unintended result of orgiastic excitement. The foundation of the Skoptsy (Castrators) sect in Russia evolved from an attempt to do away with the sexual result of the orgiastic dance (radjeny) of the *Chlyst*, which was evaluated as sinful. Sacred harlotry has had nothing whatsoever to do with an alleged 'primitive promiscuity'; it has usually been a survival of magical orgiasticism in which every ecstasy was considered 'holy'. And profane heterosexual, as well as homosexual, prostitution is very ancient and often rather sophisticated. (The training of tribades occurs among so-called *aborigines*.)

The transition from such prostitution to legally constituted marriage is full of all sorts of intermediary forms. Conceptions of marriage as an economic arrangement for providing security for the wife and legal inheritance for the child; as an institution which is important (because of the death sacrifices of the descendants) for destiny in the beyond; and as important for the begetting of children – these conceptions of marriage are pre-prophetic and universal. They therefore have had nothing to do with asceticism as such. And sexual life *per se* has had its ghosts and gods as have every other function.

A certain tension between religion and sex came to the fore only with the temporary cultic chastity of priests. This rather ancient chastity may well have been determined by the fact that from the point of view of the strictly stereotyped ritual of the regulated community cult, sexuality was readily considered to be specifically dominated by demons. Furthermore, it was no accident that subsequently the prophetic religions, as well as the priest-controlled life orders, have, almost without significant exception, regulated sexual intercourse in favor of *marriage*. The contrast of all rational regulation of life with magical orgiasticism and all sorts of irrational frenzies is expressed in this fact.

The tension of religion and sex has been augmented by evolutionary factors on both sides. On the side of sexuality the tension has led through sublimation into 'eroticism,' and therewith into a consciously cultivated, and hence, a non-routinized sphere. Sex has been non-routinized not solely or necessarily in the sense of being estranged from conventions, for eroticism is a contrast to the sober naturalism of the peasant. And it was precisely eroticism which the conventions of knighthood usually made the object of regulation. These conventions, however, characteristically regulated eroticism by veiling the natural and organic basis of sexuality.

The extraordinary quality of eroticism has consisted precisely in a gradual turning away from the naive naturalism of sex. The reason and significance of this evolution, however, involve the universal rationalization and intellectualization of culture ...

(pp. 343–4)

The last accentuation of the erotical sphere occurred in terms of intellectualist cultures. It occurred where this sphere collided with the unavoidably ascetic trait of the vocational specialist type of man. Under this tension between the erotic sphere and rational everyday life, specifically extramarital sexual life, which had been removed from everyday affairs, could appear as the only tie which still linked man with the natural fountain of all life. For man had now been completely emancipated from the cycle of the old, simple, and organic existence of the peasant.

A tremendous value emphasis on the specific sensation of an inner-worldly salvation from rationalization thus resulted. A joyous triumph over rationality corresponded in its radicalism with the unavoidable and equally radical rejection by an ethics of any kind of other- or supra-worldly salvation. For such ethics, the triumph of the spirit over the body should find its climax precisely here, and sexual life could even gain the character of the only and the ineradicable connection with animality.

But this tension between an inner-worldly and an other-worldly salvation from rationality must be sharpest and most unavoidable precisely where the sexual sphere is systematically prepared for a highly valued erotic sensation. This sensation reinterprets and glorifies all the pure animality of the relation, whereas the religion of salvation assumes the character of a religion of love, brotherhood, and neighbourly love.

Under these conditions, the erotic relation seems to offer the unsurpassable peak of the fulfilment of the request for love in the direct fusion of the souls of one to the other. This boundless giving of oneself is as radical as possible in its opposition to all functionality, rationality, and generality. It is displayed here as the unique meaning which one creature in his irrationality has for another, and only for this specific other. However, from the point of view of eroticism, this meaning, and with it the value-content of the relation itself, rests upon the possibility of a communion which is felt as a complete unification, as a fading of the 'thou.' It is so overpowering that it is interpreted 'symbolically': as a sacrament. The lover realizes himself to be rooted in the kernel of the truly living, which is eternally inaccessible to any rational endeavor. He knows himself to be freed from the cold skeleton hands of rational orders, just as completely as from the banality of everyday routine. This consciousness of the lover rests upon the ineffaceability and inexhaustibleness of his own experience. The experience is by no means communicable and in this respect it is equivalent to the 'having' of the mystic. This is not only due to the intensity of the lover's experience, but to the immediacy of the possessed reality. Knowing 'life itself' joined to him, the lover stands opposite what is for him the objectless experience of the mystic, as if he were facing the fading light of an unreal sphere.

As the knowing love of the mature man stands to the passionate enthusiasm of the youth, so stands the deadly earnestness of this eroticism of intellectualism to chivalrous love. In contrast to chivalrous love, this mature love of intellectualism reaffirms the natural quality of the sexual sphere, but it does so consciously, as an embodied creative power.

A principled ethic of religious brotherhood is radically and antagonistically opposed to all this. From the point of view of such an ethic, this inner, earthly sensation of salvation by mature love competes in the sharpest possible way with the devotion of a supramundane God, with the devotion of an ethically rational order of God, or with the devotion of a mystical bursting of individuation, which alone appear 'genuine': the ethic of brotherhood.

Certain psychological interrelations of both spheres sharpen the tension between religion and sex. The highest eroticism stands psychologically and physiologically in a mutually substitutive relation with certain sublimated forms of heroic piety. In opposition to the rational, active asceticism which rejects the sexual as irrational, and which is felt by eroticism to be a powerful and deadly enemy, this substitutive relationship is oriented especially to the mystic's union with God. From this relation there follows the constant threat of a deadly sophisticated revenge of animality, or of an unmediated slipping from the mystic realm of God into the realm of the All-Too-Human. This psychological affinity naturally increases the antagonism of inner meanings between eroticism and religion.

From the point of view of any religious ethic of brotherhood, the erotic relation must remain attached, in a certain sophisticated measure, to brutality. The more sublimated it is, the more brutal. Unavoidably it is considered to be a relation of conflict. This conflict is not only, or even predominantly, jealousy and the will to possession, excluding third ones. It is far more the most intimate coercion of the soul of the partners themselves. Pretending to be the most humane devotion, it is a sophisticated enjoyment of oneself in the other. No consummated erotic communion will know itself to be founded in any way other than through a mysterious *destination* for one another: *fate*, in the highest sense of the word. Thereby, it will know itself to be 'legitimized' (in an entirely amoral sense).

But, for the salvation religion, this 'fate' is nothing but the purely fortuitous flaming up of passion. The thus established pathological obsessive idiosyncrasy, and shifting of perspectives and of every objective justice must appear to salvation religion as the most complete denial of all brotherly love and of bondage to God. The euphoria of the happy love is felt to be 'goodness'; it has a friendly urge to poeticize all the world with happy features or to bewitch all the world in a naive enthusiasm for the diffusion of happiness. And always it meets with the cool mockery of the genuinely religiously founded and radical ethics of brotherhood ...

In the eyes of this ethic, the most sublimated unknown is the counterpole of all religiously oriented brotherliness, in three aspects: it must necessarily be exclusive in its inner core; it must be subjective in the highest imaginable sense; and it must be absolutely uncommunicable.

All this, of course, is quite apart from the fact that the passionate character of eroticism as such appears to the religion of brotherhood as an undignified loss of self-control and as the loss of orientation towards either the rationality and wisdom of norms willed by God or the mystic 'having' of godliness. However, for eroticism, genuine 'passion' *per se* constitutes the type of *beauty*, and its rejection is blasphemy.

For psychological reasons and in accordance with its meaning, the erotic frenzy stands in unison only with the orgiastic and charismatic form of religiosity. This form is, however, in a special sense, inner-worldly. The acknowledgement of the *act* of marriage, of the *copula carnalis*, as a 'sacrament' of the Catholic Church is a concession to this sentiment. Eroticism enters easily into an unconscious and unstable relation or surrogateship or fusion with other-worldly and extraordinary mysticism. This occurs with very sharp inner tension between eroticism and mysticism. It occurs because they are psychologically substitutive. Out of this fusion the collapse into orgiasticism follows very readily.

Inner-worldly and rational asceticism (vocational asceticism) can accept only the rationally regulated marriage. This type of marriage is accepted as one of the divine ordinations given to man as a creature who is hopelessly wretched by virtue of his 'concupiscence.' Within this divine order it is given to man to live according to the rational purposes laid down by it, and only according to them: to procreate and to rear children, and mutually to further one another in the state of grace. This inner-worldly rational asceticism must reject every sophistication of the sexual into eroticism as idolatry of the worst kind. In its turn, this asceticism gathers the primal, naturalist, and *un*sublimated sexuality of the peasant into a rational order of man as creature. All elements of 'passion,' however, are then considered as residues of the Fall. According to Luther God, in order to prevent worse, peeks at and is lenient with these elements of passion...

(pp. 334–49)

Max Weber

Excerpts from 'The Relationship of Religion to Politics, Economics, Art and Sexuality' (Chapter XIV of *The Sociology of Religion*)

First published in this translation by Beacon Press (1963).

The objectification of the power structure, with the complex of problems produced by its rationalized ethical provisos, has but one psychological equivalent: the vocational ethic taught by an asceticism that is oriented to the control of the terrestrial world. An increased tendency toward flight into the irrationalities of apolitical emotionalism, in different degrees and even forms, is one of the actual consequences of the rationalization of coercion, manifesting itself wherever the exercise of power has developed away from the personalistic orientation of individual heroes and wherever the entire society in question has developed in the direction of a national 'state.' Such apolitical emotionalism may take the form of a flight into mysticism and an acosmistic ethic of absolute goodness or into the irrationalities of non-religious emotionalism, above all eroticism. Indeed, the power of the sphere of eroticism enters into particular tensions with religions of salvation. This is particularly true of one of the most powerful components of eroticism, namely sexual love. For sexual love, along with the 'true' or economic interest, and the social drives toward power and prestige, is among the most fundamental and universal components of the actual course of interpersonal behavior...

(p. 236)

At the level of ethical religion, two other significant attitudes of antipathy to sexuality developed in place of the various types of magical motivation. One was the conception of mystical flight from the world, which interpreted sexual abstinence as the central and indispensable instrument of the mystical quest for salvation through contemplative withdrawal from the world. From this view, sexuality, the drive that most

firmly binds man to the animal level, furnishes the most powerful temptations to withdrawal from the mystical quest. The other basic position
was that of asceticism. Rational ascetic alertness, self-control, and
methodical planning of life are seriously threatened by the peculiar
irrationality of the sexual act, which is ultimately and uniquely unsusceptible to rational organization. These two motivations have frequently
operated together to produce hostility toward sexuality in particular
religions. All genuine religious prophecies and all non-prophetic priestly
systematizations of religion without exception concern themselves with
sexuality, from such motives as we have just discussed, generally terminating in hostility toward sexuality...

(p. 238)

The various prophets differed widely in their personal attitudes
toward and their religious teachings about woman, her place in the
community, and her distinctive feeling tone. The fact that a prophet such
as Buddha was glad to see clever women sitting at his feet and the fact
that he employed them as propagandists and missionaries, as did
Pythagoras, did not necessarily carry over into an evaluation of the
whole female sex. A particular woman might be regarded as sacred,
yet the entire female sex would still be considered vessels of sin. Yet
practically all orgiastic and mystagogic religious propagandizing,
including that of the cult of Dionysos, called for at least a temporary
and relative emancipation of women, unless such preachment was
blocked by other religious tendencies or by specific resistance to
hysterical preaching by women, as occurred among the disciples of
the Buddha and in ancient Christianity as early as Paul. The admission
of women to an equality of religious status was also resisted due to
monastic misogyny, which assumed extreme forms in such sexual
neurasthenics as Alfons of Liguori. Women are accorded the
greatest importance in sectarian spiritualist cults, be they hysterical
or sacramental, of which there are numerous instances in China.
Where women played no role in the missionary expansion of a
religion, as was the case in Zoroastrianism and Judaism, the situation
was different from the very start.

Legally regulated marriage itself was regarded by both prophetic and
priestly ethics, not as an erotic value, but in keeping with the sober view
of the so-called 'primitive peoples' simply as an economic institution for

the production and rearing of children as a labor force and subsequently as carriers of the cult of the dead. This was also the view of the Greek and Roman ethical systems, and indeed of all ethical systems the world over which have given thought to the matter. The view expressed in the ancient Hebrew scriptures that the young bridegroom was to be free of political and military obligations for a while so that he might have the joy of his young love was a very rare view. Indeed, not even Judaism made any concessions to sophisticated erotic expression divorced from sexuality's natural consequence of reproduction, as we see in the Old Testament curse upon the sin of Onan (coitus interruptus). Roman Catholicism expressed the same rigorous attitude toward sexuality by rejecting birth control as a mortal sin. Of course every type of religious asceticism which is oriented toward the control of this world, and above all Puritanism, limits the legitimation of sexual expression to the aforementioned rational goal of reproduction. The animistic and semi-orgiastic types of mysticism were led by their universalistic feeling of love into only occasional deviations from the central hostility of religion toward sexuality...

(p. 239)

Despite the widespread belief that hostility toward sexuality is an idiosyncrasy of Christianity, it must be emphasized that no authentic religion of salvation had in principle any other point of view. There are a number of reasons for this. The first is based on the nature of the evolution that sexuality itself increasingly underwent in actual life, as a result of the rationalization of the conditions of life. At the level of the peasant, the sexual act is an everyday occurrence; primitive people do not regard this act as containing anything unusual, and they may indeed enact it before the eyes of onlooking travellers without the slightest feeling of shame. They do not regard this act as having any significance beyond the routine of living. The decisive development, from the point of view of the sociological problems which concern us, is the sublimation of sexual expression into an eroticism that becomes the basis of idiosyncratic sensations and generates its own unique values of an extraordinary kind. The impediments to sexual intercourse that are increasingly produced by the economic interest of clans and by class conventions are the most important factors favoring this sublimation of sexuality into eroticism. To be sure, sexual relations were never free of religious or economic regulations at any known point in the evolutionary sequence, but originally they were far less surrounded by bonds of convention, which gradually attach themselves to the original economic restrictions until they subsequently become the decisive restrictions on sexuality.

(p. 247)

THE INFLUENCE OF FREUD

Sigmund Freud

Excerpts from 'The Sexual Life of Man' (Lecture XX)
and 'The Development of the Libido and Sexual
Organizations' (Lecture XXI) in *Introductory Lectures
on Psycho-analysis*

First published by George Allen & Unwin, London, and Washington Square Press, New York.

Seriously, it is not so easy to define what the term sexual includes. Everything connected with the difference between the two sexes is perhaps the only way of hitting the mark; but you will find that too general and indefinite. If you take the sexual act itself as the central point, you will perhaps declare sexual to mean everything which is concerned with obtaining pleasurable gratification from the body (and particularly the sexual organs) of the opposite sex; in the narrowest sense, everything which is directed to the union of the genital organs and the performance of the sexual act. In doing so, however, you come very near to reckoning the sexual and the improper as identical and childbirth would really have nothing to do with sex. If then you make the function of reproduction the kernel of sexuality you run the risk of excluding from it a whole host of things like masturbation, or even kissing, which are not directed towards reproduction, but which are nevertheless undoubtedly sexual. However, we have already found that attempts at definition always lead to difficulties; let us give up trying to do any better in this particular case. We may suspect that in the development of the concept 'sexual' something has happened which has resulted in what H. Silverer has aptly called a 'covering error'. On the whole, indeed, we know pretty well what is meant by sexual.

(Lecture XX, 'The Sexual Life of Man', p. 255)

Psycho-analytic investigation has found it necessary also to concern itself with the sexual life of children, for the reason that in the analysis of symptoms the forthcoming reminiscences and associations invariably lead back to the earliest years of childhood. That which we discovered in this way has since been corroborated point by point by the direct observation of children. In this way it has been found that all the perverse tendencies have their roots in childhood, that children are disposed towards them all and practise them all to a degree conforming with their immaturity; in short, *perverted sexuality* is nothing else but *infantile sexuality*, magnified and separated into its component parts.

(Lecture XX, 'Perverted and Infantile Sexuality', p. 261)

It will be said: 'Why are you so set upon declaring as already belonging to sexuality those indefinite manifestations of childhood out of which what is sexual later develops, and which you yourself admit to be indefinite? Why are you not content rather to describe them physiologically and simply to say that activities, such as sucking for its own sake and the retaining of excreta, may be observed already in young infants, showing that they seek pleasure in their organs? In that way you would have avoided the conception of a sexual life even in babies which is so repugnant to all our feelings'. Well, I can only answer that I have nothing against pleasure derived from the organs of the body; I know indeed that the supreme pleasure of the sexual union is also only a bodily pleasure, derived from the activity of the genital organ. But can you tell me when this originally indifferent bodily pleasure acquires the sexual character that it undoubtedly possesses in later phases of development? Do we know any more about this 'organ-pleasure' than we know about sexuality? You will answer that the sexual character is added to it when the genitalia begin to play their part; sexuality simply means genital. You will even evade the obstacle of the perversions by pointing out that after all with most of them a genital orgasm occurs, although brought about by other means than the union of the genitalia. If you were to eliminate the relation to reproduction from the essential characteristics of sexuality since this view is untenable in consequence of the existence of the perversions, and were to emphasize instead activity of the genital organs, you would actually take up a much better position. But then we should no longer differ very widely; it would be a case of the genital organs *versus* the other organs. What do you now make of the abundant evidence that the genital organs may be replaced by other organs for the purpose of gratification as in the normal kiss, or the perverse practices of loose living, or in the symptomatology of hysteria? In this neurosis it is quite usual for stimulation phenomena, sensations, innervations, and even the process of erection, which properly belong to the genitalia, to be displaced on to other distant areas of the body (e.g. the displacement from below upwards to the head and face). Thus you will find that nothing is left of all that you cling to as essentially characteristic of sexuality; and you will have to make up your minds to follow my example and extend the designation 'sexual' to include those activities of early infancy which aim at 'organ pleasure'.

(Lecture XXI, 'Development of the Libido and Sexual Organizations: On Sexuality and Organ Pleasure', p. 273)

For from the third year onwards there is no longer any doubt about sexual life in the child; at this period the genital organs begin already to show signs of excitation; there is a perhaps regular period of infantile masturbation, that is, of gratification in the genital organs. The mental and social sides of sexual life need no longer be overlooked; choice of object, distinguishing of particular persons with affection, even decision in favour of one sex or the other, and jealousy, were conclusively established independently by impartial observation before the time of psycho-analysis; they may be confirmed by any observer who will use his eyes. From about the sixth or eighth year onwards a standstill or retro-gression is observed in the sexual development, which in those cases reaching a high cultural standard deserves to be called a *latency period*. This latency period, however, may be absent; nor does it necessarily entail an interruption of sexual activities and sexual interests over the whole field. Most of the mental experiences and excitations occurring before the latency period then succumb to the infantile amnesia, already discussed, which veils our earliest childhood from us and estranges us from it ...

From the third year onward the sexual life of children shows much in common with that of adults; it is differentiated from the latter, as we already know, by the absence of a stable organization under the primacy of the genital organs, by inevitable traits of a perverse order, and of course also by far less intensity in the whole impulse. But those phases of the sexual development, or as we will call it, of the *libido-development*, which are of the greatest interest theoretically lie before this period ...

Thus we can now define the forms taken by the sexual life of the child before the primacy of the genital zone is reached; this primacy is prepared for in the early infantile period, before the latent period, and is permanently organized from puberty onwards. In this early period a loose sort of organization exists which we shall call *pre-genital*; for during this phase it is not the genital component-instincts, but the *sadistic* and *anal*, which are most prominent. The contrast between *masculine* and *feminine* plays no part as yet; instead of it there is the contrast between *active* and *passive*, which may be described as the forerunner of the sexual polarity with which it also links up later. That which in this period seems masculine to us, regarded from the standpoint of the genital phase, proves to be the expression of an impulse to mastery, which easily passes over into cruelty. Impulses with a passive aim are connected with the erotogenic zone of the rectal orifice, at this period very important; the impulses of skoptophilia (gazing) and curiosity are powerfully active; the function of excreting urine is the only part actually taken by the genital organ in the sexual life. Objects are not wanting to be component-instincts in this period, but these objects are not necessarily all comprised in one object. The sadistic-anal organization is the stage immediately preceding the phase of primacy of the genital zone. Closer study reveals how much of it is retained intact in the later final structure, and what are the paths by which these component-instincts are forced into service of the new *genital organization*. Behind the sadistic-anal phase of the libido-development we obtain a glimpse of an even more primitive stage of development, in which the erotogenic mouth zone plays the chief part. You can guess that the sexual activity of sucking (for its own sake) belongs to this stage; and you may admire the understanding of the ancient Egyptians in whose art a child, even the divine Horus, was represented with a finger in the mouth.

(Lecture XXI, 'The Phases of Sexual Organization', pp. 273–5)

Keep in view at the moment the idea that the sexual life – the *libido-function*, as we call it – does not first spring up in its final form, does not even expand along the lines of its earliest forms, but goes through a series of successive phases unlike one another; in short, that many changes occur in it, like those in the development of the caterpillar into the butterfly. The turning-point of this development is the *subordination of all the sexual component-instincts under the primacy of the genital zone* and together with this the enrolment of sexuality in the service of the reproductive function. Before this happens the sexual life is, so to say, disparate – independent activities of single component-impulses each seeking *organ-pleasure* (pleasure in a bodily organ). This anarchy is modified by attempts at *pre*-genital 'organizations' of which the chief is the sadistic-anal phase, behind which is the oral, perhaps the most primitive...

To-day we will follow up another aspect of this development – namely the relation of the sexual component-impulses to an *object*; or rather, we will take a fleeting glimpse over this development so that we may spend more time upon a comparatively late result of it. Certain of the component-impulses of the sexual instinct have an object from the very beginning and hold fast to it; such are the impulse to mastery (sadism), to gazing (skoptophilia) and curiosity. Others, more plainly connected with particular erotogenic areas in the body, only have an object in the beginning, so long as they are still dependent upon the non-sexual functions, and give it up when they become detached from these latter. Thus the first object of the oral component of the sexual instinct is the mother's breast which satisfies the infant's need for nutrition. In the act of sucking for its own sake the erotic component, also gratified in sucking for nutrition, makes itself independent, gives up the object in an external person, and replaces it by a part of the child's own person. The oral impulse becomes *auto-erotic*, as the anal and other erotogenic impulses are from the beginning. Further development has, to put it as concisely as possible, two aims: first, to renounce auto-erotism, to give up again the object found in the child's own body in exchange again for an internal; and secondly to combine the various objects of the separate impulses and replace them by one single one. This naturally can only be done if the single object is again itself complete, with a body like that of the subject; nor can it be accomplished without some part of the auto-erotic impulse-excitations being abandoned as useless.

The processes by which an object is found are rather involved and have not so far received comprehensive exposition. For our purposes it may be emphasized that, when the process has reached a certain point in the years of childhood before the latency period, the object adopted proves almost identical with the first object of the oral pleasure impulse, adopted by reason of the child's dependent relationship to it; it is, namely, the mother, although not the mother's breast. We call the mother the first *love*-object. We speak of 'love' when we lay the accent upon the mental side of the sexual impulses and disregard, or wish to forget for a moment, the fundamental physical or 'sensual' side of the impulses. At about the time when the mother becomes the love-object, the mental operation of repression has already begun in the child and has withdrawn from him the knowledge of some part of his sexual aims. Now with this choice of the mother as love-object is connected all that which, under the name of *the Oedipus complex*', has become of such great importance in the psycho-analytic explanation of the neuroses, and which has had a perhaps equally important share in causing the opposition against psycho-analysis.

(Lecture XXI, 'The Oedipus Complex', p. 277)

There is no possible doubt that one of the most important sources of the sense of guilt which so often torments neurotic people is to be found in the Oedipus complex. More than this: in 1913, under the title of *Totem and Taboo* I published a study of the earliest forms of religion and morality in which I expressed a suspicion that perhaps the sense of guilt of mankind as a whole, which is the ultimate source of religion and morality, was acquired in the beginning of history through the Oedipus complex ...

Now what does direct observation of children, at the period of object-choice before the latency period, show us in regard to the Oedipus complex? Well, it is easy to see that the little man wants his mother all to himself, finds his father in the way, becomes restive when the latter takes upon himself to caress her, and shows his satisfaction when the father goes away or is absent. He often expresses his feelings directly in words and promises his mother to marry her; this may not seem much in comparison with the deeds of Oedipus, but it is enough in fact; the kernel of each is the same. Observation is often rendered puzzling by the circumstance that the same child on other occasions at this period will display great affection for the father; but such contrasting – or better, *ambivalent* – states of feeling, which in adults would lead to conflicts, can be tolerated alongside one another in the child for a long time, just as later on they dwell together permanently in the unconscious. One might try to object that the little boy's behaviour is due to egoistic motives and does not justify the conception of an erotic complex; the mother looks after all the child's needs and consequently it is due to the child's interest that she should trouble herself about no one else. This too is quite correct; but it is soon clear that in this as in similar dependent situations, egoistic interests only provide the occasion on which the erotic impulses seize. When the little boy shows the most open sexual curiosity about his mother, wants to sleep with her at night, insists on being in the room while she is dressing, or even attempts physical acts of seduction, as the mother so often observes and laughingly relates, the erotic nature of this attachment to her is established without a doubt. Moreover, it should not be forgotten that a mother looks after a little daughter's needs in the same way without producing this effect; and that often enough a father eagerly vies with her in trouble for the boy without succeeding in winning the same importance in his eyes as the mother. In short, the factor of sex preference is not to be eliminated from the situation by any criticisms. From the point of view of the boy's egoistic interests it would merely be foolish if he did not tolerate two people in his service rather than only one of them...

When the other children appear, the Oedipus complex expands and becomes a family complex. Reinforced anew by the injury resulting to the egoistic interests, it actuates a feeling of aversion towards these new arrivals and an unhesitating wish to get rid of them again. These feelings of hatred are as a rule much more often openly expressed than those connected with the parental complex...

The first choice of object in mankind is regularly an incestuous one, directed to the mother and sister of men, and the most stringent prohibitions are required to prevent this sustained infantile tendency from being carried into effect. In the savage and primitive peoples surviving to-day the incest prohibitions are a great deal stricter than with us...

The clinical fact which confronts us behind the form of the Oedipus complex as established by analysis now becomes of the greatest practical importance. We learn that at the time of puberty, when the sexual instinct first asserts its demands in full strength, the old familiar incestuous objects are taken up again and again invested by the libido. The infantile object-choice was but a feeble venture in play, as it were, but it laid down the direction for the object-choice of puberty. At this time a very intense flow of feeling towards the Oedipus complex or in reaction to it comes into force; since their mental antecedents have become intolerable, however, these feelings must remain for the most part outside consciousness. From the time of puberty onward the human individual must devote himself to the great task of *freeing himself from the parents*; and only after this detachment is accomplished can he cease to be a child and so become a member of the social community. For a son, the task consists in releasing his libidinal desires from his mother, in order to employ them in the quest of an external love-object in reality; and in reconciling himself with his father if he has remained antagonistic to him or in freeing himself from his domination if, in the reaction to the infantile revolt, he has lapsed into subservience to him. These tasks are laid down for every man; it is noteworthy how seldom they are carried through ideally, that is how seldom they are solved in a manner psychologically as well as socially satisfactory. In neurotics, however, this detachment from the parents is not accomplished at all; the son remains all his life in subjection to his father, and incapable of transferring his libido to a new sexual object. In the reversed relationship the daughter's fate may be the same. In this sense the Oedipus complex is justifiably regarded as the kernel of the neuroses.

(Lecture XXI, 'The Oedipus Complex in Neurotics', p. 283)

Wilhelm Reich

Excerpts from *The Sexual Revolution*

First published by Farrar, Straus and Giroux Inc., New York.

There are people who say that sex-economic living will destroy the family. They babble about the 'sexual chaos' which would result from a healthy love life, and the masses are impressed by them because they are professors or the authors of best-sellers. One has to know what one is talking about. It is a matter, first of all, of eliminating the economic enslavement of women and children. And their authoritarian enslavement. Not until that is done will the husband love his wife, the wife the husband, and will parents and children love each other. They will no longer have any reason to hate each other. What we want to destroy is not the family, but the hatred which the family creates, the coercion, though it may take on the outward appearance of 'love.' If familial love is that great human possession it is made out to be, it will have to prove itself. If a dog which is chained to the house does not run away, nobody will, for this reason, call him a faithful companion. No sensible person will talk of love when a man cohabits with a woman who is bound hand and foot. No half-way decent man will be proud of the love of a woman whom he buys by supporting her or by power. No decent man will take love which is not given freely. Compulsive morality as exemplified in marital duty and familial authority is the morality of cowardly and impotent individuals who are incapable of experiencing through natural love capacity what they try to obtain in vain with the aid of the police and marriage laws.

('On Sex-Economic "Morality"', p. 29)

The foremost breeding place of the ideological atmosphere of conservatism is the compulsive family. Its prototype is the triangle: father, mother, child. While the family, according to conservative concepts, is the basis, the 'nucleus' of human society as such, the study of its changes in the course of historical development and of its social function at any given time reveals it to be the result of definite economic constellations. Thus, we do not consider the family the cornerstone and basis of society, but the product of its economic structure (matriarchal and patriarchal family, Zadruga, polygamous and monogamous patriarchy, etc.). If conservative sexology, morality and legislature keep pointing to the family as the basis of 'state' and 'society', they are correct insofar as the authoritarian compulsive family is indeed part and parcel, and at the same time, prerequisite, of the authoritarian state and of authoritarian society. Its social significance lies in its following characteristics:

1. *Economically:* In the early days of capitalism, the family was the economic unit of enterprise and still is among the farmers and small tradesmen.

2. *Socially:* In authoritarian society, the family has the important task of protecting the woman and the children who are deprived of economic and sexual rights.

3. *Politically:* In the pre-capitalistic phase of home-industry and in early industrial capitalism the family had immediate roots in the familial economy (as is still the case in the economic set-up of small farms). With the development of the means of production and the collectivization of the work process, however, there occurred a change in the function of the family. Its immediate economic basis became less significant to the extent to which the woman was included in the productive process; its place was taken by the political function which the family now began to assume. Its cardinal function, that for which it is mostly supported and defended by conservative science and law, is that of serving as a factory for authoritarian ideologies and conservative structures. It forms the educational apparatus through which practically every individual of our society, from the moment of drawing his first breath, has to pass. It influences the child in the sense of a reactionary ideology not only as an authoritarian institution, but also on the strength of its own structure; it is the conveyor belt between the economic structure of conservative society and its ideological superstructure; its reactionary atmosphere must needs become inextricably implanted in every one of its members. Through its own form and through direct influencing, it conveys not only conservative ideologies and conservative attitudes toward the existing social order; in addition, on the basis of the sexual structure to which it owes its existence and which it procreates, it exerts an immediate influence on the sexual structure of the children in the conservative sense. It is not by accident that the attitude of adolescents toward the existing

social order, pro or contra, corresponds to their attitude pro or contra the family. Similarly, it is not by accident that conservative and reactionary youths, as a rule, are strongly attached to their families while revolutionary youths have a negative attitude toward the family and detach themselves from it...

('The Compulsive Family as Educational Apparatus', p. 72)

Wilhelm Reich

Excerpts from *The Mass Psychology of Fascism*

Translated by Vincent Carfagno; first published by Farrar, Straus and Giroux Inc., 1970.

Preface to the third edition

... Since fascism, whenever and wherever it makes its appearance, is a movement borne by masses of people, it betrays all the characteristics and contradictions present in the character structure of the mass individual. It is not, as is commonly believed, a purely reactionary movement – it represents an amalgam between *rebellious* emotions and reactionary social ideas ...

Fascist mentality is the mentality of the 'little man' who is enslaved and craves authority and is at the same time rebellious. It is no coincidence that all fascist dictators stem from the reactionary milieu of the little man. The industrial magnate and the feudal militarist exploit this social fact for their own purposes, after it has evolved within the framework of the general suppression of life-impulses. In the form of fascism, mechanistic, authoritarian civilization reaps from the suppressed little man only what it has sown in the masses of subjugated human beings in the way of mysticism, militarism, automatism, over the centuries. This little man has studied the big man's behaviour all too well, and he reproduces it in a distorted and grotesque fashion. The fascist is the drill sergeant in the colossal army of our deeply sick, highly industrialized civilization. It is not with impunity that the hullabaloo of high politics is made a show in front of the little man. The little sergeant has surpassed the imperialistic general in everything; in martial music; in goose stepping; in commanding and obeying; in cowering before ideas; in diplomacy, strategy, and tactic; in dressing and parading; in decorating and 'honorating' ...

From 'Ideology as Material Force' (Chapter 1)

Narrow-minded economy has repeatedly failed to see that the most essential question does not relate to the workers' consciousness of social responsibility (this is self-evident!) but to what it is that *inhibits the development of this consciousness of responsibility* ...

Sex-economic sociology's line of questioning, which is based on these discoveries, is not one of the typical attempts to supplement, replace, or confuse Marx with Freud or Freud with Marx. In an earlier passage we mentioned the area in historical materialism where psychoanalysis has to fulfill a scientific function, which social economy is not in a position to accomplish: the comprehension of the structure and dynamics of ideology, not of its historical basis. By incorporating the insights afforded by psychoanalysis, sociology attains a higher standard and is in a much better position to master reality; the nature of man's structure is finally grasped. It is only the narrow-minded politician who will reproach character-analytic structure-psychology for not being able to make immediate practical suggestions. And it is only a political loudmouth who will feel called upon to condemn it in total because it is afflicted with all the distortions of a conservative view of life. But it is the genuine sociologist who will reckon psychoanalysis' comprehension of childhood sexuality as a highly significant revolutionary act.

It follows of itself that the science of sex-economic sociology, which builds upon the *sociological* groundwork of Marx and the *psychological* groundwork of Freud, is essentially a mass psychological and sex-sociological science at the same time. Having rejected Freud's philosophy of civilization, it begins where the clinical psychological line of questioning of psychoanalysis ends.

Psychoanalysis discloses the effects and mechanisms of sexual suppression and repression and of their pathological consequences on the individual. Sex-economic sociology goes further and asks: *For what sociological reasons is sexuality suppressed by the society and repressed by the individual?* ...

If one studies the history of sexual suppression and the etiology of sexual repression, one finds that it cannot be traced back to the beginnings of cultural development; suppression and repression, in other words, are not the presuppositions of cultural development. It was not until relatively late, with the establishment of an authoritarian patriarchy and the beginning of the division of the classes, that suppression of sexuality begins to make its appearance. It is at this stage that sexual interests in general begin to enter the service of a minority's interest in material profit; in the patriarchal marriage and family this state of affairs assumes a solid organizational form. With the restriction and suppression of sexuality, the nature of human feeling changes; a sex-negating religion comes into being and gradually develops its own sex-political organization, the church with all its predecessors, the aim of which is nothing other than the eradication of man's sexual desires and consequently of what little happiness there is on earth. There is good reason for all this when seen from the perspective of the now-thriving exploitation of human labor.

To comprehend the relation between sexual suppression and human exploitation, it is necessary to get an insight into the basic social institution in which the economic and sex-economic situations of patriarchal authoritarian society are interwoven. Without the inclusion of this institution, it is not possible to understand the sexual economy and the ideological process of a patriarchal society. The psychoanalysis of men and women of all ages, all countries, and every social class shows that: *The interlacing of the socio-economic structure with the sexual structure of society and the structural reproduction of society takes place in the first four or five years and in the authoritarian family.* The church only continues this function later. Thus, the authoritarian state gains an enormous interest in the authoritarian family: *It becomes the factory in which the state's structure and ideology are moulded.*

We have found the social institution in which the sexual and the economic interests of the authoritarian system converge. Now we have to ask *how* this convergence takes place and *how* it operates. Needless to say, the analysis of the typical character structure of reactionary man (the worker included) can yield an answer only if one is at all conscious of the necessity of posing such a question. The moral inhibition of the child's natural sexuality, the last stage of which is the severe impairment of the child's *genital* sexuality, makes the child afraid, shy, fearful of authority, obedient, 'good,' and 'docile' in the authoritarian sense of the words. It has a crippling effect on man's rebellious forces because every vital life-impulse is now burdened with severe fear; and since sex is a forbidden subject, thought in general and man's critical faculty also become inhibited. In short, morality's aim is to produce acquiescent subjects who, despite distress and humiliation, are adjusted to the authoritarian order. Thus, the family is the authoritarian state in miniature, to which the child must learn to adapt himself as a preparation for the general social adjustment required of him later. *Men's authoritarian structure* – this must be clearly established – *is basically produced by the embedding of sexual inhibitions and fear in the living substance of sexual impulses . . .*

The result is conservatism, fear of freedom, in a word, reactionary thinking.

It is not only by means of this process that sexual repression strengthens political reaction and makes the individual in the masses passive and nonpolitical; it creates a secondary force in man's structure – an artificial interest which actively supports the authoritarian order. When sexuality is prevented from attaining natural gratification owing to the process of sexual repression, what happens is that it seeks various kinds of substitute gratifications. Thus, for instance, natural aggression is distorted into brutal sadism, which constitutes an essential part of the mass-psychological basis of those imperialistic wars that are instigated by a few . . .

The sexual morality that inhibits the will to freedom, as well as those forces that comply with authoritarian interests, derive their energy from repressed sexuality. Now we have a better comprehension of an essential part of the process of the 'repercussion of ideology on the economic basis': *sexual inhibition changes the structure of economically suppressed man in such a way that he acts, feels, and thinks contrary to his own material interests.*

From 'The Authoritarian Ideology of the Family in the Mass Psychology of Fascism' (Chapter 2)

. . . For one thing, the political and economic position of the father is reflected in his patriarchal relationship to the remainder of the family. In the figure of the father the authoritarian state has its representative in every family, so that the family becomes its most important instrument of power.

The authoritarian position of the father reflects his political role and discloses the relation of the family to the authoritarian state. Within the family, the father holds the same position that his boss holds toward him in the production process. And he reproduces his subservient attitude toward authority in his children, particularly his sons. Lower middle class man's passive and servile attitude toward the führer-figure issues from these conditions. Without really divining it, Hitler was building upon this lower middle class attitude when he wrote:

The people in their overwhelming majority are so feminine by nature and attitude that sober reasoning determines their thoughts and actions far less than emotion and feeling.

And this sentiment is not complicated, but very simple and all of a piece. It does not have multiple shading; it has a positive and a negative; love or hate, right or wrong, truth or lie, never half this way and half that way, never partially, or that kind of thing. [*Mein Kampf*, p. 183]

This is not a question of an 'inherent disposition,' but of a typical example of the reproduction of an authoritarian social system in the structures of its members.

What this position of the father actually necessitates is the strictest sexual suppression of the women and the children. While women develop a resigned attitude under lower middle class influence – an attitude reinforced by repressed sexual rebellion – the sons, apart from a subservient attitude toward authority, develop a strong identification with the father, which forms the basis of the emotional identification with every kind of authority. How it comes about that the psychic structures of the supporting strata of a society are so constructed that they fit the economic framework and serve the purposes of the ruling powers as precisely as the parts of a precision machine will long remain an unresolved riddle. At any rate, what we describe as the structural reproduction of a society's economic system in the psychology of the masses is the basic mechanism in the process of the formation of political ideas ...

To what extent the *unconscious* struggle against one's own sexual needs gives rise to metaphysical and mystical thinking cannot be discussed in detail here. We will mention only one example, which is typical of the National Socialist ideology. Again and again we run across series such as this: *personal honor*, *family honor*, *racial honor*, *national honor*. This sequence is consistent with the various layers in the individual structure. However, it fails to include the socio-economic basis: *capitalism, or rather patriarchy; the institution of compulsive marriage; sexual suppression; personal struggle against one's own sexuality; personal compensatory feeling of honor; etc.* The highest position in the series is assumed by the ideology of 'national honor,' which is identical with the irrational core of nationalism. To understand this, however, it is necessary to turn aside from our main theme again.

Authoritarian society's fight against the sexuality of children and adolescents, and the consequent struggle in one's own ego, takes place within the framework of the authoritarian family, which has thus far proven to be the best institution to carry out this fight successfully. Sexual desires naturally urge a person to enter into all kinds of relations with the world, to enter into close contact with it in a vast variety of forms. If they are suppressed, they have but one possibility: to vent themselves within the narrow framework of the family. Sexual inhibition is the basis of the familial encapsulation of the individual as well as the basis of individual self-consciousness. One must give strict heed to the fact that metaphysical, individual, and familial sentimental behavior are only various aspects of one and the same basic process of sexual nega- tion.

Wilhelm Reich

Excerpts from *The Function of the Orgasm*

Translated by Vincent Carfagno; first published by Farrar, Straus and Giroux Inc., New York.

The theory of sex-economy and its investigation of living phenomena can be stated in a few sentences.

Psychic health depends upon orgastic potency, i.e., upon the degree to which one can surrender to and experience the climax of excitation in the natural sexual act. It is founded upon the healthy character attitude of the individual's capacity for love. Psychic illnesses are the result of a disturbance of the natural ability to love. In the case of orgastic impotence, from which the overwhelming majority of people suffer, damming-up of biological energy occurs and becomes the source of irrational actions. The essential requirement to cure psychic disturbances is the re-establishment of the natural capacity for love. It is dependent upon social as well as psychic conditions.

Psychic illnesses are the consequences of the sexual chaos of society. For thousands of years, this chaos has had the function of physically subjecting man to the prevailing conditions of existence, of internalizing the external mechanization of life. It has served to bring about the psychic anchoring of a mechanized and authoritarian civilization by making man incapable of functioning independently.

The vital energies regulate themselves naturally, without compulsive duty or compulsive morality – both of which are sure signs of existing antisocial impulses. Antisocial actions are the expression of secondary drives. These drives are produced by the suppression of natural life, and they are at a variance with natural sexuality.

People who are brought up with a negative attitude toward life and sex acquire a pleasure anxiety, which is physiologically anchored in chronic muscular spasms. This neurotic pleasure anxiety is the basis on which life-negating, dictator-producing views of life are reproduced by people themselves. It is the core of the fear of an independent, freedom-oriented way of life. This fear becomes the most significant source of strength for every form of political reaction, and for the domination of the majority of working men and women by individual persons or groups. It is a biophysical fear, and it constitutes the central problem of the psychosomatic field of investigation. It has been until now the greatest obstruction to the investigation of the involuntary functions of life, which the neurotic person can experience only in a mysterious and fear-ridden way.

The character structure of modern man, who reproduces a six-thousand-year-old patriarchal authoritarian culture, is typified by characterological armoring against his inner nature and against the social misery which surrounds him. This characterological armoring is the basis of isolation, indigence, craving for authority, fear of responsibility, mystic longing, sexual misery, and neurotically impotent rebelliousness, as well as pathological tolerance. Man has alienated himself from, and has grown hostile toward, life. This alienation is not of a biological but of a socio-economic origin. It is not found in the stages of human history prior to the development of patriarchy.

Since the emergence of patriarchy, the natural pleasure of work and activity has been replaced by compulsive duty. The average structure of masses of people has been transformed into a distorted structure marked by impotence and fear of life. This distorted structure not only forms the psychological basis of authoritarian dictatorship, it enables these dictatorships to justify themselves by pointing to human attitudes such as irresponsibility and childishness. The international catastrophe through which we are living is the ultimate consequence of this alienation from life.

The structuring of masses of people to be blindly obedient to authority is brought about not by natural parental love, but by the authoritarian family. The suppression of the sexuality of small children and adolescents is the chief means of producing this obedience.

Nature and culture, instinct and morality, sexuality and achievement become incompatible as a result of the split in the human structure. The unity and congruity of culture and nature, work and love, morality and sexuality, longed for from time immemorial, will remain a dream as long as man continues to condemn the biological demand for natural (orgastic) sexual gratification. Genuine democracy and freedom founded on consciousness and responsibility are also doomed to remain an illusion until this demand is fulfilled. Helpless subjugation to chaotic social conditions will continue to typify human existence. The destruction of life by means of coercive education and war will prevail.

Herbert Marcuse

Excerpts from *Eros and Civilization*

First published by Beacon Press, Boston, Mass.

The hidden trend in psychoanalysis

The concept of man that emerges from Freudian theory is the most irrefutable indictment of Western civilization – and at the same time the most unshakable defense of this civilization. According to Freud, the history of man is the history of his repression. Culture constrains not only his societal but also his biological existence, not only parts of the human being but also his instinctual structure itself. However, such constraint is the very precondition of progress. Left free to pursue their natural objectives, the basic instincts of man would be incompatible with all lasting association and preservation: they would destroy even where they unite. The uncontrolled Eros is just as fatal as his deadly counterpart, the death instinct. Their destructive force derives from the fact that they strive for a gratification which culture cannot grant: gratification as such and as an end in itself, at any moment. The instincts must therefore be deflected from their goal, inhibited in their aim. Civilization begins when the primary objective – namely, integral satisfaction of needs – is effectively renounced.

The vicissitudes of the instincts are the vicissitudes of the mental apparatus in civilization. The animal drives become human instincts under the influence of the external reality. Their original 'location' in the organism and their basic direction remain the same, but their objectives and their manifestations are subject to change. All psychoanalytic concepts (sublimation, identification, projection, repression, introjection) connote the mutability of the instincts. But the reality which shapes the instincts as well as their needs and satisfaction is a socio-historical world. The animal man becomes a human being only through a fundamental transformation of his nature, affecting not only the instinctual aims but also the instinctual 'values' – that is, the principles that govern the attainment of the aims. The change in the governing value system may be tentatively defined as follows:

from	*to*
immediate satisfaction	delayed satisfaction
pleasure	restraint of pleasure
joy (play)	toil (work)
receptiveness	productiveness
absence of repression	security

Freud described this change as the transformation of the *pleasure principle* into the *reality principle*. The interpretation of the 'mental apparatus' in terms of these two principles is basic to Freud's theory and remains so in spite of all modifications of the dualistic conception. It corresponds largely (but not entirely) to the distinction between unconscious and conscious processes. The individual exists, as it were, in two different dimensions, characterized by different mental processes and principles. The difference between these two dimensions is a genetic-historical as well as a structural one: the unconscious, ruled by the pleasure principle, comprises 'the older, primary processes, the residues of a phase of development in which they were the only kind of mental processes.' They strive for nothing but for 'gaining pleasure; from any operation which might arouse unpleasantness ("pain") mental activity draws back.'[1] But the unrestrained pleasure principle comes into conflict with the natural and human environment. The individual comes to the traumatic realization that full and painless gratification of his needs is impossible. And after this experience of disappointment, a new principle of mental functioning gains ascendancy. The reality principle supersedes the pleasure principle: man learns to give up momentary, uncertain and destructive pleasures for delayed, restrained, but 'assured' pleasure.[2] Because of this lasting gain through renunciation and restraint, according to Freud, the reality principle 'safeguards' rather than 'dethrones,' 'modifies' rather than denies, the pleasure principle.

However, the psychoanalytic interpretation reveals that the reality principle enforces a change not only in the form and timing of pleasure but in its very substance. The adjustment of pleasure to the reality principle implies the subjugation and diversion of the destructive force of instinctual gratification, of its incompatibility with the established societal norms and relations, and, by that token, implies the transubstantiation of pleasure itself.

With the establishment of the reality principle, the human being, which, under the pleasure principle, has been hardly more than a bundle of animal drives, has become an organized ego. It strives for 'what is useful' and what can be obtained without damage to itself and to its vital environment. Under the reality principle, the human being develops the function of *reason*: it learns to 'test' the reality, to distinguish between good and bad, true and false, useful and harmful. Man acquires the faculties of attention, memory and judgement. He becomes a conscious, thinking *subject*, geared to a rationality which is imposed upon him from outside...

However, neither his desires nor his alteration of reality are henceforth his own: they are now 'organized' by his society. And this 'organization' represses and transubstantiates his original instinctual needs. If absence from repression is the archetype of freedom, then civilization is the struggle against this freedom.

The replacement of the pleasure principle by the reality principle is the great traumatic event in the development of man – in the development of the genus (phylogenesis) as well as of the individual (ontogenesis)...

The reality principle materializes in a system of institutions. And the individual, growing up within such a system, learns the requirements of the reality principle as those of law and order, and transmits them to the next generation.

The fact that the reality principle has to be re-established continually in the development of man indicates that its triumph over the pleasure principle is never complete and never secure. In the Freudian conception, civilization does not once and for all terminate a 'state of nature.' What civilization masters and represses – the claim of the pleasure principle – continues to exist in civilization itself. The unconscious retains the objectives of the defeated pleasure principle. Turned back by the external reality or even unable to reach it, the full force of the pleasure principle not only survives in the unconscious but also affects in manifold ways the very reality which has superseded the pleasure principle. The *return of the repressed* makes up the tabooed and subterranean history of civilization...

(pp. 1–15)

The origin of the repressed individual

... our subsequent discussion is an 'extrapolation', which derives from Freud's theory notions and propositions implied in it only in a reified form, in which historical processes appear as natural (biological) processes.

Terminologically, the extrapolation calls for a duplication of concepts: the Freudian terms, which do not adequately differentiate between the biological *and* the socio-historical vicissitudes of the instincts, must be paired with corresponding terms denoting the specific socio-historical component. Presently we shall introduce two such terms:

(a) *Surplus-repression:* the restrictions necessitated by social domination. This is distinguished from (basic) *repression*: the 'modifications' of the instincts necessary for the perpetuation of the human race in civilization.

(b) *Performance principle:* the prevailing historical form of the *reality principle*.

Behind the reality principle lies the fundamental fact of Ananke or scarcity (Lebensnot), which means that the struggle for existence takes place in a world too poor for the satisfaction of human needs without constant restraint, renunciation, delay. In other words, whatever satisfaction is possible necessitates *work*, more or less painful arrangements and undertakings for the procurement of the means for satisfying needs. For the duration of work, which occupies practically the entire existence of the mature individual, pleasure is 'suspended' and pain prevails. And since the basic instincts strive to the prevalence of pleasure and for the absence of pain, the pleasure principle is incompatible with reality, and the instincts have to undergo a repressive regimentation.

However, this argument, which looms large in Freud's metapsychology, is fallacious in so far as it applies to the brute *fact* of scarcity what actually is the consequence of a specific *organization* of scarcity, and of a specific existential attitude enforced by this organization. The prevalent scarcity has, throughout civilization (although in very different modes), been organized in such a way that it has not been distributed collectively in accordance with individual needs, nor has the procurement of goods for the satisfaction of needs been organized with the objective of best satisfying the developing needs of the individuals. Instead, the *distribution* of scarcity as well as the effort of overcoming it, the mode of work, have been *imposed* upon individuals – first by mere violence, subsequently by a more rational utilization of power ...

The various modes of domination (of man and nature) result in various historical forms of the reality principle. For example, a society in which all members normally work for a living requires other modes of repression than a society in which labor is the exclusive province of one specific group. Similarly, repression will be different in scope and degree according to whether social production is oriented on individual consumption or on profit; whether a market economy prevails or a planned economy; whether private or collective property. These differences affect the very content of the reality principle, for every form of the reality principle must be embodied in a system of societal institutions and relations, laws, and values which transmit and enforce the required 'modification' of the instincts. This 'body' of the reality principle is different at the different stages of civilization. Moreover, while any form of the reality principle demands a considerable degree and scope of repressive control over the instincts, the specific historical institutions of the reality principle and the specific interests of domination introduce *additional* controls over and above those indispensable for civilized human association. These additional controls arising from the specific institutions of domination are what we denote as *surplus-repression*.

For example, the modifications and deflections of instinctual energy necessitated by the perpetuation of the monogamic-patriarchal family, or by a hierarchical division of labor, or by public control over the individual's private existence are instances of surplus-repression pertaining to the institutions of a *particular* reality principle. They are added to the basic (phylogenetic) restrictions of the instincts which mark the development of man from the human animal to the *animal sapiens*. The power to restrain and guide instinctual drives, to make biological necessities into individual needs and desires, increases rather than reduces gratification: the 'mediatization' of nature, the breaking of its compulsion, is the human form of the pleasure principle. Such restrictions of the instincts may first have been enforced by scarcity and by the protracted dependence of the human animal, but they have become the privilege and distinction of man which enabled him to transform the blind necessity of the fulfillment of want into desired gratification...

Smell and taste give, as it were, unsublimated pleasure *per se* (and unrepressed disgust). They relate (and separate) individuals immediately, without the generalized and conventionalized forms of consciousness, morality, aesthetics. Such immediacy is incompatible with the effectiveness of organized *domination*, with a society which 'tends to isolate people, to put distance between them, and to prevent spontaneous relationships and the "natural" animal-like expressions of such relations'.[3] The pleasure of the proximity senses plays on the erotogenic zones of the body – and does so only for the sake of pleasure. Their unrepressed development would eroticize the organism to such an extent that it would counteract the desexualization of the organism required by its social utilization as an instrument of labor.

Throughout the recorded history of civilization, the instinctual constraint enforced by scarcity has been intensified by constraints enforced by the hierarchical distribution of scarcity and labor; the interest of domination added surplus-repression to the organization of the instincts under the reality principle. The pleasure principle was dethroned not only because it militated against progress in civilization but also because it militated against a civilization whose progress perpetuates domination and toil ...

The modification of the instincts under the reality principle affects the life instinct as well as the death instinct; but the development of the latter becomes fully understandable only in the light of the development of the life instinct, i.e., of the repressive *organization of sexuality*. The sex instincts bear the brunt of the reality principle. Their organization culminates in the subjection of the partial sex instincts to the primacy of genitality, and in their subjugation under the function of procreation. The process involves the diversion of libido from one's own body toward an alien object of the opposite sex (the mastery of primary and secondary narcissism). The gratification of the partial instincts and of non-procreative genitality are, according to the degree of their independence, tabooed as perversions, sublimated, or transformed into subsidiaries of procreative sexuality. Moreover, this latter is in most civilizations channeled into monogamic institutions. This organization results in a quantitative and qualitative restriction of sexuality: the unification of the partial instincts and their subjugation under the procreative function alter the very nature of sexuality: from an autonomous 'principle' governing the entire organization it is turned into a specialized temporary function, into a means for an end. In terms of the pleasure principle governing the 'unorganized' sex instincts, reproduction is merely a 'by-product.' The primary content of sexuality is the 'function of obtaining pleasure from zones of the body'; this function is only 'subsequently brought into the service of that of reproduction' ...

In introducing the term *surplus-repression* we have focused the discussion on the institutions and relations that constitute the social 'body' of the reality principle. These do not just represent the changing external manifestations of one and the same reality principle but actually change the reality principle itself. Consequently, in our attempt to elucidate the scope and the limits of the prevalent repressiveness in contemporary civilization, we shall have to describe it in terms of the specific reality principle that has governed the origins and the growth of this civilization. We designate it as *performance principle* in order to emphasize that under its rule society is stratified according to the competitive economic performances of its members. It is clearly not the only historical reality principle: other modes of societal organization not merely prevailed in primitive cultures but also survived into the modern period.

The performance principle, which is that of an acquisitive and antagonistic society in the process of constant expansion, presupposes a long development during which domination has been increasingly rationalized: control over social labor now reproduces society on an enlarged scale and under improving conditions. For a long way, the interests of domination and the interests of the whole coincide: the profitable utilization of the productive apparatus fulfills the needs and faculties of the individuals. For the vast majority of the population, the scope and mode of satisfaction are determined by their own labor; but their labor is work for an apparatus which they do not control, which operates as an independent power to which individuals must submit if they want to live. And it becomes the more alien the more specialized the division of labor becomes. Men do not live their own lives but perform pre-established functions. While they work, they do not fulfill their own needs and faculties but work in *alienation*. Work has now become *general*, and so have the restrictions placed upon the libido: labor time, which is the largest part of the individual's life time, is painful time, for alienated labor is absence of gratification, negation of the pleasure principle. Libido is diverted for socially useful performances in which the individual works for himself only in so far as he works for the apparatus, engaged in activities that mostly do not coincide with his own faculties and desires.

However – and this point is decisive – the instinctual energy thus withdrawn does not accrue to the (unsublimated) aggressive instincts because its social utilization (in labor) sustains and even enriches the life of the individual. The restrictions imposed upon the libido appear as the more rational, the more universal they become, the more they permeate the whole of society. They operate on the individual as external objective laws and as an internalized force: the societal authority is absorbed into the 'conscience' and into the unconscious of the individual and works as his own desire, morality and fulfillment. In the 'normal' development, the individual lives his repression 'freely' as his own life: he desires what he is supposed to desire; his gratifications are profitable to him and to others; he is reasonably and often even exuberantly happy. This happiness, which takes place part-time during the few hours of leisure between the working days or working nights, but sometimes also during work, enables him to continue his performance, which in turn perpetuates his labor and that of the others. His erotic performance is brought in line with his societal performance. Repression disappears in the grand objective order of things which rewards more or less adequately the complying individuals and, in doing so, reproduces more or less adequately society as a whole.

The conflict between sexuality and civilization unfolds with this development of domination. Under the rule of the performance principle, body and mind are made into instruments only if they renounce the freedom of the libidinal subject-object which the human organism primarily is and desires. The distribution of *time* plays a fundamental role in this transformation. Man exists only *part*-time, during the working days, as an instrument of alienated performance; the rest of the time he is free for himself. (If the average working day, including preparation and travel to and from work, amounts to ten hours, and if the biological needs for sleep and nourishment require another ten hours, the free time would be four out of each twenty-four hours throughout the greater part of the individual's life.) This free time would be potentially available for pleasure. But the pleasure principle which governs the id is 'timeless' also in the sense that it militates against the temporal dismemberment of pleasure, against its distribution in small separated doses. A society governed by the performance principle must of necessity impose such distribution because the organism must be trained for its alienation at its very roots – the *pleasure ego*.[4] It must learn to forget the claim for timeless and useless gratification, for the 'eternity of pleasure.' Moreover, from the working day, alienation and regimentation spread into the free time ...

(pp. 32–43)

The dialectic of civilization

However, repression is largely unconscious and automatic while its degree is measurable only in the light of consciousness. The differential between (phylogenetically necessary) repression and surplus-repression may provide the criteria. Within the total structure of the repressed personality, surplus-repression is that portion which is the result of specific societal conditions sustained in the specific interest of domination. The extent of this surplus-repression provides the standard of measurement: the smaller it is, the less repressive is the stage of civilization. The distinction is equivalent to that between the biological and the historical sources of human suffering ...

The superiority of nature and the organization of societal relations have essentially changed in the development of civilization. Consequently, the necessity of repression, and of the suffering derived from it, varies with the maturity of civilization, with the extent of the achieved rational mastery of nature and of society. Objectively, the need for instinctual inhibition and restraint depends on the need for toil and delayed satisfaction. The same and even a reduced scope of instinctual regimentation would constitute a higher degree of repression at a mature stage of civilization, when the need for renunciation and toil is greatly reduced by material and intellectual progress – when civilization could actually afford a considerable release of instinctual energy expended for domination and toil. Scope and intensity of instinctual repression obtain their full significance only in relation to the historically possible extent of freedom ...

At the end, under the rule of the fully developed performance principle, subordination appears as implemented through the social division of labor itself (although physical and personal force remains an indispensable instrumentality). Society emerges as a lasting and expanding system of useful performances; the hierarchy of functions and relations assumes the form of objective reason: law and order are identical with the life of society itself. In the same process, repression too is depersonalized: constraint and regimentation of pleasure now become a function (and 'natural' result) of the social division of labor ...

(pp. 80–81)

The ideology of today lies in that production and consumption reproduce and justify domination. But their ideological character does not change the fact that their benefits are real. The repressiveness of the whole lies to a high degree in its efficacy: it enhances the scope of material culture, facilitates the procurement of the necessities of life, makes comfort and luxury cheaper, draws ever-larger areas into the orbit of industry while at the same time sustaining toil and destruction. The individual pays by sacrificing his time, his consciousness, his dreams; civilization pays by sacrificing its own promises of liberty, justice, and peace for all.

The discrepancy between potential liberation and actual repression has come to maturity: it permeates all spheres of life the world over. The rationality of progress heightens the irrationality of its organization and direction. Social cohesion and administrative power are sufficiently strong to protect the whole from direct aggression, but not strong enough to eliminate the accumulated aggressiveness. It turns against those who do not belong to the whole, whose existence is its denial ...

(pp. 90–91)

Notes

1. 'Formulations Regarding the Two Principles in Mental Functioning', *Collected Papers,* IV (London: Hogarth Press, 1950), 14.
2. ibid., p. 18.
3. Ernest Schactel, 'On Memory and Childhood Amnesia', in P. Mullahy (ed.), *A Study of Interpersonal Relations* (New York: Hermitage Press, 1950).
4. To be sure, every form of society, every civilization has to exact labor time for the procurement of the necessities and luxuries of life. But not every kind and mode of labor is essentially irreconcilable with the pleasure principle. The human relations connected with work may 'provide for a very considerable discharge of libidinal component impulses, narcissistic, aggressive and even erotic' (*Civilization and Its Discontents*, p. 34n.). The irreconcilable conflict is not between work (reality principle) and Eros (pleasure principle), but between *alienated* labor (performance principle) and Eros.

John David Ober

On Sexuality and Politics in
the Work of Herbert Marcuse

First published in *Critical Interruptions*, edited by P. Brienes (Herder and Herder, 1970).

Herbert Marcuse uniquely transgresses the current 'traditional wisdom' of the mass media which by the end of the decade of the sixties had in concert proclaimed the advent of *the* sexual revolution in America. Those who announced or participated in the upheaval and its commercial institutionalization tend to split into two camps: those who deplore the collapse of traditional Christian codes of conduct and those who applaud and help to create the supposed emancipation from the older verities.

Marcuse belongs to neither camp. He has always been the foe of the hair-brained enthusiasts who have tried to impose sexual codes of conduct on others in the name of transcendental ethical systems, especially those who invade the realm of privacy in their efforts to unmask and denounce carnal pleasure as sin. One of the most repressive features of Western culture has been the long-established dualism of the spirit and the flesh.[1] But Marcuse is no less the foe of all who reduce the definition of human liberation to the dimension of pure sexuality, a reduction which leads in the end to the simplistic equation that unhampered sexual intercourse (on- or off-stage, in public or private) is identical with freedom. Not unlike the erstwhile Christian moralists, the advocates of sexual reductionism (especially scientists with calipers and computers) establish and disseminate information about normative standards and techniques which may serve to replace the old taboos with more stringent codes of behaviour against which the individual must match his own performance and 'degree of liberation'.

Marcuse has most frequently been misunderstood in his opposition to the implications of the so-called sexual revolution. His unique position among contemporary social critics consists in his rejection of both Puritan taboos and the wanton sexual abandon which emerged during the past decade. Marcuse's rejection of both previous restrictions and current sexual reductionism is neither self-contradictory nor utopian, neither a defense of libertinism nor a self-styled neo-puritanism.

What, then, is the source of the confusion? Apparently it lies in an unbridged gap between *Eros and Civilization* and *One-Dimensional Man*, in the unclear relationship between the concept 'surplus-repression' in the former and the concept 'repressive desublimation' in the latter. More precisely, 'surplus-repression' would seem to conjure up the very sexual rebellion which is occurring against the lingering taboos in an effort to remove the surplus.[2] 'Repressive desublimation' would seem, on the contrary, to imply a harsh condemnation of the recent sexual emancipation. Marcuse himself is aware of the scant treatment given the latter concept and of the resulting criticism that either he has modified his position between the two books or has unwittingly contradicted his earlier views. To date he has had no occasion to discuss the relationship between 'surplus-repression' and 'repressive desublimation,' both of which play major roles in his general critique of advanced industrial society.

This study will attempt to explore the relationship between the two and to respond to the charge of inconsistency by demonstrating that the content of the sexual revolution is neither revolutionary nor liberating, but rather the extension and solidification of the most repressive features of advanced industrial society. To be sure, the new forms of domination and control operate within a broader and more lenient framework than the old. But in terms of the individual's psychological development, the decrease in both acknowledged and unacknowledged limitations on sexual behavior by no means demonstrates by itself that repression has declined or that mental health has improved. The sexual explosion does not herald the coming of the non-repressive, sublimated civilization envisaged in *Eros and Civilization*. On the contrary, the rampant commercialization, not only of sex, but of the sexual revolution itself, may well indicate an increase in the ability of the established society to tolerate more, and more divergent, forms of behavior because the shrinking of the human psyche and imagination by means of technological manipulation has rendered impotent such formerly dangerous forms of behavior.

Human freedom, for Marcuse, has always been and remains far more than a matter to be decided by individual opinion alone. The belief that thinking oneself to be free makes it so, reeks of ritual magic and is a regressive throwback to the concept of 'inner' freedom which arose during the early Reformation period. Similarly, freedom is more than the right to do anything one wants, especially if what one wants is contrary to the continuation of human civilization and is the result of the preconditioning of goals, desires, and beliefs. Freedom, even sexual freedom, is a question of politics, but a politics which transcends the accepted present and omnipresent situation in which the vote and the candidates are marketed and sold as proof of freedom.

No attempt to discuss Marcuse's theory of psychological development would be accurate if it failed to take into account the relationship between the individual personality and the socio-historical content embodied in the forces of socialization at the present time. And today more than ever, those forces are an amalgamation of political pressures operating for the preservation of the established powers. The inter-connection between sexuality and politics at present reveals itself paradoxically as an increase in the toleration of divergent sexual behavior coupled with an increase in control over individual self-realization by utilizing that toleration. The release of libidinal energy continues to serve the interests of domination. And it is only political behavior which can undermine the existence and the need for the existence of institutions which convince men to participate in their own unfreedom while believing themselves to be free.

I

In the earlier of the two books Marcuse introduces the concepts 'surplus-repression' and 'performance principle' in order to clarify the ambiguity in the Freudian theory between biological, individual instinc-tual development and the historical vicissitudes of the instincts.[3] The specific institutions and values of a given society play a major role in accounting for variations in the socialization process from one society to another.

Freud defined repression operating within the individual as 'a pre-liminary stage of condemnation, something between flight and condem-nation.'[4] In the course of psychosexual development repression arises, and can only arise, after the split between unconscious and conscious mental activity has occurred; for the role of repression is 'simply in turning something away, and keeping it at a distance, from the con-scious.'[5] The fundamental result of repression is to transform instinctual pleasures into painful experiences which continue to be rejected from consciousness:

> The fulfillment of these wishes would no longer produce an affect of pleasure, but one of pain; and it is just this conversion of affect that constitutes the essence of what we call 'repression.'[6]

Freud himself considered the discovery of repression together with the unmasking of infantile sexuality to be the two greatest achievements of psychoanalysis.[7]

For Freud, repression, and even growing repression, is an essential precondition for and an indigenous part of human civilization. But Marcuse argues – against the neo-Freudian revisionists – that there are passages in Freud which counteract Freud's own denial of the possibilities of a society without repression, or better, the reversal of the process of increasing repression.[8] And, indeed, if repression as an individual psychic phenomenon emerges only after or concurrently with the development of consciousness, then the term necessarily includes the social dimension, the institutions and agents of the socialization process. As Marcuse indicates, these institutions and agents are not mere abstractions; they are imbued with the specific content of a specific socio-economic set of arrangements. Freud's Reality Principle, therefore, is not a formal or reified structure which functions in the same way at all times and places in order to prepare individuals for their social roles in the conquest of scarcity in the struggle for existence. Different socio-economic systems socialize in qualitatively different ways.[9]

In order to clarify the fact that the specific content of the Reality Principle varies historically, Marcuse introduces his second concept, the 'performance principle', which is defined as 'the prevailing historical form of the *reality principle*'.[10] For Marcuse, then, the concept of repression must be understood in its twofold dimensions: as a technical psychic mechanism of the individual to deny the entrance of painful instincts into consciousness; and as a social process which transforms libidinous energy into channels which are useful to the preservation and perpetuation of the on-going society. Neither Freud nor Marcuse would deny for an instant that throughout human history, it is repression which has made possible all human society by curtailing and transforming the polymorphously perverse sexual energy of the individual into sublimated, deflected activities through sublimation.

The historians of civilization seem to be unanimous in the opinion that such deflection of sexual motive powers from sexual aims to new aims, a process which merits the name of *sublimation*, has furnished powerful components for all cultural accomplishments. We will, therefore, add that the same process acts in the development of every individual . . .[11]

But is Marcuse justified in his assumption that in the work of Freud himself there is a socio-historical 'performance principle'? The justification can be seen only by elucidating the fundamental lack of clarity in certain aspects of Freud's own career and work. First, he always viewed himself as a scientist, a practicing physician, and not as a speculative philosopher or sociologist. 'His political thought, accordingly, is neither systematically developed nor logically unified.'[12] Second, his theories underwent almost constant re-working in the light of new evidence acquired in the course of his practice.[13] Third, in spite of the difficulties in piecing together a complete socio-political theory from Freud's writings, Roazen has shown effectively that Freud '. . . was not as insensitive to historical change as some seem to assume.'[14] For example, on occasion Freud comments on the changes in mental health and illness wrought by historical changes in the specific values of society.[15] In his paper of 1908, '"Civilized" Sexual Morality and Modern Nervous Illness', Freud launches a virulent attack on the 'spread of modern nervous illness' due to the fact that 'the demands made on the efficiency of the individual in the struggle for existence have greatly increased and it is only by putting out all his mental powers that he can meet them.' The increase in nervous illness and the emergence of new forms of mental illness under established technological arrangements are exacerbated by the stringent and unmanageable sexual restrictions imposed by the ethical norms of Victorianism; the demands of the specific civilization lead to a curtailment of behavior which surpasses the limits of human endurance.

In addition, Freud distinguishes three historical stages in the evolution of the sexual instinct in culture. The three move from the free exercise of the instinct without regard to the aims of reproduction to 'present-day "civilized" sexual morality,' in which all of the sexual instinct is suppressed except what serves the aim of *legitimate* reproduction'.[16] Here is an example of 'surplus-repression': the subordination of excessive amounts of libidinal energy to *specific* laws, customs, and institutions – laws, customs, and institutions which may subvert freedom through external aggression and by extracting too great a toll from the resources of the individual. As envisaged by Marcuse, the reversal of the process of increasing surplus-repression would not mean the collapse of civilization into barbarism, but the transformation of an overly demanding form of civilization into one which recognizes the instinctual needs of men as well as the limits of human tolerance in terms of repression. By analogy, one might say that Marcuse has added the fully developed social dimension to the Freudian theory in much the same way that Locke introduced the concept of society into the theory of Hobbes. For Hobbes, the successful attack upon sovereignty destroys the contract and hurls man back into anarchy; for Locke, the leaders and even the form of the government can be changed without destroying civilization. But the theory presupposes the existence of autonomous individuals and thereby reveals itself as belonging to the pre-industrial period. Similarly, the society of which Freud was a part differed radically from the one which emerged from the dust and trenches of the First World War.

In that pre-War stage of historical development the suppression and control of sexuality was still achieved by means of moral and legalistic prohibitions and by rigidly defining and causing the introjection of the accepted channels of 'legitimate' sexuality. The rules were enforced by religious and legal disapprobation against all deviance. To be sure, Freud argued that such narrow limits produce neurosis by imposing demands upon the individual which he cannot meet in health. The result of such 'surplus-repression' was the sublimation of the sexual instincts beyond the human capacity for sublimation,[17] and the perpetuation of a particular society with its repressive performance principle at the expense of the health and relative happiness of the individual. For Marcuse, as we shall see, the repression continues today; but it is created and reinforced by the new dynamic of advanced industrial society.

Many other instances of Freud's awareness of the importance of specific social institutions, values, and relationships can be found, together with his condemnation of societies which extract too much by means of repression. In *Civilization and Its Discontents* he remarks that it is 'unquestionable that an actual change in men's attitudes to property' would help to lessen the threat of aggression and enhance human happiness to some degree.[18] Nor did Freud believe that fundamental social change was impossible. He was much too aware of the importance of socio-historical changes upon the development of the individual psyche in the past to ignore the possibilities for future changes. The principal problem with Freud's historical thought, according to Roazen, is that 'he was tempted to construct historical stages on scanty evidence ... Ultimately, he was more interested in illustrating timeless truths than in learning about unique historical developments.'[19]

Surplus-repression for Marcuse is repression over and above that required for the continuation of the human race in civilization. It is 'the restrictions necessitated by social domination; these additional controls arising from specific institutions of domination are what we denote as *surplus-repression*.' And there have been various modes of domination which result in various historical forms of the Reality Principle.[20] The relationships of any given society form a constellation which gives that society an identifiable character; and the values of that society, values which obviously figure in the socialization process, reflect the institutional arrangements of the society as a whole.[21] A given institution or value can only be understood in terms of the whole, and social change necessarily involves a change in the whole constellation.

In the paper '"Civilized" Sexual Morality', Freud reiterates a constant theme that the retardation and suppression of sexual development and behavior (functions which are performed by the agents of socialization – parents, educational institutions, religious institutions) are necessary not only to the survival of civilization, but also to the perpetuation of the specific form of civilization in which socio-economic arrangements permit the young of 'the educated classes' to attain independence and earn a living only after twenty or more years of life. Sexual repression works in the service of a specific form of social and economic dependence:

> This reminds one, incidentally, of the intimate interconnection between all our cultural institutions and of the difficulty of altering any part of them without regard to the whole.[22]

Freud expresses the same view even more strongly at the conclusion of his paper, 'The Sexual Enlightenment of Children.' He praises the growth of secular education against church-dominated instruction, but notes the critical omission of sexual enlightenment even among the former. Authentic enlightenment, change, emancipation can never result from isolated instances of revision and reform:

> Here, once again, we see the unwisdom of sewing a single silk patch on to a tattered coat – the impossibility of carrying out an isolated reform without altering the foundations of the whole system.[23]

The preceding discussion attempted to demonstrate that there are legitimate reasons for assuming that the seeds of a socio-political critique of contemporary forms of civilization exist within the works of Freud himself, in spite of ambiguities in his theory between the permanent elements of the psyche and the historical vicissitudes they have undergone and will surely continue to undergo.

Eros and Civilization is first and foremost an attempt to present the possibilities and processes for the removal of surplus-repression by the radical transformation of a society whose continued existence necessitates such repression, regardless of the specific agents of repression. It becomes increasingly clear that the not-so-civilized domination exercised by the technological father is replacing the domination exercised by the 'civilized' morality of the Victorian father. But indications abound that the change in the agents and even the dynamic of socialization has not changed the performance principle and has not, therefore, led to the decline in surplus-repression. The Freudian analysis stands vindicated once again: the growth of material and technological progress continues hand in hand with the growth of repression under the performance principle of advanced industrial society.[24] And the truth of the Freudian analysis is the condemnation of a society whose governing principle is the excessive utilization of libidinal energy for preconceived social projects, many of which curtail the imagination, destroy the well-springs of human relationships, and negate human freedom at the instinctual and social levels. But there is more. The anarchistic release of men from the control of repression and surplus-repression without a sweeping transformation of the present society and the performance principle by which it survives would lead not to freedom, but to the very opposite. Civilization itself would be overwhelmed in a burst of brutal and aggressive energy, which, for too long, has been accustomed to serving the interests of a brutal and aggressive society.

The question whether a 'non-repressive sublimated' society is possible is from the very first a question of politics, of transforming the established society into one in which the need for domination and surplus-repression no longer exists. Beyond that, the degree to which repression itself can be eliminated is an open issue. For Freud, repression is the irreversible price of civilization; for Marcuse, men living under different social, political, and economic conditions might in turn create freer institutions under which the need for repression would be greatly diminished.

'Sex and politics' is more than a mere slogan. For the degree of control exercised over the population of advanced industrial societies is rooted in manipulation at the instinctual level on a scale impossible prior to the advent of the means and the products of industrialization. The prescription of channels for the expression of libidinous energy in directions which are politically useful to the ruling powers has also been enhanced by technology. The result is a population which is increasingly docile *and* aggressive, content in domination while hating and destroying the things one is supposed to hate and destroy. The masters emerge stronger than ever.

Non-repressive civilization can only be considered as the outcome of political changes which would re-program the computers from overkill and moonshots to the satisfaction of human needs and would abolish the performance principle under which most men toil for the benefit of a few. The political break in the chain of control might, indeed, lead to a break in the chain of unequal, alienated toil and the establishment of a society of non-repressive, sublimated libidinal relationships in the place of the universal cash-nexus. But it is only a political transformation that offers the hope that the destruction of one historical form of the performance principle is not tantamount to the destruction of civilization.

Eros and Civilization raises the possibility of a society without surplus-repression; but the work is not a call for immediate or 'unrestricted gratification' of the sexual instinct:

> Freud did not define the 'essence' of love as sexual desire, but as the inhibition and sublimation of sexual desire by tenderness and affection, and he saw in this 'fusion' one of the greatest achievements of civilization. Consequently, Freud could not have 'had the idea' (and I did not) that 'the emancipation' of man lies in the complete and unrestricted satisfaction of his sexual desire.[25]

At the same time, Marcuse agrees with Freud's scathing denunciation of the excessive repression imposed on human sexuality by the erstwhile codes and practices of Victorianism.[26] But emancipation from surplus-repression requires far more than the unhampered release of private desires and hostilities in private and public.

II

With *One-Dimensional Man* Marcuse moves from the possibilities for a non-repressive society to the analysis of the factors in advanced industrial society which perpetuate unfreedom and repression. The work involves an examination of the important cultural changes which occurred during the period between the wars and led to new forms of repression and domination. This critique of prevailing trends leads Marcuse to conclude that the new-found freedoms of the decade are not the harbingers of the emancipation rendered possible by the available technological liberation from toil and scarcity, but, in many instances, the signs of a new and more effective control at the deepest levels of man's instinctual being. But even superficially, the events of the decade in the sphere of sexual behavior have, if anything, strengthened the illusion of freedom in other areas and, by that very token, have served the interests of control behind the backs of individuals through the coordination of control at the economic, political, and social levels. Once again Marcuse insists that the authentic emancipation of the individual from his own superfluity of repression depends upon the elimination of institutions which serve as the agents of repression and demand the rigged release of sublimated and desublimated energy for their survival. The release of repressed energy within the confines of the established order is the return to barbarism and the end of civilization – the process of regression which Freud warned against.

What are the new forces of repression which operate through the socialization process in advanced technological society? In order to discover what these forces are and how they operate in the formation of the individual personality, it is necessary first to examine the sweeping changes which have taken place in the economic, political, and social spheres since Freud's day. These changes include, first, the emergence of organized competition on the national and supra-national scale; second, the growing concentration of control by total administration and co-ordination of technology, culture, and politics; third, self-perpetuating mass production and consumption stimulated by advertising and the creation of artificial needs; fourth, the growing invasion and negation of privacy – physical, mental, and emotional – by manipulation and indoc-trination.

According to Marcuse, these tendencies have the most serious and far-reaching consequences for both the individual whose psyche is formed under the prevailing features and, conversely, for the society made up of such individuals. For example, the father and the patriarchal family, which were formerly the chief agents of socialization, have been increasingly replaced by direct socialization through the mass media, education, sport teams, peer groups. The earliest psychic conflicts and subsequent repression emerged in the long struggle with the father; with the decline in the role of the father, the ego is increasingly formed directly 'from outside', before consciousness can be shaped as the individual and relatively independent force which mediates between the id and the superego, between one's *self* and *others*.[27]

These changes in the process and agents of socialization render the individual himself one-dimensional because the content of the ego is infused from outside by the vested interests of the society. Similarly, immediate identification with the goals and projects of that society is greatly enhanced, for the individual quickly learns to experience the needs of the social system as his own personally felt needs. He is the object, conscious and unconscious, of the administered creation and satisfaction of such needs. The victims of the established performance principle are less autonomous, less capable of distinguishing Self from Other, freedom from unfreedom. The weakening of the ego in advanced industrial society helps to account for the unending stream of prose and verbalization about 'identity crises'. But the weakening of the ego also helps to explain the formation of 'masses' and the emergence of the authoritarian personality who seeks to supplant the emptiness with the introjection of external authority, opinion, and the soothing balm of the expert. What can one say of an alleged democracy when the *demos* consciously and intentionally relinquishes its sovereignty and power of ultimate arbitration to the military-industrial experts who 'know more'?[28]

The shrinking of consciousness leads to the predominance of the emotions over consciousness and conscience. The behavior of individuals is less mediated than immediate; action flows from the desire to achieve instant gratification. But even the channels for gratification are administered by and through the control and management of free time, the 'massification' of privacy.

But it would seem that the substitution of the impersonal goals and aims of society and its agents of socialization for the individual's own processes of selection is less effective as a source of gratification to the individual. The problem is twofold: first, identification with the external ego-ideal evokes anxiety, hostility in competition with others, the impossibility of satisfactorily living up to expectations which often transcend individual potentialities – a situation which prevails more often than not with the hero idols of advertising and entertainment. The frustration of competition and failure activates aggressive energy. Second, identification with the external ego-ideal means that the aggressive goals of the repressive society are easily accepted as one's own. In turn, the aggressive energy, once mobilized, is available for direct cathexis in the defense of the performance principle and its specific features of aggression at home and abroad, its wasteful ventures which satisfy no known human need. (As bigger and more expensive weapon systems replace last year's model it is increasingly possible to find earlier models in parks as playthings.) But the impersonal aims and objects which are the result of 'massified socialization' seem not to provide adequate gratification. Increased frustration in such circumstances would lead to an 'escalation of psychic aggression'.[29]

In *One-Dimensional Man* Marcuse speaks of 'repressive desublimation' or 'institutionalized desublimation.' In the face of the obvious changes in sexual mores and practices, the so-called Puritan or Victorian morality of earlier periods has essentially the same status today as the concept of free, private enterprise – a shibboleth which is reiterated daily. Both are largely mythological and have long ago ceased to function in any crucial way in determining the character of the society as a whole. Both the moral and the economic myth, however, are still effective as ideology and propaganda. The myth of unhampered free competition is apparently an important component of the illusion of freedom created in the socialization process in advanced industrial society. Similarly, the myth of the predominance of Puritan standards of sexual conduct is an important ideological ingredient in the commercialization of sex on and off Broadway and in the market place. The myth of a revolution against a tradition which has long been weak or hypocritical is undoubtedly profitable. (One need not take seriously the remark of the woman from the hinterlands who wished to see *The Boys in the Band* because she thought it was a Broadway musical.)

For Marcuse, repressive desublimation extends liberty while intensifying domination. Previous societies imposed authoritarian restrictions on sexual behaviour. But prior to the advent of technology, some restrictions were necessary for the survival of civilization as long as scarcity and the struggle against nature demanded perpetual toil. Advanced industrial society, paradoxically, has increased its control over the individual by extending the boundaries of freedom in regard to sexual behavior through prescribed channels of institutionalized desublimation, the integration of sexuality into commerce and industry, advertising, and entertainment. At the same time, sexuality is carefully isolated from the broader erotic components which, in the Freudian theory, provide the basis for all civilized human relationships. Individuals who seem no longer capable of utilizing their own faculties in work and in leisure time find solace in the packaged and structured outlets provided by the billion-dollar entertainment business. Indeed, the sexual revolution itself is largely the brainchild of that industry for profit. The commercialization and externalization of sex has meant a further reduction in the available modes of erotic cathexis and the contraction of libido from erotic to mere sexual gratification without the sublimated bonds of friendship and tenderness which constituted the greatest victory of civilization against the aggressive impulses.

The diminishing of erotic expression and sublimated sexuality leads to the intensification of sexual energy, whose expression is immediate in the terms provided under the performance principle.[30] The society offers institutionalized channels for the direct expression of limited, but intensified, sexual drives: the result is the strengthening of the control over the individuals by the protective and repressive society: 'The organism is thus being preconditioned for the spontaneous acceptance of what is offered.'[31] If the autonomy of the individual, for Freud, was embodied in the allegiance he was able to retain to the Pleasure Principle in spite of the sacrifices to the Reality Principle, then today the diminished opposition and tension between the two principles serves to strengthen the latter; the individual blithely accepts the system which permits him to satisfy, at least partially but in a direct manner, his diminished instinctual needs.

If the foregoing account of the mechanism and results of the socialization process in advanced industrial society is accurate, then a new problem arises in terms of the Freudian theory. According to Freud, the opportunity for the comparatively open and non-repressive expression of libido in sublimated forms would lead to gratification. The frustration and consequent need for aggression would be lowered as a result. But today, the facts seem to indicate that the opposite is happening: greater sexual leeway together with an *increase* in aggressive behavior.

Marcuse tries to account for this phenomenon with the argument that the institutionalization and externalization of the socialization process together with the institutionalization and control of desublimated behavior would mean, in fact, the release and gratification of fragmented, partial, and localized sexuality. By calling forth only one component of the general sexual impulse, the desublimation 'would be compatible with the growth of unsublimated as well as sublimated forms of aggression'.[32] Here too, as with sexuality, the passive acceptance and approval by large portions of the population of the national purpose, above all the practice of genocidal warfare, would indicate controlled desublimation or institutionalized desublimation in the realm of aggression. Sublimated forms of aggression also seem to be on the increase as, for example, verbal abuse and aggressive propaganda from the top usurp the place of rational discourse.

Marcuse's explanation can be amplified in terms of Freudian theory: Freud proposes that the life-serving forces which enhance civilization are 'to a great extent obtained through the suppression of what are known as the *perverse* elements of sexual excitation'.[33] One of the components of sexuality is aggression (sadism) which is normally repressed and sublimated.[34] But in a society which has instituted desublimated channels of libidinal expression in the interest of aggressive national goals, any number of 'perverse' components of the sexual instinct might be expected to emerge in the expression of sex, sadism and aggression included:

Sadism would then correspond to an aggressive component of the sexual instinct which has become independent and exaggerated and has been brought to the fore by displacement.[35]

Where sadism occurs, masochism is customarily in attendance also. Evidence of both is plentiful among the young who abuse their bodies and those of others through destructive drugs, medication, and decibel count. Some recent examples may suffice. In a report on 'Rock Style', Sara Davidson quotes one rock performer as saying, 'I've come on stage lots of times, just from the music, and it's unbelievable.'[36] Another member of a rock group exposed himself on stage. Still another 'set fire to his guitar'. Other perverse components of the sexual instincts also seem rampant, sadism and masochism especially. Leather, gold rings through the nose, sound so loud as to cause pain, and sexual sadism itself. 'Most of the girls ... are interested in getting into whipping. You know, you take off your belt and kind of tease them with it, and then you start doing it harder.'[37]

There is no greater success in the commercialization of sex-as-entertainment than the Playboy Enterprises of Hugh Hefner. In a lengthy series of articles on 'The Playboy Philosophy', Hefner relies on

Ayn Rand's concept of aggressive selfishness and on the stock liberal wisdom to invent the 'playboy', the classic description of which follows:

> He can be a sharp-minded young business executive, a worker in the arts, a university professor, an architect or engineer. He can be many things providing he possesses a certain point of view. He must see life not as a vale of tears, but as a happy time; he must take joy in his work, without regarding it as the end and all of living; he must be an alert man.... a man who – without acquiring the stigma of the voluptuary or dilettante – can live life to the hilt.[38]

Life is a 'happy time' and, like work, fun. At one and the same time, Hefner defends capitalism and the status quo, and attacks Puritanism and censorship. Almost anything goes, apparently, so long as it is American, anti-socialistic, and successful. Not a word is said about poverty, alienation of labor, wars, racial discrimination, aggression at home and abroad, waste, pollution, nuclear idiocy – and nothing is said about love, friendship, or the other civilizing affections. As the 'philosophy' unfolds, it becomes clear that eroticism plays no role in the life of the playboy. Sex as fun and entertainment with all the commercial accoutrements of sex appear to exhaust the range of human desires and expression.[39]

One-dimensional man, the victim and adjunct of advanced industrial domination, is isolated from the very instinctual roots of his unconscious memory and being by the process of surplus-repression at work in the formation of the ego and the contents of consciousness, in the controlled satisfaction of needs, and in the added stimulation and toleration of heretofore forbidden modes of behavior. For Marcuse, the most frightening element of the new performance principle is the manipulation and control of the psyche itself at the conscious and unconscious levels, for here lie the socio-psychological origins of the 'tough baby', the authoritarian personality of our times,[40] the playboy. It has been noted previously that the playboy ethos 'is basically *anti-sexual*. Like the sports car, liquor and hi-fi, girls are just another *Playboy* accessory.'[41] While the statement accurately attests to the routine commercialization of sex, the term *anti-sexuality* fails to capture the reductionism of eroticism to sex: One looks in vain for the slightest hint of eroticism in the playboy network of products. The impulses which, in their sublimated forms, Freud viewed as the essence of civilization – the affections which curtail aggression and bind people into enduring relationships of friendship – have all been reduced to their purely sexual (desublimated) components: Joy becomes fun; friends become chicks or tricks; gratification becomes instant release; and Eros yields its power to instant sexuality. And sex itself has been studied, dissected, measured, observed, computerized, analyzed, quantified, standardized, sanitized, and reduced to the techniques of copulation in a thousand different books, articles, plays, and research centers. Thomas Nagel notes, '... it is tempting to regard as sadistic an excessive preoccupation with sexual technique, which does not permit one to abandon the role of agent at any stage of the sexual act.'[42]

Civilization has arrived, then, at a stage where the instruments of toleration, flexibility, and emancipation from old taboos are at the same time the vehicles of a form of domination and repression which is, perhaps, even more debilitating than the earlier patriarchal model of socialization and psychosexual development. The latter, while demanding surplus-repression, left the individual free, albeit surreptitiously in many cases, to explore his own body and the bodies of others in freedom. Today the agents of society who prescribe 'freedom' have greatly narrowed the space for psychic maneuvering and exploration. Constant panels, discussions, lectures on norms and techniques by the media and in the academies have successfully isolated and compartmentalized sexual performance with at least four novel consequences.

(1) Sexuality itself is viewed as a laboratory specimen. It is thereby reduced to a mundane aspect of human behavior, like eating an omelet,[43] and the expansive, erotic dimensions of libido are eliminated. The fullest range of relationships which are truly human is correspondingly reduced. It is as if the mock-ups of jovial and festive social gatherings which permeate the world of advertising in the media had all but replaced such gatherings and cooperative endeavors in life itself. Community projects in the arts, where they exist at all, must be the work of committees rather than the spontaneous expression of individual needs and talents.

(2) The commercialization and scientific study of sexual performance – even to the measurement of the size of genitalia and kinetic and organic sensations during orgasm – and the increasing dissemination of such information may well tend to establish norms or standards of behavior which are far more ritualistic and repressive than the outlandish standards of perfection found in romantic love, and which are every bit as impossible of attainment. The thorough-going application of technology to every aspect of sexuality robs the imagination, the source and repository of political, social, and personal alternatives,

and poses a threat to the ego more frightening than the threat of the father.

(3) The inevitable failure to match the standards set by the commercial sex idols and ideology leads to enormous profits for the cosmetic and other industries; and it also leads both to a variety of psychological malfunctions, such as frustration and increased aggressiveness, in the continual public and private competition with the idols who serve as ego-ideals, and at the same time to passive resignation and shame which leave the individual more susceptible to that which is offered.

(4) The imposition of scientific and commercial standards of 'emancipated' performance deprive the individual of the main source of his own freedom, the Pleasure Principle. For here is the most subversive discovery in the Freudian theory: sex and politics are decisively linked – not only at the conscious level and through the forms of socialization – but also in the unconscious which strives for freedom from repression. More bluntly, freedom becomes ideology and propaganda unless the individuals in a society are relatively free both in consciousness and politically to develop and explore the erotic impulses without the presupposed, externally imposed standards of either Puritan morality or scientific, institutionalized research. There is no freedom without individuals who have charted their own course between the persistent demands of the Pleasure Principle and the demands of civilization without sacrificing all to either Aphrodite or Artemis.

But is the foregoing analysis of freedom really so very different from the credo of the 'playboy'? There appear to be decisive differences which can best be illuminated through the analysis of an example – the ambiguity of the popular slogan, 'Do your own thing.' In some ways the slogan seems to capture the ambiguities of the present, both the increased domination and the possibilities for emancipation from sexual negation and sexual reductionism. The slogan contains both the passive acceptance of intolerable or even barbaric behavior and the refusal to submit to standards which are intolerable and barbaric. If the slogan means literally that anyone at the present time is justified in acting out his own whims, then civilization is surely doomed for the very reasons expounded by Freud. Not even the permissive thinkers of the Enlightenment believed that 'anything goes' or that 'one man's opinion is as good as another's.'[44] On the other hand, the slogan is subversive of existing tendencies toward massification of socialization, the public orgasm, sexual reductionism, and increasing domination through toleration and liberation. Doing one's *own* thing implies the existence of a self which is different from the others, a conscious subject which creates for itself the alternatives to the superimposed demands of the performance principle and is conscious of the available alternatives to the 'objectification' of the psyche.

Here again sex and politics are connected. The effort to survive as a free subject against the enormous pressures exerted by the established society cannot be expected to succeed as an individual undertaking or by patchwork reform:

> Here, the old conflict arises again: human freedom is not only a private affair – but it is nothing at all unless it is *also* a private affair.[45]

In the passages cited earlier, Freud himself seemed to be aware of the impossibility of piecemeal change for the lessening of human subjugation and repression without a change in the entire structure of human institutions. Changing the whole is political change, revolutionary change, the effort to substitute a less repressive performance principle for one which amalgamates and utilizes psychic energy for increasing domination, global mastery, waste of human and natural resources, and the perpetuation of violence at home and abroad.

In summation, too many critics of the sexual 'revolution' seem to have missed the decisive point. Apart from the usual voices in the wilderness announcing the moral collapse of America through copulation, there are an increasing number of voices raised against the behavioral emancipation on typical pragmatic grounds. The usual argument of late runs something like the following: 'Uncontrolled promiscuity, nudity, and the escalating defiance of the standards of taste and propriety will unleash a backlash and lead to the institution of a new age of Puritan suppression.' It is dubious whether anyone except the commercial moguls who profit from the commercialization of sex would be the poorer if some of the trash were to disappear. But the main problem with the pragmatic argument is its fundamental ahistoricity. It is highly unlikely that the restoration of Puritanical codes could succeed unless corresponding political changes occur which lead to a full-scale totalitarian society; for the present society is itself too dependent upon the release and controlled gratification of libidinous instincts.

To be sure the possibility of political regression remains as a constant alternative, given the repressive features of the established society; similarly, liberation from those repressive features remains as a constant threat to the established society. But the path to liberation depends upon the refusal to participate in the public orgasm which, in many ways, still resembles and fortifies the process which D. H. Lawrence called 'cultural masturbation'. The refusal to participate depends on an immanent critique of the forces at work in and behind the sexual revolution and, conversely, on the remembrance and re-collection of the civilizing potentialities of Eros. The voyeurism and exhibitionism of the theatre, the authoritarian tendencies in the recent productions and public displays by the Living Theatre,[46] and the anti-erotic stimulation of the new sexuality threaten to destroy the fragile victories of sublimated sexuality. Freud noted the essential sublimation of sexuality involved in art, in the concept of beauty. The concept of beauty is rooted in 'the soil of sexual stimulation ... The more remarkable, therefore, is the fact that the genitals, the sight of which provokes the greatest sexual excitement, can really never be considered "beautiful".'[47] Eros, like art, fulfills its civilized and civilizing mission not through sex alone, but through the channels of sublimation: 'Whatever fosters the growth of culture works at the same time against the threat of war.'[48] In a review of the Hungarian film *The Round Up*, Penelope Gilliat writes:

'The Round Up' is often about terror, but the style holds it back from horror, even in a scene where a naked girl has to run up and down before an obscene likeness of an honor guard, with the two lines of soldiers lashing her. The sight suddenly made me realize – maybe along with other people – why it is that the sight of the unknown naked bodies careering around stages and screens at the moment can mysteriously make you feel frightened; to anyone who remembers the films and newsreels of the Second World War these strangers without clothes summon up the concentration camps.[49]

III

Two questions remain to be discussed here: What is the precise relationship in Marcuse's theory between 'surplus-repression' and 'repressive desublimation'? What are the alternatives to the repressive ethics of Puritanism and to the repressive sexual explosion?

There is an important adjunct to the first question. What justifies Marcuse in assuming that the sexual behavior at present is not the result of a *decline* in the actual amount of repression at the individual level and a decline in its attendant phenomena, guilt and anxiety, rather than the maintenance and even increase in repression? Why not assume that the new permissiveness is the result of a freer and more humane society which can, by that very token, subsume under the rubric of *sublimated behavior* a greater variety of pluralism of sexual practices? Isn't a society which survives and thrives on sexual plurality less repressive than one which demands heterosexual, procreative, genitalized conformity and punishes deviance with the pain of guilt and, often, prison?

Yes, of course. And a question in response: What if the emancipation not only poses no threat to the established powers, but enhances the survival of a social system which threatens to liquidate civilization and life itself? What price the public orgasm if the resulting network of cathexis lends support to a society which is increasingly inimical to the preservation of civilization as it has developed?

Marcuse's historical extension of the Freudian theory necessitates an historical definition of sublimation. The term becomes meaningless if the point of reference is only the existing society, regardless of the degree to which that society threatens life and civilization, limits and distorts the imagination, and destroys the expansive and life-giving functions of the erotic impulses. Sublimation refers to those deflections of instinctual energy which enhance life and preserve the gains of civilization. And on that account, it is the established society itself which stands condemned for its reliance on behavior which is the antithesis of the fragile historical victory against ignorance and cruelty. The immediate expression and gratification of impulses – demanded, bestowed, and rewarded – belongs not to the historical realm of civilized existence, but to the primal horde. Given the objective preconditions for the survival of civilization, the tendencies of the present denote regression and *desublimation* to the degree that they suppress the remembrance and the rational defense of alternatives at both the instinctual and political levels.

But why *repressive?* Isn't the direct expression and acting out of unconscious and conscious desires indication enough that repression is on the wane? For Marcuse, the answer is no, although the content of repression may today be radically altered due to the drastic changes in the agents and processes of socialization since Freud. The raw aggressive and sexual impulses may no longer be repressed to the same extent required under the conflicts in the patriarchal society. But the compartmentalization of sexuality in advanced industrial society means that the truly erotic components of sexuality have been eliminated and repressed because of the threat they pose to the performance principle of that society.[50]

The same holds true for aggression. Sublimation has assumed a major role in the battle against the appropriation of nature for human ends. But the evidence today points to the betrayal of and expulsion from consciousness of the historical projects which led to the mastery over nature: a growing indifference to the environment (are cities in any other industrialized sector of the globe more violent, dangerous, hideous, and uninhabitable than those here?); wanton destruction, waste, pollution replace the appropriation of nature; the indifference toward and lack of concern for one's friends, neighbors, lovers. The quick trick and the one-night stand do not bespeak the language of liberation from repression, but the language of redoubled repression. Gone are the hopes for alternatives to the performance principle, only to be replaced by a weary and aggressive resignation. It is as if the Pleasure Principle had relinquished the eternal battle with the demands of the Reality Principle; or as if the Pleasure Principle itself had been repressed, forgotten, curtailed, and narrowed in exchange for the new and partial modes of satisfaction: A stupendous sacrifice. If repression had, indeed, declined, then one might expect, according to Freud, a corresponding decline in mental illness and the growth of permanent human relationships grounded in libidinal cathexis rather than cash-nexus and the 'legitimate' contractual bonds of the courts of law.

The second question – of alternatives to the repression of sexuality under Puritanism and the repression of Eros under the governing powers of the sexual explosion – is a question of political, social, and psychological revolution. But no revolution is involved in a society which freely permits the regressive behavior of the commercial orgy and its attendant escapism to Zen, mysticism, and astrology. 'Running wild in the woods, dyeing [oneself] with woad, and living on hips and haws,'[51] constitutes neither the expression of authentic individuality in the state of nature (a regressive reversal of civilization the impossibility of which Rousseau noted) nor the advent of a new emancipation in the midst of a destructive society. The belief that mysticism and ritual magic, performed by day or night, in or out of clothing, are proof of social transformation is but the latest example of repressive desublimation at the ideological level. In Haiti voodoo serves as a mask and support for carefully calculated repression by the authoritarian regime. In advanced industrial society the celebration of the public orgasm and the mystical proclamation of change by means of enrapturing trances may serve a purpose not so very different.

But what are the alternatives? If desublimated self-indulgence rein-forces the stranglehold of the prevailing destructiveness, the return to previous codes of repressive conduct, even if such a reversal were possible, could only revive and intensify the detection and punishment of 'illegitimate' sexual behavior by more efficient technological means. The spectre of Calvin with technology at hand summons up nightmares.

Authentic alternatives to sexual desublimation must emerge within and against that desublimation itself. The transformation from sex-as-performance to erotic sexuality is at once a personal and a political project. The forces which severed the pathways that placed libidinal impulses into the service of civilization are political forces. In turn, the personal dissatisfaction and illness which result from the organized control of gratification and the social and political restriction of path-ways for the expression of sublimated sexuality into channels which make any difference demand a politics which destroys and replaces the old. Under different social conditions, the pathways which currently lead to desublimation and sexual disturbances 'must in health be sup-posed to serve ... other than sexual aims, the sublimation of sexuality.'[52] For Freud, the paths are also passable in both directions; natural and social environment created from sublimated sexual cathexis would in turn serve the interests of personal stimulation and gratification without outside interference or surplus-repression.

The hope for the alternative rests with those – both young and old – who reject the established organization of their personal lives and the expropriation of their physical and psychic energy for destructive ends. If the outcome of the struggle cannot be foretold, the ambiguities of the present trends should nonetheless be exposed; for in those ambiguities lies the cause of hope and despair.

First, together with the commercial proclamation of the sexual revolu-tion, is the unannounced effort, especially among the students, to estab-lish bonds of friendships which are not based upon the prevailing drive for profit. The greater toleration and flexibility offered by the society can be appropriated for ends, personal and political, which are fundamen-tally opposed to the social goals of the sexy commercial display. The opposition to those goals may destroy the repressive link between sexu-ality and the destructive performance principle.

Second, together with the repressive scientific reduction of sexuality to charts, graphs, and techniques comes the growing consciousness and possibility of making rational distinctions between impulses which are life-serving (erotic) and those which are destructive and aggressive. The choice among alternatives, the rational control which Freud defended over the destructive impulses, depends upon knowledge. To be sure, the new knowledge is both restricting and liberating – scientific control over the fundamental source of human freedom and creativity, on the one hand; and the defiance of that control through rational distinction and personal choice, on the other hand.

Nowhere is this ambiguity more evident than in the realm of the sexual perversions. Marcuse has amply demonstrated in *Eros and Civilization* that the weakest assumption in the Freudian theory was the unexamined link between the socially prescribed limitation of sexuality to genital-procreative sex and the productive and reproductive apparatus of the capitalist societies under the performance principle of profitability. The extension of the erotic impulses to other zones of the body and to other forms of sexual behavior may threaten the established society at its most vital point because such non-productive sexuality threatens the productive apparatus which thrives on repressive sublimation and desublimation.[53] While the established society grows wealthy from the commercial exploitation of the perversions it creates, encourages, and tolerates, the perversions themselves retain their potential for disrupting the established performance principle. Here too distinctions are necessary and possible on a more rational basis than before, in the rejection by the individual himself of those 'components' of sexuality that are destructive and partial, which distort or destroy the full erotic gratification and creation of which the individual is capable. Perversion itself would then require redefinition as 'the truncated or incomplete versions of the complete configuration ... perversions of the central impulse.'[54] Narcissism, fetishism, sadism, masochism, under this redefinition, remain perverse. They are incomplete expressions of the demands of Eros. And so it is with sexual reductionism. The civilizing mission of Eros is defeated when the orgasm replaces the Pleasure Principle as the sole end of human sexuality:

> If sex were all, then every trembling hand
> Could make us squeak, like dolls, the wished-for words.
> But note the unconscionable treachery of fate,
> That makes us weep, laugh, grunt and groan, and shout
> Doleful heroics, pinching gestures forth
> From madness or delight, without regard
> To that first, foremost law ...[55]

Notes

1. See the comments of Thomas Nagel, 'Sexual Perversion', *Journal of Philosophy*, LXVI, No. 1 (16 January 1969), 12–13. Also Herbert Marcuse, *Eros and Civilization* (Boston: Beacon Press, 1955), 210–11.

2. One student informed me that Marcuse's views of sexual conduct had received their finest popular expression in 'The Playboy Philosophy' of Hugh Hefner! See the discussion below. Also see *The New York Times* of 2 October 1969 for Paul VI's amusing denunciation of Freud and Marcuse as advocates of 'disgusting and unbridled expressions of eroticism.'

3. Herbert Marcuse, *Eros and Civilization*, 35.

4. Sigmund Freud, 'Repression', *The Standard Edition of the Complete Psychological Works of Sigmund Freud*, XIV (London: Hogarth Press, 1957), 146.

5. ibid., 147.

6. Sigmund Freud, 'The Interpretation of Dreams', *The Basic Writings of Sigmund Freud* (New York: Random House, 1938), 537.

7. Sigmund Freud, *On the History of the Psycho-Analytic Movement* (New York: Norton, 1966), 16.

8. Herbert Marcuse, *Eros and Civilization*, 5.

9. Note the interesting examples cited by Karl Polanyi, *The Great Transformation* (Boston: Beacon, 1957), Chapter 4, 43 ff.

10. Herbert Marcuse, *Eros and Civilization*, 35.

11. Sigmund Freud, 'Three Contributions to the Theory of Sex', *The Basic Writings of Sigmund Freud*, 584.

12. Thomas Johnston, *Freud and Political Thought* (New York: Citadel, 1965), 15.

13. Paul Roazen, *Freud: Political and Social Thought* (New York: Knopf, 1968), Chapter II, 76 ff. According to Roazen, 'Freud was not a comprehensive thinker; as he said in a letter to Groddeck, "I have a special talent for being satisfied with a fragment"' (p. 87). How is it possible to write a book on Freud's political and social theories without a single mention of Marcuse's work?

14. ibid., 266.

15. ibid.

16. Sigmund Freud, ' "Civilized" Sexual Morality and Modern Nervous Illness', in *The Standard Edition*, IX (London: Hogarth, 1959), 189. Italics in the original.

17. Freud illustrated the limits of toleration to the suppression of sexuality at the end of his Clark University lectures with the fable of the Schilda horse which died when underfed for reasons of economy. See *The Standard Edition*, XI (London: Hogarth, 1957), 54.

18. Sigmund Freud, *Civilization and Its Discontents* (Garden City: Doubleday), 103.

19. Paul Roazen, op. cit., 266.

20. Herbert Marcuse, *Eros and Civilization*, 35 and 37.

21. See Herbert Marcuse, 'A Note on Dialectic', *Reason and Revolution* (Boston: Beacon, 1960), vii-xvi.
22. Sigmund Freud, '"Civilized" Sexual Morality and Modern Nervous Illness', *The Standard Edition*, IX, 196.
23. Sigmund Freud, 'The Sexual Enlightenment of Children', *The Standard Edition*, IX, 139.
24. Herbert Marcuse, *Eros and Civilization*, 3 ff. and 11 ff.
25. Herbert Marcuse, 'A Reply to Erich Fromm', *Dissent* (Winter 1956), 79.
26. Herbert Marcuse, *Eros and Civilization*, 200–201 and *passim*.
27. An important discussion of this problem prior to the publication of *One-Dimensional Man* occurs in a paper delivered by Marcuse in September 1963 to the American Political Science Association. The paper was translated into German and published under the title "Das Veralten der Psychoanalyse' in *Kultur und Gesellschaft*, II (Frankfurt am Main: Suhrkamp, 1965). See esp. 87 ff.
28. ibid., 94.
29. See Marcuse's discussion, 'Aggressiveness in Advanced Industrial Society', *Negations* (Boston: Beacon, 1968), 264.
30. Herbert Marcuse, *One-Dimensional Man* (Boston: Beacon, 1964), 73–4.
31. ibid., 74.
32. ibid., 78.
33. Sigmund Freud, '"Civilized" Sexual Morality and Modern Nervous Illness', *The Standard Edition*, IX, 189. See also 'Three Contributions to the Theory of Sex', *The Basic Writings of Sigmund Freud*, 553–79.
34. Sigmund Freud, 'Three Contributions', 569.
35. ibid., 569.
36. Sara Davidson, 'Rock Style: Defying the American Dream', *Harper's* (July 1969), 60.
37. ibid., 57.
38. Hugh M. Hefner, 'The Playboy Philosophy', issued as a series of four pamphlets (Chicago: December 1962), Pamphlet I, 3.
39. See the brief sketch entitled 'Tough Baby' in Theodor W. Adorno, *Minima Moralia* (Frankfurt am Main: Suhrkamp, 1951), 51–2.
40. Herbert Marcuse, *One-Dimensional Man*, 74.
41. Harvey Cox, in J. D. Brown (ed.), *Sex in the 60's* (New York: Time-Life, 1968), 40.
42. Thomas Nagel, 'Sexual Perversion', 14.
43. ibid. See Nagel's discussion of the decisive differences between hunger and sexual motivation, pp. 8–9.
44. For example, Voltaire explicitly rejects the toleration of intolerance and the evils of church-dominated education. It is only in an age which believes that there are no historically verified elements which are quintessential to civilization itself that the rhetoric of the ACLU prevails as accepted ideology. For the present, to ask the question 'Do you prefer George Lincoln Rockwell or John F. Kennedy or Ché Guevara?' seems tantamount to asking 'Do you prefer Liederkrantz, Camembert, or Brie?' in spite of the fact that for the

majority of Americans the answer to the first question is a foregone conclusion on the basis of conditioning by the media without regard to political content and projects.

45. Herbert Marcuse, *Eros and Civilization*, 224–5.
46. Robert Brustein discussed the Living Theatre in an article which appeared in the *New York Review of Books*, Vol. 12, No. 3 (13 February 1969), 30–31.
47. Sigmund Freud, 'Three Contributions', 568n.
48. Sigmund Freud, 'Why War?', in Ernest Jones (ed.), *The Collected Papers*, V (New York: Basic Books, 1959), 287.
49. Penelope Gilliat, in *The New Yorker* (17 May 1969), 127.
50. See the thorough-going discussion of this threat in *Eros and Civilization*, esp. Chapters II and X.
51. Bertrand Russell, 'Mysticism and Logic', *Mysticism and Logic* (Garden City: Doubleday, 1957), 15.
52. Sigmund Freud, 'Three Contributions', 603.
53. Herbert Marcuse, *Eros and Civilization*, 44 ff. and 161 ff.
54. Thomas Nagel, 'Sexual Perversion', 13.
55. From Wallace Stevens, 'Le Monocle de Mon Oncle', *The Collected Poems* (New York: Knopf, 1954).

SEX AS BEING

Jean Paul Sartre

Excerpts from *Being and Nothingness*

First published in 1943 under the title *L'Être et le Néant* by Gallimard (copyright © 1943 by Jean Paul Sartre). First published in English 1958 by Methuen and Co. Ltd (English translation copyright © 1958 by Philosophical Library).

[Sartre argues that we are conscious beings in the sense that we are conscious of something. A major mode of subjectivity is the mode of 'for-itself'. Consciousness seeks to establish what it is conscious of. By bringing nothingness into the world the for-itself can judge other beings by knowing what it is not. Being for-itself then is nihilation of particular beings, and also a desire for being. The crucial way in which the for-itself tries to find itself is through interpersonal relations, of which desire is an important element. I experience my existence and confirm it through the recognition of it by others.]

... neither the tumescence of the penis nor any other physiological phenomenon can ever explain or provoke sexual desire – no more than the vaso-constriction or the dilation of the pupils (or the simple consciousness of these physiological modifications) will be able to explain or to provoke fear. In one case as in the other, although the body plays an important role, we must – in order to understand it – refer to being-in-the-world and to being-for-others. I desire a human being not an insect or a mollusc, and I desire him (or her) as he *is* and as I am in a situation in the world and he is an Other for me and as I am Other for him ...

To have sex means ... to exist sexually for an Other who exists sexually for me ... The first apprehension of the Other's sexuality in so far as it is lived and suffered can be only *desire*; it is by desiring the Other (or by discovering myself as incapable of desiring him) or by apprehending his desire for me that I discover his being-sexed. Desire reveals to me simultaneously my being-sexed and *his* being sexed, *my* body as sex and *his* body ...

Desire is expressed by the caress as thought is by language. The caress reveals the Other's flesh as flesh to myself and to the Other. But it reveals this flesh in a very special way. To take hold of the Other reveals to her her inertia and her passivity as a transcendence-transcended; but this is not to caress her. In the caress it is not my body as a synthetic form in action which caresses the Other; it is my body as flesh which causes the Other's flesh to be born. The caress is designed to cause the Other's body to be born, through pleasure, for the Other – and for myself – as a *touched* passivity in such a way that my body is made flesh in order to touch the Other's body with its own passivity; that is by caressing itself with the Other's body rather than by caressing her ...

Thus the revelation of the Other's flesh is made through my own flesh; in desire and in the caress which expresses desire, I incarnate myself in order to realize the incarnation of the Other. The caress by *realizing* the Other's incarnation reveals to me my own incarnation, that is I make myself flesh in order to impel the Other to realize *for herself* and *for me* her own flesh, and my caresses cause my flesh to be born in so far as it is for the Other *flesh causing her to be born as flesh.* And so possession truly appears as double reciprocal incarnation ... The caress has for its goal only to impregnate the Other's incarnation; desire is the desire to appropriate this incarnated consciousness. Therefore desire is naturally continued not by caresses but by acts of taking and of penetration. The caress has for its goal only to impregnate the Other's body with consciousness and freedom. Now it is necessary to take this saturated body, to seize, to enter into it. But by the very fact that I now attempt to seize the Other's body, to pull it toward me, to grab hold of it, to bite it, my own body ceases to be flesh and becomes again the synthetic instrument *which I am.* And by the same token the *Other* ceases to be an incarnation; she becomes once more an instrument in the midst of the world which I apprehend in terms of its situation ... I insist on taking the Other's body but my very insistence makes my incarnation disappear ...

Sadism is an effort to incarnate the Other through violence and this incarnation 'by force' must be already the appropriation and utilization of the Other. Sadism like desire seeks to strip the Other of the acts which hid him. It seeks to reveal the flesh beneath the action. But whereas the For-itself in desire loses itself in its own flesh in order to reveal to the Other that he too is flesh, the sadist refuses his own flesh at the same time that he uses instruments to reveal by force the Other's flesh to him. The object of sadism is immediate appropriation ...

(from Chapter 3, 'Concrete Relations with Others', Section II, 'Attitudes towards others. Indifference, Desire, Hate, Sadism')

Simone de Beauvoir

Excerpts from *The Second Sex*

Le Deuxième Sexe first published 1949. This translation published by Jonathan Cape in 1953 and by Penguin Books in 1972.

Thus humanity is male and man defines woman not in herself but as relative to him; she is not regarded as an autonomous being ... And she is simply what man decrees; thus she is called 'the sex', by which is meant that she appears essentially to the male as a sexual being. For him she is sex – absolute sex, no less. She is defined and differentiated with reference to man and not he with reference to her; she is the incidental, the inessential as opposed to the essential. He is the Subject, he is the Absolute – she is the Other ...

Thus it is that no group ever sets itself up as the One without at once setting up the Other over against itself. If three travellers chance to occupy the same compartment, that is enough to make vaguely hostile 'others' out of all the rest of the passengers on the train. In small-town eyes all persons not belonging to the village are 'strangers' and suspect; to the native of a country all who inhabit other countries are 'foreigners'; Jews are 'different' for the anti-Semite, Negroes are 'inferior' for American racists, aborigines are 'natives' for colonists, proletarians are the 'lower class' for the privileged ... Things become clear ... if, following Hegel, we find in consciousness itself a fundamental hostility towards every other consciousness; the subject can be posed only in being opposed – he sets himself up as the essential, as opposed to the other, the inessential, the object.

But the other consciousness, the other ego, sets up a reciprocal claim. The native travelling abroad is shocked to find himself in turn regarded as a 'stranger' by the natives of neighbouring countries. As a matter of fact, wars, festivals, trading, treaties, and contests among tribes, nations, and classes tend to deprive the concept *Other* of its absolute sense and to make manifest its relativity; willy-nilly, individuals and groups are forced to realize the reciprocity of their relations. How is it, then, that this reciprocity has not been recognized between the sexes, that one of the contrasting terms is set up as the sole essential, denying any relativity in regard to its correlative and defining the latter as pure otherness? Why is it that women do not dispute male sovereignty? No subject will readily volunteer to become the object, the inessential; it is not the Other who, in defining himself as the Other, establishes the One. The Other is posed as such by the One in defining himself as the One. But if the Other is not to regain the status of being the One, he must be submissive enough to accept this alien point of view. Whence comes this submission in the case of woman? . . .

The reason for this is that women lack concrete means for organizing themselves into a unit which can stand face to face with the correlative unit. They have no past, no history, no religion of their own; and they have no such solidarity of work and interest as that of the proletariat. They are not even promiscuously herded together in the way that creates community feeling among the American Negroes, the ghetto Jews, the workers of Saint-Denis, or the factory hands of Renault. They live dispersed among the males, attached through residence, housework, economic condition, and social standing to certain men – fathers or husbands – more firmly than they are to other women. If they belong to the bourgeoisie, they feel solidarity with men of that class, not with proletarian women; if they are white, their allegiance is to white men, not to Negro women. The proletariat can propose to massacre the ruling class, and a sufficiently fanatical Jew or Negro might dream of getting sole possession of the atomic bomb and making humanity wholly Jewish or black; but woman cannot even dream of exterminating the males. The bond that unites her to her oppressors is not comparable to any other. The division of the sexes is a biological fact, not an event in human history. Male and female stand opposed within a primordial *Mitsein*, and woman has not broken it. The couple is a fundamental unity with its two halves riveted together, and the cleavage of society along the line of sex is impossible. Here is to be found the basic trait of woman: she is the Other in a totality of which the two components are necessary to one another . . .

At the present time, when women are beginning to take part in the affairs of the world, it is still a world that belongs to men – they have no doubt of it at all and women have scarcely any. To decline to be the Other, to refuse to be a party to the deal – this would be for women to renounce all the advantages conferred upon them by their alliance with the superior caste. Man-the-sovereign will provide woman-the-liege with material protection and will undertake the moral justification of her existence; thus she can evade at once both economic risk and the metaphysical risk of a liberty in which ends and aims must be contrived without assistance. Indeed, along with the ethical urge of each individual to affirm his subjective existence, there is also the temptation to forgo liberty and become a thing. This is an inauspicious road, for he who takes it – passive, lost, ruined – becomes henceforth the creature of another's will, frustrated in his transcendence and deprived of every value. But it is an easy road; on it one avoids the strain involved in undertaking an authentic existence. When man makes of woman the *Other*, he may, then, expect to manifest deep-seated tendencies towards complicity. Thus, woman may fail to lay claim to the status of subject because she lacks definite resources, because she feels the necessary bond that ties her to man regardless of reciprocity, and because she is often very well pleased with her role as the *Other* ...

But men profit in many more subtle ways from the otherness, the alterity of woman. Here is a miraculous balm for those afflicted with an inferiority complex, and indeed no one is more arrogant towards women, more aggressive or scornful, than the man who is anxious about his virility. Those who are not fear-ridden in the presence of their fellow men are much more disposed to recognize a fellow creature in woman; but even to these the myth of Woman, the Other, is precious for many reasons. They cannot be blamed for not cheerfully relinquishing all the benefits they derive from the myth, for they realize what they would lose in relinquishing woman as they fancy her to be, while they fail to realize what they have to gain from the woman of tomorrow. Refusal to pose oneself as the Subject, unique and absolute, requires great self-denial. Furthermore, the vast majority of men make no such claim explicitly. They do not *postulate* woman as inferior, for today they are too thoroughly imbued with the ideal of democracy not to recognize all human beings as equals ...

(pp. 16–25)

Freud never showed much concern with the destiny of woman; it is clear that he simply adapted his account from that of the destiny of man, with slight modifications ... Freud ... admits that woman's sexuality is evolved as fully as man's; but he hardly studies it in particular. He writes: 'The libido is constantly and regularly male in essence, whether it appears in man or in woman.' He declines to regard the feminine libido as having its own original nature, and therefore it will necessarily seem to him like a complex deviation from the human libido in general. This develops at first, he thinks, identically in the two sexes – each infant passes first through an oral phase that fixates it upon the maternal breast, and then through an anal phase; finally it reaches the genital phase, at which point the sexes become differentiated.

Freud further brought to light a fact the importance of which had not been fully appreciated: namely, that masculine erotism is definitely located in the penis, whereas in woman there are two distinct erotic systems: one the clitoral, which develops in childhood, the other vaginal, which develops only after puberty. When the boy reaches the genital phase, his evolution is completed, though he must pass from the auto-erotic inclination, in which pleasure is subjective, to the hetero-erotic inclination, in which pleasure is bound up with an object, normally woman. This transition is made at the time of puberty through a narcissistic phase. But the penis will remain, as in childhood, the specific organ of erotism. Woman's libido, also passing through a narcissistic phase, will become objective, normally towards man; but the process will be much more complex, because woman must pass from clitoral pleasure to vaginal. There is only one genital stage for man, but there are two for woman; she runs a much greater risk of not reaching the end of her sexual evolution, of remaining at the infantile stage and thus of developing neuroses ...

All psychoanalysts systematically reject the idea of *choice* and the correlated concept of value, and therein lies the intrinsic weakness of the system. Having dissociated compulsions and prohibitions from the free choice of the existent, Freud fails to give us an explanation of their origin – he takes them for granted. He endeavoured to replace the idea of value with that of authority; but he admits in *Moses and Monotheism* that he has no way of accounting for this authority. Incest, for example, is forbidden because the father has forbidden it – but why did he forbid it? It is a mystery. The super-ego interiorizes, introjects commands and prohibitions emanating from an arbitrary tyranny, and the instinctive drives are there, we know not why: these two realities are unrelated because morality is envisaged as foreign to sexuality. The human unity appears to be disrupted, there is no thoroughfare from the individual to society; to reunite them Freud was forced to invent strange fictions, as in *Totem and Taboo* ...

Sexuality most certainly plays a considerable role in human life; it can be said to pervade life throughout. We have already learned from physiology that the living activity of the testes and the ovaries is integrated with that of the body in general. The existent is a sexual, a sexuate body, and in his relations with other existents who are also sexuate bodies, sexuality is in consequence always involved. But if body and sexuality are concrete expressions of existence, it is with reference to this that their significance can be discovered. Lacking this perspective, psychoanalysis takes for granted unexplained facts. For instance, we are told that the little girl is *ashamed* of urinating in a squatting position with her bottom uncovered – but whence comes this shame? And likewise, before asking whether the male is proud of having a penis or whether his pride is expressed in his penis, it is necessary to know what pride is and how the aspirations of the subject can be incarnated in an object. There is no need of taking sexuality as an irreducible datum, for there is in the existent a more original 'quest of being', of which sexuality is only one of the aspects. Sartre demonstrates this truth in *L'Être et le néant* ...

Furthermore, I shall pose the problem of feminine destiny quite otherwise: I shall place woman in a world of values and give her behaviour a dimension of liberty. I believe that she has the power to choose between the assertion of her transcendence and her alienation as object; she is not the plaything of contradictory drives; she devises solutions of diverse values in the ethical scale. Replacing value with authority, choice with drive, psychoanalysis offers an *Ersatz*, a substitute for morality – the concept of normality. This concept is certainly most useful in therapeutics, but it has spread through psychoanalysis in general to a disquieting extent. The descriptive schema is proposed as a law; and most assuredly a mechanistic psychology cannot accept the notion of moral invention; it can in strictness render an account of the *less* and never of the more; in strictness it can admit of checks, never of creations. If a subject does not show in his totality the development considered as normal, it will be said that his development has been arrested, and this arrest will be interpreted as a lack, a negation, but never as a positive decision ... Thus the psychoanalysts never give us more than an inauthentic picture, and for the inauthentic there can hardly be found any other criterion than normality. Their statement of the feminine destiny is absolutely to the point in this connection. In the sense in which the psychoanalysts understand the term, 'to identify oneself' with the mother or with the father is to *alienate oneself* in a model, it is to prefer a foreign image to the spontaneous manifestation of one's own existence, it is to play at being. Woman is shown to us as enticed by two modes of alienation. Evidently to play at being a man will be for her a source of frustration; but to play at being a woman is also a delusion: to be a woman would mean to be the object, the *Other* – and the Other nevertheless remains subject in the midst of her resignation.

The true problem for woman is to reject these flights from reality and seek self-fulfilment in transcendence. The thing to do, then, is to see what possibilities are opened up for her through what are called the virile and the feminine attitudes ... To paint, to write, to engage in politics – these are not merely 'sublimations'; here we have aims that are willed for their own sakes. To deny it is to falsify all human history ...

The fact is that from the male point of view – which is adopted by both male and female psychoanalysts – behaviour involving alienation is regarded as feminine, that in which the subject asserts his transcendence as virile ... it is among the psychoanalysts in particular that man is defined as a human being and woman as a female – whenever she behaves as a human being she is said to imitate the male. The psychoanalyst describes the female child, the young girl, as incited to identification with the mother and the father, torn between 'viriloid' and 'feminine' tendencies; whereas I conceive her as hesitating between the role of *object*, *Other* which is offered her, and the assertion of her liberty. Thus it is that we shall agree on a certain number of facts, especially when we take up the avenues of inauthentic flight open to women. But we accord them by no means the same significance as does the Freudian or the Adlerian. For us woman is defined as a human being in quest of values in a world of values, a world of which it is indispensable to know the economic and social structure. We shall study woman in an existential perspective with due regard to her total situation.

(pp. 70–83)

True sexual maturity is to be found only in the woman who fully accepts carnality in sex desire and pleasure.

It is not to be supposed, however, that all difficulties are mitigated for women of ardent temperament. It may be quite the opposite. Feminine sexual excitement can reach an intensity unknown to man. Male sex excitement is keen but localized, and – except perhaps at the moment of orgasm – it leaves the man quite in possession of himself; woman, on the contrary, really loses her mind; for many this effect marks the most definite and voluptuous moment of the love affair, but it has also a magical and fearsome quality. A man may sometimes feel afraid of the woman in his embrace, so beside herself she seems, a prey to her aberration; the turmoil that she experiences transforms her much more radically than his aggressive frenzy transforms the male. This fever rids her of shame for the moment, but afterwards she is ashamed and horrified to think of it. If she is to accept it happily – or proudly, even – she must have expanded freely in the warmth of pleasure; she can acknowledge her desires only if they have been gloriously satisfied: otherwise she angrily repudiates them.

Here we come to the crucial problem of feminine eroticism: at the beginning of woman's erotic life her surrender is not compensated for by a keen and certain enjoyment. She would sacrifice her modesty and her pride much more readily if in doing so she opened the gates of paradise. But defloration, as we have seen, is not an agreeable feature of young love; for it to be so, on the contrary, is most unusual; vaginal pleasure is not attained immediately. According to Stekel's statistics – which have been confirmed by numerous sexologists and psychoanalysts – scarcely four per cent of women have orgasmic pleasure from the beginning; fifty per cent attain vaginal orgasm only after weeks, months, or even years.

In this matter psychic factors play an essential part. The feminine body is peculiarly psychosomatic; that is, there is often close connection between the mental and the organic. A woman's moral inhibitions prevent the appearance of sex feeling; not being offset by pleasure, they tend to be perpetuated and to form a barrier of increasing strength. In many cases a vicious circle is set up: an initial awkwardness on the part of the man, a word, a crude gesture, a superior smile, will have repercussions throughout the honeymoon or even throughout married life. Disappointed by the lack of immediate pleasure, the young woman feels a lasting resentment unfavourable for happier relations subsequently.

In the absence of normal satisfaction, true enough, the man can always resort to stimulation of the clitoris, affording a pleasure that, in spite of moralistic fables, can give the woman orgasm and relaxation. But many women reject this because it seems, more than vaginal pleasure, to be *imposed*; for if woman suffers from the egoism of men intent only upon their own relief, she is also offended by a too obvious effort to give her pleasure. 'To make the other feel pleasure,' says Stekel, 'means to dominate the other; to give oneself to someone is to abdicate one's will.'

Woman accepts sex pleasure much more readily if it seems to flow naturally from that felt by the man, as happens in normal coitus when successful. As Stekel remarks again: 'Women submit gladly when they feel that their partners do not wish to subjugate them'; on the other hand, when they do feel that wish, they rebel. Many find it repugnant to be excited manually, because the hand is an instrument that does not participate in the pleasure it gives, it represents activity rather than the flesh. And if the male organ, even, seems not to be desirous flesh but a tool skilfully used, woman will feel the same repulsion. Moreover, any such compensation will seem to her to confirm the existence of the block that prevents her from feeling the sensations of a normal woman. Stekel notes after much observation that the whole desire of women called frigid tends towards the normal: 'They want to obtain the orgasm after the fashion of [what they regard as] the normal woman, other methods not satisfying their moral requirements.'

The man's attitude is thus of great importance. If his desire is violent and brutal, his partner feels that in his embraces she becomes a mere thing; but if he is too self-controlled, too detached, he does not seem to be flesh; he asks the woman to make an object of herself, without her having in return any hold on him. In both cases her pride rebels; for her to be able to reconcile her metamorphosis into a carnal object with her claim to her subjectivity, she must make him her prey while she is making herself his. This is why woman so often remains obstinately frigid. If her lover lacks seductive power, if he is cool, neglectful, awkward, he fails to awaken her sexuality, or he leaves her unsatisfied; but when virile and skilful, he may still arouse reactions of refusal; the woman fears his domination: some can find enjoyment only with men who are timid, poorly endowed, or even half impotent and who are no cause for fright ...

(pp. 411–13)

Underlying this line of interpretation is that it is *natural* for the female human being to make herself a *feminine* woman: it is not enough to be a heterosexual, even a mother, to realize this ideal; the 'true woman' is an artificial product that civilization makes, as formerly eunuchs were made. Her presumed 'instincts' for coquetry, docility, are indoctrinated, as is phallic pride in man. Man, as a matter of fact, does not always accept his virile vocation; and woman has good reasons for accepting with even less docility the one assigned to her ... Woman feels inferior because, in fact, the requirements of femininity *do* belittle her. She spontaneously chooses to be a complete person, a subject and a free being with the world and the future open before her; if this choice is confused with virility, it is so to the extent that femininity today means mutilation.

(pp. 428–9)

Thomas Nagel

Sexual Perversion[1]

First published in *The Journal of Philosophy*, Volume LXVI, No. 1 (16 January 1969).

There is something to be learned about sex from the fact that we possess a concept of sexual perversion. I wish to examine the concept, defending it against the charge of unintelligibility and trying to say exactly what about human sexuality qualifies it to admit of perversions. Let me make some preliminary comments about the problem before embarking on its solution.

Some people do not believe that the notion of sexual perversion makes sense, and even those who do disagree over its application. Nevertheless I think it will be widely conceded that, if the concept is viable at all, it must meet certain general conditions. First, if there are any sexual perversions, they will have to be sexual desires or practices that can be plausibly described as in some sense unnatural, though the explanation of this natural/unnatural distinction is of course the main problem. Second, certain practices will be perversions if anything is, such as shoe fetishism, bestiality, and sadism; other practices, such as unadorned sexual intercourse, will not be; about still others there is controversy. Third, if there are perversions, they will be unnatural sexual *inclinations* rather than merely unnatural practices adopted not from inclination but for other reasons. I realize that this is at variance with the view, maintained by some Roman Catholics, that contraception is a sexual perversion. But although contraception may qualify as a deliberate perversion of the sexual and reproductive functions, it cannot be significantly described as a *sexual* perversion. A sexual perversion must reveal itself in conduct that expresses an unnatural *sexual* preference. And although there might be a form of fetishism focused on the employment of contraceptive devices, that is not the usual explanation for their use.

I wish to declare at the outset my belief that the connection between sex and reproduction has no bearing on sexual perversion. The latter is a concept of psychological, not physiological interest, and it is a concept that we do not apply to the lower animals, let alone to plants, all of which have reproductive functions that can go astray in various ways. (Think of seedless oranges.) Insofar as we are prepared to regard higher animals as perverted, it is because of their psychological, not their anatomical similarity to humans. Furthermore, we do not regard as a perversion every deviation from the reproductive function of sex in humans: sterility, miscarriage, contraception, abortion.

Another matter that I believe has no bearing on the concept of sexual perversion is social disapprobation or custom. Anyone inclined to think that in each society the perversions are those sexual practices of which the community disapproves, should consider all the societies that have frowned upon adultery and fornication. These have not been regarded as unnatural practices, but have been thought objectionable in other ways. What is regarded as unnatural admittedly varies from culture to culture, but the classification is not a pure expression of disapproval or distaste. In fact it is often regarded as a *ground* for disapproval, and that suggests that the classification has an independent content.

I am going to attempt a psychological account of sexual perversion, which will depend on a specific psychological theory of sexual desire and human sexual interactions. To approach this solution I wish first to consider a contrary position, one which provides a basis for skepticism about the existence of any sexual perversions at all, and perhaps about the very significance of the term. The skeptical argument runs as follows:

'Sexual desire is simply one of the appetites, like hunger and thirst. As such it may have various objects, some more common than others perhaps, but none in any sense "natural". An appetite is identified as sexual by means of the organs and erogenous zones in which its satisfaction can be to some extent localized, and the special sensory pleasures which form the core of that satisfaction. This enables us to recognize widely divergent goals, activities, and desires as sexual, since it is conceivable in principle that anything should produce sexual pleasure and that a nondeliberate, sexually charged desire for it should arise (as a result of conditioning, if nothing else). We may fail to empathize with some of these desires, and some of them, like sadism, may be objectionable on extraneous grounds, but once we have observed that they meet the criteria for being sexual, there is nothing more to be said on *that* score. Either they are sexual or they are not: sexuality does not admit of imperfection, or perversion, or any other such qualification – it is not that sort of affection.'

This is probably the received radical position. It suggests that the cost of defending a psychological account may be to deny that sexual desire is an appetite. But insofar as that line of defense is plausible, it should make us suspicious of the simple picture of appetites on which the skepticism depends. Perhaps the standard appetites, like hunger, cannot be classed as pure appetites in that sense either, at least in their human versions.

Let us approach the matter by asking whether we can imagine anything that would qualify as a gastronomical perversion. Hunger and eating are importantly like sex in that they serve a biological function and also play a significant role in our inner lives. It is noteworthy that there is little temptation to describe as perverted an appetite for substances that are not nourishing. We should probably not consider someone's appetites as *perverted* if he liked to eat paper, sand, wood, or cotton. Those are merely rather odd and very unhealthy tastes: they lack the psychological complexity that we expect of perversions. (Coprophilia, being already a sexual perversion, may be disregarded.) If on the other hand someone liked to eat cookbooks, or magazines with pictures of food in them, and preferred these to ordinary food – or if when hungry he sought satisfaction by fondling a napkin or ashtray from his favorite restaurant – then the concept of perversion might seem appropriate (in fact it would be natural to describe this as a case of gastronomical fetishism). It would be natural to describe as gastronomically perverted someone who could eat only by having food forced down his throat through a funnel, or only if the meal were a living animal. What helps in such cases is the peculiarity of the desire itself, rather than the inappropriateness of its object to the biological function that the desire serves. Even an appetite, it would seem, can have perversions if in addition to its biological function it has a significant psychological structure.

In the case of hunger, psychological complexity is provided by the activities that give it expression. Hunger is not merely a disturbing sensation that can be quelled by eating; it is an attitude toward edible portions of the external world, a desire to relate to them in rather special ways. The method of ingestion: chewing, savoring, swallowing, appreciating the texture and smell, all are important components of the relation, as is the passivity and controllability of the food (the only animals we eat live are helpless mollusks). Our relation to food depends also on our size: we do not live upon it or burrow into it like aphids or worms. Some of these features are more central than others, but any adequate phenomenology of eating would have to treat it as a relation to the external world and a way of appropriating bits of that world, with characteristic affection. Displacements or serious restrictions of the desire to eat could then be described as perversions, if they undermined that direct relation between man and food which is the natural expression of hunger. This explains why it is easy to imagine gastronomical fetishism, voyeurism, exhibitionism, or even gastronomical sadism and masochism. Indeed some of these perversions are fairly common.

If we can imagine perversions of an appetite like hunger, it should be possible to make sense of the concept of sexual perversion. I do not wish to imply that sexual desire is an appetite – only that being an appetite is no bar to admitting of perversions. Like hunger, sexual desire has as its characteristic object a certain relation with something in the external world; only in this case it is usually a person rather than an omelet, and the relation is considerably more complicated. This added complication allows scope for correspondingly complicated perversions.

The fact that sexual desire is a feeling about other persons may tempt us to take a pious view of its psychological content. There are those who believe that sexual desire is properly the expression of some other attitude, like love, and that when it occurs by itself it is incomplete and unhealthy – or at any rate subhuman. (The extreme Platonic version of such a view is that sexual practices are all vain attempts to express something they cannot in principle achieve: this makes them all perversions, in a sense.) I do not believe that any such view is correct. Sexual desire is complicated enough without having to be linked to anything else as a condition for phenomenological analysis. It cannot be denied that sex may serve various functions – economic, social, altruistic – but it also has its own content as a relation between persons, and it is only by analyzing that relation that we can understand the conditions of sexual perversion.

I believe it is very important that the object of sexual attraction is a particular individual, who transcends the properties that make him attractive. When different persons are attracted to a single person for different reasons: eyes, hair, figure, laugh, intelligence – we feel that the object of their desire is nevertheless the same, namely that person.

There is even an inclination to feel that this is so if the lovers have different sexual aims, if they include both men and women, for example. Different specific attractive characteristics seem to provide enabling conditions for the operation of a single basic feeling, and the different aims all provide expressions of it. We approach the sexual attitude toward the person through the features that we find attractive, but these features are not the objects of that attitude.

This is very different from the case of an omelet. Various people may desire it for different reasons, one for its fluffiness, another for its mushrooms, another for its unique combination of aroma and visual aspect; yet we do not enshrine the transcendental omelet as the true common object of their affections. Instead we might say that several desires have accidentally converged on the same object: any omelet with the crucial characteristics would do as well. It is not similarly true that any person with the same flesh distribution and way of smoking can be substituted as object for a particular sexual desire that has been elicited by those characteristics. It may be that they will arouse attraction whenever they recur, but it will be a new sexual attraction with a new particular object, not merely a transfer of the old desire to someone else. (I believe this is true even in cases where the new object is unconsciously identified with a former one.)

The importance of this point will emerge when we see how complex a psychological interchange constitutes the natural development of sexual attraction. This would be incomprehensible if its object were not a particular person, but rather a person of a certain *kind*. Attraction is only the beginning, and fulfillment does not consist merely of behavior and contact expressing this attraction, but involves much more.

The best discussion of these matters that I have seen appears in part III of Sartre's *Being and Nothingness*.[2] Since it has influenced my own views, I shall say a few things about it now. Sartre's treatment of sexual desire and of love, hate, sadism, masochism, and further attitudes toward others, depends on a general theory of consciousness and the body which we can neither expound nor assume here. He does not discuss perversion, and this is partly because he regards sexual desire as one form of the perpetual attempt of an embodied consciousness to come to terms with the existence of others, an attempt that is as doomed to fail in this form as it is in any of the others, which include sadism and masochism (if not certain of the more impersonal deviations) as well as several nonsexual attitudes. According to Sartre, all attempts to incorporate the other into my world as another subject, i.e., to apprehend him at once as an object for me and as a subject for whom I am an object, are unstable and doomed to collapse into one or other of the two aspects. Either I reduce him entirely to an object, in which case his subjectivity escapes the possession or appropriation I can extend to that object; or I become merely an object for him, in which case I am no longer in a position to appropriate his subjectivity. Moreover, neither of these aspects is stable; each is continually in danger of giving way to the other. This has the consequence that there can be no such thing as a *successful* sexual relation, since the deep aim of sexual desire cannot in principle be accomplished. It seems likely, therefore, that the view will not permit a basic distinction between successful or complete and unsuccessful or incomplete sex, and therefore cannot admit the concept of perversion.

I do not adopt this aspect of the theory, nor many of its metaphysical underpinnings. What interests me is Sartre's picture of the attempt. He says that the type of possession that is the object of sexual desire is carried out by 'a double reciprocal incarnation' and that this is accomplished, typically in the form of a caress, in the following way: 'I make myself flesh in order to impel the Other to realize *for herself* and *for me* her own flesh, and my caresses cause my flesh to be born for me in so far as it is for the Other *flesh causing her to be born as flesh*' (391; italics Sartre's). The incarnation in question is described variously as a clogging or troubling of consciousness, which is inundated by the flesh in which it is embodied.

The view I am going to suggest, I hope in less obscure language, is related to this one, but it differs from Sartre's in allowing sexuality to achieve its goal on occasion and thus in providing the concept of perversion with a foothold.

Sexual desire involves a kind of perception, but not merely a single perception of its object, for in the paradigm case of mutual desire there is a complex system of superimposed mutual perceptions – not only perceptions of the sexual object, but perceptions of oneself. Moreover, sexual awareness of another involves considerable self-awareness to begin with – more than is involved in ordinary sensory perception. The experience is felt as an assault on oneself by the view (or touch, or whatever) of the sexual object.

Let us consider a case in which the elements can be separated. For clarity we will restrict ourselves initially to the somewhat artificial case of desire at a distance. Suppose a man and a woman, whom we may call Romeo and Juliet, are at opposite ends of a cocktail lounge, with many mirrors on the walls which permit unobserved observation, and even mutual unobserved observation. Each of them is sipping a martini and studying other people in the mirrors. At some point Romeo notices Juliet. He is moved, somehow, by the softness of her hair and the diffidence with which she sips her martini, and this arouses him sexually. Let us say that *X senses Y* whenever *X* regards *Y* with sexual desire. (*Y* need not be a person, and *X*'s apprehension of *Y* can be visual, tactile, olfactory, etc., or purely imaginary; in the present example we shall concentrate on vision.) So Romeo senses Juliet, rather than merely noticing her. At this stage he is aroused by an unaroused object, so he is more in the sexual grip of his body than she of hers.

Let us suppose, however, that Juliet now senses Romeo in another mirror on the opposite wall, though neither of them yet knows that he is seen by the other (the mirror angles provide three-quarter views). Romeo then begins to notice in Juliet the subtle signs of sexual arousal: heavy-lidded stare, dilating pupils, faint flush, et cetera. This of course renders her much more bodily, and he not only notices but senses this as well. His arousal is nevertheless still solitary. But now, cleverly calculating the line of her stare without actually looking her in the eyes, he realizes that it is directed at him through the mirror on the opposite wall. That is, he notices, and moreover senses, Juliet sensing him. This is definitely a new development, for it gives him a sense of embodiment not only through his own reactions but through the eyes and reactions of another. Moreover, it is separable from the initial sensing of Juliet; for sexual arousal might begin with a person's sensing that he is sensed and being assailed by the perception of the other person's desire rather than merely by the perception of the person.

But there is a further step. Let us suppose that Juliet, who is a little slower than Romeo, now senses that he senses her. This puts Romeo in a position to notice, and be aroused by, her arousal at being sensed by him. He senses that she senses that he senses her. This is still another level of arousal, for he becomes conscious of his sexuality through his awareness of its effect on her and of her awareness that this effect is due to him. Once she takes the same step and senses that he senses her sensing him, it becomes difficult to state, let alone imagine, further iterations, though they may be logically distinct. If both are alone, they will presumably turn to look at each other directly, and the proceedings will continue on another plane. Physical contact and intercourse are perfectly natural extensions of this complicated visual exchange, and mutual touch can involve all the complexities of awareness present in the visual case, but with a far greater range of subtlety and acuteness.

Ordinarily, of course, things happen in a less orderly fashion – sometimes in a great rush – but I believe that some version of this overlapping system of distinct sexual perceptions and interactions is the basic framework of any full-fledged sexual relation and that relations involving only part of the complex are significantly incomplete. The account is only schematic, as it must be to achieve generality. Every real sexual act will be psychologically far more specific and detailed, in ways that depend not only on the physical techniques employed and on anatomical details, but also on countless features of the participants' conceptions of themselves and of each other, which become embodied in the act. (It is a familiar enough fact, for example, that people often take their social roles and the social roles of their partners to bed with them.)

The general schema is important, however, and the proliferation of levels of mutual awareness it involves is an example of a type of complexity that typifies human interactions. Consider aggression, for example. If I am angry with someone, I want to make him feel it, either to produce self-reproach by getting him to see himself through the eyes of my anger, and to dislike what he sees – or else to produce reciprocal anger or fear, by getting him to perceive my anger as a threat or attack. What I want will depend on the details of my anger, but in either case it will involve a desire that the object of that anger be aroused. This accomplishment constitutes the fulfillment of my emotion, through domination of the object's feelings.

Another example of such reflexive mutual recognition is to be found in the phenomenon of meaning, which appears to involve an intention to produce a belief or other effect in another by bringing about his recognition of one's intention to produce that effect. (That result is due to H. P. Grice,[3] whose position I shall not attempt to reproduce in detail.) Sex has a related structure: it involves a desire that one's partner be aroused by the recognition of one's desire that he or she be aroused.

It is not easy to define the basic types of awareness and arousal of which these complexes are composed, and that remains a lacuna in this discussion. I believe that the object of awareness is the same in one's own case as it is in one's sexual awareness of another, although the two awarenesses will not be the same, the difference being as great as that between feeling angry and experiencing the anger of another. All stages of sexual perception are varieties of identification of a person with his body. What is perceived is one's own or another's *subjection* to or *immersion* in his body, a phenomenon which has been recognized with loathing by St Paul and St Augustine, both of whom regarded 'the law of sin which is in my members' as a grave threat to the dominion of the holy will.[4] In sexual desire and its expression the blending of involuntary response with deliberate control is extremely important. For Augustine, the revolution launched against him by his body is symbolized by erection and the other involuntary physical components of arousal. Sartre too stresses the fact that the penis is not a prehensile organ. But mere involuntariness characterizes other bodily processes as well. In sexual desire the involuntary responses are combined with submission to spontaneous impulses: not only one's pulse and secretions but one's actions are taken over by the body; ideally, deliberate control is needed only to guide the expression of those impulses. This is to some extent also true of an appetite like hunger, but the takeover there is more localized, less pervasive, less extreme. One's whole body does not become saturated with hunger as it can with desire. But the most characteristic feature of a specifically sexual immersion in the body is its ability to fit into the complex of mutual perceptions that we have described. Hunger leads to spontaneous interactions with food; sexual desire leads to spontaneous interactions with other persons, whose bodies are asserting their sovereignty in the same way, producing involuntary reactions and spontaneous impulses in *them*. These reactions are perceived, and the perception of them is perceived, and that perception is in turn perceived; at each step the domination of the person by his body is reinforced, and the sexual partner becomes more possessible by physical contact, penetration, and envelopment.

Desire is therefore not merely the perception of a preexisting embodiment of the other, but ideally a contribution to his further embodiment which in turn enhances the original subject's sense of himself. This explains why it is important that the partner be aroused, and not merely aroused, but aroused by the awareness of one's desire. It also explains the sense in which desire has unity and possession as its object: physical possession must eventuate in creation of the sexual object in the image of one's desire, and not merely in the object's recognition of that desire, or in his or her own private arousal. (This may reveal a male bias: I shall say something about that later.)

To return, finally, to the topic of perversion: I believe that various familiar deviations constitute truncated or incomplete versions of the complete configuration, and may therefore be regarded as perversions of the central impulse.

In particular, narcissistic practices and intercourse with animals, infants, and inanimate objects seem to be stuck at some primitive version of the first stage. If the object is not alive, the experience is reduced entirely to an awareness of one's own sexual embodiment. Small children and animals permit awareness of the embodiment of the other, but present obstacles to reciprocity, to the recognition by the sexual object of the subject's desire as the source of his (the object's) sexual self-awareness.

Sadism concentrates on the evocation of passive self-awareness in others, but the sadist's engagement is itself active and requires a retention of deliberate control which impedes awareness of himself as a bodily subject of passion in the required sense. The victim must recognize him as the source of his own sexual passivity, but only as the active source. De Sade claimed that the object of sexual desire was to evoke involuntary responses from one's partner, especially audible ones. The infliction of pain is no doubt the most efficient way to accomplish this, but it requires a certain abrogation of one's own exposed spontaneity. All this, incidentally, helps to explain why it is tempting to regard as sadistic an excessive preoccupation with sexual technique, which does not permit one to abandon the role of agent at any stage of the sexual act. Ideally one should be able to surmount one's technique at some point.

A masochist on the other hand imposes the same disability on his partner as the sadist imposes on himself. The masochist cannot find a satisfactory embodiment as the object of another's sexual desire, but only as the object of his control. He is passive not in relation to his partner's passion but in relation to his nonpassive agency. In addition, the subjection to one's body characteristic of pain and physical restraint is of a very different kind from that of sexual excitement: pain causes people to contract rather than dissolve.

Both of these disorders have to do with the second stage, which involves the awareness of oneself as an object of desire. In straight-forward sadism and masochism other attentions are substituted for desire as a source of the object's self-awareness. But it is also possible for nothing of that sort to be substituted, as in the case of a masochist who is satisfied with self-inflicted pain or of a sadist who does not insist on playing a role in the suffering that arouses him. Greater difficulties of classification are presented by three other categories of sexual activity: elaborations of the sexual act; intercourse of more than two persons; and homosexuality.

If we apply our model to the various forms that may be taken by two-party heterosexual intercourse, none of them seem clearly to qualify as perversions. Hardly anyone can be found these days to inveigh against oral-genital contact, and the merits of buggery are urged by such respectable figures as D. H. Lawrence and Norman Mailer. There may be something vaguely sadistic about the latter technique (in Mailer's writings it seems to be a method of introducing an element of rape), but it is not obvious that this has to be so. In general, it would appear that any bodily contact between a man and a woman that gives them sexual pleasure, is a possible vehicle for the system of multi-level interpersonal awareness that I have claimed is the basic psychological content of sexual interaction. Thus a liberal platitude about sex is upheld.

About multiple combinations, the least that can be said is that they are bound to be complicated. If one considers how difficult it is to carry on two conversations simultaneously, one may appreciate the problems of multiple simultaneous interpersonal perception that can arise in even a small-scale orgy. It may be inevitable that some of the component relations should degenerate into mutual epidermal stimulation by participants otherwise isolated from each other. There may also be a tendency toward voyeurism and exhibitionism, both of which are incomplete relations. The exhibitionist wishes to display his desire without needing to be desired in return; he may even fear the sexual attentions of others. A voyeur, on the other hand, need not require any recognition by his object at all: certainly not a recognition of the voyeur's arousal.

It is not clear whether homosexuality is a perversion if that is measured by the standard of the described configuration, but it seems unlikely. For such a classification would have to depend on the possibility of extracting from the system a distinction between male and female sexuality; and much that has been said so far applies equally to men and women. Moreover, it would have to be maintained that there was a natural tie between the type of sexuality and the sex of the body, and also that two sexualities of the same type could not interact properly.

Certainly there is much support for an aggressive-passive distinction between male and female sexuality. In our culture the male's arousal tends to initiate the perceptual exchange, he usually makes the sexual approach, largely controls the course of the act, and of course penetrates whereas the woman receives. When two men or two women engage in intercourse they cannot both adhere to these sexual roles. The question is how essential the roles are to an adequate sexual relation. One relevant observation is that a good deal of deviation from these roles occurs in heterosexual intercourse. Women can be sexually aggressive and men passive, and temporary reversals of role are not uncommon in heterosexual exchanges of reasonable length. If such conditions are set aside, it may be urged that there is something irreducibly perverted in attraction to a body anatomically like one's own. But alarming as some people in our culture may find such attraction, it remains psychologically unilluminating to class it as perverted. Certainly if homosexuality is a perversion, it is so in a very different sense from that in which shoe fetishism is a perversion, for some version of the full range of interpersonal perceptions seems perfectly possible between two persons of the same sex.

In any case, even if the proposed model is correct, it remains implausible to describe as perverted every deviation from it. For example, if the partners in heterosexual intercourse indulge in private heterosexual fantasies, that obscures the recognition of the real partner and so, on the theory, constitutes a defective sexual relation. It is not, however, generally regarded as a perversion. Such examples suggest that a simple dichotomy between perverted and unperverted sex is too crude to organize the phenomena adequately.

I should like to close with some remarks about the relation of perversion to good, bad, and morality. The concept of perversion can hardly fail to be evaluative in some sense, for it appears to involve the notion of an ideal or at least adequate sexuality which the perversions in some way fail to achieve. So, if the concept is viable, the judgment that a person or practice or desire is perverted will constitute a sexual evaluation, implying that better sex, or a better specimen of sex, is possible. This in itself is a very weak claim, since the evaluation might be in a dimension that is of little interest to us. (Though, if my account is correct, that will not be true.)

Whether it is a moral evaluation, however, is another question entirely – one whose answer would require more understanding of both morality and perversion than can be deployed here. Moral evaluation of acts and of persons is a rather special and very complicated matter, and by no means all our evaluations of persons and their activities are moral evaluations. We make judgments about people's beauty or health or intelligence which are evaluative without being moral. Assessments of their sexuality may be similar in that respect.

Furthermore, moral issues aside, it is not clear that unperverted sex is necessarily *preferable* to the perversions. It may be that sex which receives the highest marks for perfection *as sex* is less enjoyable than certain perversions; and if enjoyment is considered very important, that might outweigh considerations of sexual perfection in determining rational preference.

That raises the question of the relation between the evaluative content of judgments of perversion and the rather common *general* distinction between good and bad sex. The latter distinction is usually confined to sexual acts, and it would seem, within limits, to cut across the other: even someone who believed, for example, that homosexuality was a perversion could admit a distinction between better and worse homosexual sex, and might even allow that good homosexual sex could be better *sex* than not very good unperverted sex. If this is correct, it supports the position that, if judgments of perversion are viable at all, they represent only one aspect of the possible evaluation of sex, even *qua sex*. Moreover it is not the only important aspect: certainly sexual deficiencies that evidently do not constitute perversions can be the object of great concern.

Finally, even if perverted sex is to that extent not so good as it might be, bad sex is generally better than none at all. This should not be controversial: it seems to hold for other important matters, like food, music, literature, and society. In the end, one must choose from among the available alternatives, whether their availability depends on the environment or on one's own constitution. And the alternatives have to be fairly grim before it becomes rational to opt for nothing.

Notes

1. My research was supported in part by the National Science Foundation.
2. Translated by Hazel E. Barnes (New York: Philosophical Library, 1956).
3. 'Meaning', *Philosophical Review*, LXVI, 3 (July 1957), 377–88.
4. See Romans 7.23; and the *Confessions*, Book 8, v.

EMPIRICAL RESEARCH ON HUMAN SEXUALITY: THE WORK OF THE KINSEY INSTITUTE

Alfred Kinsey, Wardell B. Pomeroy and Clyde E. Martin

Excerpts from *Sexual Behavior in the Human Male*

First published by W. B. Saunders and Co. (Philadelphia, 1948). Tables omitted.

Total Outlet. The frequencies of total sexual outlet vary somewhat with the educational level to which an individual belongs, although they do not differ as much as the frequencies for the several sources of outlet. Among single males, at all ages, and whether the calculations are made as means or as medians, the highest total outlets are found among those boys who go into high school but never beyond ...

(p. 335)

A finer educational breakdown ... suggests that the sexually most active group is the one that goes into high school but not beyond the tenth grade ...

The single males who have the lowest frequencies of total sexual outlet are those who belong to the college level. The boys who never go beyond eighth grade in school stand intermediate between the high school and the college groups.

The social level picture for total outlet among married males is quite the same as for single males. The married males who have the highest total outlet are those who went into high school but not beyond. This is true for every age group between 16 and 40 years of age, and may be true at older ages.

(p. 337)

If the record for total outlet is analyzed on the basis of occupational classes, it will be seen that there is as sharp and as consistent a differentiation of groups as there is on the basis of educational level. The highest rates of total outlet are to be found among the males who belong to occupational class 3 ... Since occupation class 3 is the one that includes semi-skilled workers, it contains a great many persons who do not go beyond grade school, and almost none of them go beyond high school; and the generalizations based on occupational classes agree very well with the generalizations based upon educational levels ...

The lowest rates of total outlet are to be found in occupational class 4. This is the group which includes the skilled mechanics ...

(p. 338)

In general, the white collar groups (classes 5, 6 and 7) are low in their rates; but of these class 7 shows the highest rates. This is the professional group. It usually has 17 to 20 years of schooling ...

Masturbation. Ultimately, between 92 and 97 per cent of all males have masturbatory experience ...

The highest active incidence between the ages of adolescence and 15 is to be found among the boys who never go beyond high school. In later age periods the college males have the highest incidence.

The highest frequencies of masturbation among single males, in all age periods, are in the college level ... Between 16 and 20, for instance, masturbation among the single males of college level occurs nearly twice as frequently as it does among the boys who never go beyond grade school, and the differential is still higher in the twenties. This is the great source of pre-marital sexual outlet for the upper educational levels. For that group, masturbation provides nearly 80 per cent of the orgasms during the earlier adolescent years, as against little more than half the outlet (52%) for the lower educational level. In the late teens it still accounts for two-thirds (66%) of the college male's orgasms, while the lower level has relegated such activity to a low place that provides less than 30 per cent of the total outlet. In all later age periods the relative positions of these groups remain about the same.

Differences in incidences and frequencies of masturbation at different educational levels are even more striking among married males. At the grade school level, there are only 20 to 30 per cent who masturbate in their early marital years, and the accumulative incidence figure climbs only a bit during the later years of marriage. The frequencies are very low. The high school group closely matches the grade school group in this regard. On the other hand, among the married males who have been to college, 60 to 70 per cent masturbate in each of the age periods ...

(pp. 335–9)

Nocturnal Emissions ... there are still greater differences between educational levels in regard to nocturnal emissions – a type of sexual outlet which one might suppose would represent involuntary behavior.

Nocturnal emissions occur most often in that segment of the population that goes to college. Among males of the college level the emissions begin at earlier ages than among males of lower educational levels. About 70 per cent of boys who will go to college have such experience by age 15, whereas only about 25 per cent of the grade school group has started by then. Between 16 and 30 years of age, 91 per cent of the single males of the college level experience nocturnal emissions, while only 56 per cent of the lower level boys have such experience in the same period. The active incidence figures are highest for the college males in every other age group. Ultimately, nearly 100 per cent of the better educated males have such experience, whereas the accumulative incidence figure is only 86 per cent for the high school group, and only 75 per cent for the grade school group.

Between adolescence and age 15, upper level males average nocturnal emissions nearly seven times as frequently as the boys of lower educational levels. Between 16 and 20 the frequencies among the upper level males are nearly three times those for the lower level, if the whole population is involved in the calculation. For the active populations the frequencies for the college group are still twice as high. About the same differences hold in the older age periods, at least up to 30 years of age ...

(pp. 343–4)

Heterosexual Petting. Petting is pre-eminently an occupation of the high school and college levels. For all social levels, it may begin in high school or even before; but from 16 years of age, the males and the females who are most often involved are the ones who go into high school or ultimately into college. About 92 per cent of the males of the high school and college levels engage in at least some kind of petting prior to marriage, and nearly as many (88%) of the grade school has such experience. These figures are not very far apart, but there are greater differences in the limits to which the petting techniques go in these several groups. In general, males of grade school and high school levels are more restricted in their petting behavior than males of the college level ...

(pp. 345–6)

Analyses of the record by occupational classes confirm the statement made above that petting is most characteristic of the upper social levels. The differences by occupational class are not notable in the early adolescent years, but they become greater between 16 and 20, at which age classes 6 and 7 pet to the point of climax twice as often as classes 2 or 3. In the early twenties there is a 3 to 1 difference between the two ends of the occupational scale, and the distinctions are more or less true irrespective of the occupational classes of the parents.

Pre-marital Intercourse ... Pre-marital intercourse, whatever its source, is more abundant in the grade school and high school levels, and less common at the college level. Even in the period between adolescence and 15 the active incidence includes nearly half (48% and 43%) of the lower educational groups, but only 10 per cent of the boys who will ultimately go to college. In the later teens, 85 per cent of the grade school group and 75 per cent of the high school group is having pre-marital intercourse, while the figure for the college group is still only 42%. In later years the differentials are not so great but, compared with the grade school group, it is still only about two-thirds as many of the college males who have such intercourse.

The accumulative incidence figures for pre-marital intercourse show much the same differences. About 98 per cent of the grade school level has experience before marriage, while only 84% of the high school level and 67 per cent of the college level is involved.

The frequency figures show still greater differences between educational levels. In the age period between 16 and 20, the grade school group has 7 times as much pre-marital coitus as the college group. There is not much drop in the differential even in the older age groups...

(p. 347)

Marital Intercourse ... There are social differences, however, in regard to the percentage of the total sexual outlet which is derived from marital intercourse. In the age period between 16 and 20, among males of the grade school level, only about 80 per cent of the total sexual outlet comes from marital intercourse, while extra-marital intercourse accounts for another 11 per cent of the total outlet. However, the portion of the outlet coming from marital intercourse in this grade school group rises to approximately 90 per cent in the late forties and early fifties. Among males of the high school group, marital intercourse in the early years accounts for 82 per cent, but rises to 91 per cent of the total outlet by the late forties. For the college level, marital intercourse starts out as a higher proportion of the total outlet – nearly 85 per cent; but it drops steadily through the successive years until by the middle fifties it accounts for only 62 per cent of the outlet of these males. In comparison with males of the college level, males of the grade school level, in their middle fifties, derive 26 per cent more of their total outlet from intercourse with their wives.

In the course of his marriage, the outlet of the married male of the college level has increasingly included masturbation and nocturnal dreams and, strikingly enough, extra-marital intercourse. On the other hand, the lower level males never have much masturbation in their marital histories, and the amount becomes less in the later years. During their teens and early twenties, lower level males find a considerable outlet in extra-marital intercourse, but with the advancing years they become increasingly faithful to their wives. In short, lower level males take 35 or 40 years to arrive at the marital ideals which the upper level begins with; or, to put it with equal accuracy, upper level males take 35 or 40 years to arrive at the sexual freedom which the lower level accepts in its teens. Some persons may interpret the data to mean that the lower level starts out by trying promiscuity and, as a result of that trial, finally decides that strict monogamy is a better policy; but it would be equally correct to say that the upper level starts out by trying monogamy and ultimately decides that variety is worth having. Of course, neither inter-pretation is quite correct, for the factors involve differences in sexual adjustment in marriages at the different levels, as well as the force of the mores which lie at the base of most of these class differences ...

(pp. 355–7)

Attitudes on Sexual Techniques

In addition to differences in frequencies and sources of sexual outlet, social levels differ in their attitudes on other matters of sex ...

(p. 363)

Sources of Erotic Arousal

The upper level male is aroused by a considerable variety of sexual stimuli. He has a minimum of pre-marital or extra-marital intercourse.

The lower level male, on the other hand, is less often aroused by anything except physical contact in coitus; he has an abundance of pre-marital intercourse, and a considerable amount of extra-marital intercourse in the early years of his marriage. How much of this difference is simply the product of psychologic factors and how much represents a community pattern which can be properly identified as the mores, it is difficult to say. The very fact that upper level males fail to get what they want in socio-sexual relations would provide a psychologic explanation of their high degree of erotic responsiveness to stimuli which fall short of actual coitus. The fact that the lower level male comes nearer having as much coitus as he wants would make him less susceptible to any stimulus except actual coitus...

(p. 363)

Nudity ... Most amazing of all, customs in regard to nudity may vary between the social levels of a single community. In our American culture, there is a greater acceptance of nudity at upper social levels, and greater restraint at lower social levels. Compared with previous generations, there is a more general acceptance of nudity in the upper social level today. There is an increasing amount of nudity within the family circle in this upper level. There is rather free exposure in the home for both sexes, including the parents and the children of all ages, at times of dressing and at times of bathing. Still more significant, there is an increasing habit among upper level persons of sleeping in partial or complete nudity. This is probably more common among males, though there is a considerable number of upper level females who also sleep nude. Among the males of the college level, nearly half (41%) frequently sleep nude, about one-third (34%) of the high school males do so, but only one-sixth (16%) of the males of the grade school level sleep that way.

Finally, the upper level considers nudity almost an essential concomitant of intercourse. About 90 per cent of the persons at this level regularly have coitus nude. The upper level finds it difficult to comprehend that anyone should regularly and as a matter of preference have intercourse while clothed. This group uses clothing only under unusual circumstances, or when variety and experimentation are the desired objectives in the intercourse. On the other hand, nude coitus is regularly had by only 66 per cent of those who never go beyond high school, and by 43 per cent of those who never go beyond grade school . . .

(p. 366)

Manual Manipulation. At upper social levels there may be considerable manual petting between partners, on the part of the male who has been persuaded by the general talk among his companions, and by the codification of those opinions in the marriage manuals, that the female needs extended sensory stimulation if she is to be brought to simultaneous orgasm in coitus. Upper level petting involves the manual stimulation of all parts of the female body.

Manual manipulation of the female breast occurs regularly in 96 per cent of the histories of the married males of the upper level, and manual manipulation of the female genitalia is regularly found in about 90 per cent of the histories. The upper level believes that this petting is necessary for successful coital adjustment; but preliminary calculations indicate that the frequency of orgasm is higher among lower level females than it is among upper level females, even though the lower level coitus involves a minimum of specific physical stimulation.

The manual manipulation of the female breast occurs in only 79 per cent of the married male histories at lower levels, and the manipulation of the female genitalia occurs in only 75 per cent of the cases. Even when there is such stimulation, it is usually restricted in its extent and in its duration. The lower level female agrees to manipulate the male genitalia in only 57 per cent of the cases. The record is, therefore, one of more extended pre-coital play at the upper levels, and of a minimum of play at the lower levels. Many persons at the lower level consider that intromission is the essential activity and the only justifiable activity in a 'normal' sexual relation . . .

(pp. 367–9)

Oral Eroticism. Many persons in the upper levels consider a certain amount of oral eroticism as natural, desirable, and a fundamental part of love making. Simple lip kissing is so commonly accepted that it has a minimum of erotic significance at this level . . . Many a college male will have kissed dozens of girls, although he has had intercourse with none of them. On the other hand, the lower level male is likely to have had intercourse with hundreds of girls, but he may have kissed few of them. What kissing he has done has involved simple lip contacts, for he is likely to have a considerable distaste for the deep kiss which is fairly common in upper level histories...

Mouth-breast contact does occur at all social levels, but it is most elaborately developed again in the upper social level...

Mouth-genital contacts of some sort, with the subject as either the active or the passive member in the relationship, occur at some time in the histories of nearly 60 per cent of all males...

Mouth-genital contacts (of any kind) occur much more often at high school and college levels, less often in the grade school group. In the histories of the college group, about 72 per cent of the males have at least experimented with such contacts, and about 65 per cent of the males who have gone into high school but not beyond. Among those males who have never gone beyond eighth grade in school the accumulative incidence figure is only 40 per cent.

The percentages for males who have made mouth contact with female genitalia prior to marriage are 9, 10, and 18 for grade school, high school, and college levels, respectively. In marriage, such contacts are in 4, 15, and 45 per cent of the histories, for the three groups. Before marriage, the percentage of males with histories which included mouth stimulation of the male genitalia during heterosexual relations were 22, 30, and 39, for the three educational levels. In marriage, such relations have been had in 7, 15, and 43 per cent of the cases, for the three levels, respectively...

(pp. 369–71)

Positions in Intercourse ... It is not surprising to find that within our American culture there is some variation in coital positions among the social levels. Throughout the population as a whole, a high proportion of all the intercourse is had in a position with the female supine, on her back, with the male above and facing the female. Only a part of the intercourse is had with the female above the male. This occurs in about 35 per cent of the college level histories, in 28 per cent of high school histories, but in only 17 per cent of the grade school histories ... It should be emphasized that the most common variant position is the one with the female above. It is used, at least occasionally, by more than a third (34.6%) of the upper level males...

(pp. 371–3)

Patterns of Behavior

Within any single social level there are, of course, considerable differences between individuals in their choice of sexual outlets, and in the frequencies with which they engage in each type of activity. The range of individual variation in any level is not particularly different from the range of variation in each other level ...

(p. 374)

The Heterosexual-homosexual Balance

Concerning patterns of sexual behavior, a great deal of the thinking done by scientists and laymen alike stems from the assumption that there are persons who are 'heterosexual' and persons who are 'homosexual', that these two types represent antitheses in the sexual world, and that there is only an insignificant class of 'bisexuals' who occupy an intermediate position between the other groups. It is implied that every individual is innately – inherently – either heterosexual or homosexual. It is further implied that from the time of birth one is fated to be one thing or the other, and that there is little chance for one to change his pattern in the course of a lifetime ...

(pp. 636–7)

The histories which have been available in the present study make it apparent that the heterosexuality or homosexuality of many individuals is not an all-or-none proposition. It is true that there are persons in the population whose histories are exclusively heterosexual, both in regard to their overt experience and in regard to their psychic reactions. And there are individuals in the population whose histories are exclusively homosexual, both in experience and in psychic reactions. But the record also shows that there is a considerable portion of the population whose members have combined, within their individual histories, both homosexual and heterosexual experience and/or psychic responses. There are some whose heterosexual experiences predominate, there are some whose homosexual experiences predominate, there are some who have had quite equal amounts of both types of experience ...

Males do not represent two discrete populations, heterosexual and homosexual. The world is not to be divided into sheep and goats. Not all things are black nor all things white. It is a fundamental of taxonomy that nature rarely deals with discrete categories. Only the human mind invents categories and tries to force facts into separated pigeon-holes. The living world is a continuum in each and every one of its aspects. The sooner we learn this concerning human sexual behavior the sooner we shall reach a sound understanding of the realities of sex.

While emphasizing the continuity of the graduations between exclusively heterosexual and exclusively homosexual histories, it has seemed desirable to develop some sort of classification which could be based on the relative amounts of heterosexual and of homosexual experience or response in each history . . . An individual may be assigned a position on this scale, for each age period in his life, in accordance with the following definitions of the various points on the scale . . .

Based on both psychologic reactions and overt experience, individuals rate as follows:

0. Exclusively heterosexual with no homosexual
1. Predominantly heterosexual, only incidentally homosexual
2. Predominantly heterosexual, but more than incidentally homosexual
3. Equally heterosexual and homosexual
4. Predominantly homosexual, but more than incidentally heterosexual
5. Predominantly homosexual, but incidentally heterosexual
6. Exclusively homosexual . . .

(pp. 638–9)

. . . it becomes obvious that any question as to the number of persons in the world who are homosexual and the number who are heterosexual is unanswerable. It is only possible to record the number of those who belong to each of the positions on such a heterosexual-homosexual scale as is given above. Summarizing our data on the incidence of overt homosexual experience in the white male population and the distribution of various degrees of heterosexual-homosexual balance in that population, the following generalizations may be made:

37 per cent of the total male population has *at least some overt homosexual experience* to the point of orgasm between adolescence and old age. This accounts for nearly 2 males out of every 5 that one may meet.

50 per cent of the males *who remain single until age 35* have had overt homosexual experience to the point of orgasm, since the onset of adolescence.

58 per cent of the males who belong to the group that goes into *high school* but not beyond, *50 per cent of the grade school level*, and *47 per cent of the college level* have had homosexual experience to the point of orgasm if they remain single to the age of 35.

63 per cent of all males *never have overt* homosexual experience to the point of orgasm after the onset of adolescence.

50 per cent of all males (approximately) *have neither overt nor psychic* experience in the homosexual after the onset of adolescence.

13 per cent of the males (approximately) *react erotically* to other males *without having overt* homosexual contacts after the onset of adolescence.

30 per cent of all males *have at least incidental homosexual experience* or reaction (i.e., rate 1 to 6) over at least a three-year period between the ages of 16 and 55. This accounts for one male out of every three in the population who is past the early years of adolescence.

25 per cent of the male population *has more than incidental homosexual experience* or reactions (i.e., rates 2–6) for at least three years between the ages of 16 and 55. In terms of averages, one male out of approximately every four has had or will have such distinct and continued homosexual experience.

18 per cent of the males have at least *as much of the homosexual as the heterosexual* in their histories (i.e., rate 3–6) for at least three years between the ages of 16 and 55. This is more than one in six of the white male population.

13 per cent of the population *has more of the homosexual than the heterosexual* (i.e., rates 4–6) for at least three years between the ages of 16 and 55. This is one in eight of the white male population.

10 per cent of the males are *more or less exclusively homosexual* (i.e., rate 5 or 6) for at least three years between the ages of 16 and 55. This is one male in ten in the white male population.

8 per cent of the males are *exclusively homosexual* (i.e., rate a 6) for at least three years between the ages of 16 and 55. This is one male in every 13.

4 per cent of the white males are *exclusively homosexual throughout their lives*, after the onset of adolescence ...

(pp. 650–51)

Alfred Kinsey, Wardell B. Pomeroy, Clyde E. Martin and Paul H. Gebhard

Excerpts from *Sexual Behavior in the Human Female*

First published by W. B. Saunders and Co. (Philadelphia, 1953). Tables omitted.

11. *Orgasm in Marital Coitus vs. Pre-Marital Orgasm.* In the available sample, there was no factor which showed a higher correlation with the frequency of orgasm in marital coitus than the presence or absence of pre-marital experience in orgasm. Some 36 per cent of the females in the sample had married without having had such previous experience in orgasm ... Among those who had had no previous experience, 44 per cent had failed to respond to the point of orgasm in the first year of marriage. But among the females who had had even limited pre-marital experience in orgasm, only 19 per cent had failed to reach orgasm in the first year of marriage; and among those who had experienced orgasm at least twenty-five times before marriage, only 13 per cent had failed to reach orgasm in the first year of marriage.

Among those females who had never experienced pre-marital orgasm from any source prior to marriage, 25 per cent did respond in all or nearly all of their contacts during the first year of marriage; but 45 to 47 per cent of the females who had had pre-marital experience responded to orgasm in all or nearly all of their coitus during the first year of marriage. Similar trends had been evident throughout the later years of marriage, and even for fifteen years in the continuous marriages in the sample. It is doubtful if any type of therapy has ever been as effective as early experience in orgasm, in reducing the incidences of unresponsiveness in marital coitus, and in increasing the frequencies of response to orgasm in that coitus ...

The more responsive females may have been the ones who discovered orgasm in their pre-marital years, either in solitary or socio-sexual activities, and they were the ones who had most often responded in marriage. On the other hand, we have already presented data which show that the female can learn through experience to respond in orgasm, and we have also emphasized the fact that such learning is most effective in the early years, when inhibitions have not yet developed or have not yet become too firmly fixed. Early orgasmic experience may, therefore, contribute directly to the sexual effectiveness of a marriage.

12. *Orgasm in Marital Coitus vs. Pre-Marital Coital Experience.* The type of pre-marital experience which correlates most specifically with the responses of the female in marital coitus is pre-marital coitus – *provided that that coitus leads to orgasm.* For instance, among the females in the sample who had had pre-marital coitus but who had not reached orgasm in the coitus, 38 to 56 per cent failed to reach orgasm in the first year of marriage. While the percentages had decreased in the later years, there were still 11 to 30 per cent of the pre-maritally unresponsive females who had remained unresponsive in their coitus ten years after marriage. On the other hand, among the females who had had pre-marital coitus in which they had reached orgasm at least twenty-five times, only 3 per cent were totally unresponsive in the first year of marriage, and only 1 per cent in the later years of marriage. For more than half of the females in the sample, coitus without orgasm had been correlated with orgasmic failure in marriage. They had been unresponsive in marriage ten to twenty times as often as the females who had had fairly frequent pre-marital coitus in which they had reached orgasm.

Furthermore, the record indicates that two or three times as many of the females in the sample had reached orgasm in all or nearly all of their marital contacts if their pre-marital coitus had led to orgasm ... It should be emphasized that pre-marital coital experience which had not led to orgasm had not correlated with successful sexual relations in marriage. On the contrary, it showed a high correlation with failure in the marital coitus ...

(pp. 385–8)

13. *Orgasm in Marital Coitus vs. Pre-Marital Petting to Orgasm.* In the available sample, pre-marital petting which led to orgasm also showed a high correlation with sexual performance after marriage. Among the females who had never done petting to the point of orgasm before marriage, 35 per cent had never reached orgasm in the first year of marriage; but only 10 per cent of those who had reached orgasm in at least some of their pre-marital petting were unresponsive in marriage. The same sorts of differences held for at least fifteen years after marriage

... Again these correlations may be the product of selective factors or of some causal relationship between pre-marital and marital experience. The most responsive females may be the ones who most often pet to orgasm before marriage, and who similarly respond best in their marital coitus. Or petting to orgasm may have provided the experience which helped the female respond to orgasm after marriage. But whatever the explanation, there are three, five, or more chances to one that a girl who has not done pre-marital petting in which she reaches orgasm will not respond to orgasm after she marries. If she has reached orgasm in her pre-marital petting, there is a much better chance that she will respond in all or nearly all of her marital intercourse during the early years of her marriage and also in the later years of her marriage.

We have already noted that pre-marital petting is significant because it provides the first experience in orgasm for some 18 to 24 per cent of the females, particularly among the younger generations. We have also pointed out that petting is even more significant because it introduces the female to the meaning of physical contacts with individuals of the opposite sex. The unresponsiveness of many of the married females who had little or next to no experience in pre-marital petting is sometimes due to nothing more than their refusal to allow physical contacts which would be sufficient to effect erotic arousal. Experience in pre-marital petting may help educate the girl in the significance of such contacts.

14. *Orgasm in Marital Coitus vs. Pre-Marital Experience in Masturbation*. Although the correlations between pre-marital masturbatory experience that had led to orgasm and the female's subsequent responses in coitus in marriage were not as marked as the correlations with coital or petting experience, the masturbatory experience did show a definite correlation with the marital performance. Among the females who had never masturbated before marriage, or whose masturbation had never led to orgasm, about a third (31 to 37 per cent) had failed to reach orgasm in the first year, and nearly as many had failed in the first five years of their marital coitus. Among those who had previously masturbated to the point of orgasm, only 13 to 16 per cent were totally unresponsive in the first year of marriage...

Even after marriage, and even among females who are in their thirties and forties, difficulties in coital responses are sometimes cleared up if they learn how to masturbate to the point of orgasm. The techniques of masturbation and of petting are more specifically calculated to effect orgasm than the techniques of coitus itself, and for that reason it is sometimes possible for a female to learn how to masturbate to orgasm even though she had difficulty in effecting the same aim in coitus. Having learned what it means to suppress inhibitions, and to abandon herself to the spontaneous physical reactions which represent orgasm in masturbation, she may become more capable of responding in the same way in coitus. There are very few instances, among our several thousand histories, of females who were able to masturbate to orgasm without becoming capable of similar responses in coitus...

(pp. 388–91)

Married females: total outlet

... Among the females in the sample, about 97 per cent had experienced erotic arousal before marriage, but 3 per cent had never been so aroused before marriage. Some 64 per cent had experienced orgasm at least once before marriage, but 36 per cent married without understanding, through actual experience, the meaning of sexual orgasm.

Relation to Age. After marriage the frequencies of total outlet for the females in the sample had increased considerably over the frequencies which single females of the same age would have had. This depended, of course, primarily upon the fact that marital coitus had begun to provide such a regular and frequent source of sexual activity and outlet as few females had found in any type of activity before marriage.

The number of females reaching orgasm from any source after marriage (the active incidences) had begun at 78 per cent between the ages of sixteen and twenty. They had then increased steadily to 95 per cent at ages thirty-six to forty, after which they had begun to drop, reaching 89 per cent by age fifty-five and, to judge by our small sample, 82 per cent by age sixty.

The median frequencies of total outlet for married females who were ever reaching orgasm show marked 'aging effects'. The active median frequencies between sixteen and twenty had amounted to 2.2 orgasms per week, from which point they had steadily declined, reaching 1.0 per week between the ages of forty-one and forty-five, and 0.5 per week by age sixty...

(p. 528)

Relation to Decade of Birth. In the chapter on marital coitus, we found that the percentages of married females who were responding to the point of orgasm in that coitus (the active incidences) had risen more or less steadily in the four decades represented in the sample ... For instance, among the females in the sample who were between the ages of twenty-one and twenty-five some 80 per cent of those born before 1900 had reached orgasm; but of those who were born in the successive decades, 86, 90, and 92 per cent had so responded. Something of the same differences had been maintained in the subsequent age groups ...

(p. 529)

Relation to Other Factors. The incidences of total outlet for the married females in the sample had generally been a bit higher for the better educated groups, and lower for the grade school and high school groups. There seem to have been no consistent correlations between the active median frequencies of total outlet among the married females in the sample and their educational backgrounds, except that the graduate school group had slightly higher frequencies up to the age of thirty-five.

There seem to have been no correlations at all between the occupational classes of the parental homes in which the females in the sample had been raised and the incidences and frequencies of their total outlet.

On the other hand, the religious backgrounds of the females in the sample had definitely and consistently affected their total outlet after marriage. In nearly every age group, and in nearly all the samples that we have from Protestant, Catholic, and Jewish females, smaller percentages of the more devout and larger percentages of the inactive groups had responded to orgasm after marriage ... in some instances, as among the Catholic females who were married between the ages of twenty-one and twenty-five, the differences were of some magnitude: an active median frequency of 1.1 orgasms per week for the devoutly Catholic females, and 2.4 for the inactive Catholic females.

Sources of Total Outlet. Coitus in marriage had accounted for something between 84 and 89 per cent of the total outlet of the married females in the sample who were between the ages of sixteen and thirty-five. After the middle thirties, the importance of marital coitus had decreased. In the age group forty-six to fifty, only 73 per cent of the total number of orgasms were coming from that source.

Masturbation was the second most important source of sexual outlet for the married females in the sample, providing something between 7 and 10 per cent of the total number of orgasms for each of the age groups between sixteen and forty. Although 11 per cent of the total outlet had come from this source in the next ten years, the increase in importance of extra-marital coitus had reduced masturbation to a third place in the list.

Extra-marital coitus and orgasms derived in extra-marital petting had accounted, in various age groups, for something between 3 and 13 per cent of the total outlet of the married females in the sample. This had become the second most important source of outlet after age forty, providing 12 to 13 per cent of the total orgasms in that period.

Nocturnal dreams had provided between 1 and 3 per cent of the total outlet of the married females in each of the age groups in the sample. Homosexual contacts had never provided more than a fraction of 1 per cent of the orgasms experienced by the married females in the sample.

Married Females Without Orgasm. There had been an appreciable percentage of the married females who were not reaching orgasm either in their marital coitus or in any other type of sexual activity while they were married. The percentage had been highest in the younger age groups where 22 per cent of the married females between the ages of sixteen and twenty, and 12 per cent of the married females between the ages of twenty-one and twenty-five, had never experienced any orgasm from any source. The number of unresponsive individuals had dropped steadily in the successive age groups, reaching 5 per cent in the late thirties; but it had risen again to 6 and 7 per cent in the forties...

(pp. 530–32)

Social Factors Affecting Sexual Patterns. For males, we found (1948) that social factors were of considerable significance in determining patterns of sexual behavior. In the present volume we have found that social factors are of more minor significance in determining the patterns of sexual behavior among females...

(While religious restraints had prevented many of the females as well as the males from ever engaging in certain types of sexual activity, or had delayed the time at which they became involved, the religious backgrounds had a minimum effect upon the females after they had once begun such activities...)

(pp. 685–7)

Summary and Comparisons of Female and Male

We have, then, thirty-three bodies of data which agree in showing that the male is conditioned by sexual experience more frequently than the female. The male more often shares, vicariously, the sexual experiences of other persons, he more frequently responds sympathetically when he observes other individuals engaged in sexual activities, he may develop stronger preferences for particular types of sexual activity, and he may react to a great variety of objects which have been associated with his sexual activities. The data indicate that in all of these respects, fewer of the females have their sexual behavior affected by such psychologic factors...

But we have already observed that the anatomy and physiology of sexual response and orgasm do not show differences between the sexes that might account for the differences in their sexual responses. Females appear to be as capable as males of being aroused by tactile stimuli; they appear as capable as males of responding to the point of orgasm. Their responses are not slower than those of the average male if there is any sufficiently continuous tactile stimulation. We find no reason for believing that the physiologic nature of orgasm in the female or the physical or physiologic or psychologic satisfactions derived from orgasm by the average female are different from those of the average male. But in their capacities to respond to psychosexual stimuli, the average female and the average male do differ...

(pp. 687–8)

Heterosexual-Homosexual Rating. Only a small proportion of the females in the available sample had had exclusively homosexual histories. An adequate understanding of the data must, therefore, depend upon some balancing of the heterosexual and homosexual elements in each history. This we have attempted to do by rating each individual on a heterosexual-homosexual scale which shows what proportion of her psychologic reactions and/or overt behavior was heterosexual, and what proportion of her psychologic reactions and/or overt behavior was homosexual. We have done this for each year for which there is any record. This heterosexual-homosexual rating scale was explained in our volume on the male (1948: 636–659)...

(pp. 469–70)

Extent of Female vs. Male Homosexuality. The incidences and frequencies of homosexual responses and contacts, and consequently the incidences of the homosexual ratings, were much lower among the females in our sample than they were among the males on whom we have previously reported (see our 1948: 650–651). Among the females, the accumulative incidences of homosexual responses had ultimately reached 28 per cent; they had reached 50 per cent in the males. The accumulative incidences of overt contacts to the point of orgasm among the females had reached 13 per cent; among the males they had reached 37 per cent. This means that homosexual responses had occurred in about half as many females as males, and contacts which had proceeded to orgasm had occurred in about a third as many females as males. Moreover, compared with the males, there were only about a half to a third as many of the females who were, in any age period, primarily or exclusively homosexual.

A much smaller proportion of the females had continued their homosexual activities for as many years as most of the males in the sample.

A much larger proportion (71 per cent) of the females who had had any homosexual contact had restricted their homosexual activities to a single partner or two; only 51 per cent of the males who had had homosexual experience had so restricted their contacts. Many of the males had been highly promiscuous, sometimes finding scores or hundreds of sexual partners.

There is a widespread opinion which is held both by clinicians and the public at large, that homosexual responses and completed contacts occur among more females than males. This opinion is not borne out by our data, and it is not supported by previous studies which have been based on specific data ... Males, interpreting what they observe in terms of male psychology, are inclined to believe that the female behavior reflects emotional interests that must develop sooner or later into overt sexual relationships. Nevertheless, our data indicate that a high proportion of this show of affection on the part of the female does not reflect any psychosexual interest, and rarely leads to overt homosexual activity.

(pp. 474–5)

Alan P. Bell and Martin S. Weinberg

Excerpts from *Homosexualities: A Study of Diversity among Men and Women*

First published by Simon and Schuster, New York (1978); published by Mitchell Beazley, London (1979).

The Homosexual-Heterosexual Continuum

... Homosexuality-heterosexuality is not necessarily an either-or proposition. Rather, people can be distinguished on the basis of the degree to which their sexual responsiveness and behaviors are limited to persons of a particular sex (male or female). These facts should come as no surprise to anyone familiar with the literature. Kinsey and his associates (1948, 1953), using a seven-point scale to measure whether, and if so to what degree, their respondents were 'homosexual' or 'heterosexual' in their sexual behaviors, determined that nearly half of American males fell somewhere between 'exclusively heterosexual' (a score of 0 on the scale) and 'exclusively homosexual' (or 6). Women were likewise found to differ in their standings on this scale, although fewer were exclusively 'homosexual'...

(p. 53)

Respondents' ratings of themselves on the homosexual-heterosexual continuum were in agreement with their sexual histories. Those who rated themselves as exclusively homosexual were less apt ever to have engaged in sexual activity with persons of the opposite sex or ever to have been sexually aroused in a heterosexual context than were those respondents who scored in more of a heterosexual direction. As one moves from point to point along the seven-point Kinsey Scale (from 6 to 0), increasingly larger percentages reported more heterosexual experiences. At the very least, it would appear that respondents' self-ratings were valid reflections of their sexual whereabouts.

In addition, our data show evidence of more heterosexuality in the behaviors and feelings of the homosexual women than in their male counterparts. The further finding that the lesbians' ratings of themselves on the Kinsey Scale were less apt to agree with their actual sexual histories than were those of the males suggests that the women were less likely to behave sexually in accordance with their true interests. While they may have been engaged in sexual activity with males, many might have done so with little satisfaction or sexual release. It is possible that the lesbians' greater heterosexuality simply reflects a history of accommodation to males in a sexual context or of conformity to social expectations.

The extent to which our respondents' whereabouts on the homosexual-heterosexual continuum are similar to those in other samples is quite striking. None of these studies, including our own, pretends to have a representative sample of either homosexual males or females. None is chiefly interested in establishing the incidence of any particular characteristic among its homosexual subjects. However, on the basis of these several investigations it would not be unreasonable to suppose that a fairly strong heterosexual element is to be found in about one-third of those homosexual men most likely to participate in surveys of this kind. Even larger numbers of comparable women are apt to exhibit a 'partial bisexual style' (Schafer). Many homosexuals of both sexes have a history of sexual contact with persons of the opposite sex and, although they may not presently engage in such contact, sometimes are aware of their continuing potential for heterosexual sexual response. There are others, however, who have never been aroused sexually by a person of the opposite sex even though they may have engaged in some form of heterosexual contact. Clearly, among homosexual adults there is a diversity of experience on the homosexual-heterosexual continuum reflected in their sexual feelings, behaviors, dreams and fantasies...

(pp. 60–61)

Negative Feelings About Homosexuality

More women than men in our samples, although a minority in each case, had seriously considered stopping their homosexuality, and among those who considered this, more women than men had made actual attempts to do so. Nevertheless, since at the time of the interview more men than women regretted their homosexuality or wished for a pill to 'cure' it, it seems reasonable to conclude that homosexual men are more likely than lesbians to have difficulties in accepting their homosexuality. It may be that homosexuality is more frequently construed by males as a failure to achieve a 'masculine' sexual adjustment, while lesbians, many of whom have experienced considerable sexual contact with males, more often experience their homosexuality as a freely chosen rejection of heterosexual relationships.

Another obvious and understandable finding is that clinical samples of homosexual men and women are much more apt to include persons who regret their homosexuality. Unfortunately it is these conflicted people's determination to become heterosexual which has been more evident in the literature and which has promoted clinicians to believe that homosexuality is inevitably problematic for those involved. Our data show that many homosexual men and women appear to come to terms with their homosexuality ...

(pp. 127–8)

The first step in our construction of a typology of homosexual experience involved a cluster analysis of our male respondents on the basis of their standard scores on the major measures of sexual experience. Comparisons of the different group profiles that emerged suggested the existence of five major groups of homosexual males. Not all of the sexual variables were critical in distinguishing these five groups. The highly discriminating variables, already suggested by the factor analysis, included whether the respondents were 'coupled' (i.e., involved in a quasi-marriage), how much they regretted being homosexual, the number of sexual problems they had, how many sexual partners they reported having over the past year, the amount of cruising they did, and the level of their sexual activity. Using profiles of the different groups as models, specific criteria were set for respondents' standard scores on these measures. Using these procedures 485 white and black homosexual respondents (or 71% of the homosexual male sample) were assigned to five 'pure' types: (I) Close-Coupled; (II) Open-Coupled; (III) Functional; (IV) Dysfunctional; and (V) Asexual ...

(pp. 131–2)

The same method used in the assignment of the male respondents to a particular group was used in connection with the homosexual women.

Although we had no particular interest in creating comparable or even the same number of male and female groups, they happen to be identical in number, are called by the same names, and are directly comparable in most respects. The degree to which they are not exactly comparable represents our interest in classifying as many of the female respondents as possible and in doing justice to whatever is distinctive about their experience of homosexuality.

Two hundred eleven of the lesbians (or three-quarters of the entire homosexual female sample) were assigned to five groups on the basis of their standard scores on the different dimensions of sexual experience: whether they were 'coupled', regret over their homosexuality, number of sexual problems, amount of cruising, and how much sex appeal they thought they had for other females ...

(pp. 134–5)

Dimensions of Sexual Experience

It should be noted that we make no claim that the preceding typology exhausts the ways in which homosexual adults can be meaningfully classified or even that our own respondents could only be classified in these particular ways. For example, had we chosen to emphasize respondents' standings on the homosexual-heterosexual continuum, we might have ended up with quite different classifications. Our only claim is that after examining our particular respondents' whereabouts on the many different dimensions of sexual experience, we were able to come up with what appeared to be a sensible and potentially useful typology. There was no question but that our respondents could be distinguished on the basis of their involvement in a quasi-marriage (i.e., whether or not they were 'coupled') and of their management of that kind of relationship, of the degree to which their homosexuality was problematic, and of the extent to which they were disengaged from the explicitly sexual aspects of gay life. Hopefully our efforts will inspire other investigators to develop typologies of homosexual experience which are at once more comprehensive and discriminating.

Although it is not our intention to establish our typology as definitive in any sense or to draw conclusions from it with regard to homosexual men and women not interviewed in this particular study, several of its aspects do deserve additional comment. For example, it is interesting to note that almost one-quarter of the homosexual men could be considered relatively 'asexual'. That is, large numbers of them, and perhaps of homosexual men in general, defied the stereotypical notion that all homosexual males are inevitably caught up and chiefly interested in the explicitly sexual aspects of their lives. The fact that more than one-third of the males were either Close-Coupled or Functional and that only one-fifth could be classified as Dysfunctional is also worth noting. It would appear that relatively large numbers of homosexual men manage their homosexuality with little difficulty, while a homosexual way of life is problematic for only a distinct minority. It should also be noted, however, that there were many more Open-Coupleds than Close-Coupleds among the male respondents. This suggests that a monogamous quasi-marriage between homosexual men is probably difficult to achieve, and that most such relationships involve the pursuit of sexual contacts with persons other than one's partner.

Among the homosexual women, in contrast to their male counterparts, there were more Close-Coupleds than Open-Coupleds. Indeed, the former group contained more members than any other. These findings confirm our earlier impressions of how homosexual men and women differ in their experience of homosexuality. More women than men are apt to be involved in a quasi-marriage marked by a relatively high degree of sexual fidelity. In fact, since so few of the female respondents could be classified as Functional (i.e., not 'coupled' but with a good adjustment), it would appear that the most viable option of most lesbians may be that of a fulfilling and relatively monogamous 'marital' relationship with another woman. Those not involved in such a relationship may be apt to experience their homosexuality as more problematic on one count or another.[1] This has not been the case for homosexual men.

Finally, it should be noted that the various types of homosexual adults tended to differ from the overall sample on dimensions of sexual experience not used as selection criteria and in other ways that seem to provide for tests of convergent validity – e.g., the Asexual males and females had less extensive sexual repertoires than the rest of the respondents; the male Functionals, highly involved in the sexual aspects of the gay world, were younger than the average respondent; and the Asexuals were older. Differences such as these are encouraging to the extent that they can be understood as additional evidence of the validity of our measurements and selection procedures...

(pp. 135–6)

Psychological Adjustment

These data confirm our conviction that studies which compare homosexual men and women with their heterosexual counterparts in terms of
their adult psychological adjustment are more informative when homosexual types are delineated. If we had not done this ourselves, we would
have been forced to conclude that homosexual adults in general tend to
be less well adjusted psychologically than heterosexual men and women.
In fact, however, among both the males and the females, it is primarily
the Dysfunctionals and the Asexuals who appeared to be less well off
psychologically than those in the heterosexual groups.

Among the men, the Close-Coupleds could not be distinguished from
the heterosexuals on various measures of psychological adjustment and
actually scored higher on the two happiness measures. The Functionals,
as well, hardly differed at all from the heterosexual men in terms of their
psychological adjustment. Among the women, the need for delineating
the homosexual adults on the basis of 'type' is similarly striking. Like
their male counterparts, the Close-Coupleds and the Functionals looked
much like the heterosexuals psychologically. In fact, the Close-Coupled
lesbians reported less loneliness than the heterosexual women, while the
Functionals appeared to be more exuberant.

It would appear that homosexual adults who have come to terms with
their homosexuality, who do not regret their sexual orientation, and who
can function effectively sexually and socially, are no more distressed
psychologically than are heterosexual men and women. Clearly, the
therapist who continues to believe that it is by fiat his or her job to
change a homosexual client's sexual orientation is ignorant of the true
issues involved. What is required, at least initially, is a consideration of
why a particular person's homosexuality is problematic and to examine
the ways in which his or her life style can be made more satisfying. Of
particular importance, perhaps, might be the individual's failure to
establish an on-going relationship with the same-sex partner. Our data
indicate that such a failure may be even more consequential and problematic for most homosexual adults than whatever difficulties they might
have in accepting their homosexuality. Suicidal ideation and suicide
attempts are apt to occur at the time of the breakdown or dissolution of
a significant 'couple' relationship. Such extreme reactions on the part
of those involved need not lead us to conclude that homosexual adults
have some special deficit in their personalities. Rather, homosexual

partnerships may involve more mutual interdependence than is found among heterosexual couples and, for that reason alone, their disruption may be more debilitating for those involved. What is required is counselors sensitive to the special difficulties and challenges homosexuals face in their attempt to maintain viable partnerships. Such professionals should be prepared to work as frequently with homosexual couples as with individuals, either in an effort to reopen lines of communication and to modify the partners' expectations or to make their eventual parting an occasion for personal growth instead of alienation...

(pp. 215–16)

A Concluding Overview

We are pleased at the extent to which our investigations of homosexual men and women have been realized. The tables show clearly that homosexual adults are a remarkably diverse group. Seldom do we find the vast majority of a given sample responding to a particular question in exactly the same way. Whether they were reporting about an aspect of their sexual lives, their social adjustment, or their emotional feelings, our respondents tended to say widely different things. This, of course, accounts for the many useful response distributions to be found in connection with almost every item. Needless to say, if we had not obtained samples from so many different sources, or if our respondents had been very similar demographically or only men or only women, the diversity of homosexual experience would not have been so evident. Again and again our data have demonstrated the need for specifying the race, sex, age, and sometimes educational or occupational level of homosexual adults before drawing any particular conclusions about them.

In addition, we were able to delineate our respondents beyond what their demographic characteristics would suggest. Initially based on differences in how they experienced and expressed their homosexuality, our typology proved to be more comprehensive. The types demonstrate important relationships between homosexual adults' sexually related behaviors and feelings and their social and psychological adjustment. These relationships, evident in more comprehensive typologies described below, make it clear that the sexual, social, and psychological spheres of human life are inevitably related to each other, that experiences in one sphere frequently coincide with and influence what occurs in another. An important lesson to be learned from our data is that homosexual men and women are best understood when they are seen as whole human beings, not just in terms of what they do sexually, despite the connection between sex and other aspects of their lives.

Another lesson our data provide is that future research in this area should attend increasingly to differences among homosexual adults. Researchers must be made keenly aware of the necessity to develop more precise typologies than the one in the present study, and for heterosexuals as well. These should refer not only to the sexual features of people's lives but also to the variety of contexts in which sexual feelings and impulses are expressed and to their social and psychological correlates.

Our data show that using a typology of homosexual experience helps to clarify whatever differences there might be between homosexual and heterosexual adults. In many instances, a much greater amount of the variance was accounted for when the heterosexual group was compared with various types of homosexuals than when the comparisons involved simply the two undifferentiated groups. In some cases, if we had not distinguished one type of homosexual male or female from another and had not been able to compare each type with those in the heterosexual group, we would have concluded that homosexual men and women in general are quite different from their heterosexual counterparts, both socially and psychologically. In fact, however, the Close-Coupled homosexual men and women, similar perhaps to many of the married men and women in the heterosexual group, hardly differed at all from the heterosexual sample and in some cases actually appeared better adjusted; the same was true of the Functional homosexuals. Usually it was the Dysfunctional and Asexual homosexuals who differed from the heterosexual respondents, and often in much the same way that they differed from other homosexual respondents. There is no question but that the heterosexual population has its share of types equivalent to those found among homosexuals and that if we had been in a position to develop a corresponding heterosexual typology, we might have concluded that the chief difference between the groups involves only the nature of their sexual preference.

Returning to the *raison d'être* of our study, it should be clear by now that we do not do justice to people's sexual orientation when we refer to it by a singular noun. There are 'homosexualities' and there are 'heterosexualities', each involving a variety of different interrelated dimensions. Before one can say very much about a person on the basis of his or her sexual orientation, one must make a comprehensive appraisal of the relationships among a host of features pertaining to the person's life and decide very little about him or her until a more complete and highly developed picture appears.

In what follows we present composite pictures of the types of homosexual men and women that emerged from our samples, involving their standings on the various measures of sexual experience and social and psychological adjustment. The descriptions are based on comparisons reported throughout this book, and, in those instances where additional comparisons were made in order to determine the differences between particular types (the Close-Coupleds versus the Functionals, the Dysfunctionals versus the Asexuals, etc.), on our multivariate analysis of variance ... Each composite picture will include descriptions of some of the actual respondents assigned to the particular type. These descriptions are excerpts of 'thumbnail sketches' prepared for each respondent by his or her interviewer, who, of course, did not know we would be 'typing' the homosexual respondents.

Close-Coupleds

We resisted the temptation to call this group 'happily married', although some of its members described themselves that way, because we did not want to imply that heterosexual relationships and marriage in particular are standards by which to judge people's adjustment. Instead, we use the word 'close' in two senses. First, the partners in this kind of relationship are closely bound together. Second, the partnership is close in that the Close-Coupleds tend to look to each other rather than to outsiders for sexual and interpersonal satisfactions.

The ways in which the Close-Coupleds differ from respondents in other homosexual groups bear out this description. They were the least likely to seek partners outside their special relationship, had the smallest amount of sexual problems, and were unlikely to regret being homosexuals. They tended to spend more evenings at home and less leisure time by themselves, and the men in this group seldom went to such popular cruising spots as bars or baths. Although the Close-Coupleds did not have the highest level of sexual activity, they reported more than most respondents, and their sexual lives were evidently gratifying to them. They were likely to have engaged in a wide variety of sexual techniques and tended not to report the kinds of problems that might arise from a lack of communication between partners.

The Close-Coupleds' superior adjustment is demonstrated in other aspects of their lives. The men in this group had rarely experienced difficulties related to their sexual orientation such as being arrested, trouble at work, or assault and robbery. They were less tense or paranoid and more exuberant than the average respondent. The Close-Coupled lesbians were the least likely of all the groups ever to have been concerned enough about a personal problem to have sought professional help for it. Both the men and the women were more self-accepting and less depressed or lonely than any of the others, and they were the happiest of all...

The salience of a viable 'coupled' relationship among our homosexual respondents is evident in comparisons between the Close-Coupleds and the next group to be described, the Open-Coupleds. The latter are not as fully committed to their special partner, placing more reliance on a large circle of homosexual friends and less stress on the importance of their relationship with their partner. They are also less happy, self-accepting and relaxed than the Close-Coupleds. These differences seem to suggest that the Open-Coupled relationship reflects a conflict between the ideal of fulfilled monogamy and dissatisfactions within the partnership...

(pp. 217–21)

Open-Coupleds

Like their Close-Coupled counterparts, the men and women in this group were living with a special sexual partner. They were not happy with their circumstances, however, and tended (despite spending a fair amount of time at home) to seek satisfactions with people outside their partnership. For example, the Open-Coupled men did more cruising than average, and the lesbians in this group cruised more than any of the other female respondents. Concomitantly, the Open-Coupleds worried about their cruising, especially about the possibility of being arrested or otherwise publicly exposed – perhaps because of their partner's ignorance of their cruising activities. In addition, the Open-Coupleds reported more sexual activity than the typical homosexual respondent and broader sexual repertoires, but the men tended to have trouble getting their partner to meet their sexual requests, and the women had the greatest worry about their partner wanting to do unwelcome sexual things or about being unable to carry on a conversation with her.

In most respects of their social and psychological adjustment, the Open-Coupleds could not be distinguished from the homosexual respondents as a whole. For example, they were not notable in how they spent their leisure time, how often they had experienced various social difficulties connected with homosexuality, or how many other people knew about their sexual orientation. Psychologically, they were about as happy, exuberant, depressed, tense, paranoid, or worrisome as the average homosexual respondent. However, the Open-Coupled lesbians were less self-accepting than any of the other groups...

It should be noted that the Open-Coupleds were the modal type among the males but relatively rare among the females, many more of whom were Close-Coupled. Whether lesbians find it easier than do homosexual males to achieve a stable and satisfying relationship with just one person, or whether they are more strongly motivated by romantic feelings than the men are, is not clear. However, our analysis of variance did show that the Open-Coupled males expressed more self-acceptance and less loneliness than the females did. This kind of relationship, then, is apparently more trying for the lesbian than for her male counterpart.

Compared with members of the other groups, the Open-Coupleds are intermediate in their adjustment. They went out more often and also spent more time alone than the Close-Coupleds did, and, among the males, felt more lonely. On the other hand, the Open-Coupled males appear much better off than the Dysfunctional males do. The latter were less likely to have many homosexual friends or to value having a special partner, and the Open-Coupleds were significantly better adjusted psychologically, reporting more happiness and self-acceptance and less worry, paranoia, tension or depression. Since the Open-Coupled lesbians did not differ from their Dysfunctional counterparts in these ways, it seems possible that managing a less than exclusive homosexual relationship is more difficult for women than for men...

(pp. 221–3)

Functionals

If Close- and Open-Coupled respondents are in some respects like married heterosexuals, the Functionals come closest to the notion of 'swinging singles'. These men and women seem to organize their lives around their sexual experiences. They reported more sexual activity with a greater number of partners than did any of the other groups, and the Functional lesbians had been married more times than the rest of the female respondents. The Functional men and women were least likely to regret being homosexual, cruised frequently and generally displayed a great deal of involvement in the gay world. They were not particularly interested in finding a special partner to settle down with, engaged in a wide variety of sexual activities, considered their sex appeal very high, and had few if any sexual problems. They were particularly unlikely to complain about not getting enough sex or difficulties in their sexual performance. Of all the groups, they were the most interested in sex, the most exuberant and the most involved with their many friends. In addition, the Functional men had the fewest psychosomatic symptoms. They were also the most likely ever to have been arrested, booked, or convicted for a 'homosexual' offense: this may be related to their greater overtness, their high attendance at gay bars, and perhaps as well their relative lack of worry or suspicion of others – or even a certain degree of recklessness...

The Functionals' good adjustment seems to be a function of their particular personalities. They are energetic and self-reliant, cheerful and optimistic, and comfortable with their highly emphasized sexuality. One should not conclude, however, that Functionals are an ideal type as regards coping with a homosexual orientation. It is rather the Close-Coupled men and women who have made the best adjustment. For example, while the Functionals had few sexual problems and were not very depressed or unhappy, the Close-Coupleds surpass them in these respects. When the two groups are compared directly, we see that the Functionals understandably spend less time at home and see their friends more often, but the males are more tense, unhappy, and lonely than their Close-Coupled counterparts...

(pp. 223–4)

Dysfunctionals

Dysfunctionals are the group in our sample which most closely accords with the stereotype of the tormented homosexual. They are troubled people whose lives offer them little gratification, and in fact they seem to have a great deal of difficulty managing their existence. Sexually, socially, and psychologically, wherever they could be distinguished from the homosexual respondents as a whole, the Dysfunctionals displayed poorer adjustment.

In terms of their sexual lives, the Dysfunctionals were the most regretful about their homosexuality. They reported more sexual problems than any other group, and they were especially prone to worry about their sexual adequacy, how they could maintain affection for their partner, and whether they or their partner would attain orgasm. Despite fairly frequent cruising (among the males) and a relatively high number of partners, they tended to complain about not having sex often enough and were the most likely of all the groups to report that they and their partner could not agree on what kind of sexual activity should take place. In addition, the men had trouble finding a suitable partner and were the most likely to ever have experienced impotence and premature ejaculation. Not surprisingly, with all these difficulties, the Dysfunctionals tended to think they were sexually unappealing.

Other aspects of the Dysfunctionals' lives were similarly problematic for them. Among the men in this group, there were more reports of robbery, assault, extortion, or job difficulties due to their being homosexual; they were also more likely to ever have been arrested, booked, or convicted regardless of the reason. The Dysfunctional lesbians were the least exuberant and the most likely to have needed long-term professional help for an emotional problem, and their male counterparts were more lonely, worrisome, paranoid, depressed, tense, and unhappy than any of the other men...

Direct comparisons of the Dysfunctionals with other groups strengthen the impression of their general distress. The Dysfunctional men differ significantly from both the Functionals and the Open-Coupleds on virtually every measure of psychological adjustment. If we had numbered only Dysfunctionals among our respondents, we very likely would have had to conclude that homosexuals in general are conflict-ridden social misfits...

(pp. 225–6)

Asexuals

The most prominent characteristic of the Asexual men and women in our samples is their lack of involvement with others. They scored the lowest of all the groups in the level of their sexual activity, reported few partners, had narrow sexual repertoires, rated their sex appeal very low, and tended to have a fair number of sexual problems. In this regard, the Asexual males tended to mention trouble finding a partner and not having sex often enough, but they were also less interested in sex than the other men. The Asexuals were the least likely of all the groups to describe themselves as exclusively homosexual, and among the males, they were less overt about their homosexuality and had fewer same-sex homosexual friends. Both the men and the women in this group tended to spend their leisure time alone and to have infrequent contact with their friends. They described themselves as lonely and (among the men) unhappy; the Asexual lesbians were most apt to have sought professional help concerning their sexual orientation but also to have given up counseling quickly, and they had the highest incidence of suicidal thoughts (not necessarily related to their homosexuality) . . .

The Asexual life-style is a solitary one. Despite their complaints of loneliness, Asexuals are not very interested in establishing a relationship with a special partner or in any of the rewards the gay world might offer them. For example, in addition to their lack of involvement with friends, the Asexual men seldom went to gay bars and did less cruising than any of the other groups except the Close-Coupleds. When compared directly with the Dysfunctionals, the Asexuals differed from them chiefly in terms of their disengagement from others. Nevertheless, since the Asexuals of either sex did not differ from the sample as a whole in many respects of psychological adjustment or in the extent to which being homosexual had caused them difficulty, it seems reasonable to infer that these people's quiet, withdrawn lives are the inevitable product of an underlying apathy toward the panoply of human experience . . .

(pp. 226–8)

Epilogue

It would be unfortunate to conclude this study of homosexual men and women without making its meaning more explicit and urging serious attention by those for whom our findings have special import. Such persons include state legislators involved in debates over the decriminalization of homosexual conduct, community leaders addressing themselves to the matter of civil rights for gays, governmental and business executives charged with the responsibility of hiring and firing personnel, educators and lay people dealing with sex education, religious leaders who are re-examining their churches' sexual beliefs and values, counselors with homosexual clients, and, finally, homosexual men and women themselves.

Until now, almost without exception, people in general, as well as those above, have been outraged, fearful or despairing toward homosexuality because of the stereotypes they hold. Not only have they believed that homosexuals are pretty much alike, but that this similarity necessarily involves irresponsible sexual conduct, a contribution to social decay, and, of course, psychological pain and maladjustment. Given such a stereotype, it is little wonder that the heterosexual majority has seen fit to discourage the acceptance of homosexuality by criminalizing homosexual behaviors and ferreting out people who engage in them, refusing to employ homosexuals, withholding from homosexual men and women the civil rights enjoyed by the majority and by a growing number of other minority groups, trying to cure homosexuals of their 'aberration', and feeling grief or shame at the discovery that a loved one is 'afflicted' by homosexual propensities. Reactions such as these to the millions of homosexual men and women in America and elsewhere are understandable in the light of common notions about what it means to be homosexual.

The present investigation, however, amply demonstrates that relatively few homosexual men and women conform to the hideous stereotype most people have of them; in addition, it is reasonable to suppose that objectionable sexual advances are far more apt to be made by a heterosexual (usually, by a man toward a woman) than a homosexual. In the same vein, seduction of an adolescent girl by a male teacher is probably more frequent than the seduction of young people by homosexual teachers, who are more apt to regard the class as a surrogate family than as a target for their sexual interests. And outside the classroom, the seduction of 'innocents' far more likely involves an older male, often a relative, and a pre- or post-pubescent female. Moreover, rape and sexual violence more frequently occur in a heterosexual than a homosexual context. Rape (outside of prisons) generally involves sexual attacks made by men upon women, while the relatively rare violence occurring in a homosexual context is usually the result of male youths 'hunting queers' or a man's guilt and disgust over a sexual episode just concluded. Finally, with respect to homosexuals' sexual activity itself, as our study notes, it commonly begins with highly cautious pursuits in places not normally frequented by heterosexuals or in more public surroundings where heterosexuals are not aware of what is taking place. Most often it is consummated with the full consent of the persons involved and in the privacy of one of the partners' homes. Even this description, however, disregards the numerous instances in which homosexual contact occurs solely between persons whose commitment to each other includes sharing a household.

As for homosexuals' social and psychological adjustment, we have found that much depends upon the type of homosexual being considered. Many could very well serve as models of social comportment and psychological maturity. Most are indistinguishable from the heterosexual majority with respect to most of the nonsexual aspects of their lives, and whatever differences there are between homosexuals' and heterosexuals' social adjustment certainly do not reflect any malevolent influence on society on the part of the homosexuals concerned. Close-Coupleds and Open-Coupleds behave much like married heterosexuals. Functionals draw on a host of support systems and display joy and exuberance in their particular life style. To be sure, Dysfunctionals and Asexuals have a difficult time of it, but there are certainly equivalent groups among heterosexuals. Clearly, a deviation from the sexual norms of our society does not inevitably entail a course of life with disastrous consequences. The homosexual who is afraid that he might end up a 'dirty old man', desperately lonely, should be assured that such a plight is not inevitable and that, given our society's failure to meet the needs of aging people, heterosexuality hardly guarantees well-being in old age. Between the time of their 'coming out' and whatever years remain, homosexual men and women must become increasingly aware of the array of options they have in their lives.

Perhaps the least ambiguous finding of our investigation is that homosexuality is not necessarily related to pathology. Thus, decisions about homosexual men and women, whether they have to do with employment or child custody or counseling, should never be made on the basis of sexual orientation alone. Moreover, it should be recognized that what has survival value in a heterosexual context may be destructive in a homosexual context, and vice versa. Life-enhancing mechanisms used by heterosexual men or women should not necessarily be used as the standard by which to judge the degree of homosexuals' adjustment. Even their personality characteristics must be appraised in the light of how functional they are in a setting that may be quite different from the dominant cultural milieu. It must also be remembered that even a particular type of homosexual is never entirely like others categorized in the same way, much less like those whose life styles barely resemble his or her own. And while the present study has taken a step forward in its delineation of types of homosexuals, it too fails to capture the full diversity that must be understood if society is ever fully to respect, and ever to appreciate, the way in which individual homosexual men and women live their lives...

(pp. 229–31)

Note

1. With the advent of the feminist movement, however, this may change.

EMPIRICAL RESEARCH ON HUMAN SEXUALITY:
THE REPRODUCTIVE BIOLOGY
RESEARCH FOUNDATION
(NOW MASTERS & JOHNSON INSTITUTE)

William H. Masters and V. E. Johnson

Excerpts from *Human Sexual Response*

First published by Little, Brown and Co. (Boston) and J. A. Churchill (London), 1966.

The Sexual Response Cycle

... If human sexual inadequacy ever is to be treated successfully, the medical and behavioral professions must provide answers to these basic questions. The current study of human sexual response has been designed to create a foundation of basic scientific information from which definitive answers can be developed to these multifaceted problems.

The techniques of defining and describing the gross physical changes which develop during the human male's and female's sexual response cycles have been primarily those of direct observation and physical measurement. Since the integrity of human observation for specific detail varies significantly, regardless of the observer's training and considered objectivity, reliability of reporting has been supported by many of the accepted techniques of physiologic measurement and the frequent use of color cinematographic recording in all phases of the sexual response cycle.

A more concise picture of physiologic reaction to sexual stimuli may be presented by dividing the human male's and female's cycles of sexual response into four separate phases. Progressively, the four phases are: (1) the excitement phase; (2) the plateau phase; (3) the orgasmic phase; and (4) the resolution phase. This arbitrary four-part division of the sexual response cycle provides an effective framework for detailed description of physiologic variants in sexual reaction, some of which are frequently so transient in character as to appear in only one phase of the total orgasmic cycle.

Only one sexual response pattern has been diagrammed for the human male. Admittedly, there are many identifiable variations in the male sexual reaction. However, since these variants are usually related to duration rather than intensity of response, multiple diagrams would be more repetitive than informative. Comparably, three different sexual response patterns have been diagrammed for the human female. It should be emphasized that these patterns are simplifications of those most frequently observed and are only representative of the infinite variety in female sexual response. Here, intensity as well as duration of response are factors that must be considered when evaluating sexual reaction in the human female.

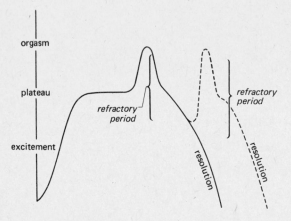

The male sexual response cycle

The first or excitement phase of the human cycle of sexual response develops from any source of somatogenic or psychogenic stimulation. The stimulative factor is of major import in establishing sufficient increment of sexual tension to extend the cycle. If the stimulation remains adequate to individual demand, the intensity of response usually increases rapidly. In this manner the excitement phase is accelerated or shortened. If the stimulative approach is physically or psychologically objectional, or is interrupted, the excitement phase may be prolonged greatly or even aborted. This first segment and the final segment (resolution phase) consume most of the time expended in the complete cycle of human sexual response.

From excitement phase the human male or female enters the second or plateau phase of the sexual cycle, if effective sexual stimulation is continued. In this phase sexual tensions are intensified and subsequently reach the extreme level from which the individual ultimately may move to orgasm. The duration of the plateau phase is largely dependent upon the effectiveness of the stimuli employed, combined with the factor of

individual drive for culmination of sex tension increment. If either the
stimuli or the drive is inadequate or if all stimuli are withdrawn, the
individual will not achieve orgasmic release and will drop slowly from
plateau-phase tension levels into an excessively prolonged resolution
phase.

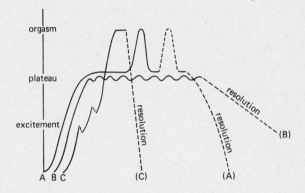

The female sexual response cycle

The orgasmic phase is limited to those few seconds during which the
vasoconcentration and myotonia developed from sexual stimuli are
released. This involuntary climax is reached at any level that represents
maximum sexual tension increment for the particular occasion. Subjective (sensual) awareness of orgasm is pelvic in focus, specifically concentrated in the clitoral body, vagina, and uterus of the female and in the
penis, prostate, and seminal vesicles of the male. Total-body involvement in the response to sexual tensions, although physiologically well-
defined, is experienced subjectively on the basis of individual reaction
patterns. There is great variation in both the intensity and the duration
of female orgasmic experience, while the male tends to follow standard
patterns of ejaculatory reaction with less individual variation.

The human male and female resolve from the height of their point in
the resolution phase if they submit to the reapplication of effective
stimulation. This facility for multiple orgasmic expression is evident
particularly if reversal is instituted at plateau tension level. For the man
the resolution phase includes a superimposed refractory period which
may extend during the involutionary phase as far as a lower excitement
level of response. Effective restimulation to higher levels of sexual

tension is possible only upon termination of this refractory period. With few exceptions, the physiologic ability of the male to respond to restimulation is much slower than that of the female.

Physiologic residuals of sexual tension are usually dissipated slowly in both the male and female unless an overwhelming orgasmic release has been experienced. Total involution is completed only after all manner of sexual stimuli have been withdrawn.

It always should be borne in mind that there is wide individual variation in the duration and intensity of every specific physiologic response to sexual stimulation. Those that occur early in the response cycle and continue without interruption during several phases are obvious (penile erection or vaginal lubrication). However, some physiologic reactions are fleeting in character and may be confined to one particular phase of the cycle. Examples are the plateau-phase color changes of the minor labia in the female and the coronal engorgement of the penis in the male.

In brief, the division of the human male's or female's cycle of sexual response into four specific phases admittedly is inadequate for evaluation of finite psychogenic aspects of elevated sexual tensions. However, the establishment of this purely arbitrary design provides anatomic structuring and assures inclusion and correct placement of specifics of physiologic response within the sequential continuum of human response to effective sexual stimulation.

The basic physiologic responses of the human body to sexual stimulation are twofold in character. The primary reaction to sexual stimuli is widespread vasocongestion, and the secondary response is a generalized increase in muscle tension. The vasocongestion may be either superficial or deep in distribution, and the myotonia reflected by voluntary or involuntary muscle contractions. The more vasocongestive and myotonic reactions are confined to plateau and orgasmic phases of the sexual cycle . . .

(pp. 3–7)

The Clitoris (and its role in orgasm)

. . . Clinical error has dominated the assignment of clitoral function in a sex tension increment for the human female. Therefore, a detailed consideration of the dual capacity of the clitoris, as both a receptor and transformer of sexual stimulation, is in order. The definitive role of the clitoris in sexual response must be appreciated if female sexual inadequacy ever is to be treated effectively . . .

Are clitoral and vaginal orgasms truly separate anatomic and physiologic entities? Attempts to answer these two questions have directed investigative interest toward a clinical evaluation of clitoral influence upon female sexual response.

While the literature contains innumerable discussions of the role of the clitoris in female sexuality, authoritative opinion has reached essential accord only in the view that the primary function of the organ is to stimulate female sexual tensions. In order to accomplish its clinical purpose, the clitoris functions in the dual capacity of both receptor and transformer of sexual stimuli regardless of whether these stimuli originally have been somatogenically or psychogenically oriented...

In the past, attempts have been made to assign to clinical variants in clitoral anatomy and physiology specific influence on the total of female sexual response. Eleven years of investigation have failed to support these concepts...

(p. 56)

The clitoral body functions as a receptor organ in an objective expression of sensual focus, as well as the subjective end-point (transformer) of neurogenic pathways...

However, the functional role (that of serving clinically as a transformer or subjective organ of sensual focus) has not been considered previously.

The subjective, or transformer, response of the clitoris to any form of effective sexual stimulation, such as reading of pornography, direct manipulation, coital connection, etc., has been vocalized by women in many ways. Some vocally identify a subjective sensation of deep pelvic fullness and warmth (possibly vasoconcentration). Others a feeling of local irritation, expansive urge, need for release, etc. (possibly glans enlargement). The clinical or functional response of the clitoris as a transformer of efferent forms of stimulation is to create in turn a subjective urge or tension increment and, ultimately, a higher cortical need for release. It is impossible to delimit this functional clitoral role of sensual focus because vocalization of the sensual response patterns varies from woman to woman. The transformer role also differs between clitoris and penis. Suffice it to say that the clitoris, serving as a receptor and transformer organ, has a role as the center of female sensual focus, and the functional response it creates easily is identifiable by any sexually oriented woman.

Any clinical consideration of clitoral response to effective sexual stimulation must include a discussion of masturbation. The techniques of and reactions to direct manipulation of the clitoral body (glans and shaft) or the mons area vary in each woman...

Marriage manuals discuss at length the importance of clitoral manipulation as the basis of adequate coital foreplay. Most discussions of initiation and elevation of female sexual tensions have included the questions of why and when to stimulate the clitoris. To date there has been little consideration of the infinitely more important questions of how to manipulate the clitoris and how much stimulation usually is required...

Not two women have been observed to masturbate in identical fashion. However, there is one facet of general agreement. Women rarely report or have been noted to employ direct manipulation of the clitoral glans...

Those women who manipulate the clitoris directly concentrate on the clitoral shaft. Usually they manipulate the right side of the shaft if right handed, and the left side if left handed. Occasionally, women have been observed to switch sides of the shaft during stimulative episodes. A relative degree of local anesthesis may develop if manipulation is concentrated in just one area for extended periods of time or if too much manipulative pressure is applied to any one area.

Women usually stimulate the entire mons area rather than concentrating on the clitoral body. Regardless of whether the clitoris is stimulated by direct means or indirectly through mons area manipulation, the physiologic responses of the clitoris to elevated sexual tensions are identical. Most women prefer to avoid the overwhelming intensity of sensual focus that may develop from direct clitoral contact. Instead, mons area manipulation produces a sensual experience that although somewhat slower to develop is, at orgasmic maturity, fully as satiating an experience as that resulting from direct clitoral shaft massage. Mons area manipulation also avoids the painful stimuli returned to many women when the clitoris is manipulated directly either with too much pressure or for too lengthy periods of time...

Another observation of female automanipulative technique should be considered for its clinical import. Most women continue active manipulation of the clitoral shaft or mons area during their entire orgasmic experience. This female reaction pattern parallels their coital pattern of demand for continued active male pelvic thrusting during the woman's orgasmic experience. This female demand for continued stimulation during the actual orgasmic expression is in opposition to the average male's reaction to his ejaculatory experience. Most males attempt the deepest possible vaginal penetration as the first stage of the ejaculatory response develops. They maintain this spastic, deep vaginal entrenchment during the second phase of the ejaculatory experience rather than continuing the rapid pelvic thrusting characteristic of preorgasmic levels of sexual tension...

The human female frequently is not content with one orgasmic experience during episodes of automanipulation involving the clitoral body. If there is no psychosocial distraction to repress sexual tensions, many well-adjusted women enjoy a minimum of three or four orgasmic experiences before they reach apparent satiation. Masturbating women concentrating only on their own sexual demands, without the psychic distractions of a coital partner, may enjoy many sequential orgasmic experiences without allowing their sexual tensions to resolve below plateau-phase levels. Usually physical exhaustion alone terminates such an active masturbatory session...

In direct manipulation of the clitoris there is a narrow margin between stimulation and irritation. If the unsuspecting male partner adheres strictly to marriage manual dictum, he is placed in a most disadvantageous position. He is attempting proficiency with a technique that most women reject during their own automanipulative experiences.

As stated previously, no two women practice automanipulation in similar fashion. Rather than following any preconceived plan for stimulating his sexual partner, the male will be infinitely more effective if he encourages vocalization on her part. The individual woman knows best the areas of her strongest sensual focus and the rapidity and intensity of manipulative technique that provide her with the greatest degree of sexual stimulation.

Finally, a brief consideration of the ... questions raised about the role of the clitoris in female sexuality: Are clitoral and vaginal orgasms truly separate anatomic entities? From a biologic point of view, the answer to this question is an unequivocal No. The literature abounds with descriptions and discussions of vaginal as opposed to clitoral orgasms...

From an anatomic point of view, there is absolutely no difference in the responses of the pelvic viscera to effective sexual stimulation, regardless of whether the stimulation occurs as a result of clitoral body or mons area manipulation, natural or artificial coition, or, for that matter, specific stimulation of any other erogenous area of the female body...

There may be great variation in duration and intensity of orgasmic experience, varying from individual to individual and within the same woman from time to time. However, when any woman experiences orgasmic response to effective sexual stimulation, the vagina and clitoris react in consistent physiologic patterns. Thus, clitoral and vaginal orgasms are not separate biologic entities...

(pp. 56–67)

The Female Orgasm

... Aside from ejaculation, there are two major areas of physiologic difference between female and male orgasmic expression. First, the female is capable of rapid return to orgasm immediately following an orgasmic experience, if restimulated before tensions have dropped below plateau-phase response levels. Second, the female is capable of maintaining an orgasmic experience for a relatively long period of time.

A rare reaction in the total of female orgasmic expression, but one that has been reduplicated in the laboratory on numerous occasions, has been termed status orgasmus. This physiologic state of stress is created either by a series of rapidly recurrent orgasmic experiences between which no recordable plateau-phase intervals can be demonstrated, or by a single, long-continued orgasmic episode. Subjective report, together with visual impression of involuntary variation in peripheral myotonia, suggests that the woman actually is ranging with extreme rapidity between successive orgasmic peaks and a baseline of advanced plateau-phase tension. Status orgasmus may last from 20 to more than 60 seconds...

(p. 231)

The Penis

Penile Fallacies

Another widely accepted 'phallic fallacy' is the concept that the larger the penis the more effective the male as a partner in coital connection. The size of the male organ both in flaccid and erect state has been presumed by many cultures to reflect directly the sexual prowess of the individual male...

The delusion that penile size is related to sexual adequacy has been founded in turn upon yet another phallic misconception. It has been presumed that full erection of the larger penis provides a significantly greater penile size increase than does erection of the smaller penis. This premise has been refuted by a small group of men selected from the study-subject population for clinical evaluation...

... there certainly is no statistical support for the 'phallic fallacy' that the larger penis increases in size with full erection to a significantly greater degree than does the smaller penis. The difference in average erective size increase between the smaller flaccid penis and the larger flaccid penis is not significant...

As Piersol has stated the size of the penis has less constant relation to general physical development than that of any other organ of the body. This statement has been made in recognition of yet another 'phallic fallacy'. It has been presumed by many cultures that the bigger the man in skeletal and muscular development, the bigger the penis, not only in a flaccid but also in an erect state. Detailed examination of the study-subject population of 312 men aged 21 to 80 years supported Piersol's contention that there is no relation between man's skeletal framework and the size of his external genitalia...

Although there is little to support the concept that erective size is proportionally greater for the larger than the smaller penis, there remains the theoretical concern of the man with the small penis as to his potential coital effectiveness. Even with erective ability of the smaller penis (less than 9cm) presumed equal to that of the larger penis (more than 10cm), the smaller penis in the flaccid state usually remains somewhat smaller in an erect state. The factor that constantly is overlooked in theoretical discussions of penile coital effectiveness is the involuntary accommodative reactions of the vagina in its functional role under coital stimulation as a seminal receptacle...

(pp. 191–3)

Vaginal Fallacies

... Full (vaginal) accommodation (of the penis) usually is accomplished with the first few thrusts of the penis, regardless of penile size. If intromission occurs early in the woman's sexual response cycle, the fully erect smaller penis can and does function as a dilating agent as effectively as a larger penis...

It becomes obvious that penile size usually is a minor factor in sexual stimulation of the female partner. The normal or large vagina accommodates a penis of any size without difficulty. If the vagina is exceptionally small, or if a long period of continence or involution due to aging intervenes, a penis of any size can distress rather than stimulate, if mounting is attempted before advanced stages of female sexual tension have been experienced...

(p. 195)

Fears of Performance

'Phallic fallacies' relating to the functional role of the penis frequently devolve from the culturally conceived role for the male partner in human coition – that of actively satisfying the female partner.

The 'fear of performance' developing from cultural demand for partner satisfaction has been in the past uniquely the burden of the responding male. Inevitably fear provides a breeding ground for misconception. Among the male members of the study-subject population and males interrogated as applicants, phallic fallacies of subjective orientation were related to decades of life experience more than to any other single factor...

For the men forty years or younger, fears of performance centered about questions of excessive ejaculatory experience and concerns for premature ejaculation. The problem of too frequent ejaculation was associated in the minds of many study subjects with possible loss of physical strength and not infrequently was presumed to be a basis for emotional instability if not severe neurosis. These misconceptions have grown from the culturally centered fear that frequent or excessive masturbation may lead to mental illness. No study subject could provide a secure personal concept of what constituted frequent or excessive levels of masturbation, nor could anyone describe an instance known to them, even by report, of mental illness resulting from masturbation. The superstition that physical or mental deterioration results from excessive masturbation is firmly entrenched in our culture, if returns from the team questioning of the total male group of study-subject applicants are any criterion.

Reported masturbatory frequency in the male study-subject group ranged from once a month to two or three times a day. Every male questioned expressed a theoretical concern for the supposed mental effects of excessive masturbation, and in every case 'excessive levels' of masturbation, although not defined specifically, were considered to consist of a higher frequency than did the reported personal pattern. One man with a once-a-month masturbatory history felt once or twice a week to be excessive, with mental illness quite possible as a complication of such a frequency maintained for a year or more. The study subject with the masturbatory history of two or three times a day wondered whether five or six times a day wasn't excessive and might lead to a 'case of nerves.' No study subject among the 312 questioned in depth expressed the slightest fear that his particular masturbatory pattern was excessive of stated frequency.

There is no established medical evidence that masturbation, regardless of frequency, leads to mental illness. Certainly there is no accepted medical standard defining excessive masturbation. It is true, of course, that many severely neurotic or acutely psychotic men masturbate frequently. If a high-frequency pattern of masturbatory activity exists, it may be but one of a number of symptoms of underlying mental illness rather than in any sense the cause of the individual distress. The vague concept of excessive masturbatory activity is a phallic fallacy widely accepted in our culture, relating specifically to the functional role of the penis in male sexuality ...

The fear of performance reflecting cultural stigmas directed toward erective inadequacy was that associated with problems of secondary impotence. These fears were expressed, under interrogation, by every male study subject beyond forty years of age, irrespective of reported levels of formal education.

Regardless of whether the individual male study subject had ever experienced an instance of erective difficulty, the probability that secondary impotence was associated directly with the aging process was vocalized constantly. The fallacy that secondary impotence is to be expected as the male ages is probably more firmly entrenched in our culture than any other misapprehension. While it is true that the aging process, with associated physical involution, can reduce penile erective adequacy, it is also true that secondary impotence is in no sense the inevitable result of the aging process ...

In most instances, secondary impotence is a reversible process for all men regardless of age, unless there is a background of specific surgery or physical trauma ...

(pp. 200–203)

William H. Masters and V. E. Johnson

Excerpts from *Homosexuality in Perspective*

First published by Little, Brown and Co. (Boston).

Clinical Discussion

Fourteen years of laboratory and clinical investigation of human homosexual function and dysfunction have provided broad-based support for the Institute's major premise that from a functional point of view homosexuality and heterosexuality have far more similarities than differences. Yet today, many decades after cultural dictum originally introduced the concept that important functional differences do exist between the two sexual preferences, the overwhelming pressure of public opprobrium still blindly reinforces this false assumption. The general public as well as many segments of the scientific community remain convinced that there are marked functional disparities between homosexual and heterosexual men and women.

This cultural precept was originally initiated and has been massively supported by theologic doctrine. The Institute has no point of contention with the relatively well-defined position of theology on the subject of homosexuality. It is not our intention to assume a role in interpreting or implementing moral judgment. These privileges and their accompanying awesome responsibilities are not within the purview of a research group devoted to psycho-physiologic aspects of human sexuality.

Actually, interviews have provided tentative support for the cultural concept of physical differences. Kinsey 0 men or women have unhesitatingly contended that homosexuality was without any semblance of psychosexual appeal because 'they (homosexuals) are different,' while Kinsey 6 individuals have been just as adamant in rejecting any possible personal interest in heterosexual interaction – and for the same reason. Unfortunately, many individuals have loosely interpreted the 'they-are-different' doctrine as meaning physically different in sexual response. Men and women representing both ends of the Kinsey spectrum have based their intractable belief in the existence of physical differences in sexual interaction entirely upon culturally engendered impressions, for they have had no personal experience with which to support or deny their socially reinforced opinions.

The bioethical problem in evaluating supposed physical differences has centered on the fact that until 15 years ago cultural prejudices were so powerful that their precepts could not even be challenged in the research laboratory. Therefore, subjective opinions, the basic fodder of cultural dictum, have neither been supported nor denied by objectively developed investigative material. Fortunately, the culture can no longer dictate this degree of blind obeisance from investigative science.

When we admit to judging the physical aspects of sexual preference on the shaky foundation of subjective impression rather than from relatively secure research objectivity, there is another and far less appealing pattern of human behavior that has consistently developed as a cultural consequence. In order to lend credence to our personal preference for a particular sexual orientation, we not only categorically deny value in 'the other way', we insist on attempting to discredit it completely. It frequently follows that those individuals who adhere to opinions and practices that are contradictory to our own in this controversial area are personally rejected.

Meanwhile, the small voice of reason has gone unheeded. For decades, Kinsey 2, 3 and 4 men and women who have had a significant amount of both homosexual and heterosexual experience have consistently contended that there was not any difference in the functional aspects of the two preference roles. These individuals may indicate a personal bias for either homosexual or heterosexual encounter, but any cultural concept of physical difference in sexual interaction has been replaced by the more pragmatic process of enjoying sensual aspects of the sexual encounter, regardless of the gender of the partner.

We are genetically determined to be male or female and, in addition, are given the ability to function sexually as men or women by the physical capacities of erection and lubrication and the inherent facility for orgasmic attainment. These capacities function in identical ways, whether we are interacting heterosexually or homosexually. When a man or woman is orgasmic, he or she is responding to sexual stimuli with the same basic physiologic response patterns, regardless of whether the stimulative technique is masturbation, partner manipulation, fellatio/cunnilingus, vaginal or rectal coitus – and also regardless of whether the sexual partner is of the same or the opposite gender.

Of course, the 'they-are-different' doctrine has had many interpretations other than the concept that homosexuals and heterosexuals function differently sexually. The Kinsey 0 considers the Kinsey 6 vastly different in many ways because he or she expresses sexual interest in a same- rather than an opposite-sex partner.

The Kinsey 0 man or woman who identifies with an opposite-sex individual as a sex object does so on an individual basis. The identification does not extend to all members of the opposite sex. In fact, although he or she might never admit the interest level openly, the Kinsey 0 man or woman is occasionally committed far more closely psychosexually with a same-sex individual than he or she ever is with many opposite-sex acquaintances. The same behavior pattern is followed by Kinsey 6 men and women, who often identify far more closely with an opposite-sex individual than with same-sex acquaintances.

In the middle of the spectrum are many men and women (Kinsey 2, 3, and 4) who closely identify with partners of both the same and opposite sex and find them equally stimulating sex objects. When responding to these partners, they react in the same physical manner regardless of the gender of the particular partner.

Finally, there are ambisexual men and women. They simply do not care whether the partner is male or female, for the gender of the partner is not an important source of sexual arousal. As abundantly demonstrated in the laboratory, ambisexuals respond in identical fashion regardless of the gender of the partner or the mode of sexual activity. Therefore, it appears that the 'they-are-different' doctrine is also consistently interpreted as 'they do not feel precisely as we do about a potential sex object'. When making this 'they-are-different' social judgment, it is always convenient to overlook the fact that we usually feel differently about a potential sex object from day to day. We tend to require consistent sexual focus on one partner or a specific type of sex object from other individuals, but not from ourselves.

Over the last 15 years, it also has become apparent that the individual's sexual orientation does not significantly alter his or her problem of sexual dysfunction. Impotence and anorgasmic states have just as devastating an effect on homosexual as on heterosexual men or women. Fears of performance and spectator roles can make a sexual cripple out of any sexually dysfunctional individual, homosexual or heterosexual. Sexual fakery is freely practiced by representatives of both sex preferences. Therefore, the Institute strongly supports the concept that sexual dysfunction be treated with the same therapeutic principles and techniques regardless of the sexual orientation of the distressed individual.

If therapeutic procedures are carried out effectively, differences in the clinical failure statistics should be minimal. Generally, there may be a lower failure rate in treating the dysfunctional homosexual than the dysfunctional heterosexual because the sexually dysfunctional homosexual does not have the extra demand for effective function during coition that is inherent in heterosexual interaction. In support of these statements a comparison of the overall failure rates in treating homosexual and heterosexual dysfunction is indicated.

Overall treatment failure rates have been compiled from a combination of acute treatment failures and both recorded and theoretical instances of renewed dysfunction during the required five-year follow-up period after termination of the acute treatment phase ... The combined (male and female) overall treatment failure rate for homosexual dysfunction was approximately 12 percent. The corresponding heterosexual statistic published in 1970 (*Human Sexual Inadequacy*) was approximately 20 percent.

The lower overall failure rate returned from treating dysfunctional homosexual men and women not only reflected the fact that effective function during intercourse was not required, but also the additional influence of another important factor. The research team had the enormous advantage of a decade of clinical experience treating heterosexual dysfunction before it initiated the homosexual treatment program. From a clinical point of view, a significant differential between the two estimated overall failure rates was to be expected.

Therapy for sexual dissatisfaction represents the 'disaster area' in the Institute's treatment program for sexually distressed homosexuals. The overall combined (male and female) failure rate was estimated at approximately 35 percent ... Actually, a significantly higher failure rate was anticipated for the treatment of homosexual dissatisfaction than that developed from treating homosexual dysfunction, but the marked differential in the failure rates was not expected. The overall failure rate for homosexual dissatisfaction was approximately three times that recorded for sexually dysfunctional homosexual men and women. This poor clinical return developed despite the fact that there was careful screening of clients in every case of sexual dissatisfaction accepted into the therapy program.

In brief, approximately one in three homosexual men and women treated for sexual dissatisfaction either failed to convert or revert to heterosexuality during the acute phase of the treatment program or actively or theoretically returned to overt homosexual interaction during the required five-year follow-up period. In comparison, approximately one in 10 homosexual men and women had a similar report of a failed therapy program for sexual dysfunction . . .

The elevated overall failure rate for the treatment of homosexual dissatisfaction is, of course, unacceptable. There should be no overall failure rate higher than 20 percent for treatment of any form of either homosexual or heterosexual inadequacy.

An important factor that has contributed significantly to failures in treating male homosexual dissatisfaction in the past should prove far less of a barrier to effective therapy in the future. It is anticipated that the degree of cooperation with the therapeutic process by those homosexual men requesting reversion or conversion therapy will improve markedly. The clients' increased confidence in the treatment modalities and, subsequently, their higher levels of clinical cooperation should come from two sources. First, the homosexual community will soon realize that there are improved therapeutic procedures available to the dissatisfied as well as the dysfunctional homosexual. This realization should, in turn, increase confidence in and cooperation with the therapeutic process. Second, there also should be a better rapport between client and therapist when there is unmistakable evidence of the health-care profession's full assumption of its professional responsibility toward the treatment of sexually distressed homosexual men and women.

There is a discrepancy between treatment programs involving sexually inadequate homosexual and heterosexual populations. This imbalance revolves about the clinical problems of dissatisfied homosexual men and women who entered treatment with the expressed interest of converting or reverting to heterosexuality . . . The problem is that there is no facet of the treatment program for the sexually distressed heterosexual population corresponding to the section for homosexual dissatisfaction. Over the 20-year period during which the Institute has been treating sexually distressed heterosexual men and women, there have only been 2 men asking for professional help in converting to homosexuality, and they were primarily impotent as heterosexuals to start with ...

With this discrepancy in mind, the only statistics that remain of more than passing interest are those that provide an open comparison between the overall failure rates of the treatment programs for all forms of heterosexual inadequacy and those for all forms of homosexual inadequacy. The overall failure rate for the heterosexual dysfunction program was estimated at a combined (male and female) total of approximately 20 percent (*Human Sexual Inadequacy*), and the overall combined failure rate for the treatment programs for homosexual dysfunction and dissatisfaction was estimated at approximately 25 percent ...

Of necessity, these are estimated statistics, for as previously stated, they are a combination of the numbers of acute treatment failures and the number of actual and theoretical failures during the required five-year follow-up program. Yet, the figures are in such close clinical parallel that they lend support to the concept of similarity, not difference, between the sexual functions and dysfunctions of the two sexual preferences.

The parallelism in overall failure rates also underscores the fact that the treatment techniques, which were essentially identical in concept and format, were generally as effective in treating homosexual as heterosexual inadequacies. Regardless of the distressed individual's sexual preference, the research team insisted upon the use of dual-sex therapy teams and requested that the sexually inadequate individual be accompanied in therapy by a partner of choice. A detailed discussion of the psychotherapeutic principles involved in the treatment of homosexual dysfunction and dissatisfaction by the dual-sex team techniques will be published at a later date.

Hormones and Homosexuality

In the last decade, research interest has been rekindled in the quest to identify biologic factors important in the genesis of homosexuality. Since the Institute's endocrine section under the direction of Robert C. Kolodny has been active in this area, we would be remiss if the current status of these research programs were not summarized.

Investigative endocrinologists have been aided by technologic advances such as radioimmunoassay techniques, which for the first time have permitted precise quantification of various hormones related to reproduction and sexual functioning. Such work has also been stimulated by related advances clarifying embryologic mechanisms of sexual differentiation – with increasing evidence that in certain instances the fetal hormonal environment may predispose individuals toward particular patterns of sexual behavior.

A large body of experimental literature, only briefly mentioned here, documents the fact that in a variety of animal species hormonal manipulation during critical phases of sexual differentiation can produce subsequent alterations in adult sexual behavior that have been interpreted as paralleling homosexual behavior in humans. While it is difficult to decide if interspecies comparisons of these behaviors provide accurate etiologic insights or, indeed, whether such behavior patterns are truly homologous, there are additional findings stemming from isolated studies of clinical situations involving humans that lend credence to the observations derived from animal studies. These diverse situations, including females with the adrenogenital syndrome (exposed in utero to high levels of androgen), men with Klinefelter's syndrome (usually marked by both a fetal and adult relative deficiency of androgen), and instances of prenatal exposure to exogenous hormonal intake (principally progestins and estrogens), seem to be associated with a higher incidence of subsequent homosexuality than would occur by chance alone.

In 1970, Margolese reported that the urinary excretion of androsterone and etiocholanolone was different in homosexual and heterosexual men. That same year, Loraine and his colleagues reported that urinary excretion of testosterone was low in two homosexual men and elevated in four homosexual women. Subsequently, work by Kolodny and his colleagues from the Institute (1971–1972) – undertaken with a degree of skepticism about such hormonal variations in homosexuals – found that plasma testosterone levels were significantly lower in young men who were either exclusively or almost exclusively homosexual (Kinsey 5 or 6) than in an age-matched group of heterosexual controls. These investigators carefully stated: 'There is no suggestion that endocrine abnormalities will be found in the great majority of homosexuals ... In fact there must be speculation that the depressed testosterone levels could be the secondary result of a ... depressive reaction relayed through the hypothalamus from higher cortical centers.'

Following this study, a large number of additional reports have appeared with considerable disagreement in results. While Evans (1972) and Margolese and Janiger (1973) separately found further evidence of altered urinary hormone metabolites in homosexual men, others have not confirmed this difference. Similarly, while Starka and co-workers (1975) described lower circulating testosterone in homosexual men than in heterosexual controls, and Rhode and his colleagues (1977) found significantly lower free plasma testosterone in 35 homosexual men than in 38 heterosexual men, studies by other investigators – including Brodie et al. (1974), Birk et al. (1973), Friedman et al. (1977), Doerr et al. (1973, 1976), Tourney and Hatfeld (1973), Pillard et al., and Barlow et al. (1974) – found no differences in circulating testosterone between homosexual and heterosexual men. To further complicate the situation, Doerr and his colleagues (1973) noted that there were significant differences in estrone and dihydrotestosterone between homosexual and heterosexual men; significant differences in luteinizing hormone secretion in these same groups were also observed by Doerr's group (1976), by Kolodny and his colleagues (1972), and by Rhode and his co-workers (1977). Similar controversy exists in hormonal studies of homosexual women, although this topic has not received such intensive investigative scrutiny.

What conclusions or inferences can be drawn from the available evidence? First, it is apparent that all of these reports are significantly handicapped by methodological limitations ranging from relatively small sample size to problems in sampling intervals. Until these problems are remedied, it is difficult to assess the evidence with any security. Second, it is apparent that homosexuality is no more a unitary phenomenon than is heterosexuality: Until it is possible to separate specific subgroups of homosexuals and heterosexuals by precise classification criteria, the heterogeneity that cuts across the basic lines of homosexual versus heterosexual – supported by the heterogeneity found in the physiologic and clinical studies reported in this text – complicates the identification of significant hormonal differences even if these exist. Third, until more is known about the origins of heterosexuality, it is difficult to believe that meaningful insights will be reached regarding the origins of homosexuality. Finally, in view of the current lack of secure information in this field, we must maintain an intellectually open stance acknowledging that in at least some instances – though clearly not in most cases – hormonal predispositions may interact with social and environmental factors to lead toward a homosexual orientation.

There is little need for further detailed comment. A start has been made. Far more sophisticated basic research in the neuro-physiology of human sexual function is next in order. In time, the neuroendocrinology of sexual response must be established. New and more effective variations in the basic therapeutic technique for sexual dysfunction and dissatisfaction must be developed. The techniques must also be combined with improved applicant screening and more effective follow-up procedures. In response to such investigative efforts, there will be progressive lowering of the overall failure rates for the treatment of both homosexually and heterosexually oriented sexual inadequacy.

(pp. 403–11)

SEX AS SOCIAL INTERACTION

J. H. Gagnon and W. Simon

Excerpts from *Sexual Conduct:
The Social Sources of Human Sexuality*

First published by Aldine Publishing Co. (Chicago, 1973).

Postadolescent Sexual Development (Chapter Three)

Young Adulthood and Later

For most persons in U.S. society the movement into adulthood that is linked to occupational life is accompanied by a movement into marriage. An extensive involvement in overt heterosexual behavior generally emerges either just prior to marriage or within the marital state. This is true for both men and women, though obviously is more characteristic of women. Indeed, the management of sexual commitments within a marital relationship characterizes the largest part of postadolescent sexual experience in our society. As with other aspects of sex behavior, it is important to underscore the real poverty of data on this topic. We presume that sexual adjustment plays an important role in overall adjustment, but this judgement is derived largely from studies of broken marriages or marriages that are in trouble. We really have very little sense of the degree to which sexual problems in troubled or dissolved marriages exceed those found in marriages that remain intact. It is possible that we have assumed an important role for sexuality and the management of sexuality in the maintenance of marital bonds because we have assumed that sex itself is an important part of most people's lives. This may not be true. Particularly after the formation of the marital unit, it is quite possible that sex – both as a psychological reward and a physical outlet – declines in salience. It may become less important than alternative modes of gratification (work, children, security, constant affection – any or all may become more significant), or the weight of these alternative gratifications may minimize the effects of any sexual dissatisfaction. It is also true that individuals learn to derive equivalent levels of gratification from non- or only partially sexual activities. This is not to offer support for the concept of sublimation but rather to point out that in the processes that follow marriage, newly learned alternative patterns of gratification may be substituted for the sexual (which may well have had only situational significance due to its salience during mate selection).

At the present time the main determinant of adult rates of heterosexual activity in our society is the level of male commitment. While interest in intercourse is highest for males and females during the early years of marriage, the peak in orgasmic responsiveness occurs much later in marriage for females (who require longer periods of time to either become de-inhibited or to learn to be sexual – depending upon your point of view). Nonetheless, coital rates in marriage decline steadily through marriage.[1] This decline, it should be noted, can only be partly attributed to declines in biological capacity on the part of the male. The decrease may derive from many things. In many cases the problem is one of relating sexually to a person whose roles have been complicated by the addition of maternal functions.[2] For lower-class males, there is a problem of not receiving homosocial support for marital intercourse, to which we might also add the disadvantage of being less trained in the use of auxiliary materials to heighten sexual interest.[3] For middle-class males, the decline is less steep, owing perhaps to their ability to find sexual stimulation from auxiliary sources – literature, movies, and the like. A greater capacity for invoking and responding to fantasy is also operative. It should be noted that for about 30 per cent of college-educated males, masturbation continues as a regular source of sexual outlet in marriage and during periods when a wife is available.[4] To this we might add an additional, but unknown, proportion who do not physically engage in masturbation but for whom the source of sexual excitement is not coital activity alone but also the fantasy elements which accompany coital activity. But even for the middle-class male, sexual activity declines in amounts that cannot exclusively be accounted for by changes in the organism. Perhaps it is simply that the conditions under which we learn to be sexual in our society make it extremely difficult to maintain high levels of sexual performance with a single partner over long periods of time. This may remain relatively unimportant in the maintenance of the family unit, however, or even with respect to the individual's sense of his own well-being because of the relative unimportance of sexual dissatisfaction or the relatively greater significance of other areas of life.[5]

Given the achievement orientation of males toward sexual activity learned in adolescence and the capacity of sexual activity to be put to a wide range of uses in human relationships, there is a tendency on the part of many males (and fewer females) to seek variety in their sexual experiences, especially after marriage and even during the period of more extensive experimentation that precedes it. This search for variation can be managed in a number of ways, all of which transgress some normative constraints on sexual behavior. The search for variety can occur within a single relationship through the expansion of the number of sexual things that people do with each other. Anal intercourse, mouth-genital contact or variety in coital positions are the most common physical techniques.[6] It is also possible to role play other social arrangements, either openly with the cooperation of the spouse or through the individual use of fantasy during coitus. In contrast, one may seek variety through contact with partners outside of marriage. It is in the violation of normative boundaries that elements of domination-submission, good and evil, enhancement of other forms of striving, or compensations or reparations for losses may be managed. The search for variety is more commonly experienced among men, though it may occur among women (either through extramarital coitus or through coitus with the spouse under new circumstances or on vacation). There are also class variations among males, with variety in technique more common in middle-class males and variety in partners among lower-class males. Even the staging of extramarital coitus may vary with class, occurring earlier in marriage for lower-status males and later in marriage for middle-class males.

It is these activities that are at the margin of conformity which introduce new elements into the marital or premarital state. Positional variation in coitus is perhaps the most frequently practiced variant. While the conventional social script for coitus has the male above and female below, a postural affirmation of the symbolic dominance of men and submission of women, this is one of the more easily eroded of all sexual taboos.[7] The problem here, as it is in initiating or maintaining nearly all forms of sexual variety, is that the novel behaviors must normally be accomplished without speaking. The female must roll over (or be rolled over) in order to gain coital entrance from the rear; she must get or be placed on top for coitus to take place with the female above. In order for this to be successfully managed, the female must usually give signs that the change in position is a source of pleasure. Commonly this is done through either having orgasm occur or making noises that are conventionally associated with sexual excitement. Textual legitimation of these positional variations (as well as other techniques) may be found in marriage manuals (or the mass women's magazines) that are more often available to women than to men, especially at lower social levels in the society.

The success of attempts to introduce positional variety depends on the flexibility of the sexual script possessed by the two partners. If the male or the female finds that the conventional position is the one in which orgasm can be achieved (not because it is more erotic or technically better, but because it is 'normal'), there will be powerful constraints to return to this position. However, the constraints on the male or female to return to this position will be quite different. The male may feel that the female above is dominating or that rear entry is degrading to a person who is to be loved. In many cases there is constraint against experimentation with the wife since she is the object of noneyrotic love preventing her from occupying (either assuming or being attributed to her) the roles that are identified with women who are sexually degraded. At the same time, women may find the sequence of behaviors that lead to orgasm requires that she be underneath, sometimes to preserve a more limited sense of 'letting go' that is part of the culturally prescribed experience of orgasm. Certain positions may be chosen since they symbolize dominance and submission or degradation which can serve to heighten sexual response through the introduction of components that either confirm or deny conventional nonsexual social postures. The sequence of physical activities (and the injunctions of the marriage manuals) is not the organizing factor in either sexual arousal or response, but it is the meaning that is attributed to the activities themselves.

Mouth-genital contact is perhaps the most tension-producing technique in sexual experimentation. The physical activity itself involves introducing the penis into the mouth of the female or the male putting his mouth on the female's vagina. Given the definitions that these organs have in terms of odor, taste, cleanliness, and excretion, putting the mouth and genitals together in an act that can be defined as pleasurable is extremely complex. Indeed, in much of conventional sexuality the genitals are out of sight or at least at arm's length, and in consequence the penis or vagina are experienced as objects of sensation, but only marginally significant in terms of manipulation. Given the strongly initiatory role that men have in sexual activity, the instigator for the largest proportion of mouth-genital activity is the male. Central to male sexual culture are a series of myths about mouth-genital contact and one of the sources of its power and significance is the desire to place the penis in a forbidden location. Since there is no meaning immanent in the activity and nothing intrinsic to the mouth that makes it a better orifice for stimulation of the penis, the meaning of the act and its capacity to arouse must be sought in extrasexual and extraphysical areas. One element in the physical character of fellatio that suggests its physical component is not central to its enjoyment is that there is a considerable constriction of the degree of freedom of movement on the part of the male – and actually only a limited number of females who could be described (from a male point of view) as technically proficient at fellatio. These two constraints suggest that it is the psychological inputs that serve to heighten arousal and not the value of the physical stimulation.

A series of symbolic meanings can be cited that heighten the significance of fellatio as a form of sexual contact. The images of filling up, choking, dominating, controlling, degrading are all immediately available, not only from pornography but from the sexual and nonsexual fantasies of males who are engaged in the behavior. Complementary elements are the expression of affection and bonding that women feel when they find that in the act they give greater pleasure to the male. The couple may act out conventional gender role models, he dominating, she submitting, while the transgression of the taboo gives both persons a heightened sense of erotic power. The etiquette of introducing mouth-genital contact into the sexual repertoire of a relationship (at least in most conventional circumstances) is commonly nonverbal, though the ubiquitous marriage manual may serve as justification. To perform the act the female must learn that the penis may be defined as an appropriate object to put into her mouth (in middle-class groups, cleanliness wars with sexual service), and she must deal with the problem of texture and taste. Even though the female is more physically active and dominating and the male more passive, the act of fellatio is symbolically constructed in terms of male dominance and female submission. This is part of the common practice found in sexual activity of relabeling physical acts to fit social definitions. Whether the male can ejaculate in the female's mouth at the culmination of fellatio remains at the edge of the taboo. The taste of semen and its consistency are not quite within the range of normal sexual stimuli and whether the semen is swallowed or not increases the psychological complexity of the relationship.

The historical nature of the male-female relationship in terms of duration is complexly related to the activity of fellatio and its etiquette. It is possible in some relationships for it to become part of the regular repertoire of sexual conduct between a couple, but this is only possible when the relationship is not narrowly conceived as being nonerotic or purely maternal. If the relationship, however, is narrowly conceived, then there will be a tendency to restrict the range of sexual activity and have what are defined as more erotic contacts with females with whom there is only a short-term relationship.

The act of cunnilingus is not physically symmetric to fellatio, though its practice may be physically reciprocal and psychologically symmetric in terms of the exchanges and of intimacy. This is frequently true in middle-class circumstances where principles of reciprocity and equality between the genders are more developed, but the normative constraints on the behavior are sufficiently powerful to require symbolic manipulation to allow normative violation. In nearly all male youth cultures, cunnilingus is viewed either ambivalently or negatively. There is a powerful component in male humor which avers to the uncleanliness of the vagina, its odors, and its peculiar (often described as fish-like) tastes. Concurrently there is the imagery that cunnilingus is somehow a homosexual act. (A version of this same belief occurs in some psychoanalytic treatises.)

At the same time, the behavior has powerful symbolic components linking it to taboo violation. The use of certain insignia by motorcycle groups to indicate that they have performed cunnilingus or, at a higher level of violation, cunnilingus with a menstruating female (whether the acts have in fact occurred or not) are techniques for the use of violations of sexual norms to stand for group solidarity and to outrage conventional onlookers. In this latter case a specific sexual act stands for male status enhancement and male collective solidarity, rather than for the bonding of two individuals as it can in a middle-class marriage. The physical activity is the same; the meanings attributed to it and the consequences are strikingly different. As with most other behavior, to search for universal meanings in the physical activity is to aim at an unknown target. Cunnilingus is usually an activity initiated by the male, as is nearly all activity in dyadic heterosexual behavior. The female may want the behavior to occur, but private speech is their mechanism for this to occur. Thus, Neil Eddington reports that 'giving head' (an argot expression for mouth-genital contact in general) is commonly referred to and expected among the pimps and prostitutes of the bright lights areas that he studies.[8] Once again, the sexual act that can be requested by the female now surfaces only in locations where the role of the female is defined as deviant. Such requests for sexual variety can occur in middle-class populations, but some mechanisms such as love, expectations of marriage, or marriage must be utilized to neutralize the deviant character that such a request might have.

The male in this case must manage the aversion that he might have to taste vaginal fluids and odors, and his touching the genitals with his tongue or mouth must be rewarded by evidence from the female that what he is doing is powerfully arousing for her. If orgasm does not ensue either during the contact or during coitus that follows, there is minimal reinforcement available for the continuation of the behavior. The act of cunnilingus is nearly always begun (and often sustained) in the context of masculine striving for the enhancement of the capacity to produce sexual pleasure in the female. The introduction of cunnilingus into the sexual repertoire of a couple once again depends on the stage of development that the relationship has. Some males introduce it with all females with whom they have intercourse as part of their regular repertoire of sexual activity. In many ongoing relationships there may well be inhibitions of the sort that we observed in fellatio; the act itself may be defined as too degrading or too excessively erotic for the definition that the nonsexual portion of the relationship maintains.

As in fellatio, there are problems of introducing cunnilingus into the normal sequence of expected sexual behavior. Nonverbal cues are developed between the couple (often stereotyped between the pair) to indicate a desire for this kind of contact. At the same time, ending cues are required to indicate whether the act will continue to orgasm or whether it will move to intercourse. These cues can either be verbal or nonverbal, but they must not intrude on what is defined as the normal sequencing of sexual excitement. Whether the act continues to orgasm or does not, there is the problem of how to manage the oral kissing behavior that often follows mouth-genital contact of any sort. Vaginal fluids or semen have meanings that are partially rooted in feelings about excretion, and for both partners such kissing frequently becomes an act of reassurance and denial. The act of oral kissing also returns the behavior to a more conventional sequence, coincidentally returning the bodies to immediately pre-coital positions. Unless previous activity has brought the male to orgasm, the sequence will typically end with coitus, since a taboo against mouth-genital contact after intromission persists among many who are otherwise committed to oral sex. Anxieties about the excremental and the homosexual combine to make postcoital mouth-genital contact fairly rare, except as it serves to celebrate a more diffuse commitment to the sexually unconventional.

Though the combining of fellatio and cunnilingus appears as a kind of sexual justice, the internal scripts that support both the additional complexity and anxieties about the violative aspects of the behavior need not have the same symmetry. For most females it may be experienced, at least initially, as a transcendent intimacy, an intimacy that licenses a right to 'indulgent' sensuality. The male, who often experiences fellatio through the metaphors of dominance, tends to experience cunnilingus through the identical modalities, seeing it as control rather than submission. Thus it is not uncommon for many men to find the performance of cunnilingus either maintaining or increasing levels of sexual arousal, despite the fact that their own genitals are not concurrently being stimulated. At the same time, moreover, a more superficial script organizes the activity as an apology for (if not a denial of) the degraded view of fellatio.

Beyond mouth-genital contact, anal intercourse becomes an additional source of elaboration. Though far less common than mouth-genital activity its occurrence tends to be facilitated by its essential resemblance to coitus, as well as the fact that male and female continue to occupy a conventional social-psychological relationship to each other in terms of dominance. This resemblance to coitus and coital positions allows for a view of anal intercourse as an extension of coital activity, rather than as 'unnatural' or aberrational ... even more complex transformations of the meaning of anal intercourse can be found in the more extreme circumstances of homosexuality in prison. In terms of complexity, the act itself may well intrude on the sequencing of sexual excitement since it often requires the use of artificial lubricants. This preparatory pause also exists when a diaphragm is used for birth control and is experienced by many females as reducing the spontaneity that is necessary in sexual activity. This suggests some of the problems for females in either avoidance of thinking about the mechanics of sex or lack of learning about how to integrate novel elements into the sexual sequence. This reflects other gender differences of the same kind – while males may wish to include more 'fetish' or 'thing' elements in sexual contacts (special clothing, objects, new roles), females tend to respond with the apparatus of the body.

Anal intercourse also involves the mastery of older symbolic forms about body odors that are strongly tabooed in Western societies. Fecal odors are to be restricted to the bathroom (notice the strong taboos on flatulence) and they must be combined with a sexual sequence that is defined quite differently. Digital manipulation of the anus may require that the odors will later be smelled during nonanal contacts, insertion of the penis into the anus commonly creates the sense of a need to defecate, and the penis should be washed for hygienic reasons after anal intercourse. Each of these activities becomes more problematic in situations where the anal intercourse is not a terminal behavior, but must be linked to further sexual activity. These problems are much more apparent in middle-class populations where cleanliness rules are powerfully learned and reinforced.

In situations where the anal intercourse is not merely a substitution for genital coitus, a transcendent set of meanings is required to legitimate the behavior. In Norman Mailer's *An American Dream*, buggery is practiced by the Jewish hero on a German female who stands for the Nazi domination of Jews. Into the 'death hole' the hero plunges, choosing to ejaculate there rather than in the vagina in order to avoid placing his own life forces symbolized by the semen in her 'life hole'.[9] Even though such a modestly complex symbolic rendering does not commonly occur as the accompaniment of anal intercourse, among those more symbolically committed to sexual activity, anal intercourse is commonly an expression of male dominance, with strong sadomasochistic overtones, at least in its originating phases. In order to breach the taboo and introduce the behavior to the female, the male must have sufficient investment in the activity to risk being turned down. The behavior is normally initiated through the use of digital contact and then later in terms of attempts to enter, at first subtly and then more insistently. The standard initiator/gate-keeper roles are assigned to the male and female, just as they are in the majority of sexual contact in the society, with the female's passive response being read as acceptance. The meaning of the act to the female in the beginning has strong elements of submission in which the normative violation can be read as an affirmation of the submissive component in femininity. Among those females with higher levels of dominance needs, such symbolic investment of specific sexual acts with submissiveness may serve as reaffirmations of femininity, which is not available to them in occupational or other spheres of life.

Orgasm in this activity is more common in the male, though it does occur in many women. The capacity for orgasm in this circumstance is evidence for our contention that specific physical sequences (the myth, for example, of the necessity of clitoral stimulation for orgasm to occur) are not necessary for the experience of orgasm on the part of females. This capacity to invest a behavior with meaning that allows it to be part of the orgasm-producing cycle is less socially supported than the sequence that invests the breasts with the same sensitivity, but while the specific ways in which sensitivity is produced are different, the outcomes are remarkably similar. What we here observe is the difference in the ways in which the body parts are put to use in the creation of ordered sequences of sexual excitement that result in sexual climax.

In addition to that between spouses in the marital state, there are three situations in which heterosexual activity may occur during adulthood. It may occur prior to, during, or after marriages have terminated. During marriage it may occur with persons other than spouses. It is this period during marriage that is of most interest here, for that which occurs after or between marriages has many of the same attributes as that which occurred prior to marriage except that sexual access seems to be more easily gained. Extramarital intercourse, adultery, or infidelity as it is variously termed by science, the law, and the participants is one of the single largest domains of normal sexual deviance.

About half of all ever-married males and a quarter of all ever-married females will engage in extramarital sexual activity at one time or another. For females there is some suggestion of a secular trend towards increases in extramarital activity from the beginning of this century to the early 1950s. This is linked to a corresponding generational rise in rates of female orgasm during this same period.[10] It is possible that these changes represent basic changes in the very nature of female sexuality. For males there are strong social class differences, with lower-class males accounting for most of the extramarital activity, particularly during the early years of marriage. This may be a direct reflection of their earlier mode of assimilation of the sexual commitment. As we previously observed, it is difficult for lower-class males to receive homosocial validation from marital sexual activity (unless, of course, it culminates in conception). This is not the case for extramarital activity, for which there is abundant homosocial validation.

In an important sense we have exhausted most of the bodily possibilities that are available (except the adding of additional bodies, which
we will discuss later) and in consequence, except in some rare instances
of narrow sexual scripts within marriage, nothing is done physically in
extramarital coitus that is not done inside of the marriage. The body
remains a physical constant, explaining little by its conformation or
shape. The sources of sexual experimentation outside of marriage must
be sought, then, in the social and psychological domain, rather than in
the specifically sexual.

As we have noted before, there are strong class variations among men
in the staging of extramarital coitus. It occurs earlier in the lives of
lower-class men and later in the lives of middle-class men. Regardless of
staging, however, the cumulative number of contacts always remains
higher among men in lower-class locations, partially because of prostitute contacts (which we will disregard) and partially because of the
continuity between sexual practices prior to marriage and during marriage. Regardless of these differences, male extramarital coitus in all
classes serves to enhance and promote feelings of masculinity and continues to create a sense of personal competence. For lower-class men
much of this derives from the male peer group, declining when the peer
group itself ceases to reward sexual experimentation. (In those societies
where the male peer group remains the major source of masculine
endorsement, the public affirmation of male extramarital coitus will
support such practices into a much later period in life, for example, in
Sicily and Southern Italy.) Among middle-class men, sexual experimentation outside of marriage begins both as reparation and as opportunity.
With rising incomes, the occupationally successful man can seek outside
of marriage that sexual experience of which he often feels that he was
cheated by his low rates of sexual activity prior to marriage, while those
feeling the tremors of occupational failure or demotion by lack of
promotion find in it reparations for losses sustained in the larger world.
The motives are simple in outline but moderately complex when put to
use. In most cases, when the relationships have an extended duration
they seem almost over-determined in character. (For an interesting
particularistic description of longer-term relationships, see Morton
Hunt's *The Affair.* [11])

For females the interest in extramarital sexual contacts is more
obscure in origin and less frequent in occurrence. Here one must deal
with the complexities of marital status. Extramarital coitus occurs

whenever one of the partners in the sexual activity is married. It does not seem unreasonable to suggest that the majority of married females who have extramarital coitus do so with married men, while for married men there might be a tendency, at least, for unmarried females to represent a larger proportion of their partners. These beliefs derive not from data (none, in fact, exist), but rather form the character of sexual and nonsexual role behavior in the society. In general, the married female has greater access to (unless she is working, and even in that case this supposition may well exist) married males. Extramarital coitus in these cases is more likely to occur among those who are known previously to the familial circle rather than to those who are known only to the female. When a female works, contacts may well be made with males who are unmarried, but with the increasing age of the female this proportion would tend to decline enormously. Given the initiatory character of the male role in sexual performances, it is apparent that a wider range of females in terms of marital status will be sought out and these contacts will include women both known and unknown to the family circle.

In large measure, most extramarital intercourse has a normal character. For most men, no matter how much they are in search of sexual adventure (and unless they make a serious pursuit of it) a female outside of the home is someone who has to be pursued and seduced. Few women ever move into a concern with sexuality that matches that of males, and in consequence males are presented with at least some of the problems (if not all, when they pursue younger females who have never married) that they faced in pursuing females when the males were premarital. These pursuits require energy, time, and money that few persons possess in great abundance. In consequence, much of extramarital coitus for the male occurs away from the home, in all-male situations (conventions of occupational or all-male social groups) and on a single-instance basis. The male may feel guilty, but the guilt can be managed by conceiving the act as insulated from the life of the family. Even when such relationships expand beyond a single encounter, in large measure the normal response is to manage guilt through the same mechanism through which most sexual guilt is generally managed: expressions of mutual passion which insulate the behavior from moral condemnation.

It is to be expected that females will be more likely to use these feelings of passion to insulate themselves from guilt than will males, given the general greater tendency of females to associate the sexual with a romantic commitment. However, in long-term relationships there is a tendency on the part of both males and females to increasingly characterize the relationship as one involving love. As the relationship becomes more intimate and more involved, there is a greater tendency for it to have consequences for a preexisting marital bond. Expressions of passion involve what Philip Slater has called 'dyadic withdrawal or social regression' (an unhappy phrase, in our opinion, but an observable phenomena) and in the building of an emotional base for the extramarital relationship there are consequences for the character of the marital relationship. In some cases such extramarital involvement decreases sexual involvement with the spouse, but there is probably an equal proportion of cases where the extramarital relationship – whether through guilt or simply heightened levels of erotic involvement – increases the rates of sexual contact with the spouse. As the actor in the extramarital relationship sees himself or herself as sexually more proficient, the sexual character of the marital relationship becomes more significant as well. This is parallel to the fact that nocturnal emissions in adolescence as often occur after other acts of sexual activity as they do before. The expression of sexual activity is as likely to feed into the dreaming life as the dreaming life to respond to sexual abstinence.

What is significant here in terms of the doing of sexual things is that the extramarital relationship can once again be linked to the dynamics of sexual performances that existed before marriage. It is in the search for tension or novelty that the significance of extramarital coitus arises, not in the avoidance of tension or the commitment to the conventional. Sex outside of marriage can be put to many social purposes by either a man or woman. For the lower-class man, it affirms the sexual prowess that he had before marriage. For young married men going to a prostitute, it may increase the bonds of maledom. For the middle-class male who is moving toward new occupational success, it is opportunity to confirm achievement in nonoccupational rewards. For the women, it is a desire for femininity to be reinforced in a way that marital coitus can rarely provide. For persons of both sexes, it is the boredom of conventional sexual or social activity transcended – the reentry into the world of risk and passion is treatment for the dailiness of regular sexual lives. The range of possibilities is wide open for those who can manage the necessary guilt that occurs with the behavior. Indeed, the search for guilt could be one of the reasons for the behavior itself. In an important sense, sex (as we note elsewhere) is part of those behaviors that represent environmental mastery, a mastery that provides at least the illusion of individuality and choice of an individuality and sense of control that is seriously eroded in a post-industrial society.

Among those involved in extramarital coitus, there are those who differ from its conventional practice. This is a domain that attracts and provokes the erotic fantasies of many in the society: wife-swapping and swinging. These represent interesting theoretical problems (they are not quite social problems), since they create conditions under which sexual behavior must become the topic of conversation between spouses and, indeed, topics that will require the creation of a new set of social and psychological categories to manage them.

Wife-swapping is that situation in which a pair (or more) of husbands and wives engage in the trading of sexual partners on an equal access, quid pro quo basis. In order for this to occur, there must be agreement between the husband and wife before the arrangement is made. This requires that the topic of infidelity (a more appropriate word in this context) has been the topic of conversation. It is possible to create a series of parodic conversations or situations in which such conversations might occur, but it seems to us that the anxiety and fear attending the beginning of such an enterprise deserve more than parody. Most commonly on the husband's initiative, sexual topics emerge in conversations with the spouse – for example, the topic of the sexual attractiveness of other men's wives. Such discussions normally follow a tentative and drifting course, a course sometimes influenced by knowledge on the part of the wife of the husband's previous extramarital behavior. In any case, the husband, for reasons of guilt (most likely), ideology (women's equality?), or ineptitude, finds himself unable to manage or get access to affairs outside of the marriage. The problem for the male is how to make available to the female an opportunity that she perhaps may not want and to make it attractive to her. It is evident that most women enter into these relationships to please (as they have in the past) their husbands' own sexual needs. There occurs a series of inconclusive conversations that finally culminate in an attempt at sexual adventure.

What has occurred is a crucial change in the marital unit. Sexuality has been changed from an activity which previously only bound the couple together into an activity that may occur with others with mutual consent. The historical limitation on sexual access has now been breached and sexuality for the couple is now a dyadic form of deviance (they have a co-partner in crime) in which sex is now both more public and significant and more casual and private. It is public between the two and significant in organizing their nonmarital behavior and more private to the couple since it is wrong and must be limited to specific audiences. At the same time, the technology and performance components of the sexual act become more important. What happens to the wife-swapping couple is what rarely occurs to any couple in the society – there are now alters who may judge not only their physical attractiveness, but also their competence as sexual partners. Both the male and the female in these situations are confronted with the requirement that they please others sexually in order to maintain the marital unit. Sex in this case binds the unit through its provision of sex to others, rather than in its provision to each other. The very need to please creates a situation of legitimated eroticism and sexual experimentation.

An important element in this relationship (however it is initiated, through the mails or with neighbors) is that the husband now possesses an object which may be used in sexual trading. It regularizes the extramarital relationships by giving him a counter to use in obtaining females, a task – given limited female commitments to sexuality – that is often not easily solvable. Hence, there are powerful constraints against the couple engaging in an individual search for sexual partners. The male in this case is at a disadvantage in most instances, given the larger proportion of males in search of females than females in search of males. One of the critical junctures in this process is when the female decides that she can search on her own, thus depriving the male of his most important token in securing sexual partners.

The engagement in this 'singling' behavior is more dangerous in terms of the development of psychopathology on the part of the female than on the part of the male. His activity falls within the limits of available social roles; males have a history and set of ideologies linked to sexual experimentation outside of marriage. The narrowness of the role sets available to women in the society suggests that when she falls outside of these narrowly limited roles there is both a greater possibility and need for role invention (a major problem for anyone) and a greater tendency for the expression of individual psychopathological behavior.

The increasingly public nature of the sexual performances increases not only the general level of sexual activity and the threats of compared sexual performance (a more difficult problem for males than females), but also serves to increase the level of eroticization of the female through degrading her. Sex with another man increases the erotic character of the wife, opposes her maternal role, and by violating the norms of sexual performance increases her desirability. At the same time there is created a set of constraints that surrounds even the rule breaking itself in order to preserve the dyad.

The Pattern of Psychosexual Development

It is not a concern of these chapters to develop a general and universal stage model of psychological development in the tradition of Erikson, since these models are generally faulty, becoming time-bound and reified, and – by becoming objects of study in themselves – fail to draw our attention to model processes. The point of the descriptive process offered here is to delineate periods in the life cycle during which certain events commonly take place in this culture. It should be noted clearly that these periods are not seen as necessary, either within or across cultures, nor necessary in some psychodynamic sense. There are roughly what has happened in between the 1930s and 1970s in a complex Western society, largely to its white working- and middle-class populations and in large measure to those persons of most ethnic and racial minorities who are attached to these model schemes of development or who have not been entirely alienated from them. There can be vast reversals and changes in the design of human sexuality, from the feelings it evokes to the kinds of things that are appropriate to or included in its performance elements. The age and moment when specific behaviors can be introduced, performed, and lived with vary enormously, so that any biological fixity in the sequence of behavior is most likely to occur in infancy and very little after that.

The following charted presentation of the sequencing of conventional sexual development is primarily of heuristic value for examining the connections among the various agents and institutions involved. Persons are selected as participants in conventional, unconventional, deviant, or criminal sexual acts from various points in this cycle. The meaning of their conventionality, their deviance, or their criminality is largely drawn from their place in this sequential collection of socializing agents, institutions, and programs. Hence the meaning of heterosexuality for two fourteen year olds who are having intercourse emerges from their stage in sexual socialization. Their motivations for the act and its consequences must be understood in terms of where they are in the developmental process. This is equally true of the two fourteen-year-old males who are having sex together; the meaning of their homosexuality arises from a specific point in the life cycle, and its significance is embedded in both that life cycle moment and the local culture (or, in complex societies, in a subculture). Thus, the interaction of fathers and daughters in incest will be meaningful in terms not of some abstract violation of the incest taboo, but in terms of the character of the family in which they live and the ages of the two participants. This is equally true in terms of the child who is the victim or participant in prepubertal sexual behavior, since the meaning of the behavior for the child is drawn from its available intellectual and emotional resources for organizing experience. The gender identity-sexual identity-family formation-reproduction pattern in this society is the central informing process for the sexual life as it is lived here.

The chart that follows, then, contains a set of stages with flexible age boundaries, the social components that are significant in either sexual or nonsexual learning that takes place during them, and finally, a rough suggestion of what is being learned or assembled. The word assembly is used quite deliberately. It was selected to indicate the collage-like, constructed, put-together, indeed artificial character of human development and to oppose an imagery of the natural flowering of an organic process.

Heuristic Stages of Conventional Stages of Sexual Development

Stage and Ages	Infancy (Ages: 0–2½ to 3)
Significant Agents	Mother to Family
Assemblies	Formation of base for conventional gender identity package

Stage and Ages	Childhood (Ages: 3–11)
Significant Agents	Family to Peers, Media increasing
Assemblies	Consolidation of conventional gender identity package; modesty-shame learning; non-sexually motivated 'sex' play; learning of sex words without content; learning of sex activities without naming; learning of general moral categories; mass media through commercials and programming content reinforcing conventional gender, sex, and family roles; media also preparing for participation in youth culture

Stage and Ages   Early adolescence (Ages: 11–15)

Significant Agents   Family, Same-sex Peers, Media

Assemblies   First societal identification as a conventional sexual performer; first overt physical sexual activity with self or others; development of sexual fantasy materials; beginnings of male/female divergence in overt sexual activity; application of gender package to sexual acts; application of moral values to emergent sexual behavior; privatization of sexual activities; same-sex peers reinforce homosocial values; family begins to lose moral control; media reinforces conventional adult content of gender roles; media attaches consumer practices to gender success; basic attachment to youth culture formed

Stage and Ages   Later adolescence (Ages: 15–18)

Significant Agents   Same-sex Peers, Cross-sex Peers increasing, Media, Family reducing

Assemblies   Increased practice of integrating of sexual acts with nonsexual social relations; movement to heterosocial values; increased frequency of sexual activity; declining family controls; continuing media re-inforcement of sexual-gender roles, and consumer and youth culture values; sexual experience with wider range of peers; common completion of sexual fantasy content; consolidation of gender differences in sexual roles and activity; good girl/bad girl-maternal/erotic distinctions completed

Stage and Ages   Early adulthood (Ages: 18–23)

Significant Agents   Same-sex and Cross-sex Peers, Media, Minimum Family of Origin

Assemblies   Mate selection, narrowing of mate choice; increased amount of sexual practice;

commitment to love by male, sex by female;
linkage of passion to love; dyadic
regressions; insulation from family judgment
and peer judgment; increasing pressure to
marry; relief from same-sex competition by
stabilization of cross-sex contacts;
legitimization of sexual activity by peers
and romantic code; media reinforces
youth culture values of romance and
virtues of marriage; experience with
falling in and out of love; termination
of protected school/student statuses

Stage and Ages	Final mate selection–Early marriage (Ages: 20–27)
Significant Agents	Fiancee(s), Spouse, Same-sex Peers, Family of Origin increases
Assemblies	Regularizes and legitimizes sexual activity; stable rates of sex activity; variation in kinds of sexual behavior; children born in most cases; increasing sexual anxiety about children; family values reinforced by children and family of origin; declining eroticism, increased maternalism; culmination of purchasing/ consumer values in wedding gifts or buying new products; routinization of sexual behavior; decreased contact with cross-sex peers unless they are married; interaction in multiple dyads; sexual activities restricted by pregnancy, children, work
Stage and Ages	Middle marriage (Ages: 28–45)
Significant Agents	Spouse, Same-sex Peers, Family of Origin, Married Peers
Assemblies	Declining sexual activity in marriage; some extramarital sexual experimentation; maturing children; conflict of erotic with maternal; emergence of sexual dissatisfaction;

increase in occupational commitments; declines in physical energy and physical beauty; fantasy competition by youth culture; continual multiple dyadic inter- actions and insulation from cross-sex peers; marriage moving to nonsexual basis for stability and continuity

Stage and Ages   Post young Children (Ages: 45 plus)
Significant Agents   Spouse, Same-sex Peers, Married Peers
Assemblies   Further decline in sexual activity; some extramarital sexual experimentation; substitution of nonsexual commitments other than children as basis of marriage; further decline in physical strength and beauty; further desexualization of gender identity; movement out of public sexual arena

This rough outline of a sexual career is the most common heterosexual pattern available in U.S. society and, even with the introduction of divorce and widowhood, the cycle does not vary except in small and minor ways. Similar modal career patterns with greater or lesser variability could be described for some of those sexual minorities who operate with alternative sexual patterns in the society. Indeed, this conventional heterosexual process is the modal sexual career that all alternative patterns must confront. The man who desires large numbers of females, the homosexual man or woman, and the sexually active women must live with the reality of this pattern, its values, and its links to the past and the future in a day-to-day way. This assembly designates the availability of sexual partners, their ages, their incomes, their point in the economic process, their time commitments, all of which shape their sexual careers far more than the minor influences of sexual desire.

Conclusion

In some places what we have been describing in terms of the integration of persons and acts into sexual scripts has been, perhaps, more dramatic than necessary. While a majority of persons might have had intercourse with the female above and the male below, only about half of the males and one-fourth of the females (even though there is some increase) engage in extramarital behavior. Mouth-genital contact is a majority experience only for the college-educated, and anal intercourse in heterosexual relations is somewhat of a rarity. By discussing the sexual at all, the sexual assumes a larger place on the stage than it deserves. What we have not noted enough are two dimensions: the first is that sex occupies very little of most people's time and energy (except those defined as sexual professionals), and the second is that most sexual behavior is accompanied by a great deal of silence.

In general, it is our feeling that sexuality and sexual activity are, by and large, derivative functions, even during adulthood. There are only a few periods in the life cycle at which there are high rates of sexual activity or sexual activity that is complicated by passion and high intensity of affective investment. These are usually adolescence in the male, the early and romantic years of marriage for both men and women, and the highly charged extramarital experiences that can be called affairs. Most of the time, sex is really a relatively docile beast, and it is only the rare individual who through the processes of self-invention or alienation from the normal course of socialization is prepared to risk occupation, present comfort, spouse and children, or the future for the chancy joys of sexual pleasure.

From this point of view it might be more proper to suggest – contrary to the Freudian point of view that sex manifests itself in other types of conduct or that other conduct is symbolic of sexual conflict – that reports of sexual conflict may in fact stand for difficulties in the more conventional zones of life. Thus, the married couple who come for counselling because of a sexual problem may be merely reporting the conventional rhetoric of the society about what they think the sources of a marital difficulty ought to be. Ovesey reports that homosexual dreams (overtly homosexual, not merely symbolic) of heterosexual men really relate to occupational problems and that the submissiveness required occupationally appears in the convenient symbolism of the 'purported' femininity of homosexual relations.[12] Indeed, many forms of both heterosexual and homosexual acting-out seem to be related to stress reactions to other life situations, rather than having specifically sexual motivations. Thus, studies of sex offenders often are overly concerned with the sexual life of the offender when this may merely be the symptom of disorders of other kinds.

While the talk about sexuality is important (and it should be observed

that in some cases people do sexual things in order to talk about them),
what is impressive is the enormous control that silence retains in the
sexual area. While one can find many locations in which the sexual is at
the service of the rest of social life, it is rarely experienced as being
continuous with other aspects of social life and is often, in fact, discontinuous with it.

While talk is significant in shaping behavior, it often does so through
its imprecisions and its absences. In a very immediate and concrete way,
most people remain untrained in the ability to talk about their own
sexual activity or scripts, particularly with persons with whom they are
having sex. There is even a major difficulty talking to the self about
matters sexual when one is in the process of a fantasy or in the midst of
sexual arousal. It is as if the aroused state were the only legitimate
condition during which an internal dialogue about sexual matters could
occur. Thinking about sexual activity in the abstract is extraordinarily
difficult for most people, and the attempt to think about it at all may
become in some cases, especially for males, the occasion for arousal.
Much of the character of the early periods of psychoanalysis involves
training the patient in how to talk without arousal about this aspect of his
life. Even when this process is successful it creates the capacity to talk
only in the context of the specialized therapeutic relationship and often
with a highly abstract vocabulary that protects both the therapist and the
patient from directly confronting sexual content. This is learning a
capacity to neutralize the topic of sexuality, not learning to talk about it
without concomitant anxiety or arousal. In an important sense even
though language is the life of man, there is a tendency to move into the
totalitarian land of silence when one moves into the sexual.

Such incapacities for speech often make the experiencing of sexual
pleasure extremely difficult. Researchers have observed that with
increasing sexual excitement and increase in general sensory thresholds
there is a declining capacity of speech, creating in this society a seeming
opposition between the physical activity of sex and the rational and
intellective processes. There are those women who have so poorly
learned the capacity to name the elements of sexual pleasure that
orgasm itself is seen as a dangerous, ego-disintegrating experience, and
the physical signs of arousal are read as premonitory symptoms of
urination or defecation. The problem here is clearly an incapacity in
assigning language to name and control the internal landscape.

One of the consequences of silence is that it produces a severe sense of discontinuity between experiencing the self in nonsexual circumstances and in sexual circumstances. It is awkward at both the transition from the conventional to sexual identity and from the sexual to the conventional, language-filled identities. A result of this discontinuity is that there are few ways of communicating to others the experience of sexual satisfaction or dissatisfaction. There seem to be no mechanisms by which the physical gestures can be converted into language so that gestures in the future can be altered or continued. For most persons the silence mounts, and with it a sense of guilt, frustration, and inadequacy. These, in turn, decline as sex itself declines in importance. And this decline is more easily managed than most would imagine. It is important to remember that people receive social recognition and support for many things, but – except for very special populations who pay different kinds of costs – there is no basis for this kind of recognition and support for sexual competence. Conversely, people may be judged failures for many things, but rarely for failing sexually, as only their partners really know, and they are equally committed to silence.

The doing of sex implies that there is some culmination to it, a moment of ecstasy or joy. Conventionally this has been identified with the moment of orgasm. Central to the work of Masters and Johnson is a description of the orgasmic cycle. Their focus is on the act (as it must be), a sequence of touching either alone or with someone else that can be described in four phases: excitement, plateau, orgasm, and resolution.[13] It is clear from much of their work that they know a good deal of the psychological component in this process, but their necessary focus is on the bounded character of the physical acts leading to orgasm. Yet even here this social and psychological component is as crucial. No one comes to age in this society with a prepared set of sociosexual repertoires that are immanent in their physical equipment. The capacity for erection or vaginal lubrication must be interpreted and linked to a suitable set of activities, people, and situations that will lead to intromission and orgasm on the part of the male and the female. The feelings that occur in the interior of the body have no immanent meaning attached to them, and they must as surely be learned and managed as is the information that is processed from the exterior of the body. Indeed, it may be that the confluence of internal sensations that is identified as orgasm is so identified because of the situation in which it occurs, rather than being a necessary connection between the sensory inputs and the central nervous system.

The problem that we have begun the tentative discussion of is the way in which physical activities are integrated into sequences that are conceived to be exciting sexually and the way in which this information ultimately becomes linked to the capacity for orgasm. Much of this linkage clearly occurs earlier in life (the capacity to identify touch as pleasurable or not, for instance) and then becomes attached to sexual activities themselves. Because we live most of our lives unself-consciously, we tend to fail to note the amount of open-ended learning that occurs early in life that is put to other uses later in life.

A sexual performance that is to end in orgasm can be as narrowly experienced as tension release or as complexly as the ritual expiation of sin. The narrow construction of the sources of sexual excitement that are overly supported in the society and the sequence of physical behaviors (from kissing to coitus) that are approved in the search for orgiastic pleasure (itself socially defined) are sufficient for most persons at least most of the time. The bodily postures assumed, the organs connected with internal sensation – these are the necessary and sufficient sequences of activity. It is only when the artificial quality of these performances is considered that it becomes apparent that they are constructions which are culturally created and normatively constrained and further built on earlier sequences of behavior that are reorganized in the performance of sexuality.

When we move beyond the physical activity and beyond the single orgasmic cycle, what becomes apparent is the inordinate complexity of the physical act of coitus as well as the integration into the act of coitus of variety in positions, variations in partners, changes in techniques or orifices of interest. The physical transitions or variations in this scripting of the arrangements is probably no more difficult (and perhaps less) than learning to ski or ride a bicycle. However, the management of bodies is also the management of meanings that are designed to constrain and organize expectations about behavior. Indeed, these expectations are the very basis for the experience of sexual excitement. We need only one further example to suggest this complexity. If one were to go further than having two in a bed and had to involve a third party in a sexual performance, what becomes apparent is that the etiquette of dyadic sexuality is totally different from the etiquette of the ménage à trois, regardless of the gender of the third person. Who does what to whom with what and in what order becomes a crucial question, a question that never occurs in the managing of two bodies, since it seems to us that there is not any problem of management (at least after we have had some practice). Yet, as we can see, there are problems of management of bodies, of attributing meaning to flaccid or tumescent penises, of managing strange fluids and odors, and of managing new and strange bodies, of managing entrances and exits so that the ordered process of increasing sexual excitement can be maintained. What enhances the limited repertoire of the body is the variety of meanings that may be attributed to those bodies, meanings that arise from the ordered and disordered connections of physical sexual activity to social life. In our present cultural state of affairs it is the possibility of transgression and normative violation that gives sex a status beyond gourmet cooking – it is the possibility of believing that one is controlling a powerful drive that allows a sense of virtue to arise from conformity and the observation of norms, and a sense of sin to arise from their violation. The wisdom of the body (at the risk of being metaphysical) is a consequence of consciousness and culture.

What is suggested here in an untentative way is that it is the sociocultural that gives sex its meaning and it is the myths of the society that give it its power. There is a sense of dismay when one makes the suggestion that sex is really just like everything else, and that there is no natural man struggling against the pressures of civilization. It tends to undermine the dramatic and powerful images of sex and leaves in its wake a sense of relatively simple and pleasant capacity that cannot fulfill the promises that have been made for it. Perhaps the last act of resistance to big brother and 1984 is properly an act of copulation – it can be allowed because it is of no danger to anyone.

Epilogue

It is only a fairly recent development in the history of man that he could begin to conceive of the possibility of social change, that he could begin to understand that his time and place did not represent the embodiment of some eternal principle or necessity but was only a point in an ongoing, dynamic process. For many it is still more difficult to conceive of the possibility of the psychological nature of man changing – and particularly changing in significant ways.[14] Much of this conservative view of man still permeates contemporary behavioral science. Thus, for many social theories, a view of man as a static bundle of universal needs supplies the necessary stability not available elsewhere in the flux of social life. A conception of man as having relatively constant sexual needs is a necessary part of this point of view. As a contrast to this conservative view, we attempt to offer a description of sexual development as a variable sociocultural invention, an invention that in itself explains little and requires much explanation.

Notes

1. A. C. Kinsey *et al.*, *Sexual Behavior in the Human Female* (Philadelphia: W. B. Saunders & Co., 1953).
2. S. Freud, 'The Most Prevalent Form of Degradation in Erotic Life', *Collected Papers*, IV (London: Hogarth Press, 1949).
3. W. Simon and J. H. Gagnon, 'Heterosexuality and Homosociality: A Dilemma of the Lower-class Family', mimeographed, 1966.
4. Kinsey *et al.*, op. cit.; Kinsey *et al.*, *Sexual Behavior in the Human Male* (Philadelphia: W. B. Saunders & Co., 1948).
5. With our increased mental health commitment to the significance of sexual activity in old age, frequent tests of sexual competence are likely with concurrent increases in dissatisfaction.
6. Extrasexual activities should be included as well, ranging from physical activity (massage, Yoga, biofeedback) to the creation of elaborate settings for sexual performances (water beds, vibrators, pillows, fireplaces).
7. This ease of transgression is probably most true for middle-class persons with a wider conception of the social and sexual capacities of a woman. Working-class men or even middle-class men with a highly restricted sense of the appropriateness of a wife's (Madonna's) sexual activity may find it more difficult to have intercourse with her on top than to have fellatio with a prostitute or even extramarital coitus. The activities and actors are differently valued in each script.
8. Neil Eddington, personal communication.
9. Norman Mailer, *An American Dream* (New York: Dial Press, 1964).
10. Kinsey *et al.*, *Sexual Behavior in the Human Female* and *Sexual Behavior in the Human Male*.
11. Morton Hunt, *The Affair* (New York: New American Library, 1971).
12. L. Ovesey, 'The Homosexual Conflict: An Adaptational Analysis', *Psychiatry*, 17 (1950), 243–50.
13. W. H. Masters and V. E. Johnson, *Human Sexual Response* (Boston: Little, Brown & Co., 1966).
14. J. H. Van Den Berg, *The Changing Nature of Man* (New York: Dell, 1964).

Ken Plummer

Symbolic Interactionism and Sexual Conduct: an emergent perspective

Three main traditions of sex research have dominated inquiries into human sexuality until very recently. The first – symbolized by Freud – is the clinical tradition which examines the emotional development of the individual person by means of intensive analytic work on childhood memories and the unconscious. The second – symbolized by Kinsey – is the social book-keeping approach which examines the frequency and social distribution of sexual behaviours by means of interviews, questionnaires and statistical computation. The third – symbolized by Masters and Johnson – is the experimental method which examines the physiology of sexual arousal by means of controlled laboratory observation. There are of course now many interconnections between these traditions but their broad collective 'control' over the field is without dispute.[1]

In contrast to the traditions mentioned above there is a fourth which has a long but undeveloped history in anthropology and a comparatively short one in sociology. Unlike the clinical, book-keeping and experimental traditions, it lacks a symbolic great name with which it can be clearly identified, as well as the generalized influence of these traditions. It consists of a growing number of disparate, small-scale, modest, often apparently trivial, primarily descriptive excursions into the minute world of contemporary contrasting varied sexual experiences. Its channels have led it firstly into exotic and simpler cultures, for example the Trobriand Islanders or the Melanesians, and latterly into the subcultures of urban life: the world of strippers, drag artists, transvestites, transsexuals, homosexuals, prostitutes, and nudists, as well as into pornographic bookstores, gynaecological examinations, massage parlours, lovers' lanes, nude beaches, abortion clinics, public conveniences, sauna baths, brothels and university bathrooms.[2] In each case, the researcher has brought back a limited focused account of life in a small realm of experience gathered through close conversation with and observation of these worlds. Now this tradition – widespread as it is slowly becoming in sociological circles – lacks a coherent, grand and systematic scheme such as the other traditions possess. Its epistemology is one which generally eschews the search for universal truths about sexual matters and shuns abstract conceptualization and grand theorization. Instead its concern pushes it towards the multiple truths of limited contexts. Its task is the relaying – and hopeful comprehension – of focused patterns of sexual experience. In contrast to the clinicians, whose prime focus is the unconscious, the book-keepers, whose prime focus is behavioural frequency, and the experimentalists, whose prime focus is sexual physiology, the concern of this tradition is with sexual meaning and the way it is socially constructed and socially patterned.

But description without theorizing is empty, and it is only in the past decade that the broad affinity between ethnography and symbolic interactionism has been detected and elaborated. Interactionism, of course, is no new theory; developing out of the pragmatist and formalist strands of thought at Chicago University in the 1920s, it sees the central features of human life as residing in socially produced, interactionally negotiated and personally sustained symbolizations.[3] Whilst humans invariably inhabit restraining material worlds (including organic ones), such worlds have to be interpreted and given sense through a dense web of negotiable symbols which are themselves historically produced. Likewise, humans come to give meaning to themselves, to the groups they identify with, to their own pasts and indeed to everything else they encounter in the world. Such meanings are never given and fixed; they are precarious and ambiguous and have to be constantly negotiated and worked at in the ceaseless stream of social interaction. Meaning thus arises in interaction, and the emergent meaning makes human life possible as we distinctively know it.

Many sociological theories have broadly similar concerns (phenomenologists, with their focus on the description and constitution of consciousness; existentialists, with their concern to study 'human experience-in-the-world'; ethnomethodologists, with their concern to investigate the procedures by which everyday life is composed) and there are affinities with other disciplines ('construct theory' and 'cognitive theory', for example, in psychology, and linguistic relativity in social linguistics),[4] but it is the interactionists who seem to have focused their general theory most forcefully on human sexuality. Not that the early interactionists showed much concern: neither Mead nor Park paid much attention to it,[5] and although one forerunner of Mead's at Chicago – W. I. Thomas – did produce a number of papers on sex, as well as a book, they are limited to idiosyncratic (and now greatly superseded) discussions on gender.[6] A few of the Chicago ethnographers provided relatively crude thumbnail sketches of sexual conduct in selected areas, but such work made little contribution to theoretical advance.[7] Likewise, the work of the Chicago 'family sociologist' Burgess (with Locke) was essentially eclectic (though acknowledging indebtedness to Cooley and Mead). Burgess also produced a short paper in 1949 – in the wake of the Kinsey turbulence – highlighting seven rather arbitrary contributions which sociology could make to the study of sex (sexual conduct, sexual roles, role inversion, change and values, extra-marital sex, change and society, research) but most importantly stressing the need to study sexuality as conduct:

> The sex behaviour of animals is motivated by instinct, that of man by his attitudes and values which reflect those of his intimate groups and of the environing society . . . The various forms of sexual outlet for man are not behaviour, they are conduct. Conduct is behaviour as prescribed or evaluated by the group. It is not simply external observable behaviour but behaviour which expresses a norm or violation.[8]

A few years later – this time in the wake of the female Kinsey volume – Kuhn (Blumer's major theoretical rival at Iowa) produced a critique that contained the clearest statement of interactionism and sexuality up to that time. For example, he wrote:

> Sex acts, sexual objects, sexual partners (human or otherwise) like all other objects towards which human beings behave are *social objects*; that is they have meanings because meanings are assigned to them by groups of which human beings are members for there is nothing in the physiology of man which gives a dependable clue as to what pattern of activity will be followed toward them. The meanings of these social objects are mediated to the individual by means of language just as in the case of all other social objects. That the communicators which involve these definitions are frequently – at least in our society – surreptitious and characterized by a huge degree of innuendo does not in any wise diminish the truth of this assertion. In short, the sexual motives which human beings have are derived from the social roles they play; like all other motives these would not be possible were not the actions physiologically possible, but the physiology does not supply the motives, designate the partners, invest the objects, with performed passion, nor even dictate the objectives to be achieved.[9]

Important as Kuhn's statement was, it was never developed and it remains 'lost' in the pages of the first volume of *Social Problems*.

The most important contemporary exponents of this perspective are John Gagnon and William Simon; both trained in Chicago in the late

1940s, going on to be senior research sociologists at the Kinsey Institute in Indiana. Since that time, in the mid sixties, they have produced a series of pathbreaking papers on the interactionist approach, culminating in their important book *Sexual Conduct*. It is their approach which has provided the litmus for much recent research – though it should be recognized that a number of other interactionists have presented similar statements.[10] Nevertheless, their account is the most innovative and distinctive. It heralded the view that sexuality should not be seen as a powerful drive but rather as a socially constructed motive; the adoption of the metaphor 'sexual script' as a framework for analysing the social construction of sexual meaning; the directive to study the social sources from which human sexualities were constructed; the need to view sexual development not as something relentlessly unwinding from within but as something constantly shaped through encounters with significant others; the need to see the importance of wider socio-historical formations in generating the meanings which people in society assumed in their identities; and the importance of stigmatic labelling in the creation of separate worlds of sexual deviance.

One of the central ideological thrusts of the work of Gagnon and Simon is the wish to take the study of human sexuality out of the realm of the extraordinary and replace it where it belongs: in the world of the ordinary. Sexuality is not to be seen as something special; it is not to be seen as a powerful drive shaping the universe or the personality; it is not to be studied by special theories which endow it with a further added significance. Instead it should be seen as an unremarkable phenomenon which can be studied in unremarkable ways using unremarkable theories.

John Gagnon summarizes this perspective in the following way:

> In any given society, at any given moment in its history, people become sexual in the same way they become everything else. Without much reflection, they pick up directions from their social environment. They acquire and assemble means, skills, and values from the people around them. Their critical choices are often made by going along and drifting. People learn when they are quite young a few of the things that they are expected to be, and continue slowly to accumulate a belief in who they are and ought to be throughout the rest of childhood, adolescence and adulthood. Sexual conduct is learned in the same ways and through the same processes; it is acquired and assembled in human interaction, judged and performed in specific cultural and historical worlds.[11]

Sexual conduct then is learnt conduct and can be studied just like any other conduct: it is only because – in the past – we have invented such a special importance for human sexuality that we have also needed to invent special theories to deal with it. Theorizing about sex has been shaped by the culture which generated it and this in turn has served to structure and fashion – indeed 'construct' – sexualities (a position arrived at more recently and from a different theoretical angle in the work of Foucault). The interactionist account of human sexuality is hence isomorphic with interactionist accounts of other everyday life phenomenon. Its central project is to unravel the social construction of meaning – in history, in interaction, and in biographies; its root metaphor for performing such a task is that of the drama; its key research tools are those which embrace 'intimate familiarity'.[12]

In order to convey something of the novelty and differentives of this approach to sexuality it is instructive to contrast it with an account of the more prevalent views. At many critical points, interactionism subverts the orthodox line, and I will briefly discuss six below.

Changing Metaphors: 'Drive' or 'Script'?

Theories are usually guided (often only implicitly) by some metaphorical image enabling something to be seen from the 'viewpoint of something else'.[13] With sexuality, the prevailing imagery has been drawn from the worlds of biology and technology – portraying it respectively as either an animal-like 'natural' eruption or a machine-like activity: hydraulic flows, orgasm mapping, energy systems. The root image is that of a *powerful biological drive*.[14] The powerful image suggests significance, importance, even centrality to life; the biological image suggests a universal essence – variability is possible only within finite organic limits; the drive image suggests driveness and determinism – sometimes, as in notions of sublimation and repression, closely linked to ideas of hydraulic pressure. This, then, is the metaphor that captures a great deal of thinking about sexuality – an imperious, insistent and often impious force that presses universally for release and satisfaction from within the human body. All shades of thought conspire to use this metaphor: from the libertarian left of Wilhelm Reich to the authoritarian right of 'traditional' Christianity, from the scientific thought of Freud and his followers to the contemporary legion of sex therapists, from the literature of Lawrence to the everyday thought of Everyperson. Variations on a theme abound; but who would challenge the 'naturalness', the significance, the bodily truth of sexuality? Even the sociologists – usually the first to stampede towards a cultural account over a biological one – have traditionally maintained the biological bedrock while merely superimposing cultural variation upon it.

The heretical task of challenging this pervasive orthodoxy has been one of the prime accomplishments of interactionism. The imagery of drive is seen to fail to do justice to either human communication or human creativity: human beings harbour the potential to *create* a diverse array of sexualities through communication with each other. For such a constructive process, the metaphor of the theatre – especially that of the script – thus becomes a crucial building block.

This dramaturgical metaphor has a long history both in sociology and out of it.[15] Despite many difficulties, it has been applied to a wide variety of phenomena: sexual scripts are merely a subset of these, 'formulated in the same ways and with the same purposes.'[16] Following on from Burke's dramatism, the metaphor directs the researcher to ponder the processes by which people come to piece together activities which are identifiable as 'sexual': the scene, the act, the agency, the agent, the purpose.[17] Human sexuality – as opposed to biological functioning – only comes to exist once it is embroiled with partners (real or imagined), activities, times, places and reasons *defined* as sexual.

This general imagery of 'script' is a vivid one in highlighting the relativity of sexual meanings, their humanly constructed nature, and in correcting biological and mechanical imagery, while a number of fruitful studies have emerged within it. But it is only a general imagery, and many problems remain.[18] In the hands of some researchers, it has become a wooden mechanical tool for identifying uniformities in sexual conduct: the script determines activity, rather than emerging through activity.[19] What is actually required is research to show the nature of sexual scripts as they *emerge* in encounters. Such encounters may be seen as stumbling, fragile and ambiguous situations in which participants gropingly attempt (through such processes as role taking, role making, altercasting and self-presentation[20]) to make 'sexual sense' of selves, situations and others. In assembling sexual meaning, there will always be elements of novelty, unpredictability and indeterminateness as actors piece together lines of action. But there will also be elements of regularity, loose 'scripts' which 'name the actors, describe their qualities, indicate the motives for the behaviour of the participants, set the sequence of appropriate activities – both verbal and non-verbal'. Regularities flow partly from personal commitments and self-lodging, partly from the existence of abstract sexual meanings, and partly from the routinization of perspectives with others. The study of the construction of the sexual is an enterprise which has only begun in recent years, and even then has primarily been restricted to areas of the unconventional. Thus there exist studies of the game manoeuvres employed in developing (often unpredictable) sexual roles in public conveniences; of the disembodied and 'work-like' properties of sexual encounters in whorehouses; of the rules employed by boy prostitutes in structuring their money-making sexual activities; of the strategies employed by nudists to render their potentially sexual conduct into non-sexual conduct; and of the emerging 'sexual' perspectives in sex-dominated occupations like striptease and taxi-cab driving.[21] Such studies as the above need to be taken seriously and extended. But the point still remains that very little is known (except by implication) about the construction of more conventional ('non-deviant') sexual encounters. While there now exist clear behavioural accounts of the unfolding of sexual acts, such as that of Masters and Johnson, social description appears to remain taboo. How, for example, do husband and wife piece together lines of conduct into a co-ordinated sexual act? How does an encounter come to be recognized as a 'romantic' one, or as a 'transient', 'commodity' one? How does a solitary individual build up a routine sexual phantasy, and how does she/he shape her/his masturbatory world?

One of the few discussions of these sorts of problems is by Gagnon.[22] In a cursory and anecdotal manner, not using empirical materials, he evokes his central concept that sexuality can be viewed as 'scripted behaviour' and presents a simple, yet telling, account of a sexual encounter between a late-adolescent, fairly inexperienced couple. He describes the settings chosen, the preliminary talk, the confused expectations and effects on self-conceptions, the kissings, the problems in undressing, the merger of public worlds with private worlds, the distractions that intrude, the taking of other's roles and the presentation of appropriate self-images, the balance sought between gaining one's own pleasure and meeting the needs of other, the 'coital mess', the feeling of 'doneness', the re-entry into the non-sexual world, and the transformed relationship. Gagnon's analysis is elementary and verges on the literary; but through the notion of script rather than drive he has placed such work at the centre of sexual analysis.

How these 'scripts' come about – historically, socially and personally –

is of prime concern to the interactionist. At once, the concept is made to bridge the most intimate human need and the boldest historical sweep. For *historically* it addresses matters such as the sources of our various cultural constructions of sexuality, and when and how we came to invest so much importance to sexuality in our general scripts.[23] *Socially* it ponders how people came to use sexual scripts for social ends, and how they come to scan their past lives, current moments and anticipated futures in order to hook them on to the available but selected sexual scripts.[24] More *personally* (and more classically) it investigates the psychic needs for individuals to gain excitement from some scripts but not others.[25] All these concerns are interdependent.

Changing Meanings: Essence or Emergent?

The metaphor of 'script' immediately suggests a composed, orchestrated construction – as something unfolding through interaction – whereas the metaphor of 'drive' suggests an essence awaiting release. A core contrast of the two views, therefore, is the way in which for drive theorists sexual meaning is relatively unproblematic: it is a given, an absolute, an essence. For interactionists this is not so; indeed their central task is to describe and theorize the *processes by which sexual meanings are constructed*. At the outset, it invariably means that all the categorizations and meanings that are routinely taken for granted by scientists and lay-persons alike have to be rendered problematic: 'sex' and 'gender' – along with their myriad derivatives – become objects of investigation. The category 'homosexual', for example, cannot be simply used as a resource to gather a sample, devise a theory or impute a personality type – as it is with other theories; rather, here, the category itself becomes the research focus. When – and for what reasons – did the category emerge? What part does it play in the wider social order? How do people come to impute such a label – to others and to self? And why can so much experience potentially capable of being so labelled escape or defy such categorization?[26] On an even grander scale, the divide between 'men' and 'women' has to be put through this analytic mill.[27] And so too, of course, must the very notion of 'sexuality'. What is this thing called 'sexuality', how do we construct it, why do we sometimes attach so much importance to it?[28]

Of course to those who view sex as a given biological force such questions may seem absurd: we know what all these things are. Naïvely, perhaps, the interactionists do not. In a striking passage, Simon reveals the relativity of sexual meaning:

> Imagine, if you will, a panel of matched penises entering an equal number of matched or randomized vaginas: the penises all thrust the identical number of thrusts, all simultaneously achieve orgasms of equal magnitude, and all withdraw at the same time, leaving all vaginas in an equal state of indifference. What can we possibly know about the character of any of these acts? Or any of the involved actors? Let me suggest, if I may, some reasonable candidates for this panel: (a) a lower-class male, having a mild sensual experience, though glowing with the anticipation of the homosocial acknowledgement he will receive as long as the vagina did not belong to his wife; (b) an upper-middle-class male crushed by his inability to bring his partner to orgasm; (c) a male achieving unusual orgasmic heights because his partner is a prostitute or someone else of equally degraded erotic status; (d) a stereotyped Victorian couple 'doing their thing' – or is it 'his thing'? – or possibly, natives of contemporary rural Ireland; (e) a husband fulfilling his marital obligations while dreaming dreams of muscular young truck drivers; (f) a couple performing an act of sexual initiation in the back seat of a VW; and (g) a Belgian nun being raped by a Hun.[29]

In a similar vein, I have remarked elsewhere:

> When a child plays with its genitals, is this 'sexual'? When a person excretes, is this sexual? When a man kisses another man publicly, is this sexual? When a couple are naked together, is this sexual? When a girl takes her clothes off in public, is this sexual? When a lavatory attendant wipes down a toilet seat, is this sexual? When a morgue attendant touches a dead body, is this sexual? When a social worker assists her client, is this sexual? When a man and woman copulate out of curiosity or out of duty, is this sexual? The list could be considerably extended; but the point I hope is made. Most of the situations above could be defined as sexual by members; they need not be. Sexual meanings are not universal absolutes, but ambiguous and problematic categories.[30]

Society and Sex: Contest or Continuity?

The notion of a powerful, 'essential' drive leads to the view that sexuality has an important role to play in the construction of social order – either as a key dynamic in the formation of stable personalities or because of its imperative claim for regulation. Unlike interactionists, who would argue that it is through social scripting that sexuality is channelled, drive theorists suggest that it is through sexuality that social order is channelled. There is both a 'right-wing' and a 'left-wing' version of this view. The former holds that the all-powerful demon of sex needs strong societal regulation for order to be maintained: any chink in the armoury of control leads to rapid moral decay, sexual anarchy, disordered personalities, and the decline of civilization. In the academic literature, such a view is to be found in Freud, Unwin and Sorokin.[31] It is also evidenced in the contemporary moral crusades in England of Whitehouse.[32] The 'left-wing' view holds that the powerful drive could be a means of creative self-fulfilment if it was not twisted and repressed by an oppressive state for its own ends: the State regulates the powerful drive through the family in order to rigidify the personality structure and render it subservient to the needs of the rulers. In the academic literature, such a view is found in the writings of Marcuse, Reich, and Reiche,[33] and more popularly in the contemporary ideologies of the Gay and Paedophile Liberation Movements.[34]

While the right-wing view sees sexuality as the demon within and the left-wing sees sexuality as the great liberator, both credit sexuality with enormous – almost mystical – powers in contributing to social order. Sex becomes the central force upon which civilizations are built up and empires crash down. Interactionists remain suspicious of the empirical validity of such a view, and suggest an alternative interpretation of powerful drives and social order: that social needs for survival and replacement have led many societies to attribute great power to sexuality – either by deification or by negation. In the latter case, a combination of sexual meanings which simultaneously encourage sexuality ('it's a powerful drive') and prohibit it ('it's sinful' etc.) lodges the sexual experience in a contradiction which may generate guilt and anxiety, and bestow an exaggerated importance on sexuality. In this view, therefore, there is a continuity between the cultural meanings and the personal experience of sexuality, and where conflicts exist in the culture they are mirrored in the person.

Sexuality as Determiner or Determined?

A further argument of drive theorists is that sexuality shapes our social conduct. Not only have we become adept at interpreting all manner of social artefacts – from chocolate flakes to motor cars – as sexual symbols; we also treat much social behaviour – collecting, neurosis, stealing, humanitarianism, artistic creation, drinking and eating – as expressions of masked sexuality. Sexual structures come to inhabit asocial worlds. Interactionists argue that instead of sexuality determining the social, it is the other way round: social meanings give shape to our sexuality.

Sexuality has no meaning other than that given to it in social situations. Thus the forms and the contents of sexual meanings are another cultural variable, and why certain meanings are learnt and not others is problematic. One important implication of this perspective is the need to analyse sexual activity in our culture for its social origins, the ways in which social experiences become translated into sexual ones. Much sexual behaviour may have 'non-sexual' sources: the health-food faddist may take sex at prescribed regular intervals in the same way as health foods and for the same purpose; the married couple may regularly have sexual activity, even when neither wants it, because each believes the other expects it; the prostitute employs sex as a means of earning a living as does the stripper; the man may seek a flow of regular sexual partners in the belief that this may sustain his public image of masculinity; and the student may masturbate out of habit or out of an association with tension-reduction.[35] In each case, sexual experiences are constructed from social motives and settings. Gagnon and Simon in one discussion on homosexuality in the prison setting suggest that:

> What is occurring in the prison situation for both males and females is *not a problem of sexual release, but rather the use of sexual relationships in the service of creating a community of relationships for satisfying needs for which the prison community fails to provide in any other forms.* For the male prisoner homosexuality serves as a source of affection, as a source of validation for masculinity, or a source of protection from the problems of institutional life.[36]

Here, sex is not merely a release used to structure experience; rather, the sexual world is itself fashioned by the social needs of the individual. These needs may centre on many issues – and it is but a short step from here to Foucault's view that 'sexuality' is 'used' as a channel for the negotiation of power.

Sexuality: Necessary or Contingent?

A related argument of drive theorists is that sex is seen as an energy which needs release – very often located within a closed reservoir system subject to the laws of the conservation of energy. The argument, in its crudest terms, suggests that the sexual energy is an absolute force which if not allowed to manifest itself in its 'natural' state will break out into other areas of life. Two key concepts here are *repression* and *sublimation*. Thus, if 'absolute sexuality' does not develop 'naturally', the energy may be *repressed*, in which case deviations and neurosis are likely to occur through the damming up of libidinal energy, or *sublimation* may arise, in which case libidinal energy may become the source of extra energy in work, especially in benevolent and artistic occupations. There are other mechanisms by which the energy may be diverted from its original sexual goal. Freud and others thereby encourage a search for the underlying sexual basis of much social behaviour; one becomes very sceptical of the apparently sexless person and imputes to him or her all manner of sublimation techniques.

Now the concepts of repression and sublimation (along with their recent counterpart 'repressive desublimation') are unproven assumptions, which have been absorbed into contemporary 'taken-for-granted' notions of sexuality. Two simple hypotheses may be deduced from the broad assumption of an energy system: (i) if people have little sexual outlet they must be repressing or sublimating their desires in some manner – and consequently, most likely, exhibiting some form of neurosis; (ii) if people have much sexual outlet their energy must be sapped away from other things – they are unlikely to be creative, active or productive. In the first case one wonders what such persons can be doing with their sexuality, where it is being sapped to; and in the second case one becomes concerned with the person's ability to perform well in other spheres of life. For both hypotheses, there is little evidence. The work of Kinsey, however, does suggest that individuals with a high degree of sexual activity can be 'of considerable significance socially' – one of his most sexually active respondents was a 'scholarly and skilled lawyer' who 'averaged over thirty [orgasms] a week for thirty years'[37] – and others have suggested that 'no genuine tissue or biological needs' are generated by a lack of sexual activity.[38]

For the interactionist, then, sex *per se* is not an absolute necessity – unlike food, one can live without it, and some societies do[39] – but neither is it ruinous if one enjoys it very often. One might of course learn to become addicted to it, and that could be damaging. But a great deal of sexual experience is not intrinsically harmful.

Becoming Sexual: Orientation or Construct?

Closely allied to this contrast is the way in which sexual development is viewed. For the 'drive' theorists the emphasis is placed upon the evolution of identities and orientations through fairly regular phases in the earlier years of life: sexuality is in a broad sense determined either by birth or by childhood. For the 'script' theorists, sexual development is a life-long learning process which is historically malleable: sexuality is in a broad sense assembled from the cultural categories currently available.

Again it is the drive view that is most common in both social science and common-sense. Biology, Freudianism and behaviourism lend support to it by tracing out the sequences of sexual development found in childhood and by suggesting the ultimate 'fiedness' of what happens there. John Money puts this view in its most flexible form:

> Each person's turn-on has rather fixed boundaries which are set before puberty. Whether the boundaries are orthodox or unorthodox, conventional or unconventional they were established in childhood as part of the differentiation of gender identity, by the coding of the schemers, and by any quirks or oddities that were incorporated into the schemers. Boundaries may first show themselves at puberty, but they are not set in puberty and they don't change much at puberty or later. Their relative unchangeability helps to explain such phenomena as why second spouse so often resembles the first. Their persistence also explains why adult obligative homosexuals can be fond of and behave affectionately towards a member of the other sex especially if the other is older, but can never fall in love with him or her. Tales of sex degenerates who go from one form of depravity to another, sampling everything, are only fiction; even so-called sex degenerates stick to their particular preferences.[40]

Side by side with this view of the development of sexual orientation is the view that identity emerges simultaneously. This means that either the identity emerges unproblematically, so that the child en route to becoming a heterosexual *being* also learns the heterosexual *identity*, or, alternatively, it means that there is a disjunction between the orientation that is built up in childhood and the identity that develops in adulthood. Thus, in this latter case, one may develop into a 'latent homosexual', where the orientation – that of 'a homosexual' – is set up in childhood but the identity acquired – that of 'a heterosexual' – is inappropriate. This model assumes that the category of heterosexual identity is here inappropriate: the person's *actual* identity is that of a homosexual. The task for some clinicians therefore would be to bring into the consciousness of that individual his or her *real* identity. It hence presumes there may be a real and essential identity – fixed in childhood – independent of members' awareness of it.[41]

In contrast, the interactionist suggests that such schemes generally *impose* taken-for-granted adult images of sexuality upon experiences that are generally incoherent, ill-formed and ill-defined while believing they are *uncovering* the true and essential nature of sexuality.

Thus, for example, studies of childhood sexuality generally fail to record shifts at the level of meaning. While there is now considerable evidence of children being involved in 'adult-defined' sexuality, these studies generally impose adult interpretations upon the behaviour rather than analysing the definitions which the child builds up. It is well documented that in other cultures children may become engaged in copulatory activities from early ages, and that in this culture children are capable of orgasms before even reaching the age of one. Likewise, it has been well established the children 'do' many 'sexual things', conjure up 'sexual fantasies' and have 'sexual things' done to them.[42] But in all of these cases it is naive to assume that children automatically 'feel' and 'recognize' these experiences in the ways that adults do. Genital play and indecent assault may both be experienced by the child in a 'non-sexual' way, because the child has not yet developed competency in the motives and feelings that adults routinely come to associate with sexuality: thus the child is merely 'playing', 'being attacked' or 'playing with an adult'. As one correspondent wrote to me:

> At about the age of eight I was coerced by a stranger to masturbate him. My chief understanding at the time was that the stranger urinated. That is, I did not understand either the ejaculation or the sexual meaning of the encounter. It struck me as bizarre, but the sexual meanings were retrospectively imposed when I learnt about orgasms.

It thus becomes clear what the thrust of the interactionist research programme on becoming sexual is.

The focus turns to the way in which individuals throughout their life cycle come to be defined by themselves and others as sexual beings, how they come to hook themselves on to the wider cultural meanings, and how these are renegotiated or stabilized. Gone is the view that socialization is concerned with the management of some inner pre-existing sexual 'condition' or 'motive'; gone is the view of 'latent' sexual conditions; gone is the view of people 'essentially being' that of which they are unaware. In its place comes a concern with the way 'sexual motives' are fashioned out of existing 'motivational ideologies'; with the ways in which individuals' self-conceptions as sexual beings shift and change through the life cycle; with the ways in which the past is constantly recast through the present. Blumstein and Schwartz have been the most ardent advocates of this view and pose the major research question as : 'What is the formula by which an actor arranges information in order to construct a sexual essence for him or herself?'[43]

Perversion or Variation?

A final significant point of contrast concerns the issue of perversion and deviance. It is the drive theorists who have primarily been responsible for establishing a new rogues' gallery of sexual perverts since – roughly – the middle of the nineteenth century: homosexuals, transvestites, trans-sexuals, sado-masochists, urolagniacs, paedophiles, fetishists and the rest.[44] In each case the 'type' has largely been discovered by clinicians, their characterization laid out, their aetiologies designated, and suggestions for remedies proposed. At the core of all this endeavour ultimately is a strong – indeed absolute – conception of what sexuality really means: coital procreation in the service of families. To the extent that sexuality has strayed a little from this purpose, it becomes worrying; to the extent that it has strayed far from it, it becomes downright perverted. In any event, most drive theorists do not merely study the pervert – they also attempt to control him.

The interactionist, yet again, moves off in a full-blown alternative direction. Given that sexuality is relative and used for different social purposes, given that it is historically constructed and bound up with specific times and places, and given that society plays an important formative role in all sexualities, then 'the pervert' loses its universal character and becomes a curious invention of our contemporary culture. It becomes, indeed, a specific category to be investigated in itself – but it cannot be clearly taken to reflect a real phenomenon. The general argument thus highlights the view that all humans are initially open to enormous sexual variations; that cultures – through their categorization systems – may restrict and narrow the seeming options to one major route and a number of minor ones; that such categorizations belie the reality of experiences which are in effect much more complex (the term 'homosexual' – like the term 'heterosexual' – hurls together an assort-ment of people with so little in common that it becomes perniciously misleading); and that finally through stigmatizing some of these diverse experiences, the foundation is laid for elevating their importance and centrality in individual lives. In this last idea there is clearly a strong affinity between interactionism and the ideas of labelling theorists who have highlighted the way in which stigma has the power to transform 'ordinary' experiences.[45]

Conclusion

Much of what has been said of the interactionist image in this article should have raised minor alarms in many readers. For its starting point in the study of human sexuality challenges much of our contemporary wisdom about sex; whereas many presume to know what sex is, interactionists do not; whereas it is commonly sensed as something special, interactionists put it on a par with everything else; whereas it is commonly sensed as being either in need or repression or as a potential source of liberation, interactionists see it as merely reflecting cultural expectations; whereas it is commonly seen as being the motive force for much human behaviour, interactionists invert this wisdom and suggest that sex is engaged in far wider social reasons; whereas 'too much' or 'too little' sex are frequently seen as problems, interactionists see no reason for this; whereas sexual development is usually seen to be determined by childhood experience, interactionists see it as much more fluid and changing; whereas certain patterns of sexual development can be *assumed* as 'perversions', the interactionists see these critically as social constructions. The interactionist is a stranger to contemporary cultural meanings and concocts a heretical view.[46]

My presentation and argument has been clearly overstated. I have lumped together many disparate views under the rubric of 'drive theorists', have performed a great injustice to the subtleties and complexities of their views; and I have polarized the differences of 'drive' and 'construct' too sharply. All of this I acknowledge. There are, I am sure, ways in which the two views can be bridged and elsewhere I have started to suggest these.[47] But before an adequate synthesis – or *didactical* revision, if you like – can be made, the logic of the counterposed position of interactionism needs to be much more thoroughly explored, empirically and theoretically. As an approach to sexuality, it is markedly different from most that have dominated thinking in the past century; it is itself scarcely a decade old in its developed form, and its more extreme arguments need careful scrutiny before it is watered down into the reigning orthodoxies.

Bibliographical Notes

1. For a good general introduction to the field of 'sex research', see P. Robinson, *The Modernisation of Sex* (Elek, 1976); E. Brecher, *The Sex Researchers* (Andre Deutsch, 1969); M. S. Weinberg (ed.), *Studies from the Kinsey Institute* (Oxford University Press, 1976). An overview of the current state of the art is to be found in 'Sex Research: Future Directions', *Archives of Sexual Behaviour*, Vol. 4, No. 4 (July 1975).

2. Examples of such ethnographic work abound. As illustrative, see E. W. Delph, *The Silent Community: Public Homosexual Encounters* (Sage, 1978), and J. Douglas and P. Rasussen, *The Nude Beach* (Sage, 1977).

3. The nature and origins of symbolic interactionism are now widely discussed, but two contrasting statements of great value are Blumer's *Symbolic Interactionism: Perspective and Method* (Prentice Hall, 1969) and Rock's *The Making of Symbolic Interactionism* (Macmillan, 1979).

4. For theories that are closely allied to symbolic interactionism, see D. Wright, 'Sex: Instinct or Appetite', in P. Nobile (ed.), *The New Eroticism* (Random House, 1970); K. R. Hardy, 'An Appetitional Theory of Sexual Motivation', *Psychological Review*, 71 (1964), pp. 1–18; and many articles in the *Journal of Social Issues*, 33.2 (1977).

5. Mead does write of the 'sexual impulse', and describes it as the impulse 'which is most important in the case of human social behaviour, and which most decisively or determinately expresses itself in the whole general form of human social organization': see G. H. Mead, *Mind, Self and Society* (University of Chicago Press, 1962), p. 228.

6. See W. I. Thomas, *On Social Organization and Social Personality*, ed. M. Janowitz (University of Chicago Press, 1966); W. I. Thomas, *Sex and Society – Studies in the Social Psychology of Sex* (University of Chicago Press, 1907), and various papers mentioned herein and published between 1898 and 1909. On Robert Park, see H. Matthews, *Quest for an American Sociology: Robert E. Park and the Chicago School* (McGill–Queens University Press, 1977).

7. For example, see N. Anderson, *The Hobo* (University of Chicago Press, 1923), Ch. 10.

8. See E. W. Burgess, 'The Sociologic Theory of Psychosexual Behaviour', in P. Hoch and J. Zubin (ed.), *Psychosexual Development in Health and Disease* (Grune and Stratton, 1949).

9. See M. Kuhn, 'Kinsey's View on Human Behaviour', *Social Problems* (1954), pp. 119–25.

10. Their work can be found in many papers, but their key books are J. Gagnon and W. Simon, *Sexual Conduct* (Aldine, 1973), and J. Gagnon, *Human Sexualities* (Scott, Foresman and Co., 1977). Other writing in this field includes I. Reiss, *The Family System in America* (Holt, Rinehart and Winston, 1971); J. Henslin, *Studies in the Sociology of Sex* (Appleton Century Croft, 1971); K. Plummer, *Sexual Stigma* (Routledge, 1975); J. DeLora and C. A. B. Warren, *Understanding Sexual Interaction* (Houghton-Mifflin,

1977); J. Petras, *The Social Meaning of Human Sexuality* (Allen and Bacon, 1978).

11. See *Human Sexualities*, p. 2.

12. The term 'intimate familiarity' is derived from John Lofland's *Doing Social Life* (Wiley, 1976). It leads to an advocacy of rigorous field work and qualitative research. For a recent overview of this see Howard Schwartz and Jerry Jacob, *Qualitative Sociology: A Method to the Madness* (Free Press, 1979).

13. On the use of metaphor in sociology, see Richard Brown, *A Poetic for Sociology* (Cambridge University Press, 1977), Ch. 4, p. 77.

14. Gagnon and Simon refer to this as 'the drive reduction model'.

15. See S. Lyman and M. B. Scott, *The Drama of Social Reality* (Oxford University Press, 1975).

16. See J. Gagnon (1977), op. cit., p. 6. A text that uses the script view throughout is Judith Long Laws and Pepper Schwartz, *Sexual Scripts: The Social Construction of Female Sexuality* (Dryden, 1977).

17. See K. Burke, *A Grammar of Motives* (George Braziller, 1955).

18. For a recent set of appraisals see J. Ditton (ed.), *The View from Goffman* (Macmillan, 1980); for an earlier one, see D. Brissett and C. Edgley, *Life as Theatre: A Dramatizical Source Book* (Aldine, 1974).

19. See Jay Ann Jemail and James Geer, 'Sexual Scripts', in Gemme and Wheeler (ed.), *Progress in Sexology* (Plenum, 1977).

20. For a clarification of such terms, see G. McCall and J. Simmons, *Identities and Interactions* (Free Press, 1966).

21. Amongst these studies are Laud Humphrey's *Tea Room Trade* (Aldine, 2nd ed. 1976); J. M. Henslin and M. A. Biggs, 'Dramaturgical Desexualization: The Sociology of the Vaginal Examination', in J. Henslin (ed.), op. cit.; G. L. Stewart, *'On First Being a John', Urban Life and Culture*, Vol. 1, No. 1 (1972), pp. 255–74; M. S. Weinberg, 'Sexual Modesty and the Nudist Camp', *Social Problems*, 12.3 (1965).

22. See John Gagnon, 'Scripts and the Co-ordination of Sexual Conduct', in *Nebraska Symposium on Motivation* (University of Nebraska Press, 1972). For an extension of this argument, see J. S. Victor, 'The Social Psychology of Sexual Arousal: A Symbolic Interactionist Interpretation', in N. K. Denzin (ed.), *Studies in Symbolic Interaction*, Vol. 1 (1978), pp. 147–80, and K. S. Rook and C. L. Hammer, 'A Cognitive Perspective on the Experience of Sexual Arousal', *Journal of Social Issues*, 33.2 (1977), pp. 7–29.

23. For an introduction to historical research on sexuality, see *Radical History Review*, 20, Spring/Summer 1979. The (now classic) statement of a history of sexuality is to be found in Michel Foucault's *History of Sexuality*, Vol. 1 (Allen Lane, 1978).

24. For an introduction to both the social uses of sexuality and sexual socialization, see Plummer (1975), op. cit., especially pp. 32–6, 56–62 and Ch. 7.

25. On this, see R. Stoller, *Sexual Excitement* (Pantheon, 1979).

26. On this, see K. Plummer (ed.), *The Making of the Modern Homosexual* (Hutchinson, 1981).

27. See S. J. Kessler and W. McKenna, *Gender: An Ethnomethodological Approach* (Wiley, 1978).
28. See Foucault, op. cit.; and also his Introduction to *Herculine Barbin: Being the Recently Discovered Memoirs of a Nineteenth Century French Hermaphrodite* (Pantheon, 1980).
29. William Simon, 'The Social, the Erotic, and the Sensual: The Complexities of Erotic Scripts', in *Nebraska Symposium on Motivation* (1973), p. 64.
30. See Plummer (1975), op. cit.
31. e.g. S. Freud, *Civilization and Its Discontents* (Hogarth Press, 1975).
32. See D. E. Morrison and M. Tracey, *Whitehouse* (Macmillan, 1979).
33. e.g. H. Reiche, *Sexuality and Class Struggle* (New Left Books, 1970).
34. e.g. Tom O'Carroll, *Paedophilia: The Radical Case* (Peter Owen, 1980); Dennis Altman, *Homosexual: Oppression and Liberation* (Outerbridge and Dienstfrey, 1971).
35. See J. Marmor, 'Sex for non-sexual reasons', in *Medical Aspects of Human Sexuality*, June 1969.
36. See Gagnon and Simon (1973), op. cit., p. 258.
37. See A. Kinsey *et al.*, *Sexual Behavior in the Human Male* (W. B. Saunders, 1948), p. 195.
38. Beech, quoted in Wright, op. cit., p. 233.
39. On 'low drive', see K. Heider, 'Dani Sexuality: A low energy system', *Man*, Vol. II, No. 2 (July 1976), pp. 188–201.
40. See J. Money and P. Tucker, *Sexual Signatures* (Abacus, 1977), p. 123.
41. I discuss this issue in 'Going Gay: Life Styles and Life Cycles in the Male Gay World', in D. Richardson and J. Hart (ed.), *The Theory and Practice of Homosexuality* (Routledge, 1981).
42. The literature on child sexuality is now considerable. A recent overview – though certainly polemical – is O'Carroll, op. cit. See also F. M. Martinson, 'Eroticism in Infancy and Childhood', *Journal of Sex Research*, Vol. 12, No. 4 (1976), pp. 251–62.
43. Although Blumstein and Schwartz have published several papers on bisexuality, at present their two most significant papers remain unpublished. These are 'The Acquisition of Sexual Identity' (American Sociological Association Annual Conference, 1976) and 'The Elements of a Sexual Identity' (American Sociological Association Annual Conference, 1980).
44. See Foucault again, op. cit.
45. See Plummer (1975), op. cit.
46. A useful commentary on the 'Stranger' in sociology is S. C. Jansen, 'The Stranger as Seer or Voyeur. A problem with the peep-show theory of knowledge', *Qualitative Sociology*, Vol. 2, No. 3 (1980), pp. 22–55.
47. See Plummer in Richardson and Hart, op. cit., and Plummer (1981), op. cit.

SEXUALITY, SEXUAL POLITICS AND CONTEMPORARY THEORY

Meaghan Morris

A Review of Michel Foucault's *La Volonté de savoir*

First published in *Working Papers*, Feral Publications, Australia. *La Volonté de savoir*, Volume 1 of *Histoire de la sexualité*, was published by Gallimard in 1976.

La Volonté de savoir ('The Will to Knowledge') is the first volume of Michel Foucault's projected six-volume work *Histoire de la sexualité*. The five volumes to come are entitled:

2 *La Chair et le corps*;
3 *La Croisade des enfants*;
4 *La Femme, la mère et l'hystérique*;
5 *Les Pervers*;
6 *Population et races*.

La Volonté de savoir is presented as an introduction to this history and as a preliminary outline of the argument to be developed and demonstrated in later volumes. As an introduction, *La Volonté de savoir* claims no demonstrative value in itself; it is rather an argued presentation of the questions to be posed, an elaboration of hypotheses and procedures, and an initial survey of the historical thesis and its theoretical counterpart – a theory (or, as Foucault prefers to say, an 'analytique') of power.

Since its appearance, *La Volonté de savoir* has been provoking both hostility and great excitement: the thesis suggested on the history of sexuality opposes current conceptions of that history as one characterized by repression and neatly coextensive with the development of capitalism; while the proposed theory of power would represent a new departure from both Marxism and psychoanalysis. So given its importance in terms of contemporary debates, what I have tried to do here is to give an account of the argument of *La Volonté de savoir* to provide a basis for discussion. What follows has no pretence to being a review; it is simply a kind of bastard translation-résumé. I have maintained no real distance from the terms of the text, except that imposed by language in the effort to summarize out of French and into English, and that created by any errors of interpretation on my part whether by unwitting misrepresentation of the text or by simple omission of essential points.[1]

One further remark I would wish to make is that *La Volonté de savoir* uses a number of terms whose meaning – and history – is best sought in Foucault's own work rather than elsewhere. These terms are particularly 'discourse', 'power' itself, 'knowledge' (savoir) and 'truth' (vérité), with the associated concepts of 'the will to truth' (la volonté de vérité) and of 'the production of true and false discourses'. On the other hand, these are phenomena of which Foucault is writing the history; but simultaneously, the terms themselves are part of his theoretical language. I am concerned that a summary such as the following runs a certain risk of encouraging a kind of substitutive reading. If the concepts of discourse, power, knowledge and truth – of their history, and the history of their interrelations – proper to Foucault's work are suppressed and replaced in the reading (consciously or otherwise) by concepts proper to other theoretical languages, the text will be misunderstood or distorted to the point of incomprehensibility. Since I have neither the space nor the intention to undertake a full scale exegesis, I can only refer the reader to the text of Foucault's inaugural address to the Collège de France, *The Order of Discourse*,[2] which contains a very clear description and explanation of the general framework and principles of his work as a whole. It would be false to regard the thesis of *La Volonté de savoir* as the direct realization of the projects announced in *The Order of Discourse*, since it represents, in fact, a fairly explicit change of direction and emphasis,[3] but the address itself remains an indispensable introduction to Foucault's work.

I. Nous Autres, Victoriens

The first chapter of *La Volonté de savoir* opens with an evocation of a text which, in its very title, embodies a widely accepted conception of the history of sexuality in what is still 'our' era; Stephen Marcus' *The Other Victorians*. The world of complex, diverse and perverse sexualities was and is condemned to be 'other' – hidden, furtive, disguised and covered by a blanket of hypocrisy. The Victorians themselves, in their official, public stances, represent still the essence of our regime of repression, standardized sexuality, censorship and enforced silence about sex.

In broad terms, this theory goes that right until the seventeenth century a certain freedom and frankness about sex flourished happily; in an uninhibited age, people lived on terms of tolerant familiarity with the illicit, the sexuality of children was recognized and was, along with all other forms of sexual behaviour, an occasion for healthy and open ribaldry. With increasing rapidity, however, as the nineteenth century approaches, bourgeois 'victorianism' takes hold of sexuality, represses it, reserves it for the conjugal family, subordinates it to the reproductive function, and imposes the legitimate, procreative couple as model and norm. The only recognized 'place' for sexuality is the parents' bedroom. Other sexualities, such as that of children, are regarded as non-existent or else reinscribed in profit circuits such as prostitution and psychiatry. Above all, a regime of silence develops; 'other' sexualities are denied even a verbal existence. The imperative of 'decency' in purified speech denies the existence of other sexualities while protecting the privacy and sanctity of the conjugal couple. Everywhere modern puritanism has imposed on sexuality a triple degree of interdiction, non-existence and mutism. We still have not freed ourselves from this regime; Freud and Reich represent some progress but this is far, very far from enough. And it is only to be expected that we cannot free ourselves without great pain and difficulty since repression, we are told, has been since the classical age the fundamental mode of liaison between power, knowledge and sexuality. To combat it we need a politics of transgression, a lifting of all bans and interdictions, an irruption of speech, a restitution of pleasure in the real, and a whole new economy in the mechanisms of power.

Foucault observes that this discourse on the modern repression of sex holds up well, since it is a very easy one to uphold. It is protected by a solemn and serious guarantee: if the birth of the age of repression can be placed in the seventeenth century, then it can be made to coincide with the development of capitalism. The bourgeois order is the embodiment of the age of repression. This has two immediate consequences. Firstly, a principle of explanation is immediately available; if sex is so severely repressed, it is because it is incompatible with a general and intensive exploitation of the labour force. Sex must be reduced to a means of reproduction of that labour force. So if, within this perspective, sex itself and its effects are still not easy to decipher, repression can on the other hand be analysed very easily indeed.

The second consequence is that sex, too, becomes part of the promised order of a better future – 'À demain le bon sexe'. The affirmation of our sexual repression is perhaps the one way left, given the experience of history, to discreetly associate the revolution and happiness, or the revolution and pleasure. An ancient prophetic function is revived in the discourse of sexual revolution; in speaking out, now, and telling the truth of sex, in denouncing all hypocrisy, we achieve a happy combination of sex, the revelation of truth, the promise of the overthrow of the law of the world, the annunciation of a New Day, and the promise of felicity. It allows us to dream once more of another city – and this prompts the question, how is it that the lyricism and religiosity which so long accompanied the revolutionary project should now, in industrial and western societies, find itself transferred, for a large part at least, onto sex?

It is at this point that Foucault wishes to situate the series of historical analyses to follow, and he describes the project in these terms:

> It is essentially a matter of interrogating the case of a society which for more than a century has been noisily chastising itself for its own hypocrisy, which speaks with prolixity of its own silence, stubbornly persists in detailing what it does not say, denounces the powers it exerts and promises to liberate itself from the laws which have made it function. I wish to examine not only these discourses, but the will which drives them and the strategic intention which sustains them. The question I wish to pose is not: why are we repressed, but why do we say, with so much passion and so much rancour against our most recent past, against our present and against ourselves, that we are repressed? By what spiral have we arrived at affirming that sex is denied, showing ostentatiously that we hide it, saying that we silence it – and this in formulating it in explicit words, seeking to expose it in its most naked reality, and in affirming it in the positivity of its power and its effects?[4]

He continues that if it is certainly legitimate to ask why sex has so long been associated with sin, we then need all the more to ask why we feel so strongly that one of the great historical faults of our society was a sin against sex.

Foucault then formulates the automatic objection: so many people today affirm our repression because that repression is historically evident; the prolixity is simply a function of the strength and solidity of the regime of repression, and especially since it is the nature of power in our societies to be repressive and to repress with particular attention useless energies, the intensity of pleasures and irregular conducts.

In relation to this 'Repression Hypothesis', three doubts are to be raised.

1. Historical question: Is the repression of sex really historically evident?

2. Historico-theoretical question: Is the mechanics of power, particularly that which is at work in a society such as ours, really, in essence, of the order of repression?

3. Historico-political question: Is there really a historical rupture between the age of repression and the critical analysis of repression?

Foucault stresses that in introducing these doubts, his purpose is not to formulate counter-hypotheses: not to claim that instead of repression we have enjoyed a regime of constant liberty, and not to assert that power is more tolerant than repressive or that the criticism of repression is simply caught in a more cunning or discreet form of power. He wishes less to show that the repression hypothesis is false, than to replace it in a general economy of discourses on sex inside modern societies since the seventeenth century. The kinds of questions to be asked are: What has been said about sexuality and why? By whom, from what situation and position and point of view? Which institutions have incited discourse on sexuality, accumulated and diffused it? What links are there between these discourses, the power effects induced by them, and the pleasures invested by them? In short, it is a question of taking into account the global 'discursive fact', the 'mise en discours'[5] of sex; and of determining, in its functioning and raison d'être, the regime of power-knowledge-pleasure which sustains the discourse on human sexuality.

Hence two important points to be pursued: to ask how has power been able, in fact, to penetrate and control everyday pleasure – with effects that can be those of refusal and build-up of barriers, but also those of incitation and intensification, the 'polymorphous techniques of power' – and secondly to determine, not whether these discursive productions and power effects lead to the formulation of the truth of sex or, on the contrary, false goods destined to obscure it, but the will to knowledge which serves them as both support and instrument.

One further insistence: Foucault is not maintaining that sex has not been prohibited or masked or misunderstood since the seventeenth century, or even that it has been less so than before. The interdiction of sex is not a red herring; what is a red herring is to make it the fundamental and constitutive element on the basis of which one could write the history of what has been said about sex in the modern epoch. 'All these negative elements ... which the repressive hypothesis regroups in a grand central mechanism destined to say No are no doubt only pieces which have a local and tactical role to play in a "mise en discours", in a technique of power, in a will to knowledge which are very far from reducible to them' (21).

The History will thus detach the analysis of sexuality from a scarcity economy in order to look for, on the contrary, the instances of discursive production, of production of power, and of productions of knowledge; it will be the history of these instances and their transformations. A first examination seems to indicate that since the end of the sixteenth century, the 'mise en discours' of sex, far from undergoing a process of restriction, has been submitted to a mechanism of increasing incitement; that the power techniques exerted on sex have not obeyed a principle of rigorous selection, but of dissemination and implantation of polymorphous sexualities; and that the will to knowledge, far from having been arrested before a taboo, has been determined to constitute a science of sexuality.

II. The Repression Hypothesis

1. The Incitation to Discourses

For the last three centuries there has been, rather than silence and censorship, a veritable discursive explosion around sex. It is true that a rigorous purification of vocabulary can be observed, and a policing of utterances with a controlling of their conditions of production; who, in other words, can say what about sex to whom and in what circumstances. There are certain definite regions of tact and discretion; between parents and children, for example, or teachers and pupils, masters and servants. But what can be observed on the level of discourse is rather a proliferation and discursive fermentation which accelerates after the eighteenth century. This activity is not 'illicit', but on the contrary institutionally incited – incited inside Christianity, medicine and then psychoanalysis and psychiatry, the judicial and penal system. (This section of *La Volonté de savoir*, which is itself only a brief outline of the historical studies to come, presents a number of examples, of which I shall mention only a few.)

One important line of development is the evolution of the Catholic pastoral and penitence sacrament after the Council of Trent – which can be examined through the history of confession manuals. The directness of the questions recommended by medieval manuals (respective positions of partners, exact motions and gestures etc.) is replaced by more and more insistent recommendations to discretion in the formulation of the questions. But at the same time the extent of confession, and the confession of the flesh, never ceases to increase. More and more importance is attached, particularly after the Counter Reform, to meticulous self-examination and to all the insinuations of the flesh. A double evolution tends to make the flesh the root of all sinfulness, and to displace the most important moment from the act itself towards desire, desire which is all-pervasive and present in the most secret of forms. There is an increasing injunction to tell, to tell everything, to tell oneself to oneself and to others, as often as possible, to tell everything which might concern the play of pleasures, sensations, thoughts which through soul and body might have something to do with sex. There is an imperative to confess not only acts against the law, but to make discourse of one's desire and of all one's desire. As far as possible nothing is to escape this formulation, even though the words used are to be carefully neutralized. In this situation the banishing of certain expressions could only be a secondary apparatus in relation to this great subjection; a way of making it morally acceptable and technically useful.

A second line can be drawn from the Christian pastoral of the seventeenth century to its projection in 'scandalous' literature. Sade, with his minute detail and extensive enumeration, relaunches the injunction to tell all, everything; and at the end of the nineteenth century the anonymous author of *My Secret Life* submits himself to the same prescription; he must make a complete account and there must be no omissions. A kind of traditional libertine, his strangest practice was to set himself the quasi infinite task of meticulously accounting for each of his actions and repeating them in discourse. Rather than a courageous escapee from 'victorianism', the author of *My Secret Life* was 'the most direct and in a way the most naïve representative of a plurisecular injunction to talk about sex'. Victorian puritanism itself can be seen as a refinement, a tactical reversal within the great process of turning sex into discourse.

Both Christianity and obscene literature hoped to produce specific effects on desire by turning sex into discourse. During the eighteenth century this production machinery was supported by other mechanisms; essentially mechanisms of 'public interest'. There is an incitation to speak of sex in discourse which would be not only moral, but rational. Sex is not only an affair for judgement, but for administration. In the eighteenth century sex becomes an affair of state, in the necessity to regulate and organize sex by useful and public discourses. 'The population' makes its appearance, a population which is not just a collection of subjects, or a 'people', but a population with its specific phenomena and its own variables; birthrate, deathrate, life expectation, fertility, state of health, frequency of illness, form of nourishment and housing. At the heart of this economic and political problem of the population is sex: it is necessary to analyse percentage of births, the marriage age, legitimate and illegitimate births, the precocity and frequency of sexual relations, the manner of rendering them fertile or sterile, the effect of celibacy and interdictions and the incidence of contraceptive practices. The future of society is tied to the use of sex; and sexual behaviour becomes both an object of analysis and a target of intervention.

Nor is the sexuality of children a case of a simple imposition of silence, first broken by the *Three Essays* and the case of Little Hans. While it is true that a certain freedom of language has disappeared, what can be observed is rather a new regime of discourse. There is no binary separation of the said and the not said; rather we need to determine the different ways of not saying, the distribution of those who can speak and those who can't, what type of discourse is authorized or what form of discretion required for and of whom. There is not silence, but silences – and they form an integral part of the strategies which underlie and traverse discourses.

There is the example of the development of colleges during the eighteenth century; their architectural design alone is a prolix statement on the sexuality of children and adolescents – a statement that it exists, in precocious, active and permanent form, and that it has become a public problem, the concern of doctors, and pedagogues and masters. Around the collegian and his sex is the proliferation of a whole literature of precepts, opinions, observations, medical counsels, clinical studies, reform schemas and plans for ideal institutions. The sexuality of children and adolescents has become an important stake around which innumerable institutional apparatuses and discursive strategies have been organized. The imposition of certain restrictions on certain ways of speaking is only a counterpart of, and perhaps a condition for the functioning of other discourses – which are multiple, interwoven, subtly hierarchized and all strongly articulated around a bundle of power relations.

A final example to mention here is the case of a French rural labourer, a simpleton, arrested in 1867 for playing the 'curdled milk' game with a young girl. The important thing about this story is its miniscule character; and that this person was the object not only of collective intolerance, but of a judicial action, a medical intervention, an attentive clinical examination and a whole theoretical elaboration. His cranium was measured, the bone structure of his face was studied, his anatomy was inspected for signs of degeneracy: he was made to talk, he was interrogated on his thoughts, inclinations, habits, sensations and judgements. And finally (acquitted of any crime) he was turned into a pure object of medicine and knowledge, hidden away to the end of his life in the hospital at Mareville, to be made known, however, to the learned world by means of a detailed analysis. No doubt, Foucault observes, the schoolmaster of the village concerned was at the same time teaching his pupils to purify their language; but this is certainly one of the conditions permitting the institutions of knowledge and power to blanket their solemn discourse over the small theatre of the everyday.

Discourses on sexuality have not multiplied outside or against power – but in the very place of exercise of power and as a means of its exercise. There is less a discourse on sexuality than a multiplicity produced by a whole series of installations functioning in institutions; there is a regulated and polymorphous incitement to discourses. At this point another objection is foreshadowed: so much stimulus to speak of sex means that there was a fundamental interdiction, which only precise necessities, economic and political, could lift, and that in limited fashion. So many strict conditions for speech mean that sex was kept hidden and secret, and still is. But, Foucault replies, it is exactly this common theme of a sex outside discourse, and to which only the removal of obstacles and the breaking of a secret can open the way, that we need to question. Isn't this part of the incitement itself, to present sex as the secret to track down, as a secret which is difficult and necessary, dangerous and precious to tell? What is proper to modern societies is not that they have condemned sex to the shadows, but that they have consecrated themselves to always speak of it, prizing it as the Secret.

2. The Perversion Implantation

The objection could be raised that it would be a mistake to see this proliferation of discourses as a simple quantitative phenomenon, as if the fact of speaking about sex were more important than the forms of imperatives imposed on it by this speech. For isn't this 'mise en discours' a way of excluding from reality forms of sexuality which do not submit to a strict reproduction economy? A way of assuring a sexuality which is economically useful and politically conservative?

Foucault replies that he does not yet know if this is, finally, the objective. But if so, it has not been sought through reduction of sexualities. The nineteenth and twentieth centuries have been rather an age of multiplication and dispersion of sexualities, of the multiple implantation of 'perversions', of the initiation of sexual heterogeneities.

Until the end of the eighteenth century, three explicit codes regulate sexual practices: canon law, the Christian pastoral, and civil law. Each fixes, in its own way, the separation of the licit and the illicit. They are all centred on matrimonial relations and conjugal duties. The sexual behaviour of the legitimate couple is submitted to a major surveillance, and overwhelmed by detailed rules, recommendations and restraints. The 'rest' remains much more obscure – for example the uncertainty of the status of 'sodomy', or the indifference of these codes to the sexuality of children. In addition, these different codes make no separation between infraction of alliance rules and deviations in relation to genitality. On the list of serious sins figures sexual relations outside the married state, adultery, kidnapping, incest – and sodomy and the reciprocal 'caress'. The tribunals condemn equally homosexuality, incest, marriage without parents' consent and bestiality. In both religious and civil orders, the 'against-nature' was only perceived as an extreme form of the 'against the law'. The prohibitions on sex were fundamentally juridical in nature; hence hermaphrodites were, by definition, considered for a long time as criminals.

The discursive explosion of the eighteenth and nineteenth centuries produced two modifications of this system centred on the legitimate couple. Firstly a centrifugal movement in relation to heterosexual monogamy; it remains the point of reference, but it is spoken of less and less often, or at least with growing sobriety. The legitimate couple has the right to more and more discretion. Secondly, what begins to be interrogated is the sexuality of children, madmen, criminals and homosexuals; these figures, once scarcely perceived, now advance to make their confession of who they are. They are disapproved, but they are listened to. If 'regular sexuality' came to be questioned once again, it was by a motion of folding back, from the basis of these peripheral sexualities.

Hence the extraction, in the field of sexuality, of a specific dimension of 'against-nature'. They assume an autonomy vis à vis other condemned acts (which are less and less condemned); there is a differentiation made between sodomy and marrying a close relative; between sadism and seducing a nun; between necrophilia and infidelity. The domain covered by the sixth commandment begins to dissociate; as does, in the civil order, the old confused category of 'debauchery'. Slowly and equivocally, the natural laws of matrimony and the immanent rules of sexuality begin to be inscribed in two distinct registers. A world of perversion designs itself – the innumerable family of perverts.

The importance of this is not to be found in the level of indulgence accorded them or the quantity of repression exerted upon them; but in the form of power exercised. The function of that power does not seem to be one of interdiction, but of four operations which are very different from simple prohibition:

1. Lines of penetration are organized, for example around the child. The 'vice' of masturbation becomes an epidemic to be combated, mobilizing the whole adult world, parents, doctors and pedagogues around the child. Masturbation is constituted as a secret, that is, constrained to be hidden in order to be discovered – surveillance apparatuses are developed, methods of spying and examining and pursuing the 'problem' to its source. Parents and educators are alerted, the suspicion is sown amongst parents that all children are guilty, and that they themselves are guilty if they are not suspicious enough; they are kept continually on the alert, what conducts prescribed and pedagogy recoded for them – a whole medico-sexual regime anchors its hold in the space of the family.

2. There is an incorporation of perversions and a new specification of individuals. Sodomy was a form of forbidden act; the homosexual of the nineteenth century becomes a character, with a history, a childhood, and also a morphology, with an indiscreet anatomy and perhaps a mysterious physiology. Since nothing which he is escapes his sexuality, it is clearly inscribed on his face and body. The sodomite was a backslider, the homosexual is a species. Species too are the perverts given strange names of baptism by nineteenth-century psychiatry; Lasegue's exhibitionists, Binet's fetishists, Krafft-Ebing's zoophiles and zooerasts, Rohleder's auto-monosexualists, the mixoscophiles, the gynecomasts, the presbyophiles, the sexoesthetic inverts and the dyspareunistic women. The machinery of power which pursues all this disparateness only pretends to suppress it by giving it an analytic, visible and permanent reality; it implants it on bodies and makes it a principle of classification and intelligibility.

3. Perpetual spirals of pleasure and power are instituted. This kind of power demands constant, curious, caressing presence, examination and

taking charge of sexuality. There is extension of the domain controlled, but also sensualization of power – there is pleasure in exercising and in evading power, and there is power soaked in pleasure pursued.

4. And hence, the apparatuses of sexual saturation,[6] characteristic of the social spaces and rites of the nineteenth century. The family, for example, is a complex web of multiple, fragmentary and mobile sexualities – as is the school and the psychiatric institution. The bourgeois society of the nineteenth century is a society bursting with sexual perversion; not in the mode of hypocrisy, or as a result of a too rigorous denial, but as a function of the type of power made to function on the body and the sex. It is a power which doesn't exclude sexuality, but includes it in the body as a mode of specification of individuals. Modern society is perverse, really and directly, as a product of the interference of a type of power on bodies and their pleasures. Polymorphous behaviours have been really extracted from people's bodies and their pleasures; or rather they have been solidified in them – by means of multiple power apparatuses, they have been brought to light, isolated, intensified and incorporated. The proliferation of specified sexualities occurs through an advance of power, its extension around and upon individual bodies (assured also by innumerable related economic profits – medicine, psychiatry, prostitution, pornography); and what is important is that it is an apparatus very different from the law which assures, by a web of interconnecting mechanisms, the proliferation of specific pleasures and the multiplication of disparate sexualities.

III. Scientia Sexualis

Supposing that the first two points are conceded: that for three centuries discourse on sex has multiplied rather than reduced, and that if it has been accompanied by prohibitions it has, in a more fundamental way, assured the solidification and implantation of a whole sexual disparate; the objection is still possible that all this simply plays a defensive role – it is, in its multiplicity, an avoidance of a real confrontation with the truth of sex. So many learned discourses on sex exist simply to obscure and disguise it; at least, until Freud. It was a discourse which shared and served a repressive morality.

And it is true that if the discourse on human sexuality in the nineteenth century is compared to the contemporary discourse on the physiology of animal and vegetable reproduction, an astounding gap appears. There is no real exchange between the medicine of sexuality and the physiology of reproduction; the former is weak not only in scientificity but in elementary rationality. Its systematic blindnesses betray an undeniable will not-to-know. But, Foucault replies, this was a refusal to see and hear which bore precisely on that which was being brought to light, forced to appear, that of which the formulation was imperiously solicited.

Not to want to see or to admit is a peripety of the will to truth; there can only be misrecognition on the basis of a fundamental relation to the truth; and it is the presence and effects of this will to truth[7] which is important. Charcot's Salpêtrière is an example – it was an immense observation apparatus, with its examinations, interrogations and experiments, but it was also a machinery of incitement with its public performances and its carefully prepared theatre. It is on the basis of this permanent incitement to discourse and to truth that the mechanisms of misrecognition come into play – thus Charcot interrupting a public consultation during which it was becoming too manifestly a question of 'That'. The important thing is not the refusal to see or accept, but the construction itself of an immense apparatus around and in relation to sex to produce the truth. Sex is constituted as one of the stakes of truth; an enterprise which does not date from the nineteenth century, even if at that time the project of a 'science' gave it a singular form.

Historically there have been two great procedures to produce the truth of sex. On the one hand there are the numerous societies – such as China, Japan, India, Rome and Arab-Islamic societies – endowed with an *ars erotica*. In erotic art, truth is to be extracted from pleasure itself, taken as practice and culled as experience. Pleasure is to be known as itself, in relation to itself; according to its intensity, specific quality, duration and reverberations in body and soul. The knowledge gained is fed back into pleasure itself, to work on it from inside and amplify its effects. The knowledge gained is constituted as a secret to conserve its efficacy and power; so the relation to the master, guide and initiator is fundamental.

Our civilization seems to have no *ars erotica*; however, it is the only one to practise a *scientia sexualis*. Or rather it has developed procedures to form a kind of power-knowledge which is rigorously opposed to the art of initiations and magisterial secrecy; the procedures of the confession.

Since the Middle Ages western societies have placed the confession among the major rituals for the production of truth: development of confessional techniques in the penitence sacrament after the Lateran Council in 1215, gradual disappearance in criminal justice of accusation procedures and trials of guilt (duels, judgements of God etc.), and the refined procedures developed by the inquisition. Confession plays a central role in the order of civil and religious powers – the development of which can be seen in the evolution of the meaning of 'avowal' itself. Once one 'avowed' or 'witnessed' on behalf of or in relation to others, this gradually becomes a recognition of one's own actions and thoughts. The individual was long authenticated by the reference of others, by the manifestation of his links and relations to others; later, he is authenticated by the true discourse he is able or obliged to hold about himself. Through the confession, the truth inscribes itself at the heart of the procedures of individualization by power.

Confession is indeed one of the most highly valorized techniques for producing the truth; in this, we are a singularly confessional society. Confession pervades the methods of our justice, our medicine, teaching, family relations, love relations, everything from daily life to the most solemn rituals. Confession can be spontaneous, imposed or extracted; confession has long been linked with torture (and this connection, a footnote informs us, will be taken up in a forthcoming book, *Pouvoir de la vérité*). Yet paradoxically we consider it, after so many centuries of its history in the exercise of power, to be a way to liberty and truth. The confession, statement, assertion of who we are seems to us to place us outside power; and this, surely, is one of the internal ruses of confession, to make us so forget how ancient is the yoke of the imperative to self-examination. Particularly in relation to sex; sex, since the developments discussed of Christian penitence up till today, has always been privileged material for confession. We need to be well and truly trapped by the ruse of confession, and have a thoroughly reversed notion of power to give censorship and interdiction a fundamental role, and to believe that all the voices which have, for so long, been urging us to 'tell' the truth are voices which speak to us of liberty. Confession has been part of the enormous work carried on for generations in the West – while other forms of labour assured the accumulation of capital – of the 'subjection' (assujetissement) of people – their constitution as subjects in the two senses of the word.

Confession is a ritual of discourse in which the subject speaking coincides with the subject of his utterance. It is also a ritual which unfolds in a power relation, for confession requires the presence, virtual at least, of a partner who is also the instance requiring the confession – imposing it, appreciating it, and intervening to judge, punish, pardon, console, reconcile; a ritual in which utterance alone produces intrinsic modifications in the speaker. For centuries the truth of sex has been culled in this discursive form, and not that of the teaching and initiation proper to *ars erotica*; and thus, through the structure of power which is immanent to it, the discourse of confession is not imposed from above, but comes from below.

An important development in the history of confession and its dissemination procedures is the institution, in the psychiatry of the nineteenth century, of a confession-science; in which can be observed the interference of two modalities of production of the true – confession procedures and scientific discursivity. How was the immense and traditional extraction of confession constituted in scientific forms? (Each of these responses is commented on in the text):

– by a clinical codification of inducement to speech.

– by the postulate of a general and diffuse causality (the principle of sex).

– by the principle of a latency intrinsic to sexuality (what must be extracted is not only what the subject wishes to hide, but what the subject hides from itself).

– by the method of interpretation (the listener is no longer the judge, but the master of truth: the listener's function is hermeneutic).

– by the medicalization of the effects of the confession (the truth heals . . .).

To return to the broad historical perspective: For over a hundred and fifty years, a complex apparatus has been in place to produce true discourse on sex – and through and across this apparatus something like 'sexuality' could appear as the truth of sex and its pleasures. This 'sexuality' is a correlative of the discursive practice of *scientia sexualis*; the fundamental characteristics of this sexuality correspond to the functional exigencies of the discourse which is to produce its truth. At the point of intersection of a confession technique and a scientific discursivity, sexuality is defined as being 'by nature' a domain penetrable by pathological processes and thus calling for therapeutic or normalizing interventions; a field of significations to decipher; a locus of processes hidden by specific mechanisms; a nest of indefinite causal relations, an obscure speech which must be both hunted down and listened to.

This leads to the posing of a general working hypothesis. The society which develops during the eighteenth century – whether it be called bourgeois, capitalist or industrial – has not opposed a fundamental refusal of recognition to sex; on the contrary it has brought into play a whole apparatus for producing true discourses about sex. As though sex contained a capital secret; and as though it was essential to inscribe it not in an economy of pleasure but in an ordered regime of knowledge. Two processes develop, mutually influencing each other – we ask sex to tell the truth of itself, and we demand that sex tell us the truth of ourselves. From this play has slowly developed a knowledge of the subject: until the point where a science of the subject begins to gravitate around the 'question' of sex.

It has often been said that western societies have been incapable of inventing new pleasures; but perhaps the only survival of an *ars erotica* in our society is precisely the invention of that new pleasure which is the pleasure of the truth of pleasure, an erotics of truth. In any case, the question is to define the power strategies which are immanent to this will to knowledge, and with the specific case of sexuality, constitute the 'political economy' of a will to knowledge.

IV. The Sexuality Apparatus

This section of the book is devoted to the formulation of some general propositions to situate the research to come, and with particular reference to a 'first sketch' of an analytics of power – some of the implications of which are developed in the book's last chapter, '*Droit de mort et pouvoir sur la vie*'. The argumentation is extremely subtle and concise, and here I only have space to present it in drastically abridged form, giving only broad indications of its direction.

A number of general questions are to be posed: What is the injunction to speak of sex? Why is there this chase for the truth of sex, and why is the knowledge held to be so precious that we have come to seek our emancipation in it? For what is, indeed, remarkable about western societies is that we have succeeded in placing ourselves almost entirely – ourselves, our bodies, our souls, our individuality, our history – under the sign of a logic of concupiscence and desire.

However, before considering some possible ways of examining these questions, it is necessary to confront the fact that there already is a critique of the simple notion of sexual repression in the form of the theory of desire put forward in modern psychoanalysis. Psychoanalysis has long abandoned the notion of a wild natural energy constrained by an order acting from above as quite inadequate for interpreting the mutual articulation of power and desire; desire is not 'repressed' for the simple reason that it is the law which is constitutive of desire and of the lack which institutes desire. The power relation is already there where desire is. Foucault has, he points out, been speaking up till this point of repression and of the law as though they were more or less the same thing, as though there were not a considerable difference in their theoretical and practical implications.

The response is that both the thematics of repression and the theory of the law-constitutive-of-desire share a certain conception of power, which it is necessary to eliminate if an analytics of power is to be possible. This conception of power can be called 'juridico-discursive'. What distinguishes the thematics of repression from the theory of the law (a distinction which might be schematized, though Foucault's text does not say this, as the distinction between classical readings of Freud and those instituted by Lacan) is the manner of conceiving the nature and dynamics of drives; it is not the manner of conceiving power. They share a common representation of power which, according to its use and supposed relation to desire, leads to two opposed consequences. If power only has an external hold on desire ('repression'), then there is the promise of a 'liberation': if power is constitutive of desire itself ('the law') then we are always already trapped.

This juridico-discursive representation of power is not only proper to those who pose the relations of power to sex; it is much more general and widespread, particularly in political analyses of power, and has its roots far back in the history of the West. Some of its principal characteristics are:

– The negative relation. Power only ever has a negative relation to sex; exclusion, refusal, masking etc. Its effects take the general form of the limit, and lack (manque).

– The instance of the rule. Power dictates the law to sex, placing it under a binary regime of permitted/forbidden. Power acts in pronouncing the rule – so the pure form of power is to be found in the function of the legislator, and its mode of action is juridico-discursive.

– The cycle of the forbidden. Power only brings a law of prohibition to bear on sex; obedience is renunciation, disobedience is punished by suppression – so the alternative is between two non-existences.

– The logic of censorship. The logic of power over sex is paradoxical; a law which articulates itself as an injunction to non-existence, non-manifestation and mutism.

– The unity of the apparatus. Power acts on sex in the same way at all levels, in uniform and massive fashion; from the State to the family, from instances of social domination to structures constitutive of the subject, we find a general form of power. This form is that of the law; whether it is given the form of the prince, the Father, the censor or the master, it is schematized in a juridical form and its effects are defined as obedience.

This is a very strangely limited notion of the supposed mechanics of power. It is a power very poor in resources, repetitive in its methods; it is a power which is only that of saying No, and thus is essentially anti-energy; and it is a power which is only juridical. The question arises why we accept this notion so easily, and elide the productive efficacy, the strategic richness and the positivity of power. A general and tactical reason seems to be that only by masking an important part of itself is power rendered tolerable; its success is in proportion to how much it can hide of its mechanisms.

But there is also a historical reason. The great institutions of power which developed during the Middle Ages – the monarchy, the State with its apparatuses – did so on the basis of, and to a certain extent acting against, a multiplicity of conflicting powers. The great institutions were able to make themselves acceptable by presenting themselves as instances of regulation, arbitration, delimitation; they functioned above and over heterogeneous rights and powers as a principle of law, with the triple character of constituting itself as a unitary ensemble, as identifying its will with the law, and as exerting itself through mechanisms of interdiction and sanction. No doubt this juridical function – *pax et justitia* – was not the only element involved in the development of the great monarchical institutions; but such was the language of power and the representation it gave of itself.

A tradition going back to the seventeenth or the nineteenth centuries encourages us to think of the monarchy as being absolutely on the side of non-law; abuse, caprice, privilege etc. But this is to forget the fundamental historical characteristics of the development of western monarchies, and that the criticism of lawless monarchy in eighteenth-century France, for example, was still juridical in nature. The monarchy may have come to break or to set itself above the law; but the critiques of its functioning present no fundamental questioning of the principle that the law should be the form of power, and that power should always be exercised in the form of law. The same postulate remains in critiques of the system of law itself as only another means of exercising violence and perpetuating 'in-justice'.

At bottom, the representation of power has remained haunted by the monarchy; the king's head has not always been cut off in political thought and analysis. Hence the prime importance still accorded in the theory of power to problems such as law and violence, law and illegality, will and liberty, and above all, the State and sovereignty (even if the latter is examined in the form of a collective being rather than in the person of the sovereign). To think power in these terms is to think it in terms of a historical form very specific indeed to our societies – the judicial monarchy. Specific, and transitory: there is the infiltration of new forms and the perpetuation of old forms of power which are probably irreducible to the representation of law. For one part, at least, these are the mechanisms which since the eighteenth century have taken in charge the life of people, people as living bodies. The new types of power function not by law but by technique and normalization, not by punishment but by positive control and are exerted at all levels and in forms which surpass the State and its apparatuses.

This juridical representation is still at work in contemporary analyses of the relations between power and sex. Whatever the status given to desire, it is still conceived of in terms of its relation to a power which is still juridical and discursive, a power which finds its central point in the enunciation of the law. We need to free ourselves of this image and of the theoretical privilege granted to law and sovereignty, if we want to analyse power in the historical and concrete play of its procedures. The project involved in a series of studies on the historical relations of power and discourse on sex is thus willingly recognized as circular, in the sense that two attempts are involved which mutually effect each other: to form a new grid of historical decipherment, in starting from a different theory of power, and to advance towards a new theory of power by observing historical material. To simultaneously think sex without the law, and power without the king.

Method

Some initial indications are necessary in relation to the word 'power'.

Power is not intended to mean 'Power' as an ensemble of institutions and apparatuses in a given State; nor a mode of subjection taking the form of a rule in opposition to violence; nor a general system of domination by an element or group, the effects of which traverse the whole social body. Power is not an institution, a structure, or a certain quality or attribute of certain persons. Power does not have its initial existence in a central point or single focus of sovereignty, from which spread derived and descending forms.

Power is rather the multiplicity of 'force relations' (rapports de force[8]) which are immanent to the domain in which they act, and are constitutive of their organization; power is everywhere, not because it englobes everything, but because it comes from everywhere; power is the name given to a complex strategic situation in a given society.

A number of propositions can be put forward following this general direction.

– power is not something which is acquired, taken or shared, but acts from innumerable points in the play of unequal and mobile relations.

– power relations are not in a position of exteriority vis à vis other types of relations (economic processes, knowledge relations, sexual relations) but are immanent to them; they are not in superstructural positions with prohibitive roles; but have, there where they act, a directly productive role.

– power comes from below: there is no great binary and global opposition of dominators and dominated, which spreads and reverberates and reproduces itself down through the whole social body. Rather, the great dominations are hegemonic effects which are continually sustained by all the multiple and local confrontations.

– power relations are simultaneously intentional and non-subjective. No power acts without a set of aims and objectives; but it does not result from the choice or decision of an individual subject or controlling group.

– wherever there is power there is resistance; but the latter is never in a position of exteriority with respect to power. This does not mean that resistances are pointless or futile; rather that they are the other term in power relations – they inscribe themselves in power relations as the irreducible vis à vis, and are thus distributed, as well, in irregular fashion. There are, sometimes, great historical ruptures, but most often it is a question of mobile and transitory points of resistance.

These propositions lead to a further specification of the question to be posed about sex and the discourse of truth which has taken it in charge. The question is

– NOT, given such and such a state structure, how and why has 'power' needed to institute a knowledge of sex.

– NOT, what global domination has been served by the care taken to produce true discourses on sex, and

– NOT, what law has presided over both the regularity of sexual behaviour and the conformity of what has been said about it.

The question is: In any given type of discourse on sex, in any given extraction of the truth which appears historically and in determined areas (around the body of the child, female sexuality etc.), what are the most immediate and local power relations at work? How do they make these kinds of discourses possible, and how do these discourses serve them as a support? How is the play of these power relations modified by their very action?

Four rules may be formulated; not as methodological imperatives, but prescriptions for prudence.

1. Rule of immanence. The starting point will be 'local sites' of power-knowledge; e.g. penitent-confessor relations, or the body of the child.

2. Rules of continuous variations. To avoid asking who has power in the order of sexuality and who does not, who has the right to knowledge and who is kept in ignorance, and to look rather for the schema of modifications and displacements implied by the very action of the relations.

3. Rule of double conditioning. To examine the relations between 'local sites' and 'transformation schemas' on the one hand, and larger strategies with their global effects on the other, not in terms of discontinuity or homogeneity, but in terms of a double conditioning – of a strategy by the specificity of possible tactics, and of tactics by the strategic envelopment which makes them function.

4. Rule of the tactical polyvalence of discourses. What is said about sex is not the simple surface projection of power mechanisms. It is in discourse that power and knowledge are articulated. So discourse is to be considered as a series of discontinuous segments whose tactical function is neither uniform nor stable; hence it is not a question of a world of discourse divided into accepted and excluded discourse, dominant and dominated, but of a multiplicity of discursive elements which can act in diverse strategies.

Domain

With these rules in mind, it is possible to define a domain of research. There is no single, global strategy bearing on the whole of society, and in uniform fashion on all manifestations of sex. Rather, four great strategic ensembles can be seen at work in various ways since the eighteenth century, developing specific apparatuses of power and knowledge in relation to sex.

- hysterization of the woman's body
- pedagogization of the child's sex
- socialization of procreative behaviours
- psychiatrization of perverse pleasure.

In the growing preoccupation with sex throughout the nineteenth century, four privileged objects of knowledge emerge; the hysterical woman, the masturbating child, the malthusian couple and the perverse adult, each being the correlative of one of the strategies which have traversed and utilized the sex of children, women and men.

The question also arises, what is going on in these strategies? Is it simply an attempt to control sexuality? Foucault suggests that rather it is a matter of the very production of sexuality itself. 'Sexuality' is not a given of nature which power is trying to checkmate, but is the name given to a historical apparatus. The elaboration of this argument involves the second problem of 'domain'; the relations between the older alliance apparatus, and the sexuality apparatus which in modern societies is superimposed on it and is tending to reduce its importance – relations which are focused in the family.

Both the alliance apparatus (marriage system, kinship rules, transmission of names and goods) and the sexuality apparatus branch over sexual partners, but in quite different models. They could be opposed term for term: the alliance apparatus functions around a system of rules defining the permitted and the forbidden, the sexuality apparatus functions according to mobile, polymorphous and conjunctural techniques of power; the alliance apparatus has a principal objective to reproduce the play of relations and to maintain the law which regulates them, while the sexuality apparatus engenders a permanent extension of domains and forms of control; for the former, it is the link between partners of defined status which is pertinent, for the latter it is the sensations of the body. Finally if the alliance apparatus is strongly articulated upon the economy because of its role in the transmission and circulation of wealth, the sexuality apparatus is linked to the economy in numerous and subtle ways, but chiefly by the body – the body which produces and consumes.

The alliance apparatus is disposed towards 'reproduction', towards a homeostasis of the social body that its function is to maintain; hence its privileged relation to the law. The raison d'être of the sexuality apparatus is not to reproduce itself but to proliferate, invert, penetrate bodies in more and more detail and control populations in a more and more global fashion. Thus we need to admit three or four theses which contradict the Repression Hypothesis. Sexuality is linked to recent power apparatuses; it has been in expansion since the seventeenth century; the arrangement which sustains it is not organized in the interests of reproduction; and it has been linked from the beginning to an intensification of the body.

It would be inaccurate to say that the sexuality apparatus has replaced that of alliance; it covers it, and historically it is around and on the basis of the alliance apparatus that that of sexuality locks in to place. The family is, clearly, the site of exchange between the two apparatuses; and the nature of this exchange can be the basis for an explanation of certain aspects of the history of the family – and also of the will to affirm the universality of the incest taboo throughout the nineteenth century. One of the lines of argument to be pursued is that if for over a century there has been a growing interest in the incest taboo, to the point of declaring it the obligatory threshold of culture itself, this has perhaps been one means of defence, not against incestuous desire, but against the extensions and implications of the sexuality apparatus and its hold on the family as a prime space for its functioning. Thus Charcot, who removed his patients immediately from their families, tried to detach the domain of sexuality from the alliance system; but in order to make individuals sexually integrable back into the family. And psychoanalysis, in withdrawing from the neurological model and bringing sexuality itself to light, puts family relations into question; but it is only to rediscover, at the heart of sexuality itself, the laws of alliance and incest.

One of the fundamental points in the whole history of the sexuality apparatus is this: with the technology of the 'flesh' in classical Christianity, the sexuality apparatus came into being by basing itself on the alliance systems and the rules regulating them; but today it plays the opposite role. It is the sexuality apparatus which tends to prop up the old alliance apparatus. Hence (among other things) the enormous consumption of psychoanalysis in societies where the alliance apparatus and the family system is in need of reinforcement.

Periodization

The Repression Hypothesis supposes two historical ruptures; one during the seventeenth century (birth of the great prohibitions, etc.) and the second, less a rupture than an inflection of the curve, during the twentieth century – critique of repression, liftings of taboos, beginnings of relative tolerance.

It is necessary to follow the chronology of these procedures; but there is also the calendar of their utilization, the chronology of their diffusion and the effects they induce. These multiple datings do not coincide with the great repressive cycle normally situated between the seventeenth and twentieth centuries.

1. The chronology of the techniques themselves goes back a long way, to the development of confessional techniques and methods of self-examination developed with particular intensity since the four-teenth century. This needs to be studied in its long theoretical elabora-tion until the end of the eighteenth century, when a new technology of sex is born – new because without being really independent of the thematics of sin, it essentially escapes from the ecclesiastical institution. Sex becomes an affair of state, an affair in which the entire social body (and each of its individuals) is called upon to put itself under surveil-lance. This develops along three axes: pedagogical (with the specific sexuality of the child an objective), medical (the sexual physiology of women) and demographic (the spontaneous or organized regulation of births). There is a visible continuity with the methods already formed by Christianity, but there is also a major transformation: the technology of sex essentially devotes itself to the medical institution, the exigency of normality and, rather than to the question of death and eternal punish-ment, to the problem of life and illness.

This mutation at the end of the eighteenth and the beginning of the nineteenth centuries opens up the way for other transformations. There is the detachment of the medicine of sex from the general medicine of the body – the opening up of the great medicopsychological domain of 'perversions'. At the same time, the analysis of heredity placed sex in a position of 'biological responsibility' with respect to the species; whence the medical and political project of administration of sex and its fecundity. The medicine of perversions and programmes of eugenics were the two great innovations of the second half of the nineteenth century; innovations which refer perpetually to each other through the theory of 'degeneration'. A genealogy of perverts became possible, but at the same time a demonstration of how sexual perversion induced exhaustion and sterility of generations to come. The solid core of the new technologies of sex was the ensemble perversion-heredity-degeneration. Certain state racisms have their roots in this. Psychoanalysis, on the other hand, resumes the project of a medical technology proper to sex, but tries to free it from all its correlations with heredity and thus with racisms and eugenics.

2. The above suggests only a dating of techniques; the history of their diffusion and their point of application is different. The Repression Hypothesis supposes, if repression is referred to the utilization of the labour force, that sexual controls have been most intense and careful when applied to the poor classes. This does not seem to be the case. The most rigorous techniques were formed and applied most intensely first of all in the economically privileged and politically dominant classes; the subtle procedures of self-examination, the medicalization of sexuality, the problematization of the sexuality of children and the psychiatrization of sex were at first accessible only to very restricted groups. The eighteenth-century collegian, the nineteenth-century 'nervous' woman did not come from the working class. The obligation to preserve one's 'health' for the safe perpetuation of family and class was felt by the bourgeoisie and the aristocracy.

The mechanisms of sexualization penetrated the masses slowly, and in three successive stages: at the end of the eighteenth century, in respect to birthrate problems when it was discovered that the masses widely understood and practised contraception and abortion; then during the 1830s campaign for the organization of the 'canonical' family, as an instrument for the political control and economic regulation indispensable for the subjection of the urban proletariat; and at the end of the nineteenth century when a judicial and medical control of perversions developed in the name of the general protection of society and the race. It can be said that the 'sexuality' apparatus, elaborated in its most complex and intense forms for and by the privileged classes, slowly diffused throughout the whole social body; but it has not always taken the same forms nor has it used the same instruments everywhere.

What is the meaning and raison d'être of the process? It is not a principle of limiting the pleasure of others, since the 'ruling classes' tried it first on themselves. It is not an ascetism, since it involves an intensification of the body and new techniques of maximilization of life. It is not the repression of another class which is to be exploited; rather, it would appear to be a matter of the self-affirmation of a class, later extended to others as a means of economic control and political subjection. After the middle of the eighteenth century the bourgeoisie was employed in giving itself a sexuality, and constituting from it a specific body, a 'class' body, a body with a health, a hygiene, descendants, a race.

There are several reasons for this; first of all, a transposition of the self-identification of the aristocracy. The aristocracy had a specificity of the body, but in the form of blood. Aristocratic blood had a genealogy, ancestors, alliances; the bourgeois body had heredity, descendants, and the health of the organism. 'The "blood" of the bourgeoisie was its sex.'

But there is more than this transposition; there is another project, that of the indefinite expansion of force, vigour, health and life. The domination of the bourgeoisie needs to be not only economic and ideological, but physical, through the valorization of the body. Hence the correlation with a racism which is very different from the essentially conservative concerns of the aristocracy – with a racism which is dynamic and expansionist. Hence also so much reluctance to recognize the body and the sex of other classes – precisely those being exploited. The living conditions given the proletariat, especially in the first half of the nineteenth century (cf. K. Marx, *Capital*, I, chap. X, 2, 'The Greed for Surplus-Labour'), do not exactly illustrate concern for its body and sex. It reproduced itself all by itself. For the proletariat to be endowed with a body and a sexuality, it took a number of conflicts, particularly in relation to urban space, economic emergencies (physical needs of heavy industry etc.) and the locking into place of a whole technology of control and surveillance which eliminated any risk of class affirmation against the bourgeoisie, since this technology remained the instrument of its hegemony. Hence no doubt the reticence of the proletariat to accept this apparatus, and its tendency to say that all that stuff about sexuality belongs to the bourgeoisie and is none of its concern.

We need to return to long disreputable formulas, and admit that there is a bourgeois sexuality, that there are class sexualities. Or rather that sexuality is originally and historically bourgeois, and that it induces, in its successive displacements and transpositions, specific class effects.

One last comment in this preliminary outline of the sexuality apparatus concerns the role actually played by the repression hypothesis in its development. When the sexuality apparatus has diffused more or less throughout the whole social body, a new differentiating element comes into play for the bourgeoisie. On the one hand, the theory of repression is linked to the diffusion of the sexuality apparatus; it justifies its authoritarian and constraining extension by declaring that all sexuality is subjected to the law, indeed, that sexuality only exists as an effect of the law; but on the other hand it compensates for the general diffusion of sexuality by the analysis of the differential play of interdictions along class lines. A discourse emerges declaring the sexuality of the bourgeoisie to be 'specially' and 'intensely' repressed; henceforth social differentiation is affirmed no longer by the sexual 'quality' of the body, but by the intensity of the repression.

Psychoanalysis inserts itself at this point, and the problem of incest is particularly important. On the one hand, the incest prohibition is posed as an absolutely universal principle, defining human culture and the individual's entry into it; but in practice, psychoanalysis gives itself the task of removing (for those in the position to have recourse to it) the effects of its repression; it permits them to articulate their incestuous desire in discourse. Now at the very moment when Freud was discovering what it was that Dora desired, and permitted her to formulate it, there was a systematic, administrative and judicial hunting down and out of incest as it existed in the country or in urban milieux to which psychoanalysis had no access. It should not be forgotten that the discovery of the Oedipus complex is contemporary with the juridical organization of loss of parental authority (such laws were passed in France in 1889 and 1898). In this way psychoanalysis, as a therapeutic practice, could play a differentiating role within a now generalized sexuality apparatus; those who had lost the privilege to have exclusive concern for their sexuality had henceforth the privilege of experiencing more than others, that which forbids sexuality, and of possessing the method which makes it possible to lift the repression.

The history of the sexuality apparatus since the seventeenth century could serve as the archaeology of psychoanalysis. It plays several simultaneous roles in that apparatus: interpinning of sexuality and the alliance system, opposition to the theory of degeneration, differentiating element in the general technology of sex, renewal of the exigencies of confession in the new sense of an injunction to retrieve that which has been repressed. The task of truth is now linked to calling the forbidden into question. This itself opens up the possibility of a considerable tactical displacement – reinterpretation of the whole sexuality apparatus in terms of generalized repression, related to generalized mechanics of domination and exploitation, linking together the processes which permit us to free ourselves from one and the other. Thus around Reich between the wars forms the historico-political critique of sexual repression. The value of this critique and its effects on reality have been considerable – partly because, in fact, this critique of repression functions always inside the sexuality apparatus, and not outside or against it. But this critique cannot, therefore, be expected to provide a grid for a history of this same apparatus. Nor can it be the principle for a movement to dismantle it.

The last chapter, 'Right of Death and Power over Life', is concerned with the elaboration of the notion of 'biopower' and its importance in the development of capitalism; a power which, articulating itself directly upon bodies, is a power over life proper to normalizing societies – and which is different from the powers of sanction and death proper to the juridical monarchies.

The difference between the ancient sovereign right of death – 'to take life and to let live' – and the functioning of a political power which administers life – 'to foster life or to disallow it to the point of death' – is discussed in terms of the significance for modern societies of massacre and genocide (wholesale slaughter practised in the name of the defence of the population, or even of the survival of the species); capital punishment (a limit, a scandal and a contradiction for a power concerned to put life in order, and a penalty increasingly reserved only for those whose monstrous crimes could be represented as posing a biological danger to others); and the privatization of death itself, together with the wane of the rituals once associated with it: death becomes power's limit, the moment which escapes it, and the most secret point of existence.

Foucault suggests that this power over life has developed in two basic forms since the seventeenth century. One of these, centring on the body as machine, was ensured by the procedures of power that characterized the disciplines: an anatomo-politics of the human body. The other, formed a little later, towards the middle of the eighteenth century, is centred upon the species-body, the body traversed by the mechanics of the living, and serving as the basis of biological processes – propagation, births and mortality, levels of health, life expectancy – which are taken in charge by a whole series of interventions and regulatory controls: a bio-politics of the population.

This biopower was, he argues, an indispensable element in the development of capitalism. Not only did this require the controlled insertion of bodies into the machinery of production and the adjustment of the phenomena of population to economic processes; it further required the growth of both these factors, and it required methods of power capable of optimizing forces, aptitudes, life in general without at the same time making them more difficult to bring into subjection.

It is against this background that the chapter examines sex as a political object with a history; a history which is partly the elaboration of the idea that sex exists as something other than bodies, organs, somatic localizations, anatomo-physiological systems, sensations and pleasures. The history of sex is the history of a fictional unity, a grouping of biological functions, anatomical elements, behaviours, sensations and pleasures – which now functions as a causal principle and omnipresent meaning. The chapter also suggests that since biopower acts upon the body, and since theories of desire and repression are parts of the apparatus which permits that action, sustained by the will to extract the truth of sex, then the basis of a counterattack against the sexuality apparatus cannot possibly be sex-desire – but bodies and their pleasures. It is the irony of the sexuality apparatus which makes us believe that it is true confession and true discourse on sex which will lead to our 'liberation'.

Notes

1. This article was published as an introduction to the text before the appearance of an English translation by Robert Hurley (Michel Foucault, *History of Sexuality*, Volume 1, *An Introduction*, New York: Pantheon Books, 1978). My translation differs from his at several points.

2. *Social Science Information*, 10 (April 1971), 7–30.

3. In *The Order of Discourse* Foucault proposes a study of discourses on sexuality in terms of interdiction, 'la parole interdite'. Which means, one assumes, that he was still thinking in the broad terms of the Repression Hypothesis at that time.

4. My translation; *La Volonté de savoir*, 16. My own text is a kind of collage of sentences, phrases, and expressions more or less translated from the French – so I have only used quotation marks in a few places, where the length of a passage directly translated, or the interest of a particularly concise sentence seemed to impose them. Otherwise the English text would have been unreadable simply for typographical reasons.

5. A 'turning, placing, putting into discourse'; in the same way the 'direction' of a play or film is in French the *mise en scène*, and bringing something into play in a given situation is a *mise en jeu*.

6. The word translated as 'apparatus' is, almost without exception, the French word 'dispositif'. Thus what I have called 'the sexuality apparatus' is, in the original, 'le dispositif de sexualité'. I chose this translation simply because of a precedent in the translation of Bachelardian texts; the translation by Robert Hurley uses the term 'deployment'. It may be important to note that this is not the same word as that used in the French for the notion of 'ideological state apparatuses'; state apparatuses are 'appareils d'État'.

7. To remove a possible ambiguity, it is worth insisting that the 'will to truth' is not a triumphalist notion or a positive value in Foucault's own thought; he regards the will to truth as a phenomenon with a history.

8. 'Rapports de force' is a term which avoids the concept of power as a superstructural effect (e.g. 'power relations') and insists on the concept of power as a positive play of energies, as expressed in the physico-biological term 'force'.

Ros Coward, Sue Lipshitz and Elizabeth Cowie

Psychoanalysis and Patriarchal Structures

First published in the *Papers on Patriarchy* (1976) by the Women's Publishing Collective, Lewes.

Introduction[1]

The locus of the concerns of this paper is the question of ideology and it is for this reason that the paper ranges across several and various disciplines. The problem of the relationship of ideology to the mode of production has been raised by the theoretical developments of the women's movement, in a way that makes it impossible to consider ideology as being of secondary importance in the dynamic of the mode of production. Ideology has long been a neglected area in Marxist thought, but recently some advances have been made under the influence of the work of Louis Althusser. His insistence on understanding society as constituted by three necessary practices, economic, political, and ideological, has at least made it possible to think of the determinancy of the ideological instance as relatively autonomous from the mode of production. This theoretical advance from the crude economism of early Marxism was felt to be valuable for the women's movement which had simultaneously, and in a way as yet unelaborated, found that the position of women could not be described or explained solely in terms of the mode of production. There were two factors which imposed attention to ideological formations and practice on the women's movement; one was the awkward fact that its apparently radical demands emerged in the context of middle-class radicalism of the late sixties. Although there was a great deal of debate about the relation of women to the economy, it was recognized, especially amongst the consciousness raising groups, that the sort of oppression experienced by women was not immediately analogous with the form of exploitation of a class which capitalist relations instituted. There was a sense of the 'traditional' role of women which extended back beyond the establishment of capitalist relations, which seemed to be centred on the role women played in the family. This was the second factor in recognizing the importance of the role played by ideology. For women, it was no longer really possible to hold to simplistic views of ideology as 'false consciousness', or an inverted image of real relations. What was encountered in consciousness raising was the fact that women were *constructed* in those socio-familial relations of capitalism; their desires and needs were the desires and needs produced in those relations, not some distorted form of the true subject of needs which underlies the notion of alienation. This was experienced as 'subjective contradiction', moments of inhibition where the revelation of the political and economic forces at work in these desires did not eradicate their efficacity in determining the subject's activity in society.

These considerations necessitated that the theory of the women's movement was extended to include an area of ideological struggle and to do this it was necessary that the notion of the subject, that is, the individual in its social relations, was extended to provide a materialist analysis of the functioning of ideology. It was in this context of work that most of us came to the work of Lacan, a French psychoanalyst, who seems to provide a materialist theory of the subject, as constructed in relation to social relations.

In this way, the theoretical developments of the women's movement ran parallel with some of the advances made by Marxist theory in the post-1968 period. Increasing political disillusion with the crude economism of the established theories and political practices which could neither account for unrest amongst students or women, nor for the backlash of political reaction except in the most economistic terms, resulted in the extension of the theoretical concerns to the area of ideology and the construction of the subject in the social process. For it was realized that implicit in such notions as alienation was an idealist view of the human being, that is, as a pure human essence, which becomes alienated under capitalist relations. Such a realization made it clear that the notion of alienation was no longer tenable by materialist thought. A new theory of the subject had to be produced, and even Althusser's formulations seem to be based on certain idealist premises. He too ultimately relies on a notion of an empty subject interpellated by ideology, rather than constructed by ideological practice in a specific relation to social relations.

The theoretical development of the Women's Movement has involved itself increasingly with an analysis of the family. This is because it is in the familial relations that we find what is specific to women's oppression. For example, a woman may work during the day but nevertheless take on herself the double burden of responsibility for all work concerned with the family. In constituting this specificity, the family has inevitably led to some very real theoretical problems. Until very recently, Marxist theory had only made rather insignificant excursions into the question of the oppression of women, and there are no founding texts even to indicate the mechanisms of the oppression of women, in the way that *Capital* could be said to provide the foundations for understanding the oppression of the working class through wage-relations. One tendency resulting from the attempt to redress this absence has been the attempt to simply transpose the mechanisms outlined in *Capital* and to apply them to the work performed by women in the home, leading to the development of the so-called 'domestic labour debate'.[2] In this way women are put into an analogous position to that of the working class, and models of productive and non-productive labour, the production of surplus value, etc., are applied. From this perspective the determinant of women's subordinate role is the relations of production and the familial relations are a sort of secondary mirroring of this determination.

There are several factors which make this form of analysis increasingly untenable. The most obvious is the fact that certain aspects concerned with women's equality belie the equation capitalism = oppression of women. Indeed some recent developments indicate that women's equal economic status is a rationalistic exigency of capitalism. Margaret Thatcher and the Equal Pay legislation are current examples. Despite all the catches of the latter it is symptomatic of the capitalist necessity to ensure a viable consumerist unit. Most of us will have encountered in one form or another the revolting tyranny of the 'professional couple', fast becoming the bedrock of the middle classes.

Another factor which challenges the tendency to view the family as a simple superstructural formation, reflecting the economic base of capitalism, has been brought forward by certain developments in China. If the family did correspond in this way, it would not now be necessary for what seems to be present in some of the current concerns of Maoism with the ideological problem of women and the need to contend with 'the thought, customs and culture which brought China to where we found her'. The refutation of Lin Piao and Confucius which played a central role in the cultural revolution is part of the struggle in the superstructures, which fully acknowledges the materiality of ideology and credits it with equal determinancy with the economic base in the social totality.

These two factors are examples of what necessitates a more complex understanding of what it is that operates to keep women in the wings of history, without any 'social' language, i.e., without the language that controls social laws and therefore political practice. It is not a question of there being something that women want to say about their essential characteristics that is consciously forbidden, nor is the assertion of the 'negative' place of women implying that women are everything that men are not. It is rather an assertion that women have formed their identity in relation to negative social relations, particularly to the relations of reproduction, and therefore are excluded from the language of political practice and the transforming relations of production. One way of formulating the negative social relations in which women appear to have been constructed is in the work of Lévi-Strauss. He suggests that the function of women as exchange in a society is what excludes them from the regulation of social laws and the formation of the body politic. This leaves men as the guardians of political power and the regulation of laws.

It is psychoanalysis that has made it possible to see these concerns in their full complexity, that is, no longer as either false consciousness nor as simple mirroring of the capitalist base. The object of psychoanalysis is the unconscious,[3] as the site of interaction between the body, history and psychic representations. Its field therefore is the production of unconscious formations, in the process of the acquisition of language. For this reason it offers a genuinely materialist route to understanding the specificity of the determinations of sexuality organized for reproductive purposes. As feminists, the development of psychoanalysis has made it possible for us to see how women are constructed in a sexuality dominated by the relations of reproduction. It has demonstrated that under patriarchy (which is the only form of culture that Western civilization has known) the acquisition of language involves an organization of sexuality which is determined by the relationships established around having and not having the phallus. Juliet Mitchell's book, *Psychoanalysis and Feminism*, represents the first significant discussion of this theoretical work in England, although it is of wide concern already in France, where the work of psychoanalyst Jacques Lacan and of Julia Kristeva has had considerable influence on the theoretical elaboration of the women's movement.

This determination of sexuality organized for reproductive purposes is what is to be understood by the 'Symbolic'[4] order which involves the production of symbolic positions, that is, desire, organized according to reproductive constraints and thus involving certain factors in the acquisition of language. The inclusion of the Symbolic as an area of concern does not involve the rejection of the ultimately determining role of economic formations and the need to analyse capitalism in its specificity. Rather it is to propose that the human labour force is part of production, and that the reproduction of this force may operate as a specific determinant in a given historical moment, which is not necessarily capitalist. Any analysis, we suggest, of the way in which the family functions to enforce the division between relations of production and relations of reproduction has to take into account both the construction of sexual difference in cultural, i.e., symbolic, relations, and also the specific ideological function of the family.

Firstly the cultural relation of sexual difference (and within this the primacy of the male) which can be relative to the particular historical circumstances and is structured in the unconscious formations.

Secondly, the subject (the individual in its social relations) finds its place as a sexed subject according to the structure of the pre-existing familial and ideological configuration. Thus ideology is not a cloud of ideas hanging over the social relations but has a materiality that structures the subject's development. For example, an expected baby in a family already has a 'place'. There is simply no way in which he or she can 'freely' choose to interpret their sexuality or culture as individuals. These two areas are central features in our analysis.

The culture in which it is each subject's task to locate him or her self (either to do this or fall ill) has historically been patriarchal. Despite the appearance of an 'undifferentiated' line of descent in the contemporary family, i.e., either child can inherit from either parent, there still remains the historical primacy of patri-linear over matri-linear inheritance of status and name, as Lévi-Strauss has shown. Even in rare matri-linear groups where the residence is in the mother's house (matrilocal), it is in fact still the fathers and brothers who govern exchange and the law of the community.

Law, that is, political organization, has belonged to the father. To say this is to situate feminism in a different problematic from an equation of 'sexism' with capitalist ideology. If women are exchanged to establish bonds between men, and this is the basis of the system of marriage that attempts to guarantee the legitimate, organized reproduction of the species, then we can attempt to see *how* the sexuality of women is structured in order to maintain and reproduce this situation.

It is only by reference to the construction of the unconscious and its hidden constraint on the formation of the individual subject that this is possible. This analysis alone can show how the subject is put in place as an individual who seems to be the point of origin for experiences or structures which always already include him or her. This is not a case of stressing the 'individual'; we all know or believe we are unique, but this conscious knowledge in no way gives us a scientific understanding of the process by which we are subjected to a structure but come to think of ourselves as point of origin of ideas and beliefs. In fact a conscious acknowledgement of this sort operates to obscure the ideological character of our identity and daily lives and actions, since it reaffirms an idealist notion of identity, essential and non-contradictory, in other words not a revolutionary notion of identity opening onto the objective contradictions of history.

The relationship of ideology to the imaginary and narcissism

In his pre-1968 writings, Althusser defines ideology as a 'system of representations . . . endowed with a historical existence and a role within a given society'. It was also said to be an imaginary relation between men and their real world. In the essay on Ideological State Apparatuses (*Lenin and Philosophy*), he redefines this, and ideology is no longer synonymous with illusion, but rather alludes to imaginary relations that are by definition 'a representation of the imaginary relationships of individuals to their real conditions of existence'.

This means that the knowledge that it is possible to get of ideology is not arrived at by unmasking an illusion, telling the truth or by just reinverting the relationships originally inverted in the camera obscura model (Marx, *German Ideology*) of fetishism. The reasons for this are (a) because the 'illusion' is structured as an *inflection* and not as an *opposition* of true and false; (b) because the process occurs in ideological apparatuses like the family that have a certain autonomy in the way they produce and reproduce themselves; and (c) because all experience partakes of ideology, one can only be in relation to it, and not outside it, ever. Scientific work is an attempt to challenge ideology, but even its starting places are in ideology.

In a Freudian account of the development of sexuality, and as extended and modified by Lacan, men enter the Symbolic order, the order of language and culture, and leave the realms dominated by the Imaginary[5] (that in which the relation to the image of the counterpart is dominant) with the formation of the superego at the resolution of the Oedipal crisis.[6] Women's entry, which is described by Freud as less convincing because, being already castrated in theory, it is not in the male way, does not, as is sometimes implied, leave them in the realms of imagination and illusion.

We maintain that their entry is negative in relation to the Symbolic, given the dominance of the phallus as signifier of meaning and women's displaced relation to it. Their entry *is* then *an* entry, and not an absence. If there were no entry, women would be unable to speak at all, unable to construct a relation to 'the Real'[7] and, living in a situation in which signifier and signified merged, could be only psychotic.

Freud is often misquoted as characterizing women as ill in this way, since in his paper on Narcissism he characterized them as dominantly narcissistic in their relationship to the world and their identification with others. The basis of such a misreading of Freud is a failure to disentangle the relationship of narcissism[8] (as in the myth of the beautiful boy who falls in love with his own image) to the theory of the development of the ego, and to confuse it as a developmental phase with its structural implications, thus not to distinguish either from that order Lacan calls the Imaginary. This we will now try to do.

The Narcissus of the myth is fixated at a particular developmental stage. He is like Lacan's child who is captivated by his own reflection in a mirror. This mirror phase[9] is the moment when the ego is constituted in the child, precisely as a misrecognition of itself as whole, in the face of an experience of his own lack of co-ordination and power. 'The jubilant assumption of his mirror image by the little man, at the infans stage still sunk in his motor incapacity and nurseling dependency, would seem to exhibit in an exemplary situation the symbolic matrix in which the I is precipitated in a primordial form, before it is objectified in the dialectic of the identification with the other, and before language restores to it, in the universal, its function as subject' (Lacan, *The Mirror Phase*). This then further structures the self/other distinction for the infant, that was first experienced in its separation from the mother's breast and then in the phase of autoerotism, and indeed there has to be such a separation or else there would be no possibility of phantasy. Narcissism organizes the sexual instincts into taking the self as love object, but in a form that is not yet genitally tending, i.e., not directly active in the interests of procreation, but rather is polymorphously pleasurable.

Now once we can imagine ourselves as whole selves, an image that is also an alienated one of self as other, we have the possibility of symbolizing. Since both sexes experience a similar process of ego construction, there is no way in which women, said to be narcissistic, can be seen as fixed prior to symbolization and condemned with pity or admiration to be like primitive man or children. Both of these groups have been mistakenly assumed to be undifferentiated from the social world, self contented, inaccessible and locked away in phantasies of omnipotence described as functional adaptation to their actual powerlessness. For if we accept the mirror phase structuring we can no longer have any conception of primary narcissism as independent of any intersubjective relationship. We are thus relieved of the burden of attempting to explain the impossible, i.e., how the infant ever escapes from the closed circle of primary narcissism and develops an ego at all out of sexual energy.

Similarly women can no longer be characterized as forces of 'nature' in this sense, feared as likely to subvert the male order, and monogamy, because they are narcissistic in an apparently asocial way. For narcissism is also commonly associated with immorality, insatiability and lack of self control, and outside of society. What in fact this analysis does mean is that by definition women's lack of a penis structures their form of the castration complex such that they have to make sense of that lack.

From this analysis we also see now where ideology finds grounds (using ideology in Althusser's sense as previously defined). It utilizes then the structuring in individuals that represents in alienation, the subject to itself as a unified whole image. These unconscious bases of ideology explain some of its force, and why it cannot be defined simply as illusory perception or false consciousness.

Women's narcissism leads to their relating to the 'other who is me' in erotic life. This other can be in the form of someone who was once part of themselves (say a child), themselves, or a past or ideal self. The female form of object love differs from that of the male because crucially of their different positions in the castration complex. The infantile sense of perfection (misrecognized in the mirror), and the experience of omnipotence, are pleasures the child only gives up reluctantly in the face of others' challenge to narcissistic satisfactions, and because of the growth of its own self-critical faculties. Both sexes form an ego-ideal[10] that enables them to retain their narcissism while evading repression and this activity is a symbolic one. For the boy, this ego-ideal becomes a part of his superego,[11] that conscience that is formed according to Freud at the resolution of the Oedipal conflict with the acceptance of female castration, of masculine identification, and of the incest taboo, hence paternal authority. Since women enter the castration complex in a negative way, there is less challenge to their infantile theories about sex difference and their knowledge of it, there is less to repress, and so the narcissistic position is not given up in the same way. The woman locates her ego-ideal in the other, rather than idealizing her love object, in her mind, as does the man the woman. This suggests her ego is depleted because she has to withdraw sexual energy (libido) from her self, thus her dependence lowers her self-esteem. The place she is in is one of referring to an image of herself that is always not-male and that cannot be denied to require a capacity to represent relationships but is characterized rather by thinking and being in a negating fashion.

According to Freud, there must always be an experience of lost satisfaction preceding, as one of the necessary conditions, the capacity to symbolize difference. There has to be an experience of there/not there, presence/absence, before there can be categories of thought. That is to say, we can describe women as always searching for the lost object, the phallus, that will be forever missing in the real but might be captured in the imaginary via satisfactory relationships with others, men or children, not ones in which the ego is simply shored up.

But men are also searching for the lost phallus that they believe their mother once possessed. All little boys imagine that their mother really has a penis too, and it is her 'castration' that faces him with the problem of sex difference, and contributes to his fear that he could be too. This lost phallus cannot be recovered in the real either, but it structures male relations to women in particular ways. For example, a man will try to create with a woman, a relationship that reaffirms the 'wholeness' felt potentially to be always threatened, since a fetishistic stage is never, more than other developmental stages for Freud ever entirely resolved. And men have unconscious ideals of women that split into that of the beloved caretaker on the one hand, and on the other there is residual hatred of feared womankind who faced them with the problem of knowledge of sex difference.

Both sexes can retreat to a primarily narcissistic position and choose only their own sex as love object (homosexual choice), or they can identify with their bisexual other aspect and take that as an ideal. None of these positions are entirely separated from the others and neither are they static nor is the ambivalence ever resolved entirely. Only in extreme narcissism, when touching one's own body becomes gratification enough, or when for a boy, the fetish object becomes a satisfactory representative part of the substitute for a loved person, are these positions pathological. So if we see narcissism as a crucial and inevitable aspect of ego-development for both sexes, there is no debate about whether women have it and men do not, but rather about its influence on the form of intersubjectivity that the sexes engage in.

The negative entry of women into the Symbolic, for example, is reinforced by the impact of puberty as a moment when meaning of physiological maturity and the real shift of a woman's relationship to her reproductive capacity and to men occurs. One would expect that here the girl re-examines her feminine identification in the light of a real shift in the social and cultural meaning of her engaging in sexual activity that could give her pleasure (autoerotic or with a partner) and yet is subject to the male in that her pleasure is to be organized genitally and for reproduction.

Entry into the Symbolic and Language

Having shown the relationship of women to the Imaginary, and stressed that it is not a case of their being restricted to the Imaginary, but rather a case of their negative entry into the Symbolic, we now intend to explain the symbolic relations and the privileged place of the phallus in the entry into the Symbolic. The Symbolic breaks up the imaginary direction of the ego, by the intervention of the third term. It is this which finally establishes the fact of difference and allows the child to take up a position in language. The third term takes the form of the father in the family drama, the father who demands that the child acknowledge the fact of sexual difference and the implications of this. In order to identify itself with a particular gender children of both sex have to give up their mother as love object. The little boy has to choose a woman other than his mother, with whom to copulate and love. He deviates in accordance with his bisexuality as Freud sees it between an active and passive orientation. For the boy wants to take his mother's place as love object for his father (the feminine attitude) and yet the father's threat of castration if he does not take on a masculine identification creates the fear that usually effectively structures the boy's choice of the masculine attitude. It is at the Oedipal moment that the physical sex differences the boy has previously noticed become important to him, since they suggest a real basis for his fear of castration. In a normal resolution of the conflict, the little boy gives up his desire for his mother, and represses it or it is literally 'smashed to pieces' and the 'Oedipus complex no longer exists even in the unconscious' being replaced by the super-ego, that internalized source of morality and conscience derived from the father. Paternal authority has been institutionalized with the abandonment of incestuous desire, that 'may be regarded as the victory of the race over the individual'.

The analysis proposed by Lacan deals with the construction of the female position as subject in symbolic relations where the phallus is the central term in the entry into these relations. In other words the relations are established around the possession or non-possession of the phallus. And this dialectic allows the child to find a position in which he or she can use language in a way ensuring social communication. These positions are only achieved by the organization of sexuality under the dominance of the genital, and as we have mentioned, the unconscious formation of this imposition is the Oedipus complex.

Lacan's claim is that the phallus is the privileged signifier in the child's entry into the Symbolic. What precisely does this mean? Before attempting an explanation, it is necessary to emphasize two factors. Firstly, Lacan's account of sexual organization is based like Freud's on the assumption of the primary bisexuality of the drives. It is only through the castration complex that the traits active/passive appear, based on having or not-having the phallus. Secondly the term phallus is used as it was in classical antiquity, as the figurative representation of the male organ: a simulacrum. Yet despite the fact that it is used as a representative of the reality of the penis, and should not be confused with it, it is still necessary to account for the paradoxical privilege of the phallus in a theory of the construction of the subject which has as its substance culture and not biology.

This privilege is based on the theory of the phallus as a signifier, that is, as in the linguistic sense of the word, as the material form of language distinct from the concept. He refers to it as such not because it appears in speech, but because it functions in the same way as the signifier, analysed by modern linguistics. This analysis is based on the work of Saussure, who established that language was only made up of differences, and that

meaning only existed according to the relations of differences contracted
in the chain of signifiers. The phallus operates in the same way, fixing
difference according to having and not having it, thus referring to a
condition outside itself which makes signification possible.[12] This condition is the situating of the subject in the symbolic order by sexual
differentiation as a necessary positionality in language in our culture. In
order to make this clearer, it is necessary to describe in a very condensed
and abbreviated way, Lacan's account of the development of the child.

This involves a notion of 'separation' or 'splitting' of the subject, first
from its sense of continuum with its mother's body: she at first is the
recipient of all the child's demands, and is the place of all narcissistic
aspects and satisfaction. Second, a separation in which the child makes
its first identification of itself in the alienating image of the mirror, and
finally, the separation by which the child finds its place in symbolization.
This construction which creates the subject and the unconscious occurs
from the moment of birth. Lacan produces a mythical hypothesis of the
child in its existence before its construction as a language-using social
being. This can only ever be mythical since any knowledge of processes
pre-existing language and the unconscious is only ever known through
language under the dominance of symbolic relations. The myth suggests
a state purely dominated by drives,[13] i.e. pressures or forces towards
certain objects. At the moment of its birth, the child is like what Lacan
calls a 'hommelette', both a little man and a broken egg, spreading
haphazardly in all directions. But submitted as they are, always and
already to social and familial constraints, the drives are limited, and
contained in what is known as 'erotogenic zones'.[14] In theories too
extensive for the space of this paper, Freud elaborated the relationship
between the structural arrangement of the drives and the construction of
the ego; indeed he even went so far as to suggest in the paper *On
Negation* that the speaking subject is a continuation of the pleasure ego,
that is, a continuation of the same process of introjection and projection[15] by which the ego sought to incorporate all that was pleasurable to
it, and expelled what created unpleasurable tension in its interaction
with the arrangement of the drives.

What is significant in this context is that according to Freud and Lacan,
the process of introjection and projection establishes, or at least traces,
marks of similarities or differences in objects. This establishes categories
by which drives come to learn or recognize differences and similarities
between objects; this accumulative recognition allows the drives to

know which objects are pleasurable or unpleasurable without having to repeat the painful process of finding out.

Thus the subject marks out separations in its surroundings, and begins to separate itself from an outside which will then be radically 'other' to itself. It is this process which forms the ego by 'cutting it out', separating it from its implication in its mother's body and its surroundings, and begins to make it possible for the subject to use language since it sets up a subject and a predictable outside. This separation is only completed by the parallel development of the mirror-phase, and the establishment of difference in the castration complex. So that although the structures of a system of differences and indeed the system of differences which is learned-language can be acquired earlier, it is only after the mirror-phase and the castration complex that the subject can find a signifying place in language where it can represent itself adequately to the structure which already includes it.

The role that the phallus plays is that it governs this positionality by which the subject can represent itself in language. These are the representations necessitated by patriarchy, representations which organize women's sexuality to the relations of reproduction. This organization occurs through the fact that women enter the Symbolic in a relation of lack. The discovery of castration – the mother lacks a penis – completes the detachment of the subject from its dependency on the mother. The phallus functions as the term representing plenitude (having the phallus) as opposed to lack (not having the phallus) when the differences previously established receive their cultural form. For this reason, the female entry is an articulation of lack, and therefore a negative entry. The positive male entry involves the fact that they find themselves in a relation of possession of *the* symbolic function, i.e. the signifier which establishes the categories of difference from which women make their identifications. In this way we are led to positing the structural function of the phallus, which establishes difference thereby ensuring sexed reproduction of the species since desire is organized according to these categories. It is this stage of difference which enables the subject to finally separate itself from dependency on the mother by situating itself in the cultural or symbolic order through identification with ideal type of its sex. Julia Kristeva describes the process in this way – '... the subject finds its identity in the symbolic, is separated from its implication in the mother, localizes its pleasure as genital and transfers the movement of the drives into the symbolic order.' The domination of the genital phase established in this organization involves a repression of any sexuality which exceeds the limits of this genital phase.

It is not to the individual woman or to women in general that the symbolic activity and social representation are refused, rather the privileged object of this repression is the wife, the sexual or genital partner, who becomes the mother of the man's children. It is the reproductive woman who is forbidden a form of expression in a society organized for the maintenance of property relations. These relations of reproduction have a more fundamental role in societies where the productive forces are under-developed and which depend therefore largely on manpower.

Thus the Lacanian position indicates that there is a structural necessity, in all societies concerned with the production of goods, which is to ensure its reproduction in having it regulated by the relations of production. This masculine power has to be maintained by keeping hidden what in woman's sexuality exceeds the organization belonging to the social power of men, i.e. phallic power. 'Pleasure', repressed in the mother, is only allowed to appear in a certain form. That is, in its contribution towards production: *reproduction*. Forms of descent that prove always in the last instance to be dependent on phallic power (organization of the law by father or brother) are a manner of subordinating procreation and unproductive expenditure of pleasure that goes with it and is inseparable from it, to the needs of the relations of production. As soon as there is a form of descent, therefore, there is paternal law, built on the genital (maternal) organization of sexuality and ensuring the procreation of the species on the vital condition that the importance and centrality of the mother in all this remains hidden or as some kind of mystery.

What relevance can this analysis have for a contemporary feminist movement? In the first place it results in a totally different understanding of the position of women at the present time. This analysis has made it possible to challenge descent as the structural limit of society and to suggest that contradictions may exist resulting from the development of the productive forces. Kristeva for example points to two contradictions: one, the family is not only no longer essential as a unit of reproduction in an economic process which is highly specialized and international, but could actually endanger the economic equilibrium of capitalism if it continues to obey the social necessities that founded it, that is, unrestrained reproduction. Two, the contraceptive measures claimed from positions as different as feminist organizations to economic specialists, challenge the automatic nature of reproduction that the family has always been asked to assure.

These have been felt increasingly since the end of the nineteenth century. Industrialization to a large extent fractured the family unit, depriving it of its economic power since feudalism. In other words, capitalism, while reforming the ideological mode of the family in a particularly repressive and exploitative mode of the nuclear family, has also developed the productive forces to the point where they are actually in contradiction with the structure.

This proposes a way of understanding the family's ideological and structural role under capitalism which suggests another political direction which can no longer pretend to be analogous with the working class. This direction refuses to retreat into marginalism and economism of the kind typifying some women's and men's liberation groups, since it insists on participating in contemporary contradictions.

It is only when ideology can be understood in this way, in the dynamic of the mode of production which would necessarily involve consideration of symbolic relations that we will be able to understand the real relations between patriarchy and capitalism. We are faced with the problem of understanding the symbolic as an order that is worked over by ideological formations but not necessarily specific to these formations, that is, having their own history. It is for this reason that the intervention of psychoanalysis has suggested a very different analysis of the role and function of women in capitalism. It has suggested that capitalism has worked over and used patriarchal formations, but has also opened up the possibility that sexual determination arising from patriarchal formations could exist in contradiction with capitalist formations.

Notes

1. This introduction was written after the original paper and its presentation at the Patriarchy Conference.
2. For a condensed account of some of the major positions adopted in this debate, see 'Relations of Production: Relations of Reproduction', Women's Studies Group in *Working Papers in Cultural Studies*, 9, Birmingham University Cultural Studies Centre.
3. It was Freud who first provided a scientific elaboration of the unconscious as we understand it in this paper. Before Freud the concept of the unconscious simply meant the 'unknown', everything not known to consciousness.

Freud's discoveries, through studying dreams ('the Royal Road to the unconscious'), parapraxes, slips of the tongue, etc., revealed the possibility of a rigorous analysis of what had previously appeared as 'illogical' and totally irrational. His analysis is particularly significant since it showed that the unconscious bore a direct relation to the construction of the repressed in the formation of the so-called normal-sexed subject. Lacan has extended this implication of Freud's work, emphasizing that the unconscious is precisely constructed in the acquisition of language. The unconscious then acquires a central position in the individual construction which displaces previous idealist notions of the individual consciousness as determining of all mental processes.

4. We discuss the term Symbolic further in the final section of this paper. It indicates the relations and positions necessitated by the fact of sociality, positions taken up in the acquisition of language, where the terms 'he', 'she', 'you', etc., become possible. It is on this assumption that Lacan asserts that there is a link between the genital organization of sexuality in the Oedipus complex and the acquisition of language. It represents the intervention of a third term, breaking up the dual relation dominant in the early imaginary identifications of the ego. For the latter, please see below.

5. The Imaginary is an order in which the ego participates in an experience of itself as an illusory totality or unity. It is not simply a stage which is terminated with the castration complex and the establishment of symbolic relations, but persists in unconscious formations such as phantasy, etc.

6. The Oedipus complex is named after the king in Sophocles' tragedy ... It is an organized body of loving and hostile wishes which the child experiences towards its parents around three to five years. The Oedipus complex is crucial in organizing the personality and sexual desire.

7. As used here, 'the Real' designates not so much the concrete, tangible world but rather a conceptual opposite on the one hand to the Imaginary – where the dual relation of the mirror phase excludes the Real fragmented body/being of the child. On the other hand the Real is opposed to the Symbolic inasmuch as it refers to that empirical realm for which the Symbolic is a coding, a structuring which gives access of articulation – 'the Real is not synonymous with external reality, but with what is real for the subject', Wilden in *The Language of the Self* (Baltimore: Johns Hopkins, 1968).

8. Narcissism: when the subject takes itself as love object. This is said to be (i) a developmental stage, common to boys and girls, when autoerotism dominates and this stage is seen as necessary and basic to becoming able to love another. For in loving oneself one constructs an ego that can meet that of another with the possibility of exchange taking place. Otherwise the other can only be seen, for example, in terms of incorporation.
(ii) Narcissism can also be structural, that is, where the energy of instincts related to all the aspects of 'love' becomes attached only to the self.

Narcissism has been described in two ways, as primary and secondary, that need elucidation since we here argue against the former's use. Primary narcissism is conceived of as a state with no referential object, where the person is locked in Imaginary relations to themselves and dominated by an image of themselves. Secondary narcissism, in contradistinction to the above, sees the love of self as deriving from the withdrawal of libidinal energy formerly attached to other objects and its attachment to the self. That is, this definition of narcissism suggests there is no state when the infant does not have some kind of object relations.

9. This is a crucially important part of Lacan's theory. It was the first work published which stressed his position that the ego, the 'I', is constructed and not pre-given. This, we believe, is crucial for feminism since the whole theoretical premise of feminism is that 'femininity' is constructed culturally and socially, and not something 'essential'.

10. The ego-ideal serves as a reference point for the ego's evaluation of itself. It is narcissistic in origin, as the ideal is the substitute for the period of childhood in which the child was its own ideal.

11. The super-ego marks the definitive identification by the child with a parent of either sex. It is heir to the Oedipus complex in that it is the resolution of incestuous desire. Through identification the child internalizes parental prohibitions and takes its place as a sexed subject within society. In addition to the functions of conscience, the super-ego includes those of self-observation and of the ideal.

12. The 'phallus' has no physical representation but is the concept, the symbolic term for the structural operation of the actual penis in the organizing of sexual difference. It is a term which posits an absence or presence – which is signifier of sexual difference but also of lack inasmuch as in signifying absence through marking presence it will signify that which is lost from being present – absent.

13. Drives: the term is usually given as 'instinct' in translations of Freud's term *Triebe*. But this is a mistranslation and we prefer to use the original term of drives which is less easily appropriated to biologism. Instinct is used in a special sense in biological writings as an inherited behaviour pattern; Freud distinguishes from this *Triebe*/Drive, which can only be known through its mental representatives, or aims. The aim of the drive is not to be confused with an object; initially the drive does not have any pre-given object. Drives can be inhibited in their aims and it is their malleability which makes them susceptible to constraint by interaction with the external world.

14. Erotogenic zones are parts of the body where excitation of a sexual nature is focused. The primary zones are the mouth, the anus, and the genitals. Within psycho-sexual development, these zones succeed each other in their importance in the child's interaction with its environment.

15. This process Freud names the Pleasure Principle, which, with the Reality Principle, constituted the two major operations by which the ego is constructed. Lacan correctly remarks that it would have been more accurate to call it the 'Unpleasure Principle' since it involves primarily the expulsion of that which produces unpleasurable tensions.

Bibliography

Althusser, L., 'Freud and Lacan' in *Lenin and Philosophy and Other Essays* (London: New Left Books, 1971).

Derrida, J., 'Freud and the Scene of Writing' in *Yale French Studies*, No. 48, 1972.

Freud, S., *Beyond the Pleasure Principle*, Standard Edition (London: Hogarth Press), Vol. XVIII; *Interpretation of Dreams*, S.E. Vol. V (London: Penguin Freud Library, 1975); *Instincts and their Vicissitudes*, S.E. Vol. XIV; *Fetishism*, S.E. Vol. XXI; *Notes Upon a Mystic Writing Pad*, S.E. Vol. XIX; *Outline of Psychoanalysis*, S.E. Vol. XVIII (Penguin Freud Library, 1975); *On Negation*, S.E. Vol. XIX; *Delusion and Dreams in Jensen's 'Gradiva'*, S.E. Vol. IX.

Hirst, Paul Q., *Problems and Advances in the Theory of Ideology* (Cambridge University Communist Party, 1976).

Kristeva, J., *et al.*, in *Edinburgh Magazine '76*, Edinburgh Film Festival.

Lacan, J., *Écrits* (London: Tavistock (English trans.) in preparation); 'The Insistence of the Letter in the Unconscious' in J. Ehrmann (ed.), *Structuralism* (New York: Anchor Books, 1970); 'The Mirror Phase as Formative of the Function of the "I"' in *New Left Review*, No. 51, 1968; 'Of Structure as an Inmixing of Otherness Prerequisite to any Subject Whatsoever' in J. Macksey and E. Donato (ed.), *The Structuralist Controversy* (Baltimore: Johns Hopkins, 1970); 'Seminar on the "Purloined Letter"' in *Yale French Studies*, No. 48, 1972.

Laplanche, J., and Pontalis, J. B., *The Language of Psychoanalysis* (London: Hogarth Press, 1973).

Laplanche, J., and Leclaire, S., 'The Unconscious: A Psychoanalytic Study' in *Yale French Studies*, No. 48, 1972.

Lemaire, A., *Jacques Lacan* (London: RKP, in preparation).

Mannoni, O., *Freud: The Theory of the Unconscious* (London: New Left Books, 1971).

Miel, J., 'Jacques Lacan and the Structure of the Unconscious' in J. Ehrmann (ed.), *Structuralism* (New York: Anchor Books, 1970).

Mitchell, J., *Psychoanalysis and Feminism* (London: Penguin Books, 1975).

Russel, J., 'Introduction to J. Lacan' in *New Left Review*, No. 51, 1968.

Schneiderman, S., 'Afloat with Jacques Lacan' in *Diacritics*, Winter 1971.

Wilden, A., *Language of the Self* (Baltimore: Johns Hopkins, 1968).

Jeff Weeks

The Development of Sexual Theory and Sexual Politics

The Politicization of Sex

The politicization of sex is not new. Concern with sexuality has been at the heart of social debate since the late eighteenth century (Foucault 1979) and it has been a continent for conscious theoretical exploration, social intervention and reforming endeavour since at least the end of the nineteenth century (Weeks 1981). Even the term 'sexual politics' has been current since the 1930s, when Wilhelm Reich employed it (Reich 1969), and the past generation has seen a host of campaigns focused on sexual issues, whether the outcrop of moral panics on subjects such as prostitution and homosexuality (Hall 1980) or the result of liberalizing campaigns (Weeks 1977). But it is only since the 1960s that a consciously radical series of movements around sexual politics has been of major social significance, a product of complex historical changes, with unpredictable social consequences. These have begun a fundamental challenge to our received ways of thinking of sex. In particular, the emergence in the 1960s and 1970s of the 'sexual liberation' movements (especially the women's and gay movements) has radically challenged the 'naturalness' and 'inevitability' of sex roles, identities and behaviours. In doing so, they have also demonstrated the inadequacies of most theories of sexuality, both liberal and self-consciously 'revolutionary'; ideologies, it should be added, which shaped the early concepts and practices of the movements themselves. What the early sex radical movements claimed to do was to speak for sexualities which more generally were seen as having been distorted or denied (such as female sexuality) or severely socially condemned and prohibitively regulated (such as homosexuality). But in speaking positively of much that had seemed, literally, unspeakable, these movements ultimately demonstrated the historically constructed nature of the categories that shape our ways of thinking of, and living, sex; and began the long-term dispersal and disintegration of these imprisoning unitary forms – at least on the level of theory. The new social movements of the past two decades have forced new ways of seeing personal and sexual relations, and in doing so have produced different ways of conceiving sexuality. There is, in other words, a difficult but definite relationship between social practices and sexual theory. Sexuality is not a realm to be discovered in ever more luxuriant detail; it is a historical edifice that has been constructed, and can be changed.

'Beneath the Cobblestones the Beach': The Problem of Naturalism

Amongst the many insights thrown up during the May events in Paris in 1968 was the striking phrase 'beneath the cobblestones the beach'. What this suggests is that underneath the thin patina of 'civilization' (a term used derisively in the nineteenth century by socialists such as Fourier and Edward Carpenter as a synonym for capitalism) there exists a natural life which can provide a basis for a better life. This naturalistic approach has been at the core of much of the recent politics of sexuality. The overwhelming tendency of the early radical exponents of 'sexual liberation' was to speak of a sexuality that had been denied, to make positive what had been negativized. So the notion of 'coming out' in the gay movement does not simply imply a social move from furtiveness to honesty; it is also an affirmation of an execrated sexuality. It implied a 'liberation' of hitherto perverse desires. The notion of 'liberation' was of course part of the whole 1960s rhetoric of radical protest, whether associated with national, ethnic or gender liberation, and formed its rhetorical echo in the counter-culture and the politics of experience and authenticity that formed the eventual backdrop to the emergence of women's and gay liberation (Weeks 1977). But with regard to sexuality it carries another weight, and one which has been central to our whole way of seeing sexuality: it counterposes itself to a sexuality that has been 'repressed'. And in this dialectic of repression–liberation we have the core of the problem. For implicit here is what may be termed a 'hydraulic theory' of sexuality, which has been common to most concepts of sex – whether conservative, liberal or radical – for over a hundred years, a theory which has had the additional advantage of appearing common-sensical and rooted in experience.

In this view sex is conceived of as an overpowering, instinctual force, whose characteristics are built into the biology of the human animal, which shapes human institutions and whose will will out, either in the form of direct sexual expression, or, if blocked, in the form of perversion or neuroses . . . Here we have a clear notion of a 'basic biological mandate' that presses on, and so must be firmly controlled by the cultural and social matrix. [Weeks 1981]

This is what Gagnon and Simon (1974) have termed the 'drive reduction' model, and what is peculiar about it is that it was until recently adopted by most theorists of sex. It was unquestionably present in the work of the nineteenth-century pioneering sexologists from Krafft-Ebing to Havelock Ellis. It is residually present in the work of Freud, despite the efforts he made to distinguish between component 'instincts' (which are biological) and drive (which is mentally shaped). And in the work of most post-Freudians an hydraulic model is often fundamentally present. Even in the case of writers like Kinsey, whose work radically demystified sexuality, and whose taxonomic efforts undermined the notions of 'normality', the concept is still traceable in the emphasis on sexual 'outlet' as opposed to beliefs or identities. Above all, with regard to our purpose here, the model is present in the writings of the Freudian left, Reich, Fromm, Marcuse, and this is particularly important because it was these theorists who crucially provided the analytic categories for the sexual liberation movements (Watney 1980). Take, for instance, a writer heavily influenced by Marcuse, Reimut Reiche, whose book *Sexuality and the Class Struggle* preceded the emergence of the women's or gay movements but is clearly a product of the same conjuncture (Reiche 1970). Sexuality for him is a biological force, like the desire for food. Its appearance is spontaneous and natural. 'The manifestations of the sexual urge in earliest childhood ... arise independently of the child's own volition' (p. 28) and have what he calls a 'natural goal' (p. 29). It is a forceful energy which the social controls in the interests of the perpetuation of a particular social order. What is surprising is that such a naturalism occurs amongst Marxists who in other regards have shown themselves anxious to challenge the notion of 'natural man'. Marx has perforce reluctantly gone to bed with a Freud married to nineteenth-century biology.

For Reiche, as for Reich and Marcuse and others before him, the social control has been in the interests of capital. But a very influential feminist position has also partaken of the same essentialism. It is noticeable that most of the views I have cited so far are male-orientated. Krafft-Ebing (1892) spoke in the nineteenth century of a 'natural instinct' which 'with all conquering force and might demands fulfilment.' The clear presupposition here is that the sex drive is male, with the female conceived of as a passive receptacle; the language used then permeates most writings on sex, so that, in appearing genderless, it actually excludes any discussion of female sexuality. But since the 1960s there has been a powerful tendency, reinforced especially by the clinical findings on female physiological response of Masters and Johnson (1966, 1970), which has stressed the superior strength and power of female sexuality, a potentiality which has been denied by patriarchy. Mary Jane Sherfey (1972), for instance, in *The Nature and Evolution of Female Sexuality* (which explicitly acknowledges the influence of Masters and Johnson) stresses the thwarted potentialities of the clitoral orgasm.

> The rise of modern civilization ... was contingent on the suppression of the inordinate cyclical sexual drive of women because (a) ... women's uncurtailed hypersexuality would drastically interfere with maternal responsibilities; and (b) ... large families of known parentage were mandatory and could not endure until the inordinate sexual demands of women were curbed. [p. 144]

In this curious transmutation of Freud, it is the suppression of female sexuality which is essential for (patriarchal) civilization. What it suggests is the sexual colonization of women by men, and a necessary struggle against men as the precondition for female liberation.

In this feminist version, the moment of liberation coincides with the freeing of female sexuality from male control. In the Freudo–Marxist version, liberation is associated with the ending of capitalist control of sexuality. But central to both views is an essentialist notion of a rebellious energy which is dammed by social repression, and a belief in a potential release and transmutation of this energy if social control is cracked.

This approach has had major implications with regard to political practice. Firstly, there is a clear assumption, which can be traced back to Fourier and nineteenth-century romantics, that the release of sexual energy would be beneficent; it is controlled precisely because its force is so disruptive and radical. In the work of Marcuse (1969) this energy is undifferentiated, both bisexual and polymorphously perverse; it is the effects of capitalism that distort and narrow this potential, so that homosexuality is the great refusal of normality. In the work of Mario Mieli, this undifferentiated Eros is originally transsexual; the heterosexual norm is based on the suppression of the homosexual potentialities in all of us, so that 'If homosexuality is liberated then it ceases to sustain this system, comes into conflict with it and contributes to its collapse' (Mieli 1980). In other words, the practice of outlawed sexualities is actually a way of breaking down the rigidly organized forms of sexuality.

It follows from this that there is a functional link between the organization of sex and the forms of capital. Sexuality is shaped in the interests of capital. In Reich's version the agency of control is the family; in Marcuse it tends to be the organizing ('one-dimensional') effect of capitalist industry itself (Marcuse 1968). But in all such cases, there is the notion of a willing, planning capitalism, which consciously regulates sexuality, usually through the organization of definite and restrictive social roles and rigid gender divisions (Brake 1976). From this stems a radical distrust of modern permissive forms of 'liberation, capitalist style'. Thus Marcuse sees the transformations in the relations of sex which have taken place in advanced capitalist countries as a form of repressive desublimation.

Sex is integrated into work and public relations and is thus made more susceptible to (controlled) satisfaction ... The range of sexually permissible and desirable satisfaction is greatly enlarged, but through this satisfaction the Pleasure Principle is reduced – deprived of the claims which are irreconcilable with the established society. Pleasure, thus adjusted, generates submission. [Marcuse 1968, p. 71]

Or, as Reiche (1970, p. 46) has put it,

Sexuality is given a little more rein and thus brought into the service of safeguarding the system.

There has been, according to this perspective, a 'partial sexual liberation', producing a false sexuality, which palliates while leaving the real structures of power untouched. Posed against this is the notion of a true sexuality which can only be found in a genuine liberation. Thus, as Ros Coward has written,

the ideas of incorporation and controlled expansion of consciousness are the two ways in which the problem of sexual liberation has been dealt with in left-wing analyses. [Coward 1980, p. 11]

Such an approach has been valuable in subjecting modern liberal sexual norms to a searching moral critique, not from the standards of the past but from the viewpoint of a potential future. But it is based on a theoretical approach which I believe to be misconceived, and which a great deal of recent work has challenged. In the first place it relies on a concept of sexuality which is essentialist and therefore ahistorical. Against this I would argue for a recognition of the social and historical construction of sexuality. Secondly, it is based on an inadequate notion of the relations of power, concentrating in a narrow way on the state and

family as agencies of repression and ignoring other forms of the regulation of sex. Thirdly it concentrates too much on the moment of liberation, rather than on the diverse forms of struggle which all the time shift
the definitions and relations of sex. Furthermore, by over-emphasizing
'liberation' it becomes all too easy to slip from an awareness of the
necessary links between social and personal change to a concentration
on *personal* liberation, a tendency which is clearly discernible in the
aftermath of the sexual radical movements in the U.S.A. (Turkle 1979,
p. 73).

Revolutions of Desire

It was the inadequacy of this model as a guide to action – whatever its
real importance as a moral critique of both traditional and permissive
attitudes towards sex – that directed many feminists in the 1970s
towards the dazzling allures of Paris – and in particular towards an
engagement with the work of Jacques Lacan and the Lacanian school of
psychoanalysis (cf. Mitchell 1974). For what Lacan had attempted was a
discovery of Freud from the biological encrustations of both immediate
post-Freudians and the Freudo–Marxists. For Lacan, Freud's work
represents the beginnings of a new science of the unconscious whose aim
is to uncover the 'truth of the subject', the individual as a sexually
constituted being (Lacan 1977, 1979). Central to Lacan's work – which
has dominated French psychoanalytic debates since the 1950s, despite
the schisms it has generated (Turkle 1979) – is the notion that society
does not influence an autonomous individual, but that the individual is
constituted by the social world, the world of language and symbols,
which come to dwell in the individual. As Sherry Turkle has put it,

> Lacan's theory of the construction of the symbolic order, when language and
> law enters man, allows for no real boundary between self and society ... Man
> becomes social with the appropriation of language, and it is language that consti-
> tutes man as a subject. [Turkle 1979, p. 74]

Such an approach offered a way of linking the relationship between the
individual and society which, say, Reich's approach could not. For in
Lacan's work there is no 'natural man' who is distorted by society;
subjectivity is formed as individuals become aware of their alienation
from themselves, in the pre-Oedipal imaginary realm, which always
remains with them; and then as through the Oedipal moment individuals
become aware of the structures of human sexuality into which they have

to be inducted by the rules of culture. The Oedipus crisis itself is instigated by the child's growing awareness of the sexual rules that are embedded in the kin relations of the culture. It is resolved by the acceptance of the prohibitions represented by the law of the Father; the emergence of the child as a sexual being, a psychological man or woman; and by the consequent creation of the unconscious as the repository of culturally impossible wishes and demands. What this means with regard to sexuality is that there is no insistent desire which pre-exists the entry into language and culture. 'Desire' is constituted in the very process of that induction, in which the component instincts and the polymorphous perversity of the young human are involuntarily 'conscripted', in Althusser's phrase (Althusser 1971), into the demands of culture. Desire is predicated upon absence, lack; upon wishes which cannot be allowed access to consciousness. So it is not a relentless physical force which is repressed, but unattainable wishes or desires which organize and unify sexual potentialities.

Lacanian psychoanalysis has had an important influence in recent Anglo-Saxon discourse in a double way: through the Althusserian theorization of ideology and subjectivity, which is heavily reliant on Lacanian theorization of the 'imaginary' realm; and through the feminist re-appropriation of Freud represented by Juliet Mitchell's *Psychoanalysis and Feminism* (1974). This latter approach has been immensely important in theorizing sexual difference and the patriarchal construction of femininity. In analysing structures of patriarchy, it has also moved away from the phallocentricity which besets Lacan's work – though at the expense of adding to the power structures of capitalism another set of relationships which are not transparently congruent with it. The result of this has been a certain ahistoricity in theories of patriarchy which Mitchell's own historical materialism does not entirely obscure (Beechey 1979; Campioni and Gross 1978).

Its crucial importance is that it has opened out the question of the psychological structuring of individuality and the theory of subjectivity in ways which complement the major concerns of the sexual liberation movements. Some writers, going beyond Mitchell's position and heavily influenced by semiological theories, have argued that the idea of the unconscious and subjectivity as produced in language simultaneously proposes their pluralism, diversity, heterogeneity and contradictoriness – and hence their potentialities for change (Coward and Ellis 1977). This is potentially a major adjunct to theories of sexual liberation. The problem remains of theorizing the relationship between the ideological categories which address particular subjects, and the processes by which individual meanings and identities are formed. This has to be both a theoretical and historical question, and as yet little work has been done in this field. The theories have remained abstract and unparticularized (but see Campioni and Gross 1978).

One step is to question the category of 'the symbolic' itself. For a Marxist like Althusser, the entry of the individual into the order of language is an entry into the human. But for many influenced by the 'revolution of desire' signalled by the May events of 1968 it was precisely this human order that was an imposition. Leaving the world of flux that precedes 'Oedipalization' and acculturation is the real human tragedy, for in that flux desire was polymorphous and hence 'revolutionary'. Out of May, in other words, grew a current of what Turkle (1979) has called a 'political naturalism' which urged, in a mode partaking in many ways of a classic irrationalism, a return to man's freedom, spontaneity and unmediated desire represented by the pre-symbolic. This approach was distanced from that of the Frankfurt–American School by its acceptance of Lacanian theories of how society enters the individual. But now society itself is condemned, along with Lacan's phallocentrism, the family, Oedipus – and psychoanalysis itself, which is crucially seen as an agent for the imposition of Oedipus and the control of desire. The major exponents of this position were Gilles Deleuze and Felix Guattari (1977) in their book *Anti-Oedipus*, first published in French in 1972.

Like Lacan, whose writing is complex and unconventional, Deleuze and Guattari attempt to challenge ordinary language as well as conventional theory, with the result that in *Anti-Oedipus* we are presented with a world whose complexity and flux defy language. For them any concept of Oedipus implies artificial restrictions on a field of the unconscious, where everything is in fact infinitely open. There is, in this flux, no given 'self', only the cacophony of 'desiring machines'. Fragmentation is universal, and is not the peculiar fate of what society defines as the schizophrenic. But the crucial point is that capitalist society cannot live with the infinite variety of potential interconnections and relationships, and imposes constraints regulating which ones are to be allowed, essentially those relating to reproduction in the family. Psychoanalysis, by accepting the familial framework, is trapped within capitalist concepts of sexuality, concepts which distort the production of desire. For, by concentrating on the Oedipal triangulation of parents and child, it reflects the social, political and religious forms of domination in modern society, and is complicit with how capitalism has constructed the family. Deleuze and Guattari argue that the individual's consciousness is not determined by a closed family system, but by a historical situation. So they can analyse and criticize the family, for example, in terms of the desires expressed during May 1968. Desire then becomes an element in the social field, an active participant in social life, not just an element in the individual's psyche. The Oedipus complex, instead of being, as in Lacan, a necessary state in the development of the human individual, is seen by Deleuze and Guattari as the only effective means of controlling the libido in capitalist society. So Freudianism plays a key role under capitalism: it is both the discoverer of the mechanisms of desire, and the organizer, through its acceptance of the Oedipus complex, of its control.

Such a position can have radical implications for sexual politics, particularly as it goes with a rejection of conventional forms of political activity and amounts to a glorification of the excluded, the marginal: the schizophrenic, the child, the 'perverse' individual. Guy Hocquenghem (1978) uses this mode to theorize gay liberation in a way which has been very influential. It is based on the assumption that 'Desire', properly speaking, is neither homosexual nor heterosexual. Desire, as Deleuze and Guattari state, is 'emergent', and its components are only discernible in the process of their expression. Homosexual desire, like heterosexual desire, is an arbitrary division of the flux of desire, an 'arbitrarily frozen frame' in an unbroken and polyvocal flux. The notion of exclusive homosexuality like that of heterosexuality is therefore an ideological misperception. But at the same time homosexuality expresses an aspect of desire, which is fundamentally polymorphous and undefined, which appears nowhere else, and which is more than just sexual activity between members of the same sex. For the direct manifestation of homosexual desire opposes the relations of roles and identities necessarily imposed by the Oedipus complex in order to ensure the reproduction of society.

The practice of homosexuality, therefore, in itself is radical, challenging the norms of civilization: homosexual promiscuity is a revolutionary act. The trouble is that both in Hocquenghem and in Mieli (1980), who shares some of the same assumptions, the homosexuality that is glorified is male, and this approach has had insurmountable problems in proposing a sexual politics that is equally relevant for women (Weeks 1978).

The Construction of Sexuality

The merits of an approach such as this, however, lie in its suggestion that categories of sex are imposed upon a sexual flux; or, to put it another way, the various erotic possibilities of the body are organized through a variety of social practices that work to produce categorizations and definitions. They are, in a word, historical constructs. This insight has not been peculiar to French theoretical work. On the contrary, a prime elaboration has come from a different theoretical area, that of post-Kinsey sex research in the U.S.A. and Britain, which has been informed by a symbolic interactionist social psychology and a labelling theory of deviance (Gagnon and Simon 1974; Plummer 1975). So, for instance, with regard to homosexuality, the focus shifts from the causes of the individual 'delinquency' to the social reactions, and the subcultural and individual responses, which together create the possibilities of a sexual identity. A gay identity is not given in nature, or a response to an essential sexuality; it is a social construct (McIntosh 1968; Plummer 1980).

A seminal essay by Mary McIntosh on the 'homosexual role', published in 1968, was a direct response to the narrow approach of the homophile organization of the time, which tended to stress homosexuality as a separate condition. Its appearance shortly before the emergence of the gay liberation movement fed into a much wider debate on the nature of sexual identities. McIntosh's essay was by way of a preliminary sketch of the problem. In later work it tended to be the processes of stigmatization that were most closely examined (Plummer 1975), and where a wider historical perspective was offered, it was heavily functionalist in its implications. It was the absence of a sense of historical process that directed attention in the late 1970s to the work of Michel Foucault (1979). There were many common themes in the approaches of the interactionists and of Foucault: in the rejection of essentialism and in the suggestion that power worked not through repression of sexuality but through regulation, organization and categorization. But Foucault's work was embedded in a historical framework that opened up the possibility of a stronger theorization of sexual categorization than hitherto (Weeks 1981, Ch. 1).

Foucault's basic interest is in the genealogy or roots of the forms of 'power knowledge' – power organized through knowledges – that characterize modern societies; the forms of discourses and practices which order the way in which we think of and conceive the 'real world'. He is concerned with the construction of specific categories of social agents and their attributes rather than with individual wills; and in modern societies the discourses on sexuality have a central organizing role. For Foucault rejects the notion that we can fruitfully interpret the history of sexuality as a regime of repression and silence. On the contrary, since the eighteenth century there has been a multiplication and proliferation of discourses on sexuality, a veritable explosion in talking about sex. What he is saying is not so much that there does not exist a universal attribute called sex; but what is defined as sexual is a function of specific discourses and forms of power relationships. And in our culture, sexuality has become a terrain of major social concern: a central object of scientific investigation, self-scrutiny, organization and desire. For it is at the axes of the two major forms of modern political technology: the particular disciplinary techniques of surveillance and control which have since the eighteenth century controlled the individual body (Foucault 1978); and the forms of power relations which have over the same period become obsessed with the size, well-being and regulation of populations.

There are several problems with this approach. A major difficulty concerns Foucault's theory of power, which is entirely relational, so there is no simple form of power, no 'power' a group or class can hold. Power, on the contrary, is omnipresent, internal to all relations. The result is a formidable and useful challenge to rigid class-based or state-orientated theories, but instead a multitude of 'micropowers' marches on to the stage of history – in a fashion which many critics have seen as being as functionalist an embodiment of total social control as the forms of deterministic Marxism that Foucault formally rejects (Poulantzas 1978). Some appropriations of his work by people in the women's and gay movements have taken his insights further, and suggested the irrelevance of the unitary categories of 'women' and 'gay' as foci for sexual-political campaigns. Foucault himself has shown little interest in feminism. As Morris has put it, he is a 'profoundly androcentric writer', and by no means a 'ladies' man' (Morris 1979), but his work on the discourses of femininity, particularly in relationship to the sexualization of the female body, eugenics, and birth control, has led a number of feminists to concentrate on the multitude of often conflicting discourses which have constructed modern womanhood.

Morris has argued, for instance, that

Feminists, both past and present, have run into some very solid brick walls through trusting too lightly to 'the obvious', assuming a continuous and evenly distributed, consistently significant, oppression of the eternal natural object 'woman' or 'women' through the ages. Much of the work going on at the moment which is questioning the 'existence' of women (within different or incompatible frameworks) is attempting to break this wall down and so solidify – or diversify – the grounds for an extension of women's struggles. [Morris 1979, p. 151]

What such an approach suggests is that feminist struggles should be organized over specific problems – of the domestic, the social – rather than around a 'false' unity such as 'the oppression of women' (Adams and Minson 1978). There are, however, dangers here. It is obviously important that the often contradictory organizations of femininity and female sexuality in discourse should be acknowledged. But what such an approach ignores is that feminism *has*, for a variety of reasons, been organized around the notion of 'womanhood' (Coward 1980). Whatever the ultimate relevance of that unification, it must be the starting point for sexual political debate precisely because it is a product of complex historical developments, and is constituted in ideology as a unitary category.

There have been similar attempts to question the relevance of gay politics (Minson 1980). While the logic of gay liberation is indeed to see the disintegration of the unitary category of 'the homosexual', to ignore the specific factors that have constructed homosexuality as an arena for political organization – though not without difficulty (Marshall 1980) – is to ignore the major transformations that have taken place in affirming homosexuality as a valid sexual experience, precisely because of the existence of gay movements.

There is a further difficulty with Foucault's approach. For in rightly recognizing the historical specificity of the western emphasis on sexuality, there is a danger that radicals – in a 'reverse discourse' – will reject its importance altogether. There have been signs of this in debates over such sensitive issues as paedophilia, and in a discussion of the even more delicate topic of rape. Foucault, Hocquenghem and others have gone a good way, in the eyes of many feminists, towards minimizing its significance altogether (see Plaza 1980). Foucault has argued that to treat rape as a sexual crime of violence is to accept that sexualization of life which is in fact social. The obvious problem with this is that if women are constituted as sexed beings (the 'sex') then the question of rape *is* about sex. To argue otherwise is to ignore the historically constituted reality, a strange distortion in a *corpus* which has an ostensibly 'historical' form.

But the major impact of Foucault has been more radical, for what he suggests is that sexual definitions are sites of contradiction and of contestation, are historically formed, and can therefore be socially changed. It is increasingly clear to those engaged in sexual politics that the organization of sex is not through a single strategy of repression in the interests of a 'ruling class' or of 'men'. On the contrary, as Mort (1980) has put it,

> We would maintain that power, or sets of power relations addressing sexuality operate through a multiplicity of practices and apparatuses (for example: medicine, psychology, sociology, education), each of which is distinguished by its specific structures of regulations which are non-reducible to a uniform or single strategy ... power operates 'positively' – it does not merely repress or prohibit, but is actively engaged in the instruction of particular forms of sexuality which will not necessarily remain constant *across* a set of social practices (for example, the construction of homosexuality in the media may well be very different from its construction in law).

Two points may be noted here. In the first place a recognition of the existence of various and contradictory ways of addressing sexual behaviour does open up the path to a more acute awareness of the best forms of intervention necessary to change the relations of power. Secondly, it is clear that there is not a transforming essence that can be released in a definite 'liberation'. There are instead various relations of sexuality, and conflicting definitions of sexuality, which are sustained by, and embedded in, a variety of social practices. Once we recognize this, then the road is open to the development of alternative practices and definitions of sexual behaviour, definitions which owe more to choice than to tradition or inherited moralities.

The Production of Desire

The project of sexual politics does not, then, relate to the release of an imprisoned secret; it is much more about the production and acceptance of alternative sexualities. But this in turn throws the debate on to quite a different plain, for it opens up the question of *who* is to produce new norms; *how* are they to be articulated; *by what means* can they be attained?

There is an apparent paradox in current practices of sexual politics. For on the one hand they start with a recognition of the contradictory nature of sexual identities, the always partial and socially constituted relationship between individual desires and available definitions and practices. On the other, identities are increasingly being constructed *around* sexuality: the effect of the gay movement, for instance, especially in the U.S.A., has been to make the gay identity almost into an ethnic identity, and the separatist tendency in the women's movement, with its emphasis on 'political lesbianism', denotes the same shift. But it is also possible to see that the very extension and broadenings of the available sexual categories as a result of the women's and gay movements point to their disintegration as unitary categories. As the Kinsey Institute recently noted, there is not one homosexuality. On the contrary there are homosexualities (Bell and Weinberg 1978), and the vast expansion of the gay subcultures in recent years has led to a proliferation of styles, specializations and a burgeoning of new identities: paedophile, sado-masochistic, leather and a host of others. As Gayle Rubin has put it,

> For almost a century, it has been women, lesbians and male homosexuals who have comprised the most vocal and organized opposition to the social, ideological, and legal structure of sexuality. More recently a veritable parade out of Krafft-Ebing has begun to lay claim to legitimacy, rights and recognition. [Rubin 1979, p. 28]

But this explosion of new categories, sub-categories, and definitions also points to another question: does this proliferation indicate a 'discovery' of pre-existing desires on the part of the individual, or the constant production and reproduction of new desires? The logic of our argument points to the latter, and if this is so, the implications are radical. For it shifts the whole axis of the debate on sexuality away from sex as an expression of self to sex as a choice of acts; and it thereby returns us to the critical question of what criteria we are to use in evaluating sexual activity.

Not surprisingly, this debate has gone furthest in the U.S.A., where, in the absence of strong class and regional loyalties on the European model, organization around sexual identity seems particularly strong. A discussion that has sprung up amongst feminists in the U.S.A. about lesbian sado-masochism will provide a useful example. *Samois*, a group of feminist lesbians positively interested in S/M, has argued that 'it can and should be consistent with the principles of feminism' (Samois 1979). To justify this they have adopted what is essentially a contract view of sex: sex activity should be based on an arrangement between people to engage in erotic activities of an agreed kind in order to attain pleasure. In this argument any form of sexual activity is justified if it is mutually agreed upon. So, for example, 'humiliation' is defined as 'An S/M game that involves deliberately lowering the status of the masochist. This lowered status is a temporary condition and exists only for erotic purposes'. The premise of this 'game' is that the rules are laid down beforehand and that in the world outside the partners should have social equality, be 'members of the same sexual caste'. Within these limitations, anything, apparently, goes.

Although this is an extreme example, the logic is present in the whole approach of radical sexual politics. It questions the relationship between sex and love, sex and relationships, sex and union: all the forms in which sexuality has generally been thought. It institutes, in its place, sex as a pleasure, as fun, as play. In doing so, it also demotes it. Sex will no longer be 'the truth of our being' (Foucault 1979); it will instead be a question of pleasurable choice. But there is a fundamental ambiguity in this, which has been well described by a critic of the lesbian S/M pamphlet, Marianne Valverde (1980).

Ever new forms of eroticism, yet more difficult positions, more bizarre pleasures ... is this not too much like the production of ever more bizarre commodities characteristic of consumer capitalism?... The time is ripe for realizing that the endless production of sexual images and sexual practices that we are experiencing today is neither completely repressive (as the guardians of morality would have it) nor is it completely progressive (as certain advocates of 'sexual liberation' would have it). As Foucault has argued, bourgeois society is *not* characterized by repression of the sexual as much as for its multiplication and intensification. There will always be yet another frontier, yet more shocking sex acts, and when faced with this sea of endlessly collapsing barriers we must stop to ask: liberation for what?

It is clear that old ways of conceiving of sexuality are no longer viable; but there is no agreement on the forms that are to replace them. A pluralism of experience, the exaltation of what Foucault calls the body and its pleasures, take the place of traditional moralities, but many radicals have lamented the forms these have taken (Fernbach 1980). The debate is still open. But henceforth it must surely be based on a recognition of the relative plasticity of sexuality; and on the real possibilities that exist for the social production of desires. If this is so then the real task of sexual politics today lies not in pursuing the will-of-the-wisp of a legendary 'liberation'. It lies in clarifying the choices we all have to make on the ultimate aim of sexual politics – to gain control of our bodies.

References

Adams, P. and Minson, J. (1978) 'The "subject" of feminism', *M/F*, No. 2.

Althusser, L. (1971) *Lenin and Philosophy* (London: New Left Books).

Beechey, V. (1979) 'On Patriarchy', *Feminist Review*, No. 3.

Bell, A. P. and Weinberg, M. S. (1979) *Homosexualities: A Study of Diversity among Men and Women* (London: Mitchell Beazley).

Brake, M. (1976) 'I may be a queer but at least I am a man', in D. L. Barker and S. Allen (ed.), *Sexual Divisions and Society: Process and Change* (London: Tavistock).

Campioni, M. and Gross, L. (1978) ' Little Hans; the Production of Oedipus', in P. Foss and M. Morris (ed.), *Language, Sexuality and Subversion* (Darlington, NSW: Feral Publications).

Coward, R. (1980) 'Socialism, Feminism and Socialist Feminism', *Gay Left*, No. 10.

Coward, R. and Ellis, J. (1977) *Language and Materialism* (London: Routledge & Kegan Paul).

Deleuze, G. and Guattari, F. (1977) *Anti-Oedipus: Capitalism and Schizophrenia* (New York: Viking Press).

Fernbach, D. (1980) 'Ten Years of Gay Liberation', *Politics and Power*, No. 2.

Foucault, M. (1978) *Discipline and Punish. The Birth of the Prison* (London: Allen Lane).

Foucault, M. (1979) *History of Sexuality*, Volume 1, *An Introduction* (trans. of *La Volonté de savoir*, Paris: Gallimard, 1976).

Gagnon, J. H. and Simon, W. (1974) *Sexual Conduct. The Social Sources of Human Sexuality* (London: Hutchinson).

Gay Left (ed.) (1980) *Homosexuality: Power and Politics* (London: Allison & Busby).

Hall, S. (1980) 'Reformism and the legislation of consent', in National Deviancy Conference (ed.), *Permissiveness and Control. The Fate of the Sixties Legislation* (London: Macmillan).

Hocquenghem, G. (1978) *Homosexual Desire* (London: Allison & Busby).

Krafft-Ebing, R. von (1892) *Psychopathia Sexualis* (London).

Lacan, J. (1977) *Écrits: A Selection* (New York: W. W. Norton).

Lacan, J. (1979) *The Four Fundamental Concepts of Psycho-Analysis* (Harmondsworth: Penguin).

Marcuse, H. (1968) *One-Dimensional Man* (London: Sphere).

Marcuse, H. (1969) *Eros and Civilization* (London: Sphere).

Marshall, J. (1980) 'The Politics of Tea and Sympathy', in Gay Left, op. cit.

Masters, W. H. and Johnson, V. E. (1966) *Human Sexual Response* (Boston: Little, Brown).

Masters, W. H. and Johnson, V. E. (1970) *Human Sexual Inadequacy* (Boston: Little, Brown).

McIntosh, M. (1968) 'The Homosexual Role', *Social Problems* (Fall 1965), republished in Plummer (1980), op. cit.

Mieli, M. (1980) *Homosexuality and Liberation. Elements of a Gay Critique* (London: Gay Men Press).

Minson, J. (1980) 'Strategies for socialists? Foucault's conception of powers', *Economy and Society*, Vol. 9, No. 1 (February 1980).

Mitchell, J. (1974) *Psychoanalysis and Feminism* (London: Allen Lane).

Morris, M. (1979) 'The Pirate's Fiancée', in M. Morris and P. Patton (ed.), *Michel Foucault. Power, Truth, Strategy* (Sydney: Feral Publications).

Mort, F. (1980) 'Sexuality: Regulation and Contestation', in Gay Left, op. cit.

Plaza, M. (1980) 'Our Costs and their Benefits', *M/F*, No. 4.

Plummer, K. (1975) *Sexual Stigma: An Interactionist Account* (London: Routledge & Kegan Paul).

Plummer, K. (ed.) (1980) *The Making of the Modern Homosexual* (London: Hutchinson).

Poulantzas, N. (1978) *State, Power, Socialism* (London: New Left Books).

Reich, W. (1969) *The Sexual Revolution* (New York: Farrar, Straus and Giroux).

Reiche, R. (1970) *Sexuality and the Class Struggle* (London: New Left Books).

Rubin, G. (1979) 'Sexual Politics, the New Right, and the Sexual Fringe', in Samois, op. cit.

Samois (1979) *What Color is your Handkerchief? a lesbian S/M Sexuality reader* (Berkeley, Ca.: Samois).

Sherfey, M. J. (1972) *The Nature and Evolution of Female Sexuality* (New York: Random House).

Turkle, S. (1979) *Psychoanalytic Politics, Freud's French Revolution* (London: Burnett Books in association with Andre Deutsch).

Valverde, M. (1980) 'Feminism Meets fist-fucking: getting lost in lesbian S & M', *Body Politic* (Feb./May 1980).

Watney, S. (1980) 'The Ideology of GLF', in Gay Left, op. cit.

Weeks, J. (1977) *Coming Out: Homosexual Politics in Britain from the Nineteenth Century to the Present* (London: Quartet).

Weeks, J. (1978) 'Preface' to Hocquenghem, op. cit.

Weeks, J. (1981) *Sex, Politics and Society: The Regulation of Sexuality since 1800* (London: Longman).

Michèle Barrett

Female Sexuality

This article is based on a section of Chapter 2 ('Femininity, Masculinity and Sexual Practice') of Michèle Barrett's book *Women's Oppression Today* (London: NLB and Verso, 1980).

The note of perplexed desperation struck by Freud when he asked 'What does a woman want?'[1] resounds through the history of attempts to analyse female sexuality. The myth that women's sexuality is more elusive, more difficult to examine and explain than men's, is one that must be confronted at the outset. It is a myth with many contributory sources, of which I shall merely suggest three. First, it would not be unduly unfair to suggest that it is a rationalization of mundane ignorance resulting from a straightforward failure to do the necessary research. Much of the literature on sexuality is implicitly or explicitly addressed to male sexuality. This is true not only of work on heterosexuality, but of studies of sexual deviance. As Annabel Faraday in her paper 'Liberating Lesbian Research'[2] forcefully points out, theories of male homo-sexuality have been elaborated in detail and then assumed to be appli-cable to the lesbian 'counterpart'. When this is unsuccessful, for the rather obvious reason that masculinity and femininity are constructed differently in our society, these researchers can by-pass the problem with a puzzled footnote.

Secondly, there is a long tradition of trying to analyse female sexuality as a negative sub-set of that of men. Freud here is an exemplary case. Having built up an extremely powerful model of the psychic and familial processes by which masculinity and male psycho-sexual maturity are developed, he later attempted to modify the theory to deal with women. The result is notoriously inadequate. We are asked, in effect, to believe that the acquisition and development of mature femininity rest on the fragile and precarious concept of penis-envy. The girl rejects her mother and takes her father as love object on recognition of her unalterable castration, the tortuous process by which she is torn from her original love object being initiated by a momentary sighting of the 'superior' male genitalia.[3] Some feminists have rightly derided Freud for this instantiation of male chauvinism, and even those otherwise convinced by Freud's work are hard put to strengthen this peculiarly weak link in the chain of his analysis. In Lacan's re-theorization of Freudian psycho-analytic work the vocabulary deployed in relation to women and femi-ninity reveals a parallel failure to consider female sexuality other than in terms of how it differs from male. For Lacan woman is defined by her *lack* of the phallus, her entry into the symbolic order a *negative* one.[4] This is not wholly innocent. The desiring sexual subject is defined as male, against which the female is negatively counterposed, and the vocabulary itself is strangely reminiscent of Simone de Beauvoir's dis-cussion of the ways in which man is constructed as 'subject' and woman as 'other'.[5] It is a perspective constituted around a polarity between masculinity and femininity whereby the latter is inevitably destined to remain marginal, ill accounted for and mythologized.[6]

Thirdly, the elusiveness of female sexuality is assumed in the frequently repeated notion that it (whatever 'it' may be) has been repressed. This view is often put forward by feminists, as well as by others, and leads inescapably to the inference that since female sexuality has never been allowed free play we cannot know what it is. Although it is clearly the case that women have been subjected to sexual violence of many kinds, have in many cases had their sexuality reduced to procreative functions, have been constricted by male efforts to secure proven paternity and so on, it is not clear that these processes are illuminated by a generalized use of a concept of repression. Attempts to argue that, contrary to appearances, female sexuality is 'really' insatiable court the obvious danger of essentialism.[7] They take no account of the ways in which, as the symbolic interaction-ists have persuasively demonstrated,[8] sexual behaviour is learnt, socially scripted behaviour on the natural determinants of which we should properly remain agnostic.

I have mentioned these three points simply to indicate that from a variety of perspectives there has been an inadequate theorization of female sexuality. It would be wrong, however, to assume that the prob-lem lies specifically with female sexuality. The illusion that the sexuality of women is less readily understood than that of men springs from the assumption that we do know what male sexuality is. But although much of the work on sexuality has implicitly addressed itself to male sexuality rather than female it has not done so directly enough to generate an adequate knowledge of masculine identity and male erotic behaviour.

Work on female sexuality therefore shares equally, but no more so, in the problems common to the field in general.

Perhaps the most general problem in assessing the different perspectives on sexuality is that we are frequently faced with a dilemma between reductionist and relativist accounts, neither of which are satisfactory. On the one hand, codes of sexual practice have often been seen as functional for particular forms of social organization. Thus we can 'explain', for instance, taboos on non-procreative sex, or a double standard of sexual morality, by reference to, say, capitalism's need for a specific family structure through which to reproduce its relations of production. Arguments of this kind have most frequently been put by Marxists seeking to provide a materialist analysis of sexual and familial ideology.[9] The main problem with reductionist accounts of this type is the difficulty they face in marshalling the variety and diversity of sexual practices at any given historical moment into the confines of the particular explanation on offer. In their most mechanical form they provide little scope for exploring the different experiential meanings of sexuality and cannot account for the range and incidence of sexual deviance. The reverse problem arises in the highly relativistic approach developed in the interactionist tradition. Here the stress on learnt definitions and 'scripted' sexual behaviour has in practice led to an emphasis on deviant sexual socialization and the role of formative subcultures.[10] So convincingly are these processes depicted that we can barely discern among the wealth of sexual variety described why or how a majority of people are socialized into normative heterosexuality.

The dilemma between reductionist and relativist accounts of sexuality rests ultimately on problems in the theory of ideology. The importance of definition and meaning in sexual practice and the degree to which ideas about sexuality are elaborated in a broader social context render it an area which must necessarily be explored through some concept of ideology. As Lawrence Stone appositely remarks, 'Despite appearances, human sex takes place mostly in the head.'[11] Yet both Marxism and sociology, the obvious candidates for a theorization of sexuality as a social practice, have a history of marginalizing and neglecting the issue and, in any case, are both locked in confusion as to how to resolve the relationship between ideology and other dimensions of the social formation.

Contemporary work on sexuality is necessarily caught up in these debates, just as it has been affected by the recent intense politicization of sexual life. The women's liberation movement, and also militant sections of the homosexual movement, have insisted on the political character of personal relations and have successfully constituted *sexual politics* as an area of struggle. Feminism and gay liberation have challenged assumptions of male aggression and female passivity, have challenged the complacent norm of heterosexuality and have introduced a note of political and moral integrity into questions such as pornography, sexual violence and sado-masochism. The vocabulary of liberation has included an important element relating to sexual choice, and perhaps the most contentious aspect of this has been the emergence of a new kind of moralism: if our sexual practice is depersonalizing or abusive to others then we can and should change it. There is a problem, however, in reconciling this politicization of sexuality with the experience of desire and pleasure. How do we understand and engage with 'incorrect' desires and practices? The question is not a trivial one, and it has thrown us back to different histories and theories of sexuality, to psychoanalysis and discourse theory, in search of a more adequate theorization of sexual pleasure.

These debates are not systematically addressed here, but they form the context in which the questions I want to raise should be seen. In attempting to consider some of the problems in dealing with female sexuality it is useful to look more closely at specific elements of the general category, and to do this I shall look first at the relationship between eroticism and gender identity and then at the relationship between procreation and sexual behaviour.

Eroticism and Femininity

The first problem I want to consider is that of the distinction between eroticism and gender identity. The acquisition of femininity and masculinity, through historically and culturally specific processes, has been much studied recently, and in particular feminists have paid considerable attention to the ways in which acceptable forms of femininity are constructed in young and adolescent girls. Yet few of these studies explicitly connect their accounts of these socialization processes with sexual practice and erotic behaviour in maturity. At the level of commonsense it is often assumed that a connection must exist between the passivity and nurturance of the feminine gender pattern and the stereotypes of female sexual behaviour, and this may be thought to explain the 'double standard' of sexual morality between men and women and the low priority attached to female sexual desire. But the ways in which a particular kind of gender socialization might lead to a particular type of erotic behaviour are rarely discussed.

It is also the case that empirical studies of erotic behaviour frequently leave unargued the connections between their findings and contemporary notions of appropriate gender identities for men and women. The study of sexology has tended to demonstrate the diversity and range of sexual behaviour without attempting to link this to dominant patterns of gender socialization. (The tradition is essentially an empiricist and descriptive one.) In relation to female sexuality, if we leave aside for a moment the claims of psychoanalytic theory to account for feminine sexual pleasure in terms of a theory of femininity, there are relatively few systematic arguments on this point. A notable exception here might be made for Angela Carter's study of the erotic writings of De Sade, which attempts to draw inferences as to the meaning of feminine gender identity in the late eighteenth century in the context of the discussion of eroticism.[12]

I want to argue here that it is useful to make an analytic separation between gender identity and eroticism: there may be an overlap between them, but it is by no means an exclusive one. At one level the descriptive information collected by Kinsey and his associates revealed a diversity of sexual behaviour which can be squared neither with some biologistic notion of appropriate behaviour for males and females, nor with the view that socially constructed gender identity determines sexual practice. Among Kinsey's findings was the fact that 37 per cent of his male respondents and 13 per cent of his female ones had experienced homosexual relations to orgasm by the age of forty-five, and he also reported the widespread practice of 'perversions' previously assumed to be very rare.[13]

A consideration of homosexuality and lesbianism throws doubt on the notion that sexual orientation and erotic behaviour are closely linked to gender identity. One of the more enduring myths about homosexuality is that it is the inevitable outcome of gender inversion (undue masculinity in women and femininity in men). The view that the 'normal' or predictable sexual orientation of a person with an inverted gender identity will be homosexual is encapsulated by Radclyffe Hall's portrait of the lesbian Steven Gordon in her novel *The Well of Loneliness*. Yet evidence suggests that this assumption is entirely untrue. The reason why Kinsey could elicit high rates of homosexual activity was that he posed his questions in terms of degrees of homosexual experience rather than in terms of consolidated homosexual or heterosexual identity. Similarly, although we now tend to think of a *choice* between heterosexuality and homosexuality, the notion of an exclusive orientation to one's own sex is a comparatively recent one. Jeffrey Weeks insists that '. . . as a starting-point we have to distinguish between homosexual behaviour, which is universal, and a homosexual identity, which is historically specific – and a comparatively recent phenomenon in Britain.'[14] A recent report on homosexuality by the Institute for Sex Research suggests that a notion of homosexuality as a displaced version of normal gender-related behaviour is completely unfounded. The authors report that among their respondents, even among those living in stable 'couple' situations, '. . . few described a domestic situation in which one partner took on only "wifely" tasks and the other the "husbandly" ones'; and they conclude that '. . . speculation about sexual "roles" (e.g. active/passive) may simply be missing the point.'[15]

We can approach the question of the relationship between femininity and female sexual behaviour from another point of view by looking again at the psychoanalytic tradition. As is now well known, Freud himself saw the normal sexual gratification of women in terms of the acquisition of a mature feminine identity. Subsequent writers in the psychoanalytic school, and perhaps most notoriously Helene Deutsch, have argued that not only is female sexual pleasure necessarily tied to vaginal penetration but that the entire erotic life of the adult woman is bound to the sacrificial nurturance of motherhood.[16] Whilst there is not the space here to go into the general controversy surrounding the relationship of psychoanalysis and feminism, nor the particular question of clitoral and vaginal orgasm, it would be useful to note that some recent developments have considerably challenged the orthodox psychoanalytic account of female sexual pleasure. Nancy Chodorow, for instance, has suggested that one neglected aspect of female psycho-sexual development is the incipient conflict engendered for women between their erotic desires and emotional attachments, and her attempt to rework psychoanalysis from a feminist point of view draws this out. She writes:

Most women emerge from their oedipus complex oriented to their father and men as primary *erotic* objects, but it is clear that men tend to remain *emotionally* secondary, or at most emotionally equal, compared to the primacy and exclusivity of an oedipal boy's emotional tie to his mother and women.[17]

This would suggest, at the least, a break in the proposed continuity between femininity as a gender identity and the forms of erotic desire characteristic of women, and as such it represents an interesting challenge to the somewhat inflexible account traditionally put forward in the psychoanalytic school.

It is necessary to reject any direct link not only between maleness and femaleness and a 'natural' orientation to heterosexual genital sexuality, but also between the socially constructed gender identities of femininity and masculinity and their assumed consequences for sexual practice. This does not, however, necessarily lead us to a radical dissociation of gender identity and eroticism. There can be no doubt that the familial and general ideological processes by which the categories of femininity and masculinity are established and reproduced in our society lead, at the very least, to a disposition towards 'appropriate' forms of eroticism.[18] But the separation I have tried to indicate here points to a need for greater awareness of an area of meaning, definition, the discourse of pleasure, and so on in our consideration of sexuality. In addition, it raises a further question as to the relationship between sexual pleasure and biological reproduction.

Procreation and Female Sexuality

The distinction between eroticism and gender identity is useful in considering the connection between sexuality and procreation, since the idea that sexuality is directly linked to biological reproduction reflects the imposition of socially constructed gender responsibilities on to a wide variety of sexual practices.

At the most general level the ideology of sexuality in our culture has, until comparatively recently, imposed severe sanctions on the most obvious forms of non-reproductive sexual behaviour. Jeffrey Weeks has pointed out that the death penalty for sodomy applied to heterosexual anal intercourse and to intercourse with animals as well as to homosexual buggery. 'The law against sodomy', he argues, 'was a central aspect of the taboo on all non-procreative sex', and indeed it had considerable flexibility since the 'crime against nature' which it sought to punish was *inter Christianos non nominandum* (not to be named among Christians).[19] Similar sanctions have been applied to the woman who attempted to dissociate sexual activity from procreation: abortion has in most western European countries been illegal except under medically authorized procedures and has even carried a death penalty in some places.

There is considerable evidence that the prohibition on non-procreative sexual activity has come to play a large part in the history of sexuality which we have inherited. Lawrence Stone cites several phenomena which clearly illustrate the strength of this proscription and its importance to the sexual practice which Christianity sought to enforce. One example of this is the view, apparently *de rigueur* in religious circles in early modern Europe, that sexual passion within marriage was no better than adultery. Stone quotes one cleric of 1584:

> The husband who, transported by immoderate love, has intercourse with his wife so *ardently* in order to satisfy his passion that, even had she not been his wife he would have wished to have commerce with her, is committing a sin.

The ideology of 'matrimonial chastity' is found also in extraordinary beliefs about the efficacy of various sexual practices for conception. Stone describes the ways in which theologians tried to interfere with sexual intercourse, proscribing any position other than the ('missionary') one of the man on top, since conception was less likely if the semen had to struggle against gravity. Curiously enough the theologians and the medical professions did not prohibit clitoral stimulation for women – they believed that both male and female fluids were necessary for conception, and even that female sexual pleasure made the mouth of the womb more receptive to male sperm, and hence they endorsed masturbation to orgasm as a legitimate part of intercourse.[20]

I say 'curiously enough' since our knowledge of sexual morality, particularly that of the Victorian period, tends to assume a denial or a 'repression' of female sexual pleasure. To some extent this view is borne out historically. The often-quoted remark of William Acton (1857) that '... the majority of women (happily for them) are not very much troubled with sexual feeling of any kind' was not necessarily representative of the period but did have some resonance in an era where the only recognized lust women indulged in was a lust for maternity. Here lies an important aspect of the relationship between sexuality and procreation – that it has been posed as a much closer one for women than it is for men. The most obvious example of this is the 'double standard' of sexual morality, according to which the crime of adultery was a much more serious one for the married woman than for the married man. Consideration of the double standard has tended to emphasize its importance to the nineteenth century's flourishing institution of prostitution, and the way in which this widespread practice preserved the sanctity of the bourgeois family and the legitimate inheritance of its property. Yet it seems to be the case that the discrepancy between the freedom of men and that of women goes further back than this period. Boswell, writing in 1776, records a conversation he had with a woman who was considering committing adultery:

I argued that the chastity of women was of much more consequence than that of men, as the property and rights of families depend upon it. 'Surely', said she, 'that is easily answered, for the objection is removed if a woman does not intrigue but when she is with child.' I really could not answer her. Yet I thought she was wrong, and I was uneasy . . .[21]

Boswell's 'unease' is significant. It is impossible to analyse the double standard in terms of solely economic criteria such as the inheritance of property, important as these may be for the bourgeoisie; the constraints on women's extra-marital sexual activity are rooted in an ideology of gender division which to some extent must be seen as historically prior to and independent of strictly capitalist social organization. Indeed the Victorian attitude to sexuality tended if anything to exert pressure against a formerly accepted double standard: in the seventeenth and eighteenth centuries the conventions on bastard children made illegitimacy considerably more open and acceptable.

The question of the double standard is frequently perceived in terms of a link between sexuality and procreation which is more forcibly maintained in the case of women than that of men. Yet this view would encounter serious problems in trying to explain why it should be the case that, in Britain at least, lesbianism has never figured in the criminal law. Looking at it from the point of view of biological reproduction, clearly there is not much to choose between male and female homosexuality, and the relatively tolerant attitude towards lesbianism requires further historical analysis.

It would seem, then, that the link between sexuality and procreation is a very complex one. Although sexual activity has never, throughout our recent history, been restricted to procreative ends the ideology that it should be restricted in this way has tended to vary. During this century major changes have taken place in the direction of freeing women from the reproductive consequences of sexual intercourse. The development and increasing acceptability of contraception are obviously the most important of these, although the resistance to them of religious and other forces should not be overlooked. Also it is clear that the liberalization of the law on homosexuality and the greater acknowledgement of non-procreative female sexual pleasure have been important features of the last two decades. It would be wrong to argue, however, that these changes have created a total dissociation of sexuality and reproduction, or that they have effected any significant liberation for women in the sphere of sexuality. The extent to which sexual practice is circumscribed by the ideology of gender and women's responsibilities for procreation can be seen quite clearly.

Sally MacIntyre, in a study of single pregnant women, analysed the assumptions underlying the treatment they received from doctors, nurses and social workers.[22] She found that although these professionals articulated a belief in a 'maternal instinct' they did not hold this to apply to unmarried women – they 'bracketed together' sex, marriage and biological reproduction and did not perceive single motherhood as medically or socially desirable. Although MacIntyre's study concerned the 'vocabularies of motive' of the professionals and the women involved, drawing out important differences in their perceptions of the situation, it is clear that these assumptions must be considered as part of a wider ideology linking pregnancy (and sexual intercourse) to the social institution of marriage. Hence the disapproval of unmarried mother-hood relates precisely to a socially constructed category of femininity and maternal responsibility.

Similarly Mary McIntosh has pointed out that neither sociologists nor sexologists have questioned the assumption that the institution of pros-titution exists to service the 'imperious' male sexual urge:

Innately, it seems, women have sexual attractiveness while men have sexual urges. Prostitution is there for the needs of the male hunchback – no one asks how the female hunchback manages.[23]

For women, it seems, even if sexual activity cannot be linked directly to procreation, it can be linked to a stable emotional relationship; for men many forms of casual experiences are not only tolerated but expected and encouraged. So although it may be true to argue that the prohibition on non-reproductive sexuality has weakened considerably in recent times, it remains a powerful component of the ideology of sexuality and affects men and women differently.

It should be clear that I have been discussing an assumed rather than a necessary link between sexuality and procreation. Clearly some connection exists at the level of biology between heterosexual intercourse and procreation. Yet the widespread practices of contraception and abortion, and the high incidence of non-procreative sexual activity, render this initial equation totally unsatisfactory as an account of sexual practice and ideology. What is more useful to consider is the variations in beliefs about the relationship between sexuality and procreation. Such beliefs are not necessarily rational in terms of our knowledge of biology in any case. The view frequently expressed, by feminists and more generally, that sexuality and procreation are more closely linked for women than men is a case in point. In one sense this view is correct, in that heterosexual intercourse may, and frequently does, leave the woman with a pregnancy to consider while the man may even remain ignorant of his impending paternity. Yet on the level of anatomy the connection for men between sexuality and procreation is much closer than it is for women. For men (except in rare cases of 'multiple orgasm') the ejaculation of sperm is absolutely co-terminous with orgastic pleasure; for women (notwithstanding the opinion of the theologians mentioned earlier) there is no relationship between orgasm and conception.

We must conclude, then, that in a society where contraceptive practices are widespread the belief that sexuality and procreation are necessarily related must form an object to be analysed as part of sexual ideology. Indeed it relates closely to the social construction of gender, as is particularly apparent in the view that female sexuality is more orientated towards procreation than is male. Such assumptions have little to do with the mechanics of sexual intercourse and cannot adequately be explained in terms of the meanings attached by individuals to eroticism. They belong to an ideology of femininity and masculinity which reproduces gendered subjects and should be considered in a broader analysis of the social context of sexual practice.

These questions have an important bearing on the issues raised at the outset. Female sexuality cannot be understood either as a mechanical expression of feminine gender socialization or in terms of the supposed dictates of procreative biology. Sexual orientation and the morality of desire are at present significant political controversies within the women's liberation movement,[24] and the feminist challenge to normative heterosexuality is in some respects related to that of the homosexual movement. Yet the two are not exactly parallel. Although feminism has treated sexual politics seriously – taking the right to autonomous sexuality as a major demand – the oppression of women is fundamentally located in gender socialization and the present structure and ideology of the family. The oppression of gays, although undoubtedly tied to the development of a particular family structure in modern society, is perhaps more specifically located in notions of appropriate sexual practice and erotic behaviour than is that of women. In order to disentangle these different aspects of oppression we need to distinguish between the role played by particular family structures, conceptions of femininity and masculinity characteristic of specific historical periods, and the socially constructed meanings of sexual practices.

Notes

1. Ernest Jones, *The Life and Work of Sigmund Freud*, abridged edition (Harmondsworth: Penguin, 1974), p. 474.
2. In *The Making of the Modern Homosexual*, ed. Kenneth Plummer (London: Hutchinson, 1980).
3. See the essay 'Some Psychical Consequences of the Anatomical Distinction between the Sexes' in the Pelican Freud Library, Vol. 7, *On Sexuality* (Harmondsworth, 1977).
4. Jacques Lacan, *Écrits* (in English) (London: Tavistock).
5. *The Second Sex* (Harmondsworth: Penguin, 1972).
6. See Terry Lovell, *Pictures of Reality* (London: British Film Institute, 1980).
7. See Mary Jane Sherfey, *The Nature and Evolution of Female Sexuality* (New York: Random House, 1972).
8. See J. H. Gagnon and W. Simon, *Sexual Conduct* (Chicago: Aldine, 1973).
9. For a functionalist account of homosexual oppression in these terms, see David Fernbach, 'Toward a Marxist Theory of Gay Liberation', *Gay Marxist*, No. 2 (1977).
10. For instance, Kenneth Plummer, *Sexual Stigma* (London: Routledge & Kegan Paul, 1975).
11. *The Family, Sex and Marriage in England 1500–1800* (London: Weidenfeld & Nicolson, 1977), p. 483.
12. *The Sadeian Woman* (London: Virago, 1979).
13. A. C. Kinsey *et al.*, *Sexual Behavior in the Human Male* and *Sexual Behavior in the Human Female* (Philadelphia, 1948 and 1953).
14. *Coming Out* (London: Quartet, 1977), p. 3.
15. Alan P. Bell and Martin S. Weinberg, *Homosexualities: A Study of Diversity among Men and Women* (London, 1978), pp. 101 and 111.
16. Helene Deutsch, *Psychology of Women* (New York: Grune and Stratton, 1944, 2 vols.).

17. *The Reproduction of Mothering: Psychoanalysis and the Sociology of Gender* (University of California Press, 1978), p. 193.

18. See Jeffrey Weeks, 'Discourse, Desire and Sexual Deviance: Some Problems in the History of Homosexuality', in Plummer (1980), op. cit.

19. *Coming Out*, p. 14.

20. See *The Family, Sex and Marriage*, pp. 483–500.

21. Quoted by Stone, op. cit., pp. 506–7.

22. '"Who Wants Babies?" The Social Construction of "Instincts"', in *Sexual Divisions and Society*, ed. D.L.Barker and S.Allen (London:Tavistock, 1976).

23. 'Who Needs Prostitutes? The Ideology of Male Sexual Needs', in *Women, Sexuality and Social Control*, ed. C. and B.Smart (London: Routledge, 1978).

24. See, for example, Beatrix Campbell, 'Feminist Sexual Politics', *Feminist Review*, No. 5 (1980).

Monique Plaza

'Phallomorphic Power' and the Psychology of 'Woman': A patriarchal chain

First published in *Questions Féministes*, 1 (1978). This translation by Miriam David and Jill Hodges was first published in *Ideology and Consciousness*, IV (Autumn 1978).

Preface: On the subject of criticism . . .

Certain articles which appear in this review submit to criticism the methods, perspectives, inquiries . . . in short, the discourses of feminist women. This practice seems to me not only legitimate, but even indispensable for the radicalization of the feminist movement.

Nevertheless, in the current situation, this is often conceived by many of us as destructive, a drain on our energies etc. In my view, we must free ourselves from this anxiety which is not in our interest and threatens very soon to shut us in an impasse because it *individualizes* and *moralizes* a problem which must not be posed in individualist, moral terms.

A discourse is socially constituted. What interests us, in the feminist critique of a discourse, is the location of its *social determinants*, the analysis of what gives it its sociological weight. In this sense, any idea of a 'personal attack' on the author is foreign to our project. What does concern us, on the other hand, is the 'envelopment' of the author in rules, schemas external to her.

'But even so, to attack women . . .,' someone will say. It is nevertheless precisely at the level of that which we produce about our oppression that we must be the most rigorous. This doesn't mean an absence of solidarity: feminist solidarity doesn't consist in a grand symbiosis (the Sacred Union), rather it is constituted by *bringing to light and questioning our contradictions,* by *revealing the cunning, pernicious ways of oppression, even inside our own struggle.*

'But criticism is destructive . . .' It is true that the notion of criticism is ambiguous and disliked because it often includes the idea of a negative, nihilist method. Now criticism is positive not only in that it allows the installation of a non-moralistic form of political solidarity, but also insofar as it necessarily proceeds from a *full* and *positive* analysis of our oppression, from a militant practice *fully* and *positively* against our oppression.

'Phallomorphic Power' and the Psychology of 'Woman'

Feminist analyses show the existence of woman's multi-dimensional oppression by the social system. In delineating this oppression they reveal the manifestations and workings of a patriarchal order which prescribes rigid functions for men and women on the basis of 'natural differences'.

When they discover diverse systems of exploitation and alienation of which they are the victims, women often ask themselves these questions: 'What are we, what would we be without this social mould? What, basically, is a woman?' An understandable and inevitable question: the oppression happens as an abusive restriction of existence, as a mutilation. Stating that woman is invalidated in discourse, exploited in practice, we cannot avoid demanding our liberation (this term, despite its ambiguities, has a concrete political value) and asking ourselves what we are.

There are many replies to this questioning which is going on at the moment, in a number of publications and various magazine articles. The most interesting are those which are written by women who have broken the bonds of patriarchy, because they exemplify the stake and limits of our struggle. But it seems as if our gains are constantly threatened with annihilation, our discoveries undermined from within. There is nothing surprising in that, since our arguments are part of a patriarchal structure, on which they are always partly dependent.

An answer to the problem of our reality comes to us at this moment, from our discussions about ourselves. It posits that woman is to be sought, discovered, brought into the open. The reasoning by which it proceeds affirms, in the first place, that woman does not exist, by dint of patriarchal oppression. This statement is based on a quasi-exclusive analysis of discourses (philosophical, literary ...). Sometimes this non-existence is judged in terms of the domain of value: woman exists, but ideology devalues her existence; or it is posed from a deeper point of view of essence: woman, because of an oppressive schema, has not yet arrived at her being.[1] In the second place, it is postulated that at this moment woman is in the process of birth: 'the young newborn woman'[2]; our task as women is to delineate our subjective position, to discover our relationship with the world, to seek our essence. In short, to promote our specificity.

This research project attracts lots of us. Because it seems full and positive, doesn't it distance us from the claimants, suffragettes, shrews, hysterics and other frustrated women ... labels which are showered freely on feminists. Mariella Righini congratulates Annie Leclerc on the publication of her book *The Nuptials*, which precisely opposes the negativism of the feminist critique:

> Instead of eternally and interminably striking the balance between, on the one hand, oppressions, repressions; prohibitions, sanctions, limitations on women and ... on the other, the ramblings, lamentations, complaints and recriminations ... she does not declaim.[3]

Denunciation, described as tedious, is supplanted by a project which seems to be immediately constructive, because it questions woman from the evidence of her own characteristics:

> She allows what lives freely in her to speak ... She goes straight to the essential: what is important to her heart and body ... She announces a new way of living, with happiness and pride, her woman's body (which has been given to her) and her woman's world (which she has made for herself).[4]

To let the body speak for itself ... That is precisely the proposition that arouses our critical attention. Would not woman's specificity derive in the last instance from her body, supposed to be the natural site of sex differences? However, suggesting the body and demanding our 'difference' is already to participate in a social and oppressive system: nature does not speak the difference, it supplies indications which we interpret as a function of social relations. The individual does not have a 'natural' existence, he is always-already socialized, including in his 'biological irreducibleness'. We shall not find 'true' woman by eliminating the social from our questioning. Because the social is always there, imposing its oppressive construction. If we set it aside from our thinking, from the logic of our rules, the flowering of our sex, it will inevitably overtake us again: it will impel our construction of ourselves. On the contrary, we must constantly be made aware of it so that it does not enmesh us in its nexus of evidence. Believing that we can economize on critical analyses by being attuned to the rhythms of our bodies, is to imprison ourselves totally in the patriarchal logic which has constituted our knowledge of sex difference and the nature of woman.

But if we assume a critical procedure at the start of our investigation, will we perhaps be able to construct a second stage, ourselves in our genuine being? This is the procedure which Luce Irigaray seems to assume. She postulates that an irreducible 'X', 'Woman', has been excluded from the production of western discourse and has been defined as a function of masculine parameters. For Luce Irigaray, the study of Platonic discourse and Freudian theory leads to the statement that woman does not exist at the moment; she is concealed by discourse and distorted in her psyche. To construct woman, we have then to project her in a conditional prospective: what would she be if her specificity were respected? This procedure, supported by 'critical' thinkers, seems also to have 'conservative' connections, to the extent that it does not postulate oppression in an effective way. The critique elaborated by Luce Irigaray seems problematic in that it poses the existence of a psychological schema of 'transformation-deformation' which woman undergoes because of masculine domination. This is what brings her to search for a being 'before the transformation', that is, to pose the existence of a feminine which the West would have deformed and mutilated.

The Irigarayan schema involves three postulates:

— 'Woman' exists in an irreducible way, in terms of an essence hitherto unrecognized.

— This feminine essence gives women the potentiality of psychic existence which the West crushes and hides.

— This feminine essence can only be discovered outside the oppressive social framework, that is to say *in the body of woman*.[5]

The potential existence of woman depends therefore on the discovery of her essence, which lies in the specificity of her body. As long as her body does not declare her specificity, woman will not exist. In the end, the potentiality of the existence of woman is related *to the potentiality of her pure biological reality*. That is to say *when woman is no longer a social being*.

So the question of our reality, at the moment, seems to end in the elaboration of a prospective of our bodies in which oppression is purely and simply put on one side, or apparently cast in the form of a critique, but used to invalidate our present existence. Is this question therefore premature? Should we reject it as void? Not at all: the energy which it increasingly channels amongst us shows that it constitutes a vital stake for feminism. Far from scratching it out, we should, on the contrary, include it *in the theory of our oppression*, in the project of our existence. This should allow us to grasp in what way and how our problematic may backfire against us. In fact, by projecting woman in a conditional way, by arguing from her present non-existence, we remain prisoners of our oppression:

1. First in that we confuse the ideological description that is given of women, of their oppression and of their very existence. The various oppressive processes which woman must submit to may be refuted; but this delineation, to be operative, must

(a) include the notion of contradiction in its formal arrangement without referring implicitly to a moral systematization[6];

(b) take as its fundamental premise the statement that woman exists: there is nothing evanescent about woman, either on the psychological or the sociological plane;

(c) rest on a conceptual system which theorizes oppression without putting forward an equation 'woman at present = nothing'. For that equation, which seems to summarize our oppression, in fact, doubles it: we ask woman not what we are, how we exist, but what she could become, in her essence. It is here: in the society in which we live, and now, that we must situate our reality as women, and not in the timeless splits of our body or of our essence. The stake is important: we run the risk of paralysing the struggle, of invalidating it and wiping it out. Because we distance ourselves from the social scene where our oppression is produced, to lose ourselves in the search for the feminine 'interior'. Because of the impossibility of imagining what woman could be, would be and will be, we impute to her the most traditional feminine characteristics based on the specificity of her body. So the oppressive knot encloses us: we form ourselves into a 'natural' group, referring to the notion of 'difference'. It is at this level that our second imprisonment intrudes:

2. Precisely because the oppression of women is based on the surprising first principle of sex difference. The fact that men and women have specific genital organs, that woman has the 'privilege' of gestation, does not imply that anatomical sex should prescribe the psychic and social existence of the individual. The ability to urinate from a distance[7] does not necessarily lead to the prerogative of founding civilization. Bearing children does not signify exclusive rights over their education. The existence of woman does not boil down to her periods, to the form of her sex or to her pregnancies.

To found a field of study on this belief in the inevitability of natural sex differences can only compound patriarchal logic and not subvert it: to pose woman as the specific object of oppression, we hide the fact that she is the object of oppression, *through* the specific. Far from taking the Difference as the basis of our project, we should demolish it and denounce its falsity. Analysing how and why it takes on an ineluctable character: I must be man or woman; neither both nor something else ... at the risk of getting lost. In this sense, building a solidarity indispensable to our survival, may not rest on the elaboration of a feminine universe, on the idea of a shared nature of women. Which does not signify either that we are going to 'deny' our bodies, or want 'to be men'. The oppression of women is based on the appropriation of their bodies by patriarchy, on the restriction of sexuality within the framework imposed by the masculine-feminine opposition, the subjection of the woman in confinement to medical power, the contemptuousness of menstruation, the lack of recognition of sexuality. But recognizing this vast sexual oppression of women must not lead us to the conclusion that oppression derives from the body, or from sex; or that the body explains social oppression. Woman's sex is denied, unrecognized. But that does not mean that woman's oppression derives from that lack of recognition. We must guard ourselves from a form of reflective 'pan-sexualism' which is only a coarse, disguised naturalism. If the category of sex has such an important position in patriarchal logic, this is not because sex gives its shape to the social; it is because the social is able to make sexual forms seem obvious and thereby hide oppressive systems.

Determining what constitutes our specificity cannot be done until we have elucidated

– what is the reality of woman from the point of view of her present existence;

– the precise functioning of the category of sex in the oppressive system;

– the central position which the notion of 'Difference' occupies in it.

It is by examining the work of one of us that I am going to ask these questions. Why this mediation? Because, at first reading, I was attracted by the work of Luce Irigaray: doesn't it propose, in the psychoanalytic domain, a subversive theory of patriarchal power and a tempting definition of woman? However, I began to feel uneasy when I heard Luce Irigaray, during a conference, read one of her articles and maintain that woman thinks about nothing ... I then had the impression that the structure was full of traps, all the more dangerous because it went along with the 'shelters of transgression'. In this sense, Luce Irigaray's method of analysing and synthesizing which I am proposing only has value in clarifying *our* problematic. For me, it's a question of how our subversive insights can be reduced to nothing by the process of diverse 'under-minings'. That's to say it's not a question of an argument about words: the patriarchal 'chain' tends to annihilate our struggles. I deliberately use this word, which has the sense both of a logical closure and a spatial encirclement.

Luce Irigaray seems to have a double objective in producing the two writings to which I will refer here.[8] In the first place, she tries to reconstitute the philosophical and psychological premises of western 'Logos',[9] describing in it the objectification and belittling of woman. The woman that she is studying is the object of man's discourse. Second, she tries to define what woman is when she is subjected to this phallomorphic and phallocentric 'Logos' and tries to define woman's potential being if left to herself. Juggling with these heterogeneous objects of study presents a substantial difficulty which Luce Irigaray does not seem to be able to get around without simplification and trivialization.

A. The Ultimate Axioms of 'Western Logic'[10]

1. Elements of a strategy

Luce Irigaray maintains that subject/man dominates the scene of knowledge. Why does he dominate? She does not seem to ask that question and we should be grateful to her for her prudence. In fact, that question often invokes the search for origins and invites all the myths about the prehistory of humanity. It would certainly be useful to know how this oppression was established, but this research is made virtually imposs-ible by the falsity of the archives at our disposal.

Nevertheless, even if Luce Irigaray does not ask the question, she provides an implicit answer in looking for an origin in the realm of Ideas within western Logic. *And what she finds is nothing more than man as western discourse presents him.*

Man dominates because he is man

For Luce Irigaray man seems to be an essential-biological-psychological entity, equipped with his own particular characteristics: so he is narcis-sistic, aggressive. And above all, he has the luck to have a visible sex:

If the boy is made narcissistic, made like Moses (*moisé*), via his penis because this is valued in the sexual market and culturally overestimated because it is visible, suggestive, fetishizable... [*Speculum*, p. 81]

Luce Irigaray fastens the notion of 'form' to that of 'phallic' and postulates an isomorphism between western discourse and the masculine sex (the privilege of erection):

In fact it can be shown that all western discourse presents a certain isomorphism with the masculine sex: the privilege of unity, form of the self, of the visible, of the specularizable, of the erection (which is the becoming in a form)...[11]

Now it is not because of its intrinsic qualities that the penis is valued to the detriment of the vulva or the breasts which are themselves also *visible*. It is to the extent that culture is androgenous, patriarchal that the phallus is raised to the level of a symbol. The 'phallic superiority' of man is nothing other than the interpretation, in terms of nature and hierarchy, of women's oppression by men. If one had to justify women's domination of men an ideology could just as easily claim that men lacked breasts, are mutilated because they can't give birth, and have a monstrous outgrowth in the place of a vulva. We would be as much convinced by the evidence of their 'nothing to show'. Luce Irigaray confuses 'social' man and 'anatomical' man. Man, like woman, is a social product whose characteristics are related to the place which society gives him and the subjectivity which it lends him. Men are not aggressive by nature. *Nor are they masters of their existence.* Their dominant social position does not imply that they do not need to seek domination. However, it is this plan that Luce Irigaray imputes to them, on the basis of an irrepressible psychological determination.

The denial of the uterus

Man, according to Luce Irigaray, turns away from his matriarchal origins: he does not want to recognize that he is born of woman, of a mother. This process escapes him totally because it is absolutely impossible for him to reproduce himself. So he develops his argument by an obliteration of motherhood:

So every enunciation, every affirmation, will develop and certify the recovery of the obliteration of the immutable connection of the being to the material mother. [*Speculum*, p. 202]

The claim by certain men that they have a horror of their mothers could certainly have a descriptive or even a clinical validity. Let's remember Artaud:

... it is not just Jesus Christ whom I want to seek out among the Tarahumaras but myself, me, M. Antonin Artaud born the 4 September 1896 at Marseilles, 4 rue de Jardin des Plantes, from an uterus that I had nothing to do with and with which I have never had anything to do before, because to be copulated and masturbated for 9 months by the membrane, the brilliant membrane which, without teeth, devours, as the UPANISHADS say, is no way to be born and I know that I was born in another way, through my works and not from a mother, but my MOTHER wanted to take me, and you can see the result in my life. I was born from my sadness alone and would that you could do the same too, Mr Henri Parisot. And we must believe that the uterus approved this sadness, since it wanted to take it for itself and feed off it under the disguise of maternity.[12]

Horror of one's mother and the desire to be born by oneself are clearly expressed by Artaud, and the violence of his words evokes the virulence of psychoanalysts and psychiatrists against the 'wicked mothers of psychotics' and the 'wicked wives of alcoholics'. Must we therefore suggest the horror of motherhood as a constituent element of masculine psychology? The hypothesis could be restrictive. *Because women also show a desire for self-propagation.* Men and women, long before the question of their sexual identity comes to the fore, undergo the 'primary violence' of their dependence on an adult (the mother in our societies): in fact, if the psyche functions from the start on the postulate of self-propagation,[13] this postulate is contradicted by the impotence of the child who realizes the weight of another's power over him.

On the other hand, as soon as one considers the negation of mother as a fantasy, one cannot precisely relate it to a sexual characteristic: the concept of fantasy invokes the symbolic and not the anatomical. The fantasy derives from primary elements provided by symbolic cultural schemas. The symbolic order – if we wish to refer to the Lacanian concept – is ordered around signifiers. But these signifiers construct and interpret 'nature' as a function of social organization (this sociological interpretation of the symbolic order doesn't exist (as such) in psycho-analytic statements which remain nearer to nature. I go beyond psycho-analytic theory to give the concept of the symbolic order a social significance). So the signifiers 'Phallus' and 'the Name of the Father' confirm sex differences and the duality of the positions of father and mother which social organization has instituted.

Every individual, man or woman, is from the start caught in the 'defiles of the signifiers' to which he must render himself subject. An essentially patriarchal order which Freud has described (metaphorically) in *Totem and Taboo*. Nothing for human beings escapes the symbolic ordering of language. 'Mother's body', gestation, are not only experiences mediated by socio-cultural organization but are constituted by it. In fact, psychic reality only becomes meaningful by the addition, to the 'thing-presentation' – insofar as this concept can be grasped – of a 'word-presentation'. Even if one postulates the inscription in the archaic unconscious level of a thing presentation (mother's body), one cannot avoid suggesting that this thing presentation becomes psychically meaningful through the inscription of a word presentation 'mother's body'. And, precisely, the fantasy about mother's body can only appear as a psychic production at the point when the psychic apparatus assimilates *the significance that another gives to the utterance 'mother's body'*. All these psychic elaborations of the body and of the mother rely necessarily on this signifying system limited by a language. When psychoanalysis refers, for example, the castration complex back to an anatomical observation it is making a theoretical error since it postulates that a thing presentation could be inscribed by a look outside any signifying system. Luce Irigaray is similarly reductive when she suggests 'matrial implantation' in the realm of 'feeling' and when she makes of its concealment the fundamental principle of 'western Logos'.

First operation of the passage from sensation to understanding which will produce – somewhat mysteriously – a schema which will never give back to sensibility what it owes it. Because the imaginary, its most subtle faculty, will stay to serve the understanding ... Thus the transcendental scheme would have as its function the negation of a particularity of feeling, which would not recover. Strongly closed in its initial empirical naivety. And what would, from this fact, have to be set aside in the diversity of its feelings in order to elaborate the concept of object, is the immediacy of the *relationship to the mother*. [*Speculum*, p. 254]

The scotomization of the Difference: farcical phallic

Man, Luce Irigaray proposes, strongly denies the existence of the sexual difference. This denial (just like his forgetting the uterus) is explained by his psychic economy. He makes the woman bear the burden of castration (she has no sex) because he finds it intolerable to imagine that she has a sex that can't be seen:

The possibility that something absent to sight, something that can't be mastered by looking, specula(riza)tion, might have some reality, in fact, would be unbearable to man because it would come and threaten the theory and practice of the representation through which he would have sublimated, or dressed up the prohibition of, masturbation [*Speculum*, p. 57]

From this fear, which he has because he is man (with a penis) comes the origin of the concept man elaborates about woman. To answer his wish for omnipotence and satisfy his phobia of the unknown, man will construct woman in his own image – a quaint double which he dispossesses of the delectable attribute of power: the penis. So man resolves the 'problem of his (phallic) principle' by basing himself on the 'a priori of the Same' which assures him of the domination of *his* only *desire*. In doing this he forgets that woman is different from him; he refuses to see in the woman anything other than a man. The only small difference between them must consist in the possession or non-possession of a penis.

It is curious that Luce Irigaray in calling this movement the 'a priori of the Same', distinguishes it from the step of differentiation. For the 'a priori of the Same', far from being an autonomous construction, is, on the contrary, *the logical complementary concept of the Difference*: the Difference refers the Other (woman) to the One (man) placed in the dominant position. The Other is always the negative of the One, the Same. The notion of Difference necessarily founds the constitution of a dominant referent (the Same) and a referred dominated (the Other). It is to be feared insofar as it implies the idea of a hierarchy when it orders social relations. It consists of a double movement: it accords primacy to one term that it erects as a norm and casts the Other into the negative, the monstrous.

When Luce Irigaray proposes that 'western logic' has discredited the Difference to satisfy man's narcissism, she makes a reductionist and hence false interpretation. *On the one hand*, to the extent that she does not see that western logic has, on the contrary, integrated the concept of Difference (which ideologically orders the relations of domination between men and women), thus suggesting the existence of an irreducible sex difference, that is to say of a hierarchy where women are differentiated and, in the same movement, negatively evaluated in relation to the referent. *On the other hand*, in that she psychologizes her investigation: she proposes the existence of a 'man', with an *eternal psyche* and hostile to everything which escapes him: she transforms a *descriptive* fantasy element into an *explanatory* characteristic: she confers on man an *original power, an initial wish for domination* (however unconscious she regards this wish as being). And above all, she produces a *psychological analysis* of the 'logic' when she studies a discourse, a theory.

Recourse to psychology certainly allows the fate of what Freud calls 'the instinct for knowledge' to be described in the particularity of certain cases: one can then give an account of the way in which a particular individual placed in a particular historical dimension constitutes himself as a knowing subject. In this decidedly psychological viewpoint, one thus relates productions (theoretical, artistic . . .) to the history of the subject which produces them; Luce Irigaray does not do this since she psychologically analyses Platonic discourse without so much as referring to the non-amnestic elements which Freud used.

Luce Irigaray thus seems to place herself between two types of analysis: psychological, although she does not have the necessary material at her disposal; ontological (since she wants to study the place of Man and not the place of a certain man 'X'), but carrying out a psychological reduction: she claims to take account of the content of Platonic statements with reference to man's wish. Now that psychological reduction is unjustified to the extent that a discourse is created in a particular social formation of which it is a product. Every discourse – even if endowed with its own historicity – necessarily orders epistemological themes current in the society, is supported by institutional determinants and responds to economic imperatives. In this sense, the subject who participates in the Discourse – the author – is enveloped in rules exterior to his psychology. One can certainly describe psychologically how an author A or B has managed to invest his 'instinct for knowledge' in such and such a domain of knowledges, but one cannot claim to reduce the content of the discourse to that investment.[14]

What can one state rigorously about the relation of men to discourse?

1. That men are the privileged, speaking modalities of language: they are the ones who produce the vast majority of statements.

2. That placed in an androcentric social organization, dominated by women's oppression, men have produced statements that are mutilated and false. Statements certain of which are phallo*centric*, but not at all phallo*morphic*. This distinction is essential: men's discourse is not caused by the form of their sex but complies with patriarchal organization.

The equivalence that Luce Irigaray establishes between 'western

Logos' and 'sexist statements made by men', the psychological interpretation which she gives to schemes of thought, lead her to conclusions
which are at the very least abusive concerning women. We shall come
back to this.

For Luce Irigaray the falsification of 'western Logos' is based on an
exclusion of the 'irreducible sensibility', 'empirical': the feminine sex
and the maternal body. Her exclusive study of discourse and her inscription in the epistemological site of psychoanalysis lead her to take as the
origin what is the consequence and to be caught in the naturalistic trap.
In fact, the kind of analysis that she elaborates does not allow her to
show the status of the category of sex in the development of western
logic.

One can show that the discourses occurring in the West have taken as
the basis of ordering, in certain of their statements, the notion of 'natural
sex differences' and that this ordering allows the perpetuation of an
oppressive social system. But one cannot pretend that this oppression
consists in a concealment of woman's nature: *recourse to nature is, on the
contrary, fundamental to the justification and masking of the social
oppression of women.* [15] It is *secondarily* that the nature of woman is in a
certain way concealed; *everything happens as if it were necessary to
connote the natural existence of woman, but impossible to give it a positive
content: woman can only be described as emptiness in relation to man's
fullness.*

The category of sex introduced into discourse, via the expedient of
the 'Difference', a masking of the social existence of women, an incomplete description of their place. Thus the discourses, far from
forgetting the Difference, constitute it. The oppression is doubly
determined: by the naturalism of the investigation and by the integration of the concept of 'Difference'. Thus Naturalism and Difference
refer in a perfectly synchronized way to oppressive processes, which they
hide through the mode of evidence and fatality. Let's go into the 'evidence' precisely. A woman is different from a man: denial of that is
rooted in neurosis and madness. However, the 'evidence' raises a question. It is not the idea of the *specificity* of each sex which is so problematic
but the *differential questioning* by which woman cannot be described
except in terms of 'less than man' and in terms of her 'nature'. When
people speak of the differences of the sexes, they do not stick to a
description of man and woman in their genital specificity but make out
that the reason for woman's social oppression is the nature of woman;

the psychic and social existence of woman is entirely laid down by deficient anatomy.

2. The discursive tactic: cheating utterances

Luce Irigaray establishes from Plato to Freud a continuum founded on the existence of western logic, i.e. on 'man's' 'desire'. This psychologistic and reductionist construction does not permit her to analyse rigorously patriarchal strategy. At the very most it allows her to set out certain tactics.

Thus, for Freudian discourse – where every metaphor created since Antiquity can be found expressed – Luce Irigaray formulates a certain number of critiques against patriarchal organization. One could in fact read in *Speculum* a critique of the prescription of the psychic by the anatomic (p. 12); a denunciation of the seductive function of the Law (p. 39); a demystification of the positions of father and mother (pp. 40–41); a questioning of the assimilation of the present psychic functioning to eternal laws (p. 120). This dissection makes us think that Luce Irigaray postulates an oppression of women based upon a sociological stance, which is concretized in *Speculum* by reference to Marxist theory:

> . . . . *what economic infrastructure commands the conception of the role of woman in Freud's work?* One which squares with the lack of abilities – sexual, psychological, social, cultural etc. – with which he reproaches her. A misogyny which can be understood as an ideological caution to the prosperity of property regimes. [*Speculum*, pp. 150–51]

Likewise, in *Ce sexe qui n'en est pas un*, Luce Irigaray exposes the necessity of a political interrogation of psychoanalysis:

> We have not finished enumerating the questions that psychoanalysis could ask itself with regard to the destiny, particularly the sexual one, allowed to woman. A destiny, too often imputed to anatomy, biology, which would explain, among other things, the very high incidence of female frigidity. *But the historical determinations of this destiny should be questioned.* That implies psychoanalysis reconsidering the very limits of its theoretical and practical field, imposing on itself the detour of 'interpretation' of the cultural base and the economy, especially political, which have left their mark on it without it so realizing. And asking itself whether it is possible to argue, regionally, about female sexuality insofar as woman's status in the general economy of the West has not been established. [*Ce sexe qui n'en est pas un*, p. 62]

However, she seems to forget most of her criticisms as soon as she has formulated them. This is the result of the ambiguity of her project:

... I try, as I have already indicated, to retraverse the masculine imaginary, to interpret how it has reduced us to silence, to mutism, or to mimicry, and I try, starting from there and *at the same time*, to (re)-find a possible space for the feminine imaginary. [ibid., p. 159, my italics]

B. The 'Consequences' of 'Phallomorphism': Woman does not exist

Hysteria: mime and pretence

Man, then, has constituted the 'Logos' in such a way as to resolve the problem of his principle, leaving to woman the elements least readily taken upon oneself – death, for example (cf. *Speculum*, pp. 61–3). The impasse in which man confines woman deprives the latter of language, of her sex, making her like an hysteric:

her drives are in some way on holiday: not really invested in the structuration of a 'psychosis', nor in auto-eroticism, nor in the setting up of a narcissism, nor in desire, love, for her first object, nor in appropriation, possession – were this even by means of sublimation – of her sexuality, of her sex etc. *Only hysteria is left to her.* Hysterical psychosis? neurosis? On an interruption, in an interruption of the economy of her original drives, she will do 'as' she is asked. 'As if' she were doing what one asked her. But an 'as', 'as if', which for her are not mastered, nor really elements of play, even if they sometimes appear so. [*Speculum*, pp. 85–6]

Luce Irigaray takes account again of Freudian theory and questions it from the inside. She reconstructs the psychological journey imposed upon little girls in becoming woman and searches for clinical, conceptual equivalences: would the woman be produced as a psychotic, a melancholic? [*Speculum*, pp. 78 ff.]. She ends up with a hysteric, as do Freud and Lacan. This poses two questions:

1. Isn't it abusive to propose a psychopathological category to define that which is acknowledged to be a psycho-sociological path: the subjection of the girl to femininity, which Freud exactly recognized would not be defined in psychoanalytic terms?[16]

2. What content should be given to the concept of hysteria? Luce Irigaray puts the notion of 'mime' at the centre of this concept. Certainly, the hysterical *symptom* appears as the likeness – but not an exact one – of organic symptoms, which limit medical power (frequently since Freud the hysterical symptom in this sense has been questioned). But does this amount to saying that the hysterical *structure* (assumed thus to define a woman) comes under the aegis of 'mime'? The hysteric would then be defined as 'pretence': for woman it would consist in doing what

man expects, in full. For example, if the analyst expects woman to feel penis-envy, she will feel it:

> Of course, let's not ignore the fact that the hysterical woman is particularly prone to submission, suggestion, even invention, in what concerns the discourse – desire of the other ... So she will utter, and repeat, her envy of the male organ. [*Speculum*, pp. 64–5]

Luce Irigaray integrates, in that interpretation of hysteria, the very traditional scheme of *influence*, which makes out that a power relationship rests on the *aptitude* of the dominated for weakness, and the aptitude of the dominant for force. Put in this way, the concept of hysteria allows a complete equivalence to be made between

– the ideological positions offered to women by discourse:
– woman as 'subject' fixed in a psychic social existence.

Thanks to the concept of hysteria, woman can be completely defined by the discourse of Freud, for example, it is enough to allow that woman – empty thing – fills herself with the role that man gives her.

How has Luce Irigaray managed to reduce woman to this automaton? Reading Freud's observations on the celebrated 'hysterics' Elizabeth Von R., Emmy Von N., Dora ... does not lead one to the conclusion that hysteria is mime, obedient and submissive to man's desire. The women whom Freud depicts for us are rather in revolt against their situation as women. Was not Dora enraged, among other things, at being object of exchange for her father? Freud himself was obliged to point it out!

> When she was feeling embittered she used to be overcome by the idea that she had been handed over to Herr K. as the price of his tolerating the relations between her father and his wife; and her rage at her father's making such a use of her was visible behind her affection for him.[17]

And hasn't she abandoned Freud to his manifest incomprehension? ... How can we forget that Anna O. became, in spite of Breuer's dropping her, and her multiple sufferings, a resolute, militant feminist?[18]

Certainly, Freud depicted woman's destiny: her subjection to the patriarchal law ... but he has also been obliged to admit that women revolted against that Law, not being able to really '(get) rid of her masculinity complex and ... emotionally accept without a trace of resentment the implications of her female role'[19] ... this to the extent that 'being the actual vehicle of the sexual interests of mankind', women, 'who, though they may find a sufficient substitute for the sexual object in an infant at the breast, do not find one in a growing child –

experience shows, I repeat, that women, when they are subjected to the disillusionments of marriage, fall ill of severe neuroses which permanently darken their lives.'[20]

Doesn't hysteria pose the problem of the present impasse of 'sexual identity'? Psychoanalytic literature develops at length the theme that hysterical women manifest an inability to know their sex. Certainly. But how could it be otherwise when 'being woman' is equivalent to 'leading a confined and dependent existence'? Hysteria reveals the contradictions of the structure and the impossibility for women of being what they are expected to be! Hysteria is between subjection and revolt.

On the other hand, Luce Irigaray's definition seems very restrictive. It seems to follow from her insufficient questioning of psychoanalysis: has Freud purely and simply enclosed woman within a reductive discourse, or has he taken account of her alienation by patriarchy? Where is the trickery and where the description of present psychological functioning? These are questions which ought to precede a study of Freud. For they begin the constitution of a theory of oppression, without which a study of women is reductionist. To economize here is to risk implicitly doubling the oppressive patterns. In the disintegration, the rupture of the reflection which accompanies ideological demystifications, one cannot do without a guiding thread. Luce Irigaray seems at certain moments to have lost that thread, between armchair and couch.

The repute given to Freud under the guise of his disrepute

So Luce Irigaray replies to Freud on 'women's minimal sense of justice', which he puts forward as a characteristic of women. She replies to it as if it were a question of evidence:

> To return to the question of justice, to the 'sense of justice', one should ask oneself how woman will achieve it, *given her exclusion from the practice of exchange(s), except under the heading of merchandise.* [*Speculum*, p. 147]

Luce Irigaray accepts Freud's fact and tries to justify it. Now it would have been more expeditious and pertinent to question Freud on the concept of justice, which his theory has never elaborated, and to show that his assertion rested on a crude misogynistic joke. The malevolence which breaks through Freud's propositions is the same as that which drives his reflections on weaving, women's only invention, supposedly to hide her anatomical diminution! His remarks constitute a *falsehood* which invalidates a social realization in putting it forward as a consequence of an anatomical anomaly (which is a normative conception without great interest), and, what is more, as unique (which is false: women have produced inventions which men have appropriated, or which they have denied as inventions...).

Perhaps it is convenient to consider psychoanalysis in a contradictory way. What status can we give it on the question of woman's oppression? Luce Irigaray manifestly does not succeed in replying. Sometimes her critiques let us believe that she regards Freud's assertions as fictions (e.g. the penis-envy which women feel). But at other times she seems to incorporate psychoanalytic hypotheses. Hence her pessimistic remarks on hysteria.

Three types of approach, whose distinction is essential, seem possible in Freudian theory.

First approach

Psychoanalysis lays out a general theory of psychic functioning on the basis of mixed (men, women) clinical material. This theory, which one can put forward as a 'metapsychology', establishes the laws of psychic functioning and their mode of structuration: conscious, unconscious, preconscious dimensions; problematic of drives; function of the symptom; structure of wish ... What do we perceive then? *That the psychic apparatus does not have a sex.*

Second approach

Psychoanalysis establishes a theory of 'culture'. Freud describes the (patriarchal) structure and the (repressive) functionings of the cultural order, thus giving us a sort of reconstruction of the symbolic patriarchal organization of society. He proposes that the domain of sexuality is that on which 'culture' is based, exacting from the individual a renunciation (incest taboo, restriction of sexual life) and a submission to the Law of the Father. The cultural order imposes the category of the 'Lack' differentiating masculine/feminine sex. It 'castrates' woman and raises the phallus to the level of symbol (the symbol as murderer of the thing). This differentiation-hierarchization ensures that the patriarchal structure keeps functioning (through the existence of an empty space which makes possible the play of elements), and justifies its oppressive functioning: it maintains ideologically a division of labour which places woman outside the social circuit, an appropriation of woman by man.

Psychoanalysis, whose clinical material constitutes itself from the subjective positions of individuals, takes account of the psychological course which the child follows to acquire adult identity, sexed and submitted to the patriarchal Law. It describes the process of subjection, in differentiating girl and boy, before each slips into the position that patriarchy, I say, anatomy, Freud says, gives them.

Psychoanalysis overflows, ceaselessly, the framework of a limited statement of socio-cultural organization, to constitute a naturalist dogma. However, by using psychoanalytic constructions despite themselves, one succeeds in comprehending the acute character taken on by the steps of sexual differentiation in patriarchal society. This permits breaking with the very imprecise psychosociological notion of 'role' which does not take account of the violent, inescapable and unmistakable character which the process of sexual identification takes for individuals.

Despite itself, psychoanalysis shows us then that 'sex difference' can only be established and become meaningful psychically through violence, and that its inescapable character comes from its being amalgamated with basic human problems by the confusion of individuality and sexed identity. The scope and the implications of this confusion deserve further consideration.

The child is confronted with the patriarchal symbolic as soon as he is caught up in the mesh of language. A certain number of imaginary constructions are imposed on him (infantile sexual theories, Oedipus, castration) which mediate and order his approach to sexual reality. The notion of 'Difference of the sexes' holds a central place in this passage of fantasy. It is imposed on the infant as

1. being the natural order;
2. requiring a hierarchy;
3. indispensable for acquiring an identity.

It is introduced in some way by force in the psyche of the child and makes him conceive of the masculine and feminine sexes as radically opposed – the feminine sex as 'nothing to be seen', the masculine sex as 'everything to be seen'.

The child, to whom the question of sexual identity does not pose itself at first, reorders after the event all his previous multiple experiences of lack, under the primacy of castration. *Hence the central place which this introduction of the sexual difference holds at the psychological level.* For the psyche can only establish a liveable functioning to the extent that it includes the dimension of the object separated from the body, of the Other separated from itself. Every process of fusion is antithetical to the constitution of individuality through which the psychic functioning takes on meaning. No one would think of contesting that.

But psychoanalysis, whose reflections are supported by an 'epistemological basis' common to the human sciences, takes for itself the notion of 'Difference', whose foundation is hierarchy. Through this and to the extent that it cannot dissociate psychic functioning from the symbolic functioning of the 'culture', it is constrained to amalgamate – as this same symbolic system makes it do – the paradigm 'Necessary individuality – separation – loss of the object' and the paradigm 'Identity – Difference = Hierarchy – Primacy of the phallus'.

Effectively there is a 'Fatum'[21] of the human being, of which the loss, the lack, the break are the principal points. But the rock of death does not have the same status as the rock of castration. Why does psychoanalytic theory merge them? Without doubt because it refers to that which, faute de mieux, I call 'the patriarchal ordering' which places the dimension of sex to the fore, but simultaneously sets it up as being a forbidden dimension. This ordering sets up men and women as different (i.e. man as 'positive', woman as 'negative of the positive') and extends the dimension of sex to the entire universe: sex is everywhere but sexual relations impossible. This coincides admirably with the present impasse of man-woman relations, which psychoanalysis, on account of its object, cannot fail to describe.[22]

In this present framework, constituting one's identity is thus acquiring a sexed identity, that is, integrating the difference, or further recognizing castration as a threat to boys, as carried out for girls. The effect of the psychic violence which this system exerts, must be to allow individuals to be pushed into their positions and to be kept there.

In my view, psychoanalysis did not invent the patriarchal structure and its impact on subjectivity. It looks as if our psychic system could be said *here and now* to function thus. Rather the problem that psychoanalysis poses appears when it transforms itself into a 'conception of the world', and when it judges what it states to be inevitable. Because, through this judgement, it distorts the meaning of the speaking material which it gathers.

If we summarize what psychoanalysis – on balance – teaches us, one can say that there is no anatomical sex difference which is primary or of the order of feeling. There is an anatomy which the child symbolizes in the functioning of the imaginary schemes which are imposed on him, schemes of the Difference-hierarchy.

In a non-patriarchal symbolic system, the dimension of sex would have 'its' place. The particularity of individuals would not then be summed up by their sexual identity. Moreover, psychoanalysis also teaches us that in the present framework the fusion of individuality and sexed identity is not total: in earliest life the child becomes an autonomous subject independent of every reference to his anatomical sex.[23]

Third approach

Finally, psychoanalytic discourse gives a portrait of 'woman'. 'Woman' is described as marginal, unknown, dark continent, mysterious. But also as inferior, irreducibly passive, masochistic, neurotic, feeble-minded, egoistic, shrewish, castrator ... in short, since phallic supremacy orders everything ... castrated. This description of 'woman' that Freud develops in his articles on 'female sexuality' is a coarse fabric woven of elements of the theory of culture, of statements from analytic practice (erected on normal and normative laws) and of traditional misogynistic stereotypes. But it scarcely includes psychological theorizing, properly so called: hence its flagrant contradictions, its imprecisions, its lack of rigour.

It is, however, this description of woman that has been retained from Freud's work. And with reason: this portrait of woman is integrally inscribed in the patriarchal system. In fact it differentiates woman and under the guise of deciphering her 'mystery', her 'specificity', it encloses her in a reductionist, naturalist, normative and pejorative language which defines her solely as 'woman'.

Thus this theory kills two birds with one stone: it justifies the oppression of woman (which has been denounced since the beginning of the nineteenth century) and it establishes it inescapably: it conceals that which psychoanalytic theory otherwise demonstrates, the knowledge that woman is not only woman, a being made marginal and inferior, she is also the general-individual.

Luce Irigaray is a victim of this ideological subterfuge. She overlooks the fact that difference of the sexes does not order the entirety of Freudian theory, she confies herself to *the portrait of woman that Freud has superimposed on a general canvas*: she takes this cracked canvas for a work of art and concludes: woman does not exist:

> Woman, as such, will not be. Will not exist, unless in the mode of *not yet* being. [*Speculum*, p. 207]

This statement of non-existence (which she modifies somewhat in *Ce sexe qui n'en est pas un* but keeping the same premises, which lead to very much the same conclusion – I shall return to this) – this statement bears not only on the 'being' of woman but also on her possibilities of breaking out.

The invalidation of feminism

Woman, a cardboard figure dispossessed of language, seems to Luce Irigaray to be incapable of formulating an acceptable critique of patriarchy:

> For if sexual emancipation is a claim, notably 'feminist', those terms are sometimes, often, badly posed, badly evaluated, too little elaborated, giving rise to derision – easy irony for someone who commands language and does not have to acquire the practice in order then to subvert it. [*Speculum*, p. 148]

This critique which stresses the awkwardness and insufficiency of feminist discourses explicitly takes man (his derision, his irony) as a normative reference. It seems to derive from an idea of the oppression of women, a pessimistic idea according to which women do not have language at their disposal. Now this assertion is false. Woman has always talked and thought at the same time as man, just as she has participated in history. But she has been excluded from discourses, struck out of the archives. This has taken two forms: either it has been impossible for her to occupy certain places; or her effective participation has been killed, denied.[24] Gradually and to the extent that they reach places of speaking modalities (which is very difficult, because barred to them), women bring to light this burying, this erasure, this invalidation of their existence. Such is one of the activities of awkward feminism...

Luce Irigaray completes her critique of feminism by reflecting on the political perspectives deemed to guide it:

> And in ignorance, unconscious of that which belongs to her, of her merits, her value, the eventual specificity of her role in exchange economy, woman can only 'envy' and reclaim powers equal, or 'equivalent' to those of man. A moment, doubtless inevitable, when she (will) represent herself as subjected, victim, the butt of fortune, of penile narcissism, in the only goal possessed of such privileges. A sexual revolt, revolution which would simply overturn things, and which risks perpetuating an eternal return to the same. Thus, Freud was in some way right to disagree with the 'feminists', except that the reasons that he invoked are open to

challenge and testify to his misunderstanding of the importance of the question. [*Speculum*, p. 148]

Thus without knowing it the feminists will aim only at a perpetuation of phallocentrism: in simply overthrowing things (how many struggles, fights are condensed in this 'simply'), unconscious of their value, they will undertake a struggle which is to be condemned – by Freud, Irigaray – based on the fact of their misunderstanding of the primacy of the Same.

The anti-feminism which Luce Irigaray expresses seems to rest on a theory of the alienation of women – which invalidates their research on the grounds of insufficiency of thought and language; based on a preconception about feminism (a presumption which assimilates feminism and demands for sexual liberation; now feminism denounces sexual repression as one of the domains of oppression: it is not limited only to that); and on a problematic of the destruction of phallocentrism: the initial sameness must be destroyed and the Difference re-established, giving woman back their true value. A triple approach which puts Luce Irigaray outside the group of women – who do not know how to handle language, far from the feminists – unconscious of their value and their perspectives on struggle, close to Freud but more perspicacious than him.

Oppressive theory or theory of oppression?

Luce Irigaray provides not so much a theory of oppression as a reconstitution of the ideological place of 'woman' that patriarchy offers women. She does not describe for us what women are, because *women are not the object, 'woman', of the masculine discourse*: one cannot confuse the 'woman' that ideology describes and women in their social existence. The image of woman that discourse delineates does not take account of the psychic-social existence of women.

But, we may ask, has she not retraced the series of acts of violence that the girl undergoes to become the woman that patriarchy is expecting? Not at all; even if one takes the strictly psychological point of view – of the imaginary investments of subjects and their subjective positions – one cannot conceive the ideological subjection to femininity as defining, entirely and without contradiction, the 'psyche' of women. There is no doubt that to understand the alienation of women, one has to call upon the notion of *division* rather than that of *totalization*.

The danger of psychoanalytic discourse (and its practice) is to make out that castration defines women, summarizes their psychic existence.

Now the castration fantasy is a violence towards women which *tends to break their identification as a 'general being'*, to impose on them the signifier 'woman = castrated' to define them. As for penis-envy, it is nothing other than the expression, in the terms imposed by the patriarchal symbolic order, of woman's desire to be something other than 'woman' ('woman = castrated'). It only signifies 'being like man' to the extent that the androcentric social organization confuses general and masculine.[25]

Woman is produced as divided, split in two on the psychic plane: she is both the same and the other. In order to understand, to describe this division without being a victim of psychologism, it is helpful to establish a connection (for the moment, metaphorical and not explanatory: mechanistic hypotheses are so sterile) between psychological and sociological registers.

Let's consider, for example, the status of woman in theoretical discourses. One sees that the category 'woman' introduces a forcing of the difference which tends very precisely to exclude women from the general where they were really inserted. It all happens as if there were a falsehood which produces a mystification: that of making out that women are elsewhere, by their nature as women (elsewhere than in civilization, than in language, than in thought or sexuality). By stressing the difference of the sexes, the *discourses seem to propose that women are 'elsewhere': in the register of a nature.*[26]

Now women are, in a certain way, well immersed in an 'elsewhere' but in an elsewhere that owes nothing to nature: they form part of the patriarchal mode of production, ensuring its reproduction.[27] It is precisely in this that they are not elsewhere than in society, but well *into society*. However, to make this statement, one must leave the analytic categories of classical sociology and economics[28]; indeed, these two disciplines know nothing of the patriarchal mode of production, the totality of the society that they theorize is a totality where women are absent.

Women are not then excluded from the *reality* of the 'general' social but from the *representation* that the dominant discourse provides of it. This representation desocializes women's existence by pushing forward the notion of 'Woman' as entirely defined by naturalistic criteria. With this, *the more 'woman' exists, the less women exist*: the more they are limited in their activites, the more their existence is restricted only to the familial dimension, the more their bodies are appropriated, the more their individual bodily autonomy is limited.[29] The difficulty for us is to affirm the reality of women without sinking into the mystification of differences. Our method must consist in, at one and the same time, revealing women's specific exploitation, and affirming their existence as 'general' individuals, *from this point on*.

Woman then is produced as split in two: social individual, she carries out work, she has an existence; 'woman', she leads an allegedly natural life looking after her family. But this is not to say that this division opposes the concrete and the ideological. Because the notion of 'Woman' is imbricated in the materiality of existence: women are *enclosed* in the family circle and work *for free*. The patriarchal order is not only ideological, it is not in the simple domain of 'value'; it constitutes a specific, material oppression. To reveal its existence and lay bare its mechanisms, it is necessary to bring down the idea of 'woman', that is, to denounce the fact that the category of sex has invaded gigantic territories for oppressive ends.

At the psychological level, it is the signifier 'woman' which must summarize for the woman the whole of her existence. The weight of this signifier in her psychic system is made possible by her subjection to the patriarchal symbolic arrangements. A course which tends to annihilate the individual in the interests of the woman alone. And in which the paradox is to impose on woman a definition which is the *negative* of the referent, man. The 'excess' of woman only defines her negatively, as 'less' than the man. There domination goes one better, leading to contradiction and giving rise to illness (hysterics, who, it is said, do not know what their sex is!) or to revolt among women (lesbians, feminists who refuse the patriarchal framework and possession by man).

Women cannot fail to notice and draw attention to the fact that it is not a 'genuine' difference of the sexes which regulates the patriarchal system. This is why at present they are insisting on promoting their specificity, on *truly* establishing the difference. But this (protofeminist) method remains imprisoned by the patriarchal scheme, since it hides that woman is nothing but woman. It is as abusive to define a woman by a man as to postulate her radical difference from him.

Women always experiment at certain moments in their life with the view that 'femininity' is a pretence. This garment that they must don often transforms itself into an unbearable shell. Whence 'women's complaints', their 'lack of satisfaction', their 'recriminations'... How not to talk of 'Love', deemed to rule the totality of their existence: isn't it for love of a man that they must become submissive, desirable, devoted wives, and self-sacrificing mothers of families? This signifier 'Love' which they have associated with that of 'woman' and in which they tend to lose themselves. Quest for an absolute, an impossible. A model for alienation which they sometimes push to the sublime, to madness.[30]

Woman then has a psychic existence subject to the general laws of psychic functioning. She talks, thinks, dreams, desires. But her subjection to the patriarchal symbolic order confronts her with the signifier 'woman', inducing her to feel always, somewhere inside her, unworthy. Unworthy to speak, to think, to dream, to desire ... outside of the place where her existence is necessary: the place of the family, subjects to do with love ... And what she has been able to elaborate in this restricted space is not nothing. We can neither deny it, nor reify it as ascribable to eternal 'femininity'.

To say that woman does not exist, is then to produce a falsified statement of the psychological and sociological reality of woman. To have an exploited existence, does not at all signify not being. To undergo a division which engenders psychic suffering, in no way signifies not being.

Woman exists too much as signifier. Woman exists too much as subjected, exploited individual. The 'not enough', 'not yet' situates itself not on the side of woman's being, but on the reverse side of the material and psychic autonomy of women. That is something that cannot be constructed in a problematic of the Difference. Nor in a prospective of the unutterable.

Taking the contradiction into account?

Luce Irigaray, in *Ce sexe qui n'en est pas un*, repeatedly asks the question of whether woman reduces herself to this function of mime (of non-existent) which she postulates as hers. This is an important question; it involves a theory of oppression. In her second work, Luce Irigaray puts forward statements which seem less summary than those dealt with in *Speculum*, and appear to introduce a contradictory analysis. Did she not write in one of her articles:

> ... if women mime so well, it is because they are not simply absorbed in that function. *They also remain elsewhere*: another insistence of 'matter', but also of 'jouissance' (pleasure). [*Ce sexe qui n'en est pas un*, p. 74]

At the same time, she puts forward the ambiguity of hysteria:

> But this 'pathology' is ambiguous, because it signifies equally well *something else being kept in reserve*. To put it differently, in hysteria there is always a power in reserve at the same time as a power which is paralysed. [ibid., p. 136]

Nevertheless, the same basic ambiguity remains, deriving from the *naturalism underlying the investigation*. Indeed, when Luce Irigaray asks the question about women's current existence, she replies to it with an appeal to essences:

> .. if women can play at mimicry, it is in that they can refuel its functioning. That they have always fed its functioning? Is not the 'first' stake of mimicry that of (re)-producing nature? Of giving it shape, so as to appropriate it for oneself? As guardians of 'nature', are not women the ones who uphold mimesis and thus make it possible for men, for the logos, to draw on it. [ibid., p. 74]

The appeal to essences and to nature constitutes a 'blind spot', from which the oppressive shackles will close back upon Luce Irigaray. Dealing with the present existence of woman as a pure nothing, she will seek a 'prior to any deformation', in other words, a feminine essence.

The absence of a theory of oppression, the belief in the unavoidable and irreducible sexual Difference, the psychologistic reduction, the inflation of the notion of 'woman' which one finds in Luce Irigaray's investigation, can only result in this essentialist quest. In the gap left by the statement of woman's non-existence, Luce Irigaray will set up a 'new' conception of woman. A conception which is not surprising, since all she can do is to project into the unknown the too well known misogynistic ideology.

C. The Newborn Woman: The Eternal Feminine

Luce Irigaray postulates that woman does not yet exist. Contrary to man, who has more or less resolved the problem of his principle, woman will not know the form of her wish, misunderstanding the density of her difference. Luce Irigaray questions woman in her 'specificity', that is to say in her body.

Obscurity, the unutterable, the feminine syntax

Luce Irigaray tries to describe woman's attempt to get outside the 'masculine Logos'. This breaking through into the realm of Ideas can only be abstract and obscure, limited to word-games.

A blind breaking out from the closed room of the philosopher, from the speculative womb in which he has cloistered himself to consider everything clearly. An escape from the 'soul' outside her which cuts out a cave mouth through which she will be able to (re)enter herself. A breaking of the enclosing wall, an infringement of the/her distinction between inside/outside. Ex-tasies in which she soon risks losing herself, or at least risks seeing vanish the assurance of her own identity.* Doubtless, this will not happen all at once, caught as she already is in multiple representations and enveloping layers, in diverse configurations and chains which lead her back bit by bit to her unity. To the assembling of *what she would be ideally, in her own pure form or substance.* [*Speculum*, pp. 239–40, my emphasis]

The ex-tasies and the cave mouths risk immersing us in a particularly enveloped chimera . . . if we do not pay attention to that which gives its full meaning to this phrase: 'form', 'own substance' of woman.

The impossibility of description, the poetics of envelopment which arise in the text, play in a contradictory way. On the one hand, they seem to take account of the difficulties woman meets in her breaking out. But on the other, they end in a petrification where no struggle can be expressed. The fugitive from the realm of Ideas is completely immersed in the unspeakable:

What is expected is neither a *this* nor a *that*, not even a *here* any more than a *there*. Without being, nor time, nor place which can be designated. Better, then, to refuse all discourse, to be silent or to confine oneself to some clamour, barely articulated enough to shape it into a *song*. And with a ready ear for any quiver announcing a return. [*Speculum*, p. 241]

The unutterable of the 'feminine syntax'; woman will indeed be able to make use of a syntax of her own, isomorphic with her sex, which Luce Irigaray should have begun to develop in her *Speculum*.

What remains embarrassing is that the claim to the unutterable is necessarily accompanied – for whoever speaks of it – by something like a 'theoretical somersault':

To claim that the feminine should be able to speak itself in the form of a concept, is to let oneself be caught again within a system of 'masculine' representations, where women trap themselves in an economy of meaning which subserves the self-love of the (masculine) subject. Though it is indeed a question of disputing 'femininity', it is not a question of elaborating another 'concept', unless a woman gives up her sex and wants to speak like men. [*Ce sexe qui n'en est pas un*, p. 122]

*The French here reads 'l'assurance de son identité à elle (comme) même.' It thus also has the meaning of 'her identity as the same.'

The refusal of the term concept applied to the feminine ... what is it other than conceptual work? ... and how could it be formulated outside of that very concept?[31]

Isomorphism with her *sex*; it is indeed as a statue that woman is best described. A dumb statue subjected to our view, a mummified-statue whose bandages are being unwrapped, a body sized up in its 'specificity' ...

The incomplete woman

Luce Irigaray, for her part, is not petrified by the unspeakable. And the place from which she describes woman to us is not 'neutral':

> Now woman is neither closed or open. Indefined, infinite, in-finite, *the form does not end there.* She is not infinite, but no more is she a unity: letter, figure, number in a series, proper noun, unique object (of a) perceivable world, simple ideality of an intelligible whole, entity of a substructure etc. This incompleteness of her form, of her morphology permits her, at each instant, to become something else, which is not to say that she will ever be unequivocally nothing. [*Speculum*, p. 284]

To what norm do Luce Irigaray's statements about our bodies refer, in positing our form as incomplete? What becoming is taken to be ordained by this 'incompleteness'? The way in which she assimilates the notion of 'form' to that of 'phallus' leads her to place our sex in the domain of the formless/ill-formed. Which is no more correct than regarding it as 'nothing to be seen'.

The eternal, unsated, woman

Luce Irigaray interprets woman's sex as a plurality whose specificity will be somewhat virginal: a sex closed in on itself by virtue of its two lips which touch each other. The form of woman's pleasure, principally auto-erotic, will depend on this anatomical arrangement:

> *Woman* touches herself, by herself and in herself without the necessity of mediation and before any possible distinction between activity and passivity. Woman touches herself all the time and nothing external can forbid her to do so because her sex is made of two lips which kiss each other continually. [*Ce sexe qui n'en est pas un*, p. 24]

Luce Irigaray provides here an interpretation of anatomy which certainly tends to oppose the conception of sex-as-a-hole, but at the cost of a generalization which is, to say the least, surprising. A surprising metaphor: does she not lend us the capacity for uninterrupted pleasure (which is not unrelated to Freud's concept of 'polymorphously perverse' 'girls')? Further, she prescribes feminine pleasure in terms of anatomical sex which can only lead one to endless speculations ... if one conceives of woman's sex as a hole, one will postulate that the filling of its abyss gives her her pleasure; if one defines her sex as a closed flower, one will suggest that the closure of her petals gives her her pleasure ...

For Luce Irigaray the morphology ordains the pleasure. But also the wish:

> Woman's wish would not speak the same language as man's, and it has been buried by the logic which has dominated the West since the time of the Greeks. [*Ce sexe qui n'en est pas un*, p. 55]

The notions of 'pleasure', 'wish' are difficult to grasp. However, from the strict Freudian point of view, the experience of wishing does not refer to the category of sex. Further, the wish does not have an autonomous existence. It is born in a power relation where the child absolutely cannot satisfy its vital needs. Then it is channelled ceaselessly into the schemes which prescribe its form and its content.

How can one postulate the existence of a wish outside of social frameworks without falling into naturalism, that is, into the present oppression? One must denounce the oppressive patterns which channel the wish into sidings, and promote relations which will not be 'master-slave'. But one must guard against looking for the 'language' of the feminine wish ... because the quest will hold no surprises. More's the pity.

The eternal idiot

Luce Irigaray pursues her construction, cheerfully prescribing woman's social and intellectual existence from her 'morphology'. This prescription cannot fail to astonish us, when we remember that Luce Irigaray criticized Freud's prescription of the psychical by the anatomical. Certainly, for her own part, she privileges the concept of morphology over that of anatomy, seemingly wishing to refer to something which would be more empirical, less of a construction? Despite this distinction, her method remains fundamentally naturalist and completely under the influence of patriarchal ideology. For one cannot describe morphology as though it presented itself to perception, without ideological mediation. The positivism of the Irigarayan construction is here matched by a flagrant empiricism.

And what follows from it for us is terribly negative. Luce Irigaray closes us in the shroud of our own sex, reduces us to the state of child-women; illogical, mad, prattling, fanciful ...: thus is woman:

'She' is indefinitely other in herself. It is doubtless because of this that she is said to be capricious, incomprehensible, fanciful, agitated ... Without going so far as evoking her language, where 'she' sets off in every sense without 'him' locating the coherence of any sense. Contradictory words, a little mad for the logic of reason, inaudible to those who listen with ready-made grids, with a code already worked out. In her speaking too – at least when she dares to – woman re-touches herself all the time. She moves away with trouble from a prattling, an exclamation, a half-confidence, a phrase left in mid-air. [*Ce sexe qui n'en est pas un*, pp. 28–9]

Surprise. Every mode of existence which ideology imputes to women as part of the Eternal Feminine and which for a moment Luce Irigaray seemed to be posing as the result of oppression, is from now on woman's essence, woman's being. All that 'is' woman comes to her in the last instance from her anatomical sex, which touches itself all the time. Poor woman ...

But before such a destiny of non-existence, Luce Irigaray can only turn her attention away from us and address her prospective to those who speak, men:

Useless then to trap women in the exact definition of what they are trying to say, to make them repeat themselves so as to get it clearer, they are already elsewhere than in this discursive machinery where *you* claim to catch them unawares. They are turned in on themselves. Which you must not understand as the same way as on yourselves. They do not have the interiority which you have, which perhaps you suppose them to have. In themselves, that is to say in the *intimacy of this silent, multiple, diffuse touch*. And if you ask them insistently what they are thinking about, they can only reply nothing. Everything.

Mystery of our absence. Of our nothing. Of our silence. But then who is speaking to/about us? (... *qui nous parle?*)

What I call metaphorically the 'patriarchal chain' is an ideological configuration which arose after the emergence of feminism. That is, after women's oppression by the social system was recognized. It consists in invalidating this discovery, in channelling women's research into a perspective which allows the concealment and perpetuation of patriarchy. It manages this invalidation in several stages. The patriarchal 'strategic plan' is not always applied in its entirety. Sometimes, the introduction of only one of its elements is sufficient to block the whole investigation. In this respect, Luce Irigaray's work is interesting for it has necessitated the detonation of several minefields and so reveals to us the tactics of the patriarchal Genius (I apologize for this military vocabulary, nevertheless so adequate to its object!). I give an account of it in a *structural* and not a chronological form.

This is a montage, a schematic reconstruction of that which seems to me to be patriarchal ideology. My aim is to describe how the Patriarchy recuperates the subversive postulates advanced by feminists. I have chosen to set up imaginary characters in opposition to one another: this mechanical division is of course an arbitrary separation of two instances which play in the same discourse (Luce Irigaray's procedure has served me here as a model), but it has the merit of describing a dynamic in concrete form, of showing how our subversive questionings are undermined by patriarchal setbacks.

I shall use initials to designate the characters:

W = woman producing a discourse against the patriarchy.

P = patriarchal Commandment.

I

W's first denunciation: 'Woman is the object of a multiple oppression. She is described negatively and with extreme misogyny by the dominant discourse. She is psychologically subjected to a schema made by/for man.'

P's first rebuttal: consists in a confusion introduced between one level of discourse, that of the theory *about* 'woman', and another which concerns the existence of women. Oppression is driven to a caricature because 'woman', necessarily the object of man's discourse, is confounded with women. The discourse which man holds about woman dominates those which women can hold on their oppression, or what women are in their existence.

II

W's new question: 'Woman, object of an oppression, is reduced to being nothing. But why this misrecognition of woman?'

P's new rebuttal: he proposes as a causal schema for this misrecognition the idea of 'Man' as essence, as biological entity. This causal schema is tautological:

– 'man' is dominant because he is 'man' ('man' = 'virile', which allows him to impose himself by force),

– 'man' is dominant because he isn't woman (incapable of reproduction, he is jealous of woman who gave birth to him, which is inconsistent with his archaic wish for auto-creation).

III

W insists: 'But *how* does man dominate?'

P's third rebuttal: he plays a trick card, the bluff of the 'Same': 'Man dominates thanks to the primacy of the Same, he constructs the world in his own image (the same as him).' P thus suggests, through this bluff, that W take as a liberatory hypothesis the postulate of sexual difference: if the Same oppresses woman, its opposite, 'Difference', will liberate her.

IV

W's hypothesis: 'Woman is subjected to a pattern which does not correspond to her, which, to the extent that all is centred on man and the Same, reduces her to nothing.' W, trapped in the play of the Same, takes up for herself the hypothesis suggested by P: let us liberate ourselves from the Same and try to promote the difference of the sexes. We do not know the real difference between the sexes and this ignorance implies that woman, whose shape is unknown, does not exist.

P extends this 'fact' to every sphere of woman's existence and amalgamates psychology, ideology, social life ... Women, confounded with woman, are posed as not existing.

V

W's conclusion: 'Woman doesn't exist, it's not yet possible for her to exist.'

P has been cornered and has to give in because the 'yet' is dangerous to him: it could set off a struggle of women united against oppression. And so, in order to separate W from the feminist movements which have demonstrated the existence of an oppression, P makes use of fending-off notions designed to give W a simplistic and caricatured image of feminism: creating a pejorative stereotype.

VI

W's judgement against those to whom she was drawn: feminists are mistaken, they must necessarily be wrong, they want in fact to perpetuate phallocentrism, they are sexist because they would be content to invert the existing order of things.

VII

W cannot stop herself from pursuing her interrogation: 'Woman doesn't exist at present, but then what is she in her being?'
P lays down the mechanism of myths: projection into the future, into the unknown, into that which was the starting point, that is to say, into that which ideology gives us to hear and to see.

VIII

W constructs a prospective of woman: 'Woman will be that which is her difference.'
P perfects his destructive work in suggesting 'if women do not exist, this prospective cannot be the destiny of their being'.

IX

W encloses us in a shroud: 'If you ask them insistently what they are thinking about, they will answer you: about nothing. Everything.'

Notes and references

Translators' notes

a. Where articles and books referred to in the French text have been translated into English, we have cited the appropriate *English* work. References to Freud use the Standard Edition ('S.E.'; London: Hogarth Press).
b. Some of the quotations from Irigaray's works carry multiple meanings which are lost in the translation into English. With one or two exceptions, we have not attempted to point out where the translation fails to capture the full meaning of the French. Interested readers should consult the original texts.

Author's notes

1. Annie Leclerc refers to the first thesis, Luce Irigaray to the second.
2. Title of a work (*La jeune née*) by Hélène Cixous and Cathérine Clement (Paris: Union Générale d'Éditions, 1975).
3. Mariella Righini (1976), 'Le sang d'une femme poète', *Le Nouvel Observateur*, 621, p. 65.
4. ibid.

5. Luce Irigaray's findings are completely unsurprising. cf. the critical analysis that Christine Delphy has made of *Parole de femme* by Annie Leclerc in 'Proto-feminism and anti-feminism' in *The Main Enemy* (London: WRRC, 1977).

6. A moral denounced by Christine Delphy in her debate with Danièle Léger (in *The Main Enemy*) and which, for example, allows the invalidation of certain domestic tasks by bourgeois women. The moral condemnation of labour considered to be superfluous allows women who perform it to be placed as outside the patriarchal system, as not concerned with oppression.

7. I am here taking up a formulation of Freud's on the fact that men, being able to urinate at a distance, were allowed to 'put out the fire'. Whence the attribution that women, because of the anatomical impossibility of realizing this 'prowess', only had to 'keep the home fires burning'...

8. Luce Irigaray's two books are *Speculum. De l'autre femme* (referred to in the text as *Speculum*; Paris: Éditions de Minuit, 1974), and *Ce sexe qui n'en est pas un* (referred to in the text by its full title; Paris: Éditions de Minuit, 1977).

9. Irigaray seems to give the 'logos' the sense of 'discourse', 'understanding', 'logical function' and 'imaginary'. This imprecise conceptualization immediately confuses her investigation.

10. My titles and subtitles.

11. Luce Irigaray (1977), 'Women's exile: interview with Luce Irigaray', *Ideology and Consciousness*, I, 62–7.

12. Antonin Artaud, letter to Henri Parisot (7 September 1945), *Œuvres complètes* (Paris: Gallimard), vol. IX, 64–5.

13. A hypothesis clearly demonstrated by Piera Castoriadis-Aulagnier in *La violence de l'interprétation* (Paris: PUF, 1975).

14. And this even when one refers to the language of a man whom society judges 'alienated', that is to say 'outside of society'. The famous mad jurist Schreber who published his memoirs in 1903 was made the object of a psychological analysis by Freud, who tried to discover the relationship of the individual Schreber to his delirious language. The themes addressed by Schreber inscribe themselves in the discourse of his own time: the constitution of a racist problematic, the place of 'discipline' (as described by Michel Foucault in *Discipline and Punish*, London: Allen & Unwin, 1975).

15. cf. Colette Guillaumin, 'Pratique du pouvoir et idée de nature' (communication to a British/French seminar SSRC/MSH on 'Categories of sex and class/Economic relations in domestic group', London, 1975): 'The physical characteristics of those who are physically appropriated appear to be the *causes* or the reasons for the domination to which they submit. Their physical characteristics are said to be for them (and *them alone*) the cause of their social characteristics, and the final explanation of the latter.'

16. In *The Psychogenesis of a Case of Homosexuality in a Woman* (S.E. XVIII, 145–72), Freud notes: 'But psychoanalysis cannot elucidate the intrinsic nature of what in conventional or in biological phraseology is termed "masculine" and "feminine": it simply takes over the two concepts and makes them the foundation of its work.'

17. Sigmund Freud (1905), *Fragment of an Analysis of a Case of Hysteria* (S.E. VII, 7–122).

18. cf. Phyllis Chessler, *Women and Madness* (New York: Avon, 1973).

19. Sigmund Freud (1937), *Analysis Terminable and Interminable* (S.E. XXIII, 216–53).

20. Sigmund Freud (1908), 'Civilized Sexual Morality and Modern Nervous Illness' (S.E. IX, 181–204).

21. What French word can one find to express the inescapable character of death, a tragic and total destiny?

22. Thus the psychoanalyst Eugénie Lemoine-Luccioni in *Partage du femme* (Paris: Seuil, 1976) elaborates a theoretico-clinical construction which starts from the statement of a 'crisis-state' today of 'women's complaints'. She notes: 'Also, I cannot fail, at the present point of surveying the Freudian field, to ask myself, a woman, about "what a woman wants", even if I run the risk of discovering that she precisely wants to disappear as woman.' But faced with this central question she refuses to push to the end the logic of the 'risk' and quickly closes the breach by concealing the present functioning in Eternity: 'No sexual revolution will change the lines of division, neither that which passes between man and woman nor that which divides woman', and in holding on to the uncertainty: 'it is really true that woman finds herself caught in paradigms and systems of virile representations. But I do not conclude from this that she should *not* be caught there. I know nothing about it.' Luce Irigaray, on the contrary, puts forward this necessity.

23. D. W. Winnicott (1971), 'Transitional objects and transitional phenomena', in *Playing and Reality* (London: Tavistock; also in Penguin). Winnicott, whom one cannot suspect of feminism, has noted that the constitution of the 'transitional space' follows the same law for boys and girls: the choice of object is indifferent: and the modalities of its appearance are a function of the relations of the child with its primordial object – the mother, not necessarily the biological mother.

24. For example, we are only now in the process of discovering the writings of feminists or revolutionary women: these writings are not included in the archives, or the history taught us at school.

25. This is the object of work currently in progress. Indeed, the question is one of knowing what place language currently leaves to the category of sex, how the process of sexual identification can set itself up in a *contradictory* manner, whether the androcentrism of language allows a possibility of play.

26. cf. Nicole Claude-Mathieu (1973), 'Homme-culture et femme-nature?', *L'Homme* XIII, 101–13; and (1977) 'Paternité biologique, maternité sociale ... De l'avortement et de l'infanticide comme signes non reconnus du caractère culturel de la maternité', in Andrée Michel (ed.), *Femmes, sexisme et sociétés* (Paris: PUF).

27. cf. Christine Delphy, *The Main Enemy*.

28. cf. Christine Delphy (1977), 'Le classement des femmes dans les études de stratification: une manœuvre pour masquer leur classe réelle', in *Femmes, sexisme et sociétés*.

29. This is why *all* women (whatever their social class) undergo the same oppression, though certainly with variations in the modalities.
30. The sublime of Marguerite Duras depicting the impossible quest for absolute Love (*Le ravissement de Lol V. Stein*, Paris: Gallimard, 1964, reed. 1976, coll. Folio, No. 810); the madness of Emma Santos (*J'ai tué Emma S.*, Éd. Des Femmes, 1976); and of Jeanne Champion (*Le cri*, Paris: Juilliard).
31. Moreover, one could question the political project of taking up certain philosophical themes such as 'loss of meaning', 'polysémie', rejecting the term concept in order to define the 'feminine', so fashionable in certain current intellectual circles.

INDEX

ABOUT THE AUTHOR

Mike Brake was born in Plymouth, England. He received his B.A. from Leeds University, his M.Sc. and Ph.D. from the London School of Economics, and is currently professor of social work at Carleton University in Ottawa, Canada. Dr. Brake is the author of *The Sociology of Youth Culture and Subcultures*, and co-author of *Radical Social Work*.